Collective Investment Schemes Administration

The Official Learning and Reference Manual

APPROVED WORKBOOK

5th Edition, December 2008

This Workbook relates to syllabus version 4.0 and will cover examinations from 1st January 2009 to 31st December 2009.

PROFESSIONALISM | *INTEGRITY* | *EXCELLENCE*

SECURITIES & INVESTMENT INSTITUTE

COLLECTIVE INVESTMENT SCHEMES ADMINISTRATION

Welcome to the Collective Investment Schemes Administration study material for the Securities & Investment Institute's *Investment Administration Qualification (IAQ)*. This workbook has been written to prepare you for the Securities & Investment Institute's IAQ Collective Investment Schemes Administration examination.

PUBLISHED BY:

Securities & Investment Institute
© Securities & Investment Institute 2008
8 Eastcheap
London
EC3M 1AE
Tel: 020 7645 0600
Fax: 020 7645 0601

WRITTEN BY:

Clive Shelton, FSI, Risk and Compliance Director, International Financial Data Services (UK) Ltd

This is an educational manual only and the Securities & Investment Institute accepts no responsibility for persons undertaking trading or investments in whatever form.

While every effort has been made to ensure its accuracy, no responsibility for loss occasioned to any person acting or refraining from action as a result of any material in this publication can be accepted by the publisher or authors.

All rights reserved. No part of this publication may be reproduced, stored in a retrieval system, or transmitted, in any form or by any means, electronic, mechanical, photocopying, recording or otherwise without the prior permission of the copyright owner.

Warning: Any unauthorised act in relation to all or any part of the material in this publication may result in both a civil claim for damages and criminal prosecution.

A Learning Map, which contains the full syllabus, appears at the end of this workbook. The syllabus can also be viewed on the Institute's website at www.sii.org.uk and is also available by contacting Client Services on +44 (0) 20 7645 0680. Please note that the examination is based upon the syllabus. Candidates are reminded to check the 'Examination Content Update' (ECU) area of the Institute's website (www.sii.org.uk) on a regular basis for updates that could affect their examination as a result of industry change.

Workbook version: 5.1 (December 2008)

FOREWORD

Learning and Professional Development with the SII

The SII is the leading professional body for the securities and investment industry in the UK. 40,000 of its examinations are taken each year in the UK and around the world. This learning manual (or 'workbook' as it is often known in the industry) provides not only a thorough preparation for the appropriate SII examination, but is a valuable desktop reference for practitioners. It can also be used as a learning tool for readers interested in knowing more, but not necessarily entering an examination.

The SII official learning manuals ensure that candidates gain a comprehensive understanding of examination content. Our material is written and updated by industry specialists and reviewed by experienced, senior figures in the financial services industry. Exam and manual quality is assured through a rigorous editorial system of practitioner panels and boards. SII examinations are used extensively by firms to meet the requirements of the UK regulator, the FSA. The SII also works closely with a number of international regulators which recognise our examinations and the manuals supporting them.

SII learning manuals are normally revised annually. It is important that candidates check they purchase the correct version for the period when they wish to take their examination. Between versions, candidates should keep abreast of the latest industry developments through the Content Update area of the SII website. SII is also pleased to endorse the workbooks published by 7City Learning and BPP for candidates preparing for SII examinations.

The SII produces a range of elearning revision tools such as *Revision Express*, *Regulatory Refresher* and *eIAQ* that can be used in conjunction with our learning and reference manuals. For further details, please visit www.sii.org.uk

As a Professional Body, 41,000 SII members subscribe to the SII Code of Conduct and the SII has a significant voice in the industry, standing for professionalism, excellence and the promotion of trust and integrity. Continuing professional development (CPD) is at the heart of the Institute's values. Our CPD scheme is available free of charge-to-members, and this includes an online record keeping system as well as regular seminars, conferences and professional networks in specialist subject areas, all of which cover a range of current industry topics. Reading this manual and taking an SII examination is credited as professional development within the SIICPD scheme. To learn more about SII membership visit our website at www.sii.org.uk

We hope that you will find this manual useful and interesting. Once you have completed it you will find helpful suggestions on qualifications and membership progression with the SII.

Ruth Martin
Managing Director

Contents

Chapter 1:	Introduction to Collective Investment Schemes	1
Chapter 2:	Regulatory Controls	19
Chapter 3:	Constitution	65
Chapter 4:	Roles and Responsibilities	83
Chapter 5:	Investment and Borrowing Powers (IBP)	97
Chapter 6:	Buying and Selling Units/Shares	117
Chapter 7:	Registration and Settlement	153
Chapter 8:	Distribution of Income	173
Chapter 9:	Investor Communications	191
Chapter 10:	Taxation of Collective Investment Schemes	211
Glossary		241
Appendix		259
Sample Multiple Choice Questions		321
Index		329

It is estimated that this workbook will require approximately **70** hours of study time.

INTRODUCTION TO COLLECTIVE INVESTMENT SCHEMES

1.	ORIGINS OF THE COLLECTIVE INVESTMENT SCHEME (CIS) INDUSTRY	3
2.	INVESTING IN A COLLECTIVE INVESTMENT SCHEME	5
3.	FEATURES OF A COLLECTIVE INVESTMENT SCHEME	11
4.	HOW DO COLLECTIVE INVESTMENT SCHEMES COMPARE WITH OTHER INVESTMENTS?	14
5.	INVESTMENT OBJECTIVES AND THE USE OF COLLECTIVE INVESTMENT SCHEMES	16

This syllabus area will provide approximately 3 of the 50 examination questions

INTRODUCTION

Collective Investment Schemes (CISs) enable investment in shares or other securities, either direct into the CIS or via a tax-wrapper such as an ISA. Investors' contributions are pooled and invested on their behalf by professional fund managers.

The two main types of CIS in the UK authorised by the Financial Services Authority (FSA) for sale to the public are the Unit Trust and the OEIC (Open-Ended Investment Company). While these two types of scheme are broadly the same, there are some differences due to the evolution of the CIS fund industry.

Note: Throughout this workbook the term 'OEIC' is employed, being the term generally used in the industry. In many of the official publications from the FSA the term ICVC (Investment Company with Variable Capital) is used. Both OEIC and ICVC describe the same type of CIS.

1. ORIGINS OF THE COLLECTIVE INVESTMENT SCHEME (CIS) INDUSTRY

LEARNING OBJECTIVES

1.1.1 Know why Collective Investment Schemes were introduced and how they are used

1.1.2 Know the influence of the following on the development of schemes: launch of fixed trusts; introduction of flexible trusts; EU and the introduction of UCITS

1.1 Unit Trusts

Unit trusts can be traced back to the last century in the US where they are referred to as mutual funds. They first appeared in the UK in 1931. Following the stock market crash of 1929, investors were wary of the risks of stock market investments. Unit trusts were aimed at encouraging investors back into the market through a reduction in risk.

The first unit trusts were fixed trusts, ie, the trust manager was not allowed to vary the investments once they had been purchased, and so the investor knew exactly how his money was invested. The manager had no ongoing discretion over investments and could only purchase further assets in the fixed portfolio of companies in the same proportion as that fixed at the launch of the fund. These trusts were also set up for a fixed period, usually a 20-year term. Of course, while this type of trust gave some protection through diversification to the investor, the manager was unable to take advantage of new securities when they were created. Hence, some investments purchased may have subsequently incurred losses but the investment was locked into the trust.

By the mid-1930s flexible trusts began to emerge. These allow the manager both to interchange investments and to increase the size of the fund. If more people decide to invest in a particular fund, the manager buys more investments and the fund grows: if more people cash in their units then the size of the fund is reduced. Funds that are able to expand and contract in this way are referred to as 'open-ended'; all authorised unit trusts (AUTs) available in the UK today are flexible unit trusts.

Many CISs are managed in line with a European standard known as **UCITS (the Undertakings of Collective Investment in Transferable Securities Directive)**. UCITS has evolved since the standard was first introduced in 1985, with the current version being known as **UCITS III**. Any changes to the UCITS standard must be reflected in UK regulation, requiring the FSA to update its rules. The FSA and UCITS regulations are discussed in greater detail in Chapter 2. The aim of the UCITS Directive is to help develop a single EU market for collective investment schemes whereby fund managers can sell to investors across the borders of member states.

1.2 Open-Ended Investment Companies (OEICs)

> **LEARNING OBJECTIVES**
>
> 1.1.2 Know the influence of the following on the development of schemes: launch of fixed trusts; introduction of flexible trusts; EU and the introduction of UCITS

While unit trusts could follow UCITS there was concern that some features of the unit trust structure placed UK fund managers at a competitive disadvantage when trying to market products in Europe. In the mid-1990s UK-based fund managers lobbied for greater freedom in arranging their products. This demand led to the introduction of a new type of collective investment scheme, the OEIC, enabling them to:

- compete effectively with other European-based collective investment schemes that are companies with variable capital, including those based in Luxembourg and Dublin where unprecedented growth was taking place;
- offer a tax-efficient vehicle which allowed distributions of income, both interest and dividend distributions, to be paid gross to non-resident investors; and
- sell funds based on a single price, rather than the traditional system of dual pricing used by unit trusts, which is unfamiliar to investors elsewhere in Europe.

The OEIC was created, including these features, together with facilities already available to unit trusts. Various changes to UK corporate law were required in order to introduce OEICs. For example, public and private companies in the UK cannot repurchase their shares from existing shareholders without a formal corporate action (due to their closed-ended share capital structure). However, it is necessary for OEIC investors to be able, on any day, to sell their holdings back to the company (ie, an open-ended structure).

After a long period of consultation with the industry, HM Treasury established new corporate legislation to enable OEICs to be launched and the FSA issued rules for the operation of such companies. The current legal and regulatory framework is provided by:

- the Open-Ended Investment Companies Regulations 2001 (as amended); and
- FSA Regulation (described in more detail in the next chapter) made under the Financial Services and Markets Act 2000 (FSMA).

OEICs were given the same tax position as unit trusts, despite hopes that they would receive special tax advantages to assist with competition in Europe. Consequently, fund managers initially focused on the flexibility offered by the OEIC as a corporate vehicle which:

- can consist of a single fund or as an umbrella type structure, with several sub-funds; and
- has the ability to offer multiple share classes designed to meet the needs of different types of investor, eg, retail and institutional investors.

While no two structures will be the same, the following diagram shows part of an umbrella OEIC. It could have 2 to 20+ sub-funds, each with different charging structures. The diagram below shows part of a structure covering two sub-funds; three share classes are shown in detail for sub-fund A for illustrative purposes.

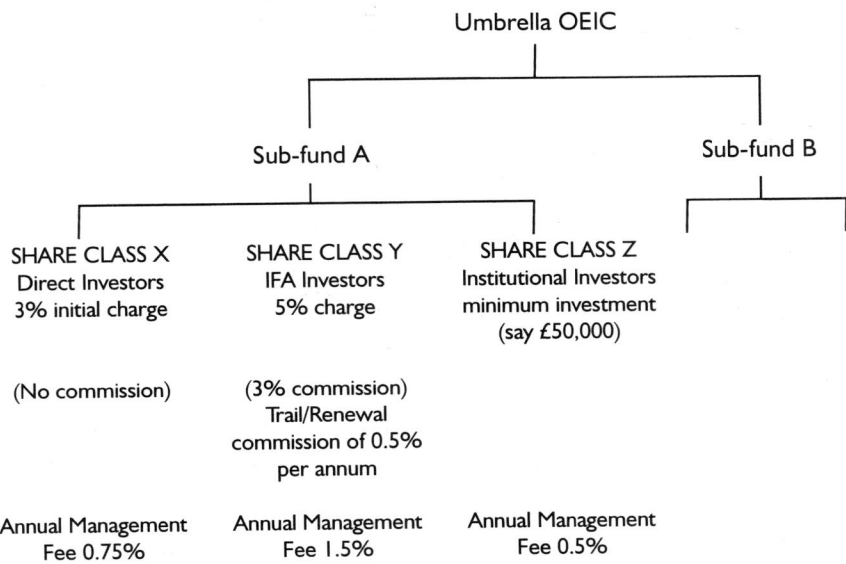

A new rulebook aligning the rules relating to both unit trusts and OEICs was introduced by the FSA in 2007. See Section 2.3 for more details.

2. INVESTING IN A COLLECTIVE INVESTMENT SCHEME

LEARNING OBJECTIVES

1.1.2 Know the influence of the following on the development of schemes: launch of fixed trusts; introduction of flexible trusts; EU and the introduction of UCITS

2.1 Growth of Popularity of CIS Investment

The following table shows how the number of UK-authorised CISs and the amounts invested have grown over recent years (in the case of umbrella schemes, each sub-fund is counted as a separate CIS).

Year End	No. of Funds	Value of Funds (£bn)
2002	1,957	194.55
2003	1,924	240.47
2004	1,975	275.37
2005	2,007	347.30
2006	2,033	410.00
2007	2,178	468.00
2008*	2,248	425.20

* figures to 30 June 2008

As mentioned earlier the first fixed trusts were introduced in 1931, following the Wall Street crash in 1929. This was a time of deep industrial depression when UK investors were in a highly nervous mood; they felt reassured by being able to see the short list of securities that underlay their trust and by knowing that these securities (representing companies of strength, such as Boots, Shell and BAT) could not be changed.

These trusts, and the early flexible trusts that followed, were successful in their investment aims and the diversification of risk. Nevertheless, growth in funds under management was slow at first, but from the late 1950s the industry began a period of steady growth until, by 1980, there were 467 funds available, worth £5bn.

The boom years of the mid-1980s saw significant growth in the number of funds and their value and this continued throughout most of the 1990s. There can be little doubt that the privatisation programme did much to raise public awareness of equity investment; the introduction of Personal Equity Plans (PEPs) and their replacement, the Individual Savings Accounts (ISAs), served to continue the industry's growth.

The number of funds and sub-funds have continued to increase steadily and the trend shows an increasing value of funds under management, albeit with an occasional market correction. 2002 was a difficult year and the difficulties in financial markets as a result of the credit crunch in 2007/8 has seen a reduction in total value of funds under management.

Despite these difficult market conditions from time to time, over the long term the trend has shown a strong growth in the use of collective investment schemes. There is a combination of factors for this growth of the industry since the late 1950s:

- increase in disposable income (but not enough to engage a stockbroker for direct equity investment);
- steady performance and investor protection offered by CISs eg, no failures whereby investors are left penniless;
- increased promotional activities by CIS companies;
- use of CISs by insurance companies for unit-linked life and pension policies, tax advantages and reduced administration costs;
- advice provided by independent financial advisers (IFAs) and the payment of commission to them;
- greater public awareness of the benefits of equity investments;
- the introduction and tax benefits of ISAs and in particular, the increase in the amount which may be invested in collective investment schemes. Currently £7,200 a stocks and shares ISA;
- the development of fund supermarkets as a distinct distribution channel;
- a broader range of funds designed to meet investor needs.

From 6 April 2008, ISAs were simplified by HM Government. Investors have a choice of a cash ISA with an annual allowance of £3,600 or a stocks and shares ISA with an annual allowance of £7,200.

The following table shows the growth in the value of CIS PEPs/ISAs since 1992.

Growth in Collective Investment Scheme ISAs and PEPs	
Year (end)	Value of Funds (£bn)
1992	3.30
1994	12.00
1996	25.07
1998	49.51
1999*	67.29
2000	75.19
2001	68.13
2002	57.91
2003	68.65
2004	75.31
2005	84.10
2006	90.50
2007	90.70
* ISAs were introduced in 1999 and with effect from 6 April 2008, PEPs were re-categorised as ISAs	

In spite of the successful growth of the industry, less than 10% of the working population of 28 million invest directly in collective investment schemes and much remains to be done to inform the public about the advantages of such investment.

Most authorised collective investment schemes are eligible for inclusion within an Individual Savings Account (ISA), the government's tax-incentivised scheme to encourage savings and investment. ISAs have proved to be popular investment vehicles, replacing PEPs and TESSAs as the vehicle for new savings and investment since 5 April 1999. Although ISAs offer a broader choice in terms of cash, insurance and stocks and shares, a substantial number of investors are attracted to invest in stocks and shares (eg, equities and bonds) – either directly or through CISs.

Since 6 April 2004 plan managers have been unable to claim the tax credit on dividend income from equity investments (including CIS investments) held within an ISA or PEP on behalf of investors. The result has been a shift towards fixed-interest investments and corporate bond funds that pay interest distributions on which plan managers can continue to reclaim the income tax deducted.

From the start of the 2008/09 tax year, a number of changes were made to simplify ISAs. PEPs were re-categorised as stocks and shares ISAs. The types of ISA available were reduced to two, namely a cash ISA or a stocks and shares ISA; the previous categories of maxi/mini ISAs were swept away. This simplification, together with raising the limit to £7,200 and allowing transfers from cash to stocks and shares ISAs, should have a beneficial impact on tax-wrapped business going forward.

2.2 The Principal Types of Fund by Asset Class and IMA Categories

LEARNING OBJECTIVES

1.1.3 Know the principal types of fund available by asset class and the IMA performance categories

Funds Available by Asset Class

Long-term investment success depends on the right mix of asset types, something determined not just by the prevailing market conditions but by what is appropriate for the investor given the stage of life they are at, their financial position and their attitude to risk. For institutional investors, eg, pension funds, the drivers may be a little different but, in principle, consideration of their investment objectives and attitude to risk will determine their overall asset allocation.

The main asset classes used by investors are:

- cash – often in the form of bank or building society deposits;
- fund of funds (multi-manager) – fettered (own funds) or unfettered (other managers funds and own funds);
- fixed-interest securities – gilts and corporate bonds;
- property – commercial and investment property;
- property (underlying portfolio in property shares and Real Estate Investment Trusts (REITs); and
- equities – shares.

The CIS funds available to the public cover all these asset classes. The use of funds will, to some extent, be determined by the availability of, and the risk associated with, alternative products; for example, in the UK the use of cash and near cash (money market instrument-based) funds is relatively small because of readily available alternatives in the form of high-interest deposit accounts with high street banks and building societies.

As well as offering funds in each asset class the industry has offered balanced funds which, although predominantly invested in one class, may offer a portfolio which contains an element of other asset classes; the aim here may be to offer a range of assets and a balance between income-producing assets (cash fixed interest securities) and those aimed at producing growth (equities). Under the former CIS Sourcebook the rules relating to the categories of funds limited the extent to which assets could be mixed; however, the removal of these categories and the introduction of so-called **mixed funds** (see Chapter 5 for more details) under the new COLL sourcebook provides much greater flexibility for fund managers to design funds to suit different investor objectives and risk profiles.

The Investment Management Association (IMA) provides statistics on funds under management broken down by asset class. The following table shows the change in make up of funds by asset class between 1995 and 2007.

Summary of funds under management by asset class (£bns)						
Year	Equity	Bonds	Money Market	Balanced	Other	Total
1995	100.4	3.7	0.4	7.4	0.6	112.5
%	89.3%	3.3%	0.3%	6.6%	0.5%	100.0%
2006	306.3	59.0	3.8	31.8	9.1	410.0
%	74.7%	14.4%	0.9%	7.8%	2.2%	100%
2007	327.6	84.2	5.2	37.9	13.1	468
%	70%	18%	1.1%	8.1%	2.8%	100.0%

Source: IMA
'Other' includes guaranteed/protected funds, pension unit trusts and unclassified sector

Most interesting is the move away from equities towards the other asset classes and notably the greater level of investment in bonds (ie, fixed-interest securities – UK gilts and corporate bonds). Concerns over stock market performance, in particular since 2002, have undoubtedly contributed to this change.

As the investment and borrowing powers for an authorised CIS are based on the FSA regulations they each operate in a similar way, but the range of industries and stock markets in which they invest is wide. This allows investors, many of whom have very different objectives, to find a CIS to meet their needs. Those concerned with long-term capital growth, eg, for retirement in the future, may choose a general or growth scheme, whereas a pensioner concerned about income to meet living expenses, when a pension is eroded by inflation, may choose to invest in a high-income scheme.

IMA Performance Categories/Sector Classification

The IMA, the industry's trade body, places CISs in more than 30 investment categories that range from general, to growth in overseas markets. The categories are intended to make performance comparisons easier and to aid investor choice. The categories are shown in Appendix 1. Other data on collective investment schemes can be found at the IMA website (www.investmentfunds.org.uk) and performance tables can be found at www.moneyobserver.com.

Statistical Returns by AFMs

LEARNING OBJECTIVES

1.1.4 Know what statistical reporting is made by AFMs to industry and government bodies

The IMA collects statistics from its members and publishes them on a monthly, quarterly and annual basis. These statistics include gross and net sales; total funds under management; breakdown by fund category, distribution channel and asset class; and performance. The IMA publishes annually an Asset Management Survey which provides a comprehensive review of the industry.

In addition to the IMA, Authorised Fund Managers (AFMs) make various statistical returns during the course of the year. Some of these are made to the FSA, the industry regulator, as a condition of carrying out business in the financial services sector. These would include returns to show that the AFM has complied with requirements on capital requirements (see Chapter 2); government departments would include HM Revenue & Customs for various forms of tax (see Chapter 9) and the FSA for returns of complaints in connection with purchase of financial products including CISs (see Chapter 2).

2.3 The Future for Collective Investment Schemes

> **LEARNING OBJECTIVES**
>
> 1.1.2 Know the influence of the following on the development of schemes: launch of fixed trusts; introduction of flexible trusts; EU and the introduction of UCITS

For some years Authorised Fund Managers (AFMs)* have been lobbying for greater flexibility. While the UCITS requirements are fixed by European legislation, the AFMs considered that the regulations should allow funds not being sold into European markets more scope to exploit niche markets. This workbook is based on the new Collective Investment Schemes rule book referred to as 'COLL' which became effective in 2007.

The COLL sourcebook will be looked at in more detail in the next chapter. The impact on the industry is that AFMs are designing transition projects to create new funds, convert old funds, and identify new market sectors in which they wish to place products. The coming years will see various new types of CIS being created, with AFMs taking advantage of the wider powers they have in product design. These powers, and the differences between the old and new rules, will be looked at in detail in Chapter 2.

The intermediary channel continues to increase its influence in the distribution of investment funds to retail investors, accounting for more than 85% of all gross retail sales in 2007. This compares to 81% in 2006 and 65% in 2003. The main reason for this trend is fund platforms/supermarkets which are continuing to grow in popularity.

The last few years have seen strong growth in the use of unfettered Fund of Funds (ie, external funds rather than in-house funds), Property Funds (although 2007 marked a change in sentiment) and although still small overall, the use of Ethical Funds. Given the current market uncertainty there is an expectation of increasing demand from retail investors for absolute return funds, ie, ones that will have an objective to deliver positive returns, irrespective of the market.

The government has announced that Individual Savings Accounts (ISAs) will be made permanent and more flexible. This means that ISAs will continue to be a key vehicle for CIS investments.

*In this workbook the term Authorised Fund Manager (AFM), unless the context requires otherwise, includes both Authorised Unit Trust Managers and Authorised Corporate Directors (or ACD) of an open-ended investment company.

3. FEATURES OF A COLLECTIVE INVESTMENT SCHEME

3.1 Authorisation and Classification of Collective Investment Schemes

> **LEARNING OBJECTIVES**
>
> 1.1.8 Know the purpose of authorising Collective Investment Schemes and the classification of those schemes by the FSA

The main purpose of authorising CISs, and the classification of these schemes by the FSA, is for the protection of investors. The CIS regulatory structure provides various means of protection – some of which are not found in other forms of retail investment.

As well as authorisation and oversight by the FSA, a CIS (and the AFM) is subject to oversight by an independent body whose duty is also to hold the assets of the fund and act solely for the benefit of the fund's investors. For a unit trust this body is called the **trustee**; for an OEIC it is known as the **depositary**. Both the AFM and the trustee/depositary have to be an authorised person under FSMA and are subject to direct regulation. Most trustee/depositary firms are part of major international banks. Both managers and trustees/depositaries have to maintain a set level of capital adequacy. This is much higher for trustees/depositaries than for managers.

The FSA's Collective Investment Scheme Sourcebook (COLL) classifies each fund into one of three categories:

- UCITS Retail Schemes (complying with the EU Directive);
- Non-UCITS Retail Schemes (NURS) (still a retail-focused fund, but with wider flexibility than a UCITS fund);
- Qualified Investor Scheme (QIS) (not intended for retail investors but focused on the needs of more sophisticated and institutional investors).

Retail investors will be able to choose from the range of UCITS and non-UCITS funds in the market (these fund types together being described as **Retail Funds**). QIS schemes are generally not available to retail investors, being designed specifically for professional and institutional investors. QIS schemes are, therefore, non-retail.

Unit trusts may be established which are not authorised by the FSA. These unauthorised funds are perfectly legal but cannot be marketed to the general public. These funds are typically set up by fund managers, stockbrokers and investment banks for investment by private clients such as pension funds. In contrast, all OEIC funds must be authorised. The rules around the establishment and operation of authorised CISs are covered in more detail in Chapters 2 and 3. This workbook does not seek to cover unauthorised unit trusts.

Most AFMs are, without obligation, also members of the IMA, which represents its members' views in discussions with the regulatory, and other relevant authorities and often on their behalf. When changes to regulations are proposed, it acts as a watchdog for the industry and regularly holds meetings for members. The trustees and depositaries have their own association: the Depositary and Trustees Association (DATA).

3.2 Advantages and Disadvantages of CIS Investment

LEARNING OBJECTIVES

1.1.5 Know the comparative features, advantages and disadvantages in contrast to other forms of investment (direct and indirect)

a. Investors can invest comparatively small amounts of money (lump sums from as little as £250 upward or, on a regular savings basis, from about £25 per month).

b. Investors can secure a much wider diversification of risk because the money they contribute is invested in between perhaps 50 and 120 separate companies' shares. If the investor puts his money (say, £500) into one company, he could lose it all if the company goes into liquidation but, with a collective investment scheme's broadly based portfolio, only a very small amount would be lost.

c. The investor's money is managed by a professional investment manager. Investment managers have access to a wide range of resources and data and some have teams of people providing information about which securities to invest in. An individual is unable to spend the time or money to obtain as much information as a professional.

d. CIS investors benefit from the investment manager's ability to deal in larger quantities of securities at lower average dealing costs, and it is easy to make investments. An investor may invest through a financial intermediary, such as an independent financial adviser (IFA), a fund supermarket or a stockbroker. Alternatively, the investor wishing to buy or sell part or all of his investment can simply contact the AFM by telephone, in person or in writing. A number of AFMs offer internet and email facilities for buying and selling.

e. Once the investor has purchased his holding, the value can be followed because the daily prices of most CISs continue to be quoted in the press and specialist personal finance publications, and may also be available through the IMA and AFM websites. In addition, investors receive an investment report from the AFM every six months.

f. The individual CIS is exempt from capital gains tax (CGT) on gains made on its own internal transactions. This provides potential for the fund to grow in value more quickly. Investors have a potential liability to CGT on any profit they make, but only when they sell their holdings – and the individuals profits are above their an annual allowance.

g. Investors can normally sell their holdings within the funds at any time, ie, there is no minimum investment period and usually no penalty for encashment. Some fund managers have dropped the initial charge in favour of an early withdrawal fee or exit charge if the securities are only held for a short time before being sold. Such exit charges may only apply for a period so that the long-term investor might pay neither an initial, nor an exit, charge.

h. An investor with just a few shareholdings, such as small holdings resulting from privatisation issues or building society conversions, may be able to exchange them for holdings within the fund without going through a stockbroker. Beneficial terms are often available.

i. One of the problems with stock market investments, including collective investment schemes, is that of timing. Often new investors will be attracted to the market when it is doing well but it may have already peaked. Having invested at the high point, they quickly become disillusioned when the market falls, along with the value of their investment.

One way to reduce the risk is to invest a little at a time. Most AFMs offer regular savings plans to make it easier for investors to adopt this strategy. The benefit of regular investment of a fixed sum is that each investment buys a larger holding when the price is low and a smaller holding when the price is high. This has the effect of making the average cost of purchases lower than the average price per unit/share over the same period. This is referred to as the **pound cost averaging**.

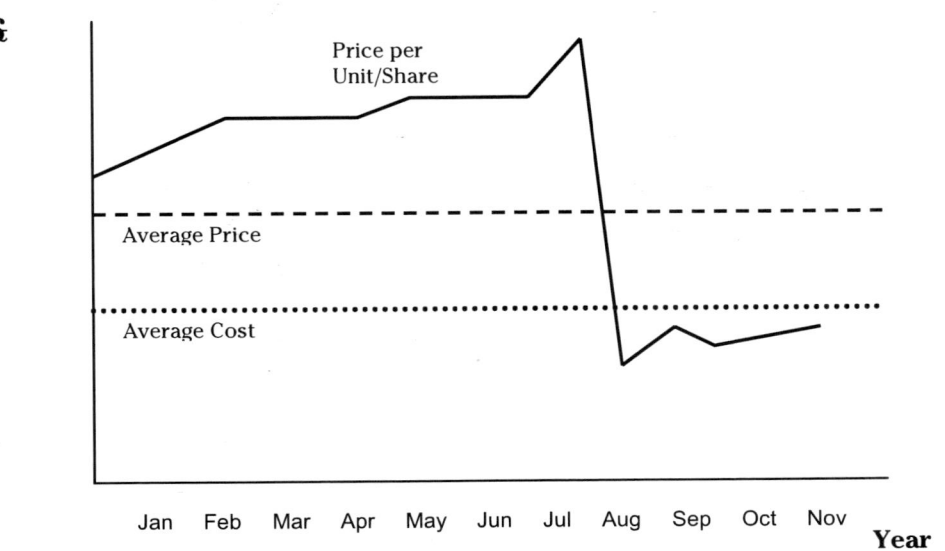

If a regular amount is invested, say £50 each month, the average cost of investment bought is lower than the average unit/share price over the same period. Over the long term, usually five years plus, the price recovers and so the investor should achieve a better return than those who invested a lump sum when the market was high. Indeed, by adopting a regular investment strategy, any short-term falls in the stock market will not be seen as something to fear but as a benefit.

j. With the safeguard of an independent trustee/depositary and the FSA regulations governing scheme operations, a CIS is a relatively safe investment – although, because prices can fluctuate, it is not risk-free.

4. HOW DO COLLECTIVE INVESTMENT SCHEMES COMPARE WITH OTHER INVESTMENTS?

LEARNING OBJECTIVES

1.1.5 Know the comparative features, advantages and disadvantages in contrast to other forms of investment (direct and indirect)

There are further types of investment against which CIS investment can be compared, but it is necessary to compare like with like. For example, National Savings Certificates give a safe return with the amount payable at the end of the five-year period known when the certificates are purchased. Therefore, they cannot be compared with CISs because of the lack of risk. Neither do they work on a collective principle. Some, more useful, comparisons are listed below.

4.1 Investment Trusts

There is often confusion over the distinction between CIS schemes and investment trusts. Both pool money to purchase the shares of companies and other investments, yet there are a number of restrictions on CISs that do not apply to investment trusts. An investment trust is not legally a trust, rather a company formed for the purposes of holding securities or other property by way of investment. The correct title is an **Investment Trust Company (ITC)**.

Investors in an ITC are shareholders, though they are separate from the company in whose name all assets are held. This is similar to the position of shareholders in an OEIC. However, the owners of units in a unit trust are beneficial owners of the property of the scheme, which is registered in the name of the trustee (who acts for the protection of investors).

ITCs have considerable freedom to borrow sums of money, so investment opportunities may be increased because of the use of these additional funds. CISs have more limited powers to borrow. This factor also helps to keep the price of CIS units/shares more stable, as the price fluctuations which may accompany gearing are less likely (see Chapter 5).

In a CIS fund, the trustee/depositary carries out monitoring for the benefit of investors to see that the AFM keeps within the FSA regulations. In an ITC, there is no equivalent protection. Both an ITC and a CIS are, however, subject to annual audit by qualified independent accountants. In an ITC, up to 15% of income from shares and securities may be retained by the management. CIS fund investors receive, at regular intervals, a distribution of the whole of the income of the scheme, less certain deductions for expenses allowed by FSA regulations. All income must be distributed at the end of the annual accounting period.

CISs are **open-ended** and their size will fluctuate as fund units/shares are issued or cancelled to match demand. ITCs are **closed-ended** funds with a fixed share capital.

The price of CIS unit/shares is based on net asset value, calculated by the manager on a regular basis (usually daily), whereas the value of shares in an ITC is fixed by the market price of shares. These fluctuate constantly, according to the economic laws of supply and demand, as with any other listed company on the Stock Exchange.

CIS units/shares are bought and sold via the AFM who calculates the price. The price may include any transaction cost, although in the case of single-priced units/shares, such costs may be shown separately or even borne by the fund, whereas (with the exception of some investment trust savings plans) buying or selling shares in an ITC requires the purchaser to buy/sell on the Stock Exchange with a stockbroker charging commission for dealing with the transaction. The broker may deal with one or more market makers when dealing on behalf of his client on the Stock Exchange.

4.2 Endowment Policies

The investor holds their policy for 10–25 years and is guaranteed a lump sum together with annual bonuses paid to date plus terminal bonuses. The investor has no CGT liability on such an investment, though the life fund is liable to CGT on transactions effected within it. There are often heavy penalties if the policyholder surrenders their policy in the early years after purchase. A CIS investor may be subject to CGT on realised gains on sale of their investment, but relief available may reduce the burden.

The CIS investor can surrender their investment over a number of years and, using their CGT allowance, avoid paying CGT. A CIS is exempt from CGT on transactions effected within it. The result is that it can grow more quickly than a life fund. This offers CISs a major tax advantage over endowment policies, especially for investors who do not otherwise use their CGT allowance.

The value of a CIS unit/share can be readily checked, either in a daily newspaper or by other means (such as by telephone or the internet). A notice of bonuses is sent to the endowment policy holder only annually.

4.3 Insurance Bonds

These are either purchased as a lump sum or taken out as a regular savings plan; the latest prices can be found in daily newspapers. The charges for bonds are usually higher to cover the life assurance element. Similar tax considerations apply as in the case of endowment policies. This usually allows a collective investment scheme to outperform a bond.

4.4 Offshore Funds

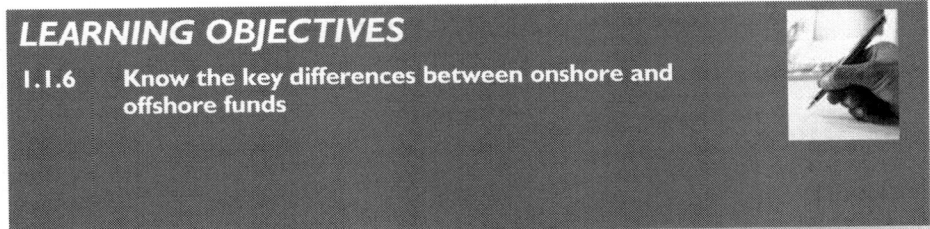

LEARNING OBJECTIVES
1.1.6 Know the key differences between onshore and offshore funds

These are typically domiciled in the Isle of Man, Channel Islands, Luxembourg or the Republic of Ireland and are often favoured by non-UK investors who, for example, do not want to remit funds to the UK and, therefore, can avoid paying UK tax, though sometimes the charges for offshore funds are higher.

Not all offshore funds give the legal protection that UK funds provide. They are a form of collective investment but, as they are not authorised in the UK by the FSA, the regulatory regime under which they are constituted may not provide the same protection as that provided by a UK-authorised CIS. However, offshore funds have to be recognised by the FSA before they may be publicly promoted in the UK. They will usually be able to distribute income gross. Unless they have distributor status, all capital gains made by those resident for tax purposes in the UK will be subject to income tax as at the date of realisation.

The last ten years have seen significant growth in the number of funds and assets based in Luxembourg and Ireland, in part at the expense of the UK. This is due to the use of the familiar corporate structure, which led to the introduction of OEICs, and a simple-single pricing regime, which again is now available in the UK and discussed later in this workbook. However, the major difference has been a more favourable and competitive tax regime in these offshore centres. There are technical tax reasons for this view, but also fund managers appear to have greater confidence and trust in offshore tax systems than they do in the UK's system.

HM Treasury is consulting on changes to improve the competitiveness of UK-based funds by shifting the burden of taxation from the fund to the investor.

5. INVESTMENT OBJECTIVES AND THE USE OF COLLECTIVE INVESTMENT SCHEMES

LEARNING OBJECTIVES

1.1.7 Understand how schemes can be used to meet different investment objectives

CISs are no longer used only by small investors. They can be used to meet various needs and today are often used by large and sophisticated investors as part of an investment portfolio. Typically, investors will look to invest for income, growth, or a combination of the two; they may also have other objectives, such as diversification. Some examples of the reasons for the use of different funds are given below. The asset allocation (see Chapter 1, Section 2.2) will often reflect the investment objectives.

5.1 Retirement Income

CISs are often used as part of retirement planning. For example, an investor may initially invest for long-term growth and then switch to income funds on retirement.

Some CISs allow monthly income payments, as opposed to the more usual half-yearly or annual payment. This allows more effective planned payment dates. Alternatively, a portfolio of equity funds with different half-yearly income payment dates can provide regular income with the prospect of rising income in the case of equity funds. Funds that invest in gilt-edged (government) securities or corporate bonds may be able to provide a higher income yield with less risk to capital.

5.2 Investing for Children

Collective investment schemes can be used as a long-term investment for grandparents and parents to invest for children. The adult buys the units/shares for the child and has them registered in an adult's name, with the child's initials as a designation, as nominee. The units/shares can be re-registered into the child's name when the child reaches 18, though some AFMs will do so when the child reaches 14. Depending upon the child's tax position they may be able to reclaim any income tax suffered on income received, though, if the money is given by a parent, this only applies if the gross income generated is not more than £100 per annum. Subject to certain restrictions, CISs are also eligible for the government's Child Trust Funds.

5.3 Overseas Investments and Specialist Sectors

The investor may have direct shareholdings in the UK and use collective investment schemes for overseas investment because dealing, eg, brokerage, as well as obtaining detailed market information, may be expensive. Similarly, investing directly in the individual shares of commodity companies dealing in, for example, copper, diamonds and oil may be risky. This risk can be reduced by investing in a wider spread of shares through a CIS specialising in commodity investments.

END OF CHAPTER QUESTIONS

Think of an answer for each question and refer to the appropriate section for confirmation.

	Question	Answer Reference
1.	Describe the differences between a fixed and a flexible unit trust.	Section 1.1
2.	Why are unit trusts and OEICs referred to as being 'open-ended'?	Section 1.1
3.	Why were OEICs introduced as a new collective investment scheme vehicle?	Section 1.2
4.	In what ways have existing UK laws changed in relation to the repurchase of shares to accommodate OEICs?	Section 1.2
5.	What is the main legislation governing OEICs?	Section 1.2
6.	How are OEICs structured?	Section 1.2
7.	Name three factors for the growth of investment in collective investment schemes.	Section 2.1
8.	What role does the IMA play within the collective investment schemes industry?	Section 2.2
9.	What are the main asset classes used by investors?	Section 2.2
10.	Explain the new three tier structure of the collective investment schemes under the 'COLL' sourcebook.	Section 3.1
11.	What is 'pound cost averaging'?	Section 3.2
12.	Name three differences between CISs and investment trusts.	Section 4.1
13.	Describe how CIS funds might be used for retirement purposes.	Section 5.1

REGULATORY CONTROLS

1.	UK REGULATION AND LEGISLATION	21
2.	DATA PROTECTION ACT (DPA) AND DIRECTIVE	29
3.	PREVENTION OF MONEY LAUNDERING	31
4.	EUROPEAN UNION (EU) DEVELOPMENTS AND PROTECTION	37
5.	UNIT/SHAREHOLDER RIGHTS AND PROTECTION	44
6.	FINANCIAL PROMOTION RULES	51
7.	CANCELLATION OF AN INVESTMENT	52
8.	STAKEHOLDER PRODUCTS	56
9.	MEETINGS OF UNIT/SHAREHOLDERS	57
10.	VOTING AT MEETINGS	60

This syllabus area will provide approximately 8 of the 50 examination questions

Collective Investment Schemes Administration

INTRODUCTION

This chapter looks at various controls exercised over the financial services sector, particularly those not dealt with in the IAQ's FSA Regulatory Environment syllabus. It will look at aspects particularly relevant to collective investment schemes. Additionally, the rights and protection of unit/shareholders will be examined.

1. UK REGULATION AND LEGISLATION

The Financial Services Act 1986 was introduced to regulate the financial services sector following a number of financial disasters. Initially, a system of self-regulatory organisations (SROs) was set up and run by the financial services industry. However, following further problems, such as the collapse of Barings Bank and pensions misselling, the government decided there was a need for further regulation and for the powers of the SROs to be brought together under a single regulator answerable to HM Treasury and Parliament. This resulted in the passing of the Financial Services and Markets Act 2000 (FSMA 2000) which replaced the Financial Services Act 1986. From 1 December 2001, the new Act created the Financial Services Authority (FSA), giving it wide powers to make new rules. These rules are contained in the FSA Handbook.

What is Principles-based Regulation?

The FSA has established 11 high level principles for businesses and these have formed the basis for successful enforcement action. They have to ensure that firms have adequate controls to mitigate the risk of breaking regulatory requirements.

The FSA handbook does, however, contain thousands of rules setting out details on how firms are to behave. Principles-based regulation is about outcomes or ends, while rules-based regulation is about means. Principles-based regulation allows firms to decide how best to achieve required outcomes and allows a much greater alignment of regulation with good business practice.

Senior management, not their regulators, are responsible for identifying and controlling risks. A more principles-based approach allows them increased scope to choose how they go about this. It is obvious that the FSA cannot devise a rule to cover every new financial situation that arises. However, firms are accountable for their actions and principles-based regulation requires management to ensure existing rules are not contravened while greater scope is given on how to conduct their business.

The changing emphasis from rule to principle-based regulation will be noted as you read through the next few pages of this chapter eg, fair value pricing and treating customers fairly.

The FSA for its part has sought over the last few years to reduce the amount of prescriptive rules in its' handbook and to set out principles for firms to follow. These principles are supplemented from time to time by guidance on best practice issued by industry trade bodies. An example of this is the guidance notes issued by the Joint Money Laundering Steering Group (JMLSG) which are drawn up by industry representatives and approved by HM Treasury.

While COLL contains a good deal of detailed rules, the FSA has tried to shorten the prescriptive rules wherever possible. The problem for the FSA is that needs to implement new EU Directives from time to time and the EU Commission appear to be issuing detailed rules which the FSA has, to a large extent, simply copied directly into the handbook.

1.1 FSA Handbook of Rules and Guidance

LEARNING OBJECTIVES

2.1.1 Know the requirements of the Conduct of Business Rules relating to authorisation of Collective Investment Schemes

The FSA handbook should be considered on two levels:

- A set of **Principles** – fundamental requirements relating to prudential soundness, market conduct and the treatment of customers.

- Detailed **Rules**, including general sections (such as authorisation to undertake investment business, training and competency, and complaints), as well as sections for specific types of business (examples include collective investment schemes, building societies and recognised exchanges).

Each separate section within the handbook is called a **sourcebook**, and each is known by a specific abbreviation (you will meet various of these in this chapter). Each chapter is numbered, as is each paragraph, so any part of the handbook can be identified by the abbreviation followed by the chapter and paragraph numbers. For example, COB 7.5.3 is a reference to the Conduct of Business Sourcebook, Chapter 7, Paragraph 5, Point 3.

The general purpose of the handbook is to assist the FSA to meet its regulatory objective of the protection of consumers by providing a regime for the UK financial services industry. Some parts of the handbook are rules that must, therefore, be complied with, whilst other parts offer guidance (an indication of good practice to aid firms in satisfying the regulations). Other parts give directions and requirements, binding on the people to whom they are addressed (such as the Statements of Principle). The handbook clearly indicates Rules by use of a bold capital letter R, while Guidance is identified by a capital letter G. Other letters are used in certain circumstances but do not fall within the content of this workbook.

All FSA documentation is available, free of charge, at its website www.fsa.gov.uk.

Conduct of Business Sourcebook (COBS)

The Business Standards block of the handbook contains all of the detailed sourcebooks relating to the way in which authorised businesses operate. Part of this block is the Conduct of Business Sourcebook (COBS).

Operating an authorised CIS, including operating as an ACD, or acting as trustee/depositary, require the person/firm to be authorised by the FSA to undertake that activity.

COBS took effect from 1 November 2007 and focuses on regulatory outcomes rather than on the procedures and processes firms should use to achieve these. COBS also implements part of the EU Markets in Financial Instruments Directive (MiFID) and other European Directives. COBS places stronger emphasis on senior management responsibility to achieve the outcomes the FSA is looking for, eg, treating customers fairly. COBS is split into a number of chapters, each dealing with a separate part of the relationship with the client. These chapters include information on:

- classification of clients;
- terms of business and client agreements;
- communicating with clients, including financial promotions – rules governing layout and content of financial promotions;
- suitability (including basic advice) governing these activities where undertaken;
- appropriateness (for non-advised services);
- dealing and managing investments on clients' behalf (including best execution);
- preparing product information and providing information to clients;
- cancellation;
- reporting information to clients;
- distance communication.

1.2 FSA Collective Investment Scheme Sourcebook (COLL)

> **LEARNING OBJECTIVES**
>
> 2.1.2 Know the framework of UK regulation and the purpose of the following: the FSA Collective Investment Schemes Sourcebook (COLL); the OEIC Regulations 2001

Previously two sourcebooks had been in operation, ie, the Collective Investment Scheme Sourcebook known by the abbreviation 'CIS' and the replacement operative from the 12 February 2007, the new Collective Investment Schemes Sourcebook abbreviated to 'COLL'. By this date all AFMs transferred the whole of the range of CISs to the COLL rules.

The main aims of the sourcebook are to:
- meet the FSA's consumer protection objective;
- ensure a high and uniform standard of protection for consumers in UK OEIC and AUT schemes.

The FSA Collective Investment Schemes Sourcebook (COLL)

The main aims of the FSA's review which led to COLL were to:
- promote confidence in authorised collective investment schemes;
- create a lighter-touch and more flexible regulatory regime for schemes aimed at more experienced investors;
- harmonise the rules for retail UK unit trusts and UK open-ended investment companies, while at the same time not compromising investor protection or prejudicing the authorised scheme brand;
- generally reduce prescription, provide durability and greater flexibility for AFMs to provide products to fit the needs of investors;
- incorporate the latest European regulatory developments, ie, the UCITS Product Directive.

The COLL details areas in which controls are required, and some guidance on the purpose and parameters of the control. However, it is for the AFM to define the actual control, agree its application with the trustee/depositary, and document the control in the literature available (eg, prospectus) to investors (enabling them to compare different products).

The reduced prescription in the new sourcebook places a greater burden on scheme documentation to clearly describe the operation and behaviour of the scheme. While the new sourcebook contains less prescriptive rules, the scheme documents must make various additional disclosures to ensure investors are correctly informed.

The effect is to shift the balance in the way CISs are governed from the regulatory rules to scheme documentation.

The FSA has recently completed a review of single- and dual-pricing methodologies used by CIS. Following consultation, the FSA has issued revised rules that allow AFMs to have flexibility in deciding which method of pricing is best suited to their funds. This flexibility applies to both authorised unit trusts and open-ended investment companies; and reflects the FSA's focus on principles based regulation with less prescriptive rules.

As indicated in Chapter 1, this workbook concentrates on the administration and rules surrounding retail funds (ie, schemes offered to the general public, whose general lack of knowledge and experience in investment matters necessitates a greater degree of protection). The new sourcebook provides for two types of authorised retail scheme: UCITS and Non-UCITS Retail. COLL has also created a new category of scheme aimed for non-retail investors, called the Qualified Investors' Scheme. As a QIS is a non-authorised CIS, it may only be promoted to non-retail investors. QIS have far greater flexibility with investment strategies than retail schemes. They are less heavily regulated than retail schemes because they are only available to more sophisticated investors and act as a halfway house between retail schemes and wholly unregulated schemes. The diagram following shows the COLL structure of schemes:

Structure of Schemes under the FSA's New Collective Investment Schemes

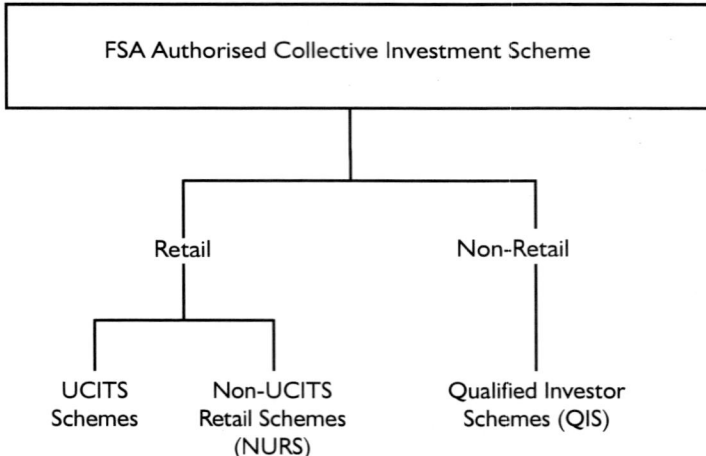

COLL measures affecting collective investment schemes in the retail sector

The FSA is adopting a three-tier approach to investor communication in relation to changes to the operation of a collective investment scheme. A change will be defined as one of three categories:

1. **Fundamental** – requiring prior approval of investors, eg, change to fund objective.
2. **Significant** – requiring 60 days' notice to investors; and
3. **Notifiable** – requiring notification to all investors, but the change may already be in place.

(See also diagram in Section 9 of this chapter.)

Introduction of Mixed Funds

COLL, for retail collective investment schemes (both UCITS and Non-UCITS Retail Scheme, known as NURS), moves away from specific categories of fund such as securities funds, money market funds and futures and options funds. Instead, COLL introduces the concept of mixed funds, ie, funds which may invest in a mixture of all the eligible asset types. This provides AFMs with greater flexibility. They can offer funds which follow the traditional asset class type classification or develop new types of fund which adopt a mixed fund approach.

The FSA's rules in respect of UCITS and NURS aim to ensure that risk is spread and that investments held can be accurately valued and readily disposed of. Details of investment and borrowing powers are covered in detail in Chapter 5.

Broader use of Derivatives

Similarly, the regulatory controls around the use of derivatives have been made more flexible: no longer are AFMs limited to use them just for hedging or efficient portfolio management purposes (such as protecting a fund from the risks of foreign exchange rate changes) but derivatives can now be used for more general investment purposes to deliver the investment objectives of the fund.

Wider use of Non-UCITS Retail Schemes

Introduction of the Non-UCITS Retail Scheme enables authorised funds to have wider investment and borrowing powers, permitting greater investment in assets restricted or prohibited by the UCITS Directive (such as real estate or gold).

Short Reports Introduced

Responding to an industry view that retail investors do not make use of the six-monthly fund report and accounts, the FSA has created a new document format, known as the Short Report. All investors in retail funds must receive a copy of the Short Report; for more details see Chapter 9. The full report and accounts must be prepared (in the format specified in the Statement of Recommended Practice, or SORP), and must be provided to any investor that requests a copy. Whilst the Short Report contains no accounting information, the FSA considers it has sufficient information for retail investors.

Initial Offer Period – Greater Flexibility

Previously, the initial offer period for launching a scheme could not exceed 21 days. COLL removes this limit, requiring only that the period should not be unreasonable when the scheme's characteristics are considered. Schemes investing significantly in physical property might, therefore, apply a longer initial offer period. See Chapter 6 for more details.

Two-hour Notification Limit Removed

Previously, the AFM had a two-hour window after the valuation point to notify the trustee/depositary of the number of units/shares to be issued or cancelled. This prescriptive two-hour limit has been removed from COLL, with the AFM and trustee/depositary required to agree an appropriate time period for the scheme.

Dealing Cut-off Point

To ease administration difficulties in determining the number of units/shares for issue and/or cancellation, for funds operating under COLL where forward pricing is operated, an AFM may introduce a cut-off point after which it will not accept instructions to deal at a price determined at the valuation point. In order to protect investors' interests, the cut-off point should be no earlier than close of business on the day before the relevant valuation point. The valuation point is discussed in more detail in Chapter 6.

Redemption Arrangements

UCITS schemes have to give investors the right to redeem at all reasonable times, valuation for these schemes must be at least twice monthly.

For Non-UCITS Retail Schemes, COLL allows schemes which invest substantially in approved immovables, or whose investment objective is to provide a specified level of return (ie, guaranteed or protected funds), to provide limited redemption arrangements which are appropriate to the schemes, objectives and aims. Periods of redemption must not be more than six months apart.

For daily priced funds there is a risk that a significant redemption might force the AFM to sell fund assets at less than their value in order to meet the redemption. In these circumstances, the unit/shareholders remaining in the scheme would be disadvantaged. To try and protect against this effect, COLL enables daily priced retail funds to use a process of **Deferred Redemption**. Where redemptions at a valuation point are significant (eg, exceeding a pre-disclosed figure, such as 10% of the scheme's value) the AFM will be able to defer redemption in excess of this limit, to the next valuation point. COLL does not specify the exact method to be used (either pro rata dealing or holding all repurchases over to the next day) but does require the method to be fair to investors and disclosed in the prospectus.

Fair Value Pricing (FVP)

There will always be certain assets for which it is difficult to establish a market price, such as equity shares in long-term suspension from trading. The AFM has always been required to determine a price in such cases, but COLL introduced a more formalised approach to how such decisions should be made. The approach, known as **Fair Value Pricing (FVP)**, outlines for the AFM the factors that should be considered in reaching a price decision though, in keeping with the overall aim of COLL in reducing prescription, each AFM must document its own procedures for how FVP will be effected within its firm.

Price Publication

Previously, AFMs were required to publish unit/share prices in at least one national newspaper. Given the various forms of media now available to investors, COLL has changed this requirement. Prices must now be published in an appropriate manner, which enables the AFM to use internet facilities or a telephone enquiry system. COLL includes guidance on matters that need to be taken into account in deciding the manner chosen as appropriate, such as cost, timing, frequency, and general availability to the public.

Charges and Expenses

AFMs are required to disclose, in the Key Features Document (KFD), information on charges and expenses and the effect of these on the fund. The prohibition of performance fees for collective investment funds has been removed under COLL. Such fees are permitted in place of, or in a combination with, the approaches previously permitted (ie, a fixed fee or a percentage of the scheme's value). Details of a performance fee must be provided in the prospectus and KFD or simplified prospectus and the charges must not be excessive when compared to the rest of the industry.

It remains prohibited for promotional payments to be made from the scheme property to any party other than the AFM where permitted under COLL. The FSA has provided guidance in COLL on what constitutes a prohibited payment. Examples are:

- commission payable to intermediaries (such payments should normally be borne by the AFM);
- payments or costs in relation to the preparation or dissemination of financial promotions (other than the preparation of key features); and
- payments to third parties, eg, nominee companies, for maintaining details of beneficial unit/shareholders.

Distributions and Income

The FSA requires that scheme documents should contain this information with appropriate disclosure in the prospectus.

1.3 Rules and Guidance for Qualified Investor Schemes (QIS)

> **LEARNING OBJECTIVES**
>
> 2.1.2 Know the framework of UK regulation and the purpose of the following: the FSA Collective Investment Schemes Sourcebook (COLL); the OEIC Regulations 2001

COLL has created a new category of non-retail authorised scheme, called Qualified Investor Scheme (QIS), which is only available to the same categories of non-retail investors to whom an unregulated CIS may be promoted. QISs are less heavily regulated than retail schemes because they are only available to more sophisticated investors. This type of fund is covered only briefly in this workbook.

Chapter 8 of COLL contains provisions for QIS funds. The FSA considered it important that the rules provide sufficient protection to distinguish them from unregulated funds and to provide market confidence in this new type of product.

AFMs must take reasonable care to ensure only eligible investors become unit/shareholders. This does not preclude expert private customers, providing that they have prior assessment by the AFM as having sufficient expertise and knowledge to understand the details and risks of the product.

Distinctive Features of QIS Funds

Unlike retail funds, the spread of risk and detailed investment limits is not stipulated by the rules. Instead, the FSA has imposed a high-level rule simply requiring the AFM to take reasonable steps to ensure there is a spread of risk, taking into account the scheme's investment objectives and policy. Suitable diversification of risk regarding capital depreciation and income stream into the fund is required and the means of spreading risk must be disclosed in the prospectus. Any limits adopted will be defined by the AFM.

The main features of QISs are:

- Derivatives (eg, traded options, financial or currency futures), precious metals and commodity contracts (if normally and regularly traded on a regulated market) will be permitted but the fund's exposure must be limited to the value of the net assets of the fund.

- Borrowing by the scheme cannot exceed 100% of the net asset value and is subject to adequate cover. There must be the facility in place to close out quickly to avoid inadequate cover.

- Limited issue and redemption for the fund to be provided but this must be allowed for in the instrument of incorporation and the details set out in the prospectus.

- Prices of shares should be published in an appropriate manner and, for limited redemptions, an indicative price should be available on request before the dealing day so investors can see how the net asset value has moved and decide whether to exercise redemption rights.

- A depositary must be appointed to oversee the AFM on valuation, pricing, income calculation and investment requirements.

- Only fundamental changes to the fund (eg, investment objective) will require approval by investors.

- The instrument of incorporation and the prospectus will require more detail than for retail funds.

Overall, while the QIS will be less regulated than retail funds allowing AFMs greater freedom to act, more details will be available to the institutional investors who will be able to interpret and use that information more easily and readily than to ordinary members of the public.

2. DATA PROTECTION ACT (DPA) AND DIRECTIVE

LEARNING OBJECTIVES

2.1.3 Know the reasons for the Data Protection Act 1998 and the responsibilities of investment groups

The EU Data Protection Directive required all Member States to have new data protection legislation in place by 24 October 1998. The government introduced the Data Protection Act to harmonise UK data protection law with the rest of the EU. All eight data protection principles in the Data Protection Act 1984 have been retained, but the law requires all controllers to comply with the principles, whether or not they are required to notify their processing to the Information Commissioner (formerly the Data Protection Registrar). The Commissioner will have greater powers to enforce the requirements of the Data Protection Act 1998.

The rules regulate the use of personal information. Any organisation that maintains personal information must comply with these rules to ensure that the data is:

- processed fairly and lawfully;
- obtained and used only for specified and lawful purpose;
- not excessive;
- accurate and updated;
- kept no longer than necessary;
- kept so that the data subject has access and the right to correct;
- protected against unauthorised access; and
- not transferred outside the European Economic Area, unless to a country with an adequate level of data protection.

The following subsections set out some further changes, additional to the strengthened powers given to the Commissioner.

2.1 Manual Records

The Act now covers any readily accessible manual data as well as computer records containing information relating to a 'data subject' (ie, a living individual). For example, paper-based complaint files are covered.

2.2 Overseas Transfers

Overseas transfers of data are controlled more strictly under the Act. Transfers of personal data outside the European Economic Area (EEA) are allowed only if there is an adequate level of protection for the rights and freedoms of data subjects being transferred. There are exceptions to the general rule prohibiting transfers outside the EEA. These are:

- with consent;
- to make or perform a contract;
- for reasons of substantial public interest;
- in legal proceedings;
- to protect the vital interests of the individual;
- if the information is on a public register;
- on terms approved by the Information Commissioner; or
- when authorised by the Information Commissioner.

2.3 Action Required by Investment Groups

Investment groups must ensure that:

- data controllers treat manual records in the same way as automated records, particularly in relation to subject access (ie, providing information to the person to whom the information relates);
- any processing of personal data is only on the basis of one of the specified criteria, including those for sensitive data;
- procedures meet all the requirements of informing individuals when obtaining or disclosing data;
- procedures to deal with requests by individuals are modified so as to provide the additional information required;
- any data transferred outside the EU receives adequate protection, or that one of the exceptions applies;
- register entries are brought up to date and, as far as possible, rationalised and consolidated;
- they keep up to date with advice from the government and the Information Commissioner.

See www.dataprotection.gov.uk (the Information Commissioner's website) for guidance notes.

3. PREVENTION OF MONEY LAUNDERING

LEARNING OBJECTIVES

2.2.1 Know the requirements of the Proceeds of Crime Act 2002, the Money Laundering Regulations 2007 and the Joint Money Laundering Steering Group guidance as they apply to: control systems; record keeping; staff training; reporting procedures; roles and responsibilities of a Money Laundering Reporting Officer

3.1 Background

The UK law relating to money laundering was initially contained in several different Acts. The Criminal Justice Act 1993 contained provisions necessary to implement the EC Money Laundering Directive and led to the introduction of the 1994 regulations. The legislation relating to anti-money laundering was consolidated within the Proceeds of Crime Act 2002. A third EU Money Laundering Directive has been agreed and required member states to bring the provisions into force by 15 December 2007. The Money Laundering Regulations 2007 came into force on 15 December 2007 as required by the EU Directive. The financial services industry, including collective investment scheme operators, introduced administration procedures in order to comply with these regulations.

FSMA 2000 gave the FSA a statutory duty to reduce the scope for financial crime. The prevention of money laundering is an important component and so the FSA provided rules in the **Money Laundering Sourcebook**.

However, the FSA are moving to a more principles-based approach to regulation, reducing prescriptive rules whenever possible and as a result the ML sourcebook was revoked on 31 August 2006. The FSA introduced new rules, in March 2006, which focused on systems and controls. Detailed guidance will be left to the Joint Money Laundering Steering Group (JMLSG). The FSA will simply require:

- firms to have effective anti-money laundering systems and controls in place to reduce opportunities for money laundering;
- approved persons (the directors and other senior management) to exercise appropriate responsibilities in relation to those anti-money laundering systems and controls.

The JMLSG, a committee of the British Bankers' Association that includes representatives from the trade associations and representative bodies of the financial services industry, has produced Money Laundering Guidance. This guidance, which provides a practical interpretation of the regulations and gives examples of good practice, is aimed at assisting members of the financial services industry to comply with the relevant legislation. The guidance is not mandatory but by, following the guidance notes, financial institutions can be confident of complying with the regulations.

These guidance notes were first brought together in a single document in 1997, covering three areas:

- institutional and private client investment business;
- banking, lending and deposit taking; and
- insurance and retail investment products.

The 2003 version of the guidance notes extended their scope slightly by clarifying that any proceeds of criminal activity should be considered together with money laundering. This requires firms to be conscious of any potential benefit fraud, tax evasion, or other financial crime within the anti-money laundering procedures it establishes.

The updated January 2007 guidance notes refers to prevention of money laundering combating the financing of terrorism. The guidance assumes that customers are not money launderers and is more risk-based. The new guidance notes now require fund operators to collect details of beneficial owners rather than just the registered holders on transfer.

Copies of the guidance notes can be obtained from the JMLSG website at www.jmlsg.org.uk

3.2 What is Money Laundering?

Money laundering is the process by which criminals attempt to disguise the origin of money from burglary, drug trafficking, terrorism or other forms of crime and exchange it for money which can then be classed as 'clean' and used for legitimate purposes. There are three stages:

Placement	The dirty money is transferred into a bank account, an insurance policy or CIS, etc.
Layering	The money is passed through a number of transactions so that its origin is difficult to detect. For example, money may be transferred from abroad to an individual in the UK where it is used to invest in a collective investment scheme or to open an ISA. Shortly after, the investment is either cancelled and a refund obtained, or simply redeemed. A cheque is then drawn by the financial institution and represents clean money to the criminal.
Integration	The money is used in a bona fide operation, eg, the buying of control of a legitimate company or an investment portfolio.

3.3 What the Regulations Require of Financial Institutions

LEARNING OBJECTIVES

2.2.5 Be able to apply the actions required if inadequate evidence is provided

2.2.8 Know the requirements firms and individuals need to meet in relation to money laundering and financial crime prevention and the implications of not meeting the requirements

The money laundering regulations require institutions, such as CIS operators to:

- establish and maintain specific internal controls, policies and procedures;
- seek satisfactory evidence of the identity of investors;
- keep records of customers and transactions, providing an audit trail for at least five years from the date when the relationship with the customer has ended;
- report any suspicious transactions recognised;

- educate and train 'relevant employees' (ie, all employees who might be dealing with customers or their transactions).

The third Money Laundering Directive Regulations will make the following changes to existing anti-money laundering controls:

- In specified cases, eg, in respect of prospective clients which are listed companies, regulated persons may be allowed to carry out what is called '**simplified due diligence**', meaning that the standard procedures can be modified.
- However, where a prospective client is classed as a '**politically-exposed person**' additional checks will have to be carried out. In such circumstances the regulated AFM will have to adopt a risk-based approach as regards the level of detail that may be looked for. In other words, they must comply with the regulations to be sure he is carrying out his responsibilities properly, bearing in mind the penalties shown further down.
- All persons who are regulated for money laundering purposes will need to be monitored and supervised for their compliance with the statutory rules.

Under the law relating to the prevention of money laundering, there are a number of offences, where not just the firm but the individual employee may be liable to prosecution, leading to imprisonment, a fine, or both.

Offence	Punishment (maximum)
Assisting a money launderer	14 years and/or fine
Tipping off, ie, informing the money launderer that he/she is under suspicion/being investigated	5 years and/or fine
Failure to report, ie, if an employee fails to report his/her suspicions	5 years and/or fine
Failing to comply with the rules including establishing and maintaining specific money laundering procedures	2 years and/or fine

The regulations also require all financial businesses to establish a central point of contact with the law enforcement agencies to handle reported suspicions. This means financial institutions must appoint a nominated officer. This person is referred to as the Money Laundering Reporting Officer (MLRO) and this role is an FSA-controlled function. This person is also responsible for oversight of the firm's compliance with the FSA's rules on anti-money laundering systems and controls.

3.4 Action to Take if Money Laundering is Suspected

> **LEARNING OBJECTIVES**
> 2.2.5 Be able to apply the actions required if inadequate evidence is provided
> 2.2.6 Understand the importance of being able to recognise a suspicious transaction and the procedures for reporting it

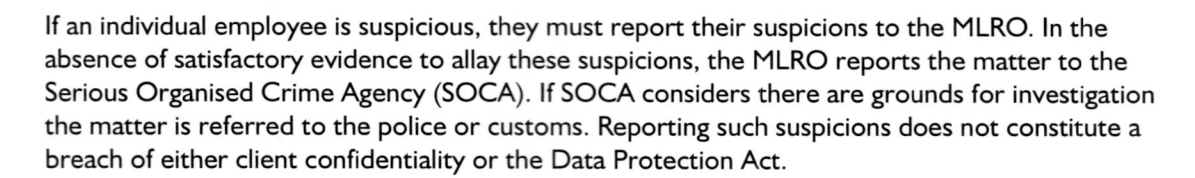

If an individual employee is suspicious, they must report their suspicions to the MLRO. In the absence of satisfactory evidence to allay these suspicions, the MLRO reports the matter to the Serious Organised Crime Agency (SOCA). If SOCA considers there are grounds for investigation the matter is referred to the police or customs. Reporting such suspicions does not constitute a breach of either client confidentiality or the Data Protection Act.

In the absence of satisfactory evidence of a client's legal identity, or if any suspicion of money laundering is aroused, the company must freeze the transaction. This means, if necessary, retaining any unit/share certificate or redemption proceeds pending resolution of the matter. The FSA has amended its rules to allow the AFM and trustee to delay the issue of such documents, if necessary.

3.5 Satisfactory Evidence of Identity and when it is Required

> **LEARNING OBJECTIVES**
> 2.2.2 Be able to apply the money laundering requirements for new and existing clients
> 2.2.3 Know what is satisfactory evidence and when it is required
> 2.2.4 Understand the importance of verification

The requirements to verify the identity of investors began in April 1994. Investors who were clients prior to that date were not required to provide evidence of identity. For new clients, and in certain cases pre-April 1994, existing clients who entered into new transactions, evidence of identity is required.

The evidence required may be in a number of alternative forms but should enable the investor's name, address and date of birth to be verified. For example, electoral register or credit reference agency searches, government-issued documents with or without a photograph, a recent utility bill (gas, electric, etc) or a bank statement are all acceptable. There are a number of exemptions and these are detailed in the guidance notes.

A concession, important to fund managers, is the **Source of Funds** concession. When business is taken and payment is sent by cheque or electronically from an account in the investor's name, drawn on a UK or EU bank account or building society, no further evidence of identity is required. A record should be made of the customer's branch sorting code and account number. This source of funds concession is reflected in the JMLSG guidance.

Although the guidance notes do not impose any obligation on AFMs it is recommended that managers take a risk-based approach to existing customers to ensure they do not represent a risk in terms of money laundering. In some cases evidence of identity may, therefore, be requested.

3.6 The Proceeds of Crime Act 2002

The Act consolidates, updates, and expands all earlier anti-money laundering legislation. Legislation has been passed to tighten control over the proceeds of money laundering and, in Part 7, it is an offence for any person to acquire or possess criminal property, or to provide assistance to any other person to launder the proceeds of any criminal conduct. There is no limit on size if a person gains benefit. The Assets Recovery Agency has been set up to recover property that has been obtained through unlawful conduct.

A mandatory reporting requirement for the regulated sector (ie, organisations regulated by the FSA, including collective investment scheme operators) is established. The offence of not reporting carries a penalty of up to five years in jail on conviction. In addition to reporting if there is knowledge or suspicion of money laundering, the Act introduces a requirement to report if there are reasonable grounds to suspect money laundering in organisations in the regulated sector. This is quite controversial as the previous **failure to report** offences required either knowledge or suspicion of money laundering. The new offence introduces an objective or 'negligence' test whereby an offence will be committed not only if there is knowledge or suspicion of money laundering, but also if there are reasonable grounds for suspicion (ie, where the firm should have been suspicious).

An additional offence of not reporting has been introduced for MLROs and appropriate persons (termed **nominated officers** in the Act). The offence applies to circumstances where a nominated officer who has received an internal report has knowledge, suspicion or reasonable grounds to suspect money laundering and does not make a report to SOCA on their disclosure form, as soon as is practicable after the internal report was received.

A time limit of seven working days has been introduced for SOCA to respond by consent or refusal when a report has been made before a transaction has been completed. If SOCA refuses consent within seven days, there is a 31 working-day moratorium period in which a law enforcement agency, eg, SOCA, must obtain a restraint order if they wish to prevent the transaction from going ahead.

Are there any defences against prosecution?

Members of staff within the regulated financial sector are provided with a defence against not reporting knowledge or suspicion of money laundering if their employer did not provide them with the training required under the regulations to recognise and report suspicions. The defence is not available if there would have been reasonable grounds to suspect.

How does this affect those employed in financial institutions?

Financial institutions should already educate and train relevant employees who may be dealing with customers or their transactions. However, this area of training may be extended to include a wider area of staff as it will be necessary to be more vigilant than previously. Relying on the defence shown above is unsatisfactory and any unwanted publicity could be embarrassing. This will also require the MLRO and others to review their systems of checking on a regular basis.

3.7 Money Laundering: the FSA's Role

> **LEARNING OBJECTIVES**
>
> 2.2.7 Understand the role of the FSA and other crime prevention agencies in relation to money laundering and financial crime prevention
>
> 2.2.8 Know the requirements firms and individuals need to meet in relation to money laundering and financial crime prevention and the implications of not meeting the requirements

The FSA has a role in relation to money laundering that differs from those of its predecessors by being:

- explicit; and
- adequately empowered.

The role comprises both setting and enforcing standards and will reflect the objective, set by statute, relating to reducing financial crime. The roles of SOCA, the police and other criminal law enforcement bodies continue unchanged. The FSA will still continue to work with these agencies but will concentrate on anti-money laundering systems and controls in the firms it regulates.

FSMA imposes on the FSA a regulatory objective to reduce financial crime, ie, to reduce the extent to which it is possible for a business carried on by a regulated person to be used for a purpose connected with financial crime. The Act specifies that financial crime includes any offence involving handling the proceeds of crime. The financial crime objective thus draws the FSA's attention to the risk of criminal proceeds being laundered through the businesses of regulated persons. Such laundering can also pose a risk to two of the FSA's other objectives, ie, maintaining market confidence and the protection of consumers.

How will the FSA use its powers?

The FSA's powers include the regulatory powers of authorisation, powers to make rules and other standard-setting pronouncements, powers relating to supervision, powers of enforcement etc. When approving firms for authorisation to carry on business, identification, record-keeping and internal reporting procedures will be inspected. The FSA will adjudicate whether the appropriate money laundering systems and training are in place.

4. EUROPEAN UNION (EU) DEVELOPMENTS AND PROTECTION

LEARNING OBJECTIVES

2.3.1 Know the purpose of the following EU directives: undertakings of Collective Investment in Transferable Securities Directive (UCITS); Eligible Assets Directive (EAD); Markets in Financial Instruments Directive (MiFID); Capital Requirements Directive (CRD); Distance Marketing Directive (DMD); Market Abuse Directive (MAD); European Savings Directive (EUSD)

EU legislation's influence on financial services in the UK is growing. A number of EU Council directives impact on the fund management industry and the administration of regulated CISs. These include:

- UCITS Directive;
- Eligible Assets Directive (EAD);
- Markets in Financial Instruments Directive (MiFID);
- Capital Requirements Directive (CRD);
- Distance Marketing Directive (DMD);
- Market Abuse Directive (MAD); and
- European Savings Directive (EUSD).

4.1 The UCITS Directive

LEARNING OBJECTIVES

2.3.1 Know the purpose of the following EU directives: undertakings of Collective Investment in Transferable Securities Directive (UCITS); Eligible Assets Directive (EAD); Markets in Financial Instruments Directive (MiFID); Capital Requirements Directive (CRD); Distance Marketing Directive (DMD); Market Abuse Directive (MAD); European Savings Directive (EUSD)

EU legislation to co-ordinate regulations relating to Undertakings for Collective Investments In Transferable Securities (referred to as the UCITS Directive) was passed by a Council Directive in 1985. This allows schemes constituted in member states to be marketed in any other member state, subject to the scheme first being authorised in its home state and obtaining recognition from the regulator in a host state. Collective investment schemes that comply with the terms of the Directive are referred to as UCITS schemes, the COLL sourcebook categorises retail schemes as either UCITS or non-UCITS funds. The AFM of any FSA-authorised fund that is UCITS-compliant will receive a certificate confirming it is a UCITS scheme. This is often referred to as a **passport** and AFMs can use it when notifying the regulators in another member state of the intention to market their fund in that member state.

The fund types listed above also reflect the assets which may be held by those UCITS funds authorised under COLL using the mixed fund approach.

The latest UCITS Directive, UCITS III, is actually made up of two parts: a Product Directive which sets out the rules for funds (see below) and a Management Directive which provides rules on the activities of collective investment scheme operators.

The UCITS Management Directive

The Management Directive:

- Introduces harmonised rules for UCITS operators across all member states making possible the grant of a single authorisation, valid throughout the EU. Such companies will be able to establish branches throughout the EU if they so wish.

- Requires UCITS operators to meet minimum capital requirements to ensure that they can fulfil their obligations.

- Enables UCITS operators to extend their permitted activities. Whilst the UCITS Directive currently limits the permitted business of UCITS operators to the management of their own collective investment schemes, the Management Directive enables them to manage and market their own funds; perform any other function/task associated with fund management activity; manage the assets of EU investment companies; undertake third party administration/fund management activities on behalf of other EU operators; and manage client portfolios, including pensions funds, subject to controlling any conflict of interests.

- Requires a UCITS operator to be authorised in the member state in which it has its registered office.

- Enables UCITS operators to utilise a new 'simplified' type of prospectus in addition to the existing full prospectus. The simplified prospectus would contain similar information as would be included in the 'full' prospectus, but it would be more user friendly, ie, clear, concise and understandable. While offering less detail it should still be a source of valuable information. The contents must include a statement that detailed information is contained in the **full** prospectus and in the yearly/half-yearly reports, which are obtainable free of charge on request. Before concluding a purchase, investors must be offered a copy of the **simplified** prospectus free of charge. Further details on these documents are included in Chapter 3.

What were the reasons for the Directive?

One of the main purposes of the EU is to allow freedom of movement of goods and services. To achieve this in terms of collective investment schemes, it was necessary to have a common set of rules to which funds could comply. Thus the rationale behind the Directive is to:

- eliminate rules which may distort competition and to ensure equivalent protection for unit holders;

- provide rules which make it easier to market schemes across the borders of member states;

- provide rules which help bring about a single European capital market.

Is recognition by the FSA of overseas schemes automatic?

The purpose of the two months notification is to allow the FSA time to consider whether the scheme meets UK regulations and ensure that the scheme complies with the UCITS Directive. Thus recognition of a scheme is not necessarily automatic. The FSA may, within the two month period, reject the scheme and notify the authorities in the host state in question as to why the scheme does not comply with UK law.

What is the UK's position?

The UK, as a member state, must follow the provisions of the UCITS Directive. This has a direct impact on the operation and regulation of collective investment schemes. The FSA COLL sourcebook categorises funds as either UCITS or non-UCITS.

The UCITS Product Directive

This has extended the investment powers of UCITS schemes. See Chapter 5 Section 2.1 for more details.

4.2 Eligible Assets Directive (EAD)

The EU Eligible Assets Directive (EAD) and the related Committee of European Securities Regulators (CESR) sets out guidelines for operators of UCITS schemes. The EAD helps with the definition of which assets are eligible for UCITS schemes to invest in.

The UCITS Directive lays down a set of rules covering which financial instruments a UCITS scheme can invest in. This directive defines those as being transferable securities (eg, shares) and other liquid financial assets (eg, derivatives). However, in a fast-changing world it has been agreed that hedge fund indices may be included. Hedge funds are usually international funds subscribed by wealthy individuals run by managers seeking to achieve above average returns. They do this by investing in currencies and special situations in the world's markets. They frequently gear up (ie, substantially increase) their investments with borrowed money.

For a UCITS scheme to gain exposure to a hedge fund index the index must be sufficiently diversified to represent a benchmark, and it must be published in an appropriate manner. The methodology of the index must provide for the selection and re-balancing of the components (eg, the basis of the investment strategy of the selected hedge funds) and treatment of defined components, whether the index represents an adequate benchmark for the kind of hedge funds to which it refers.

The AFM should of course carry out due diligence on any investment he proposes to make. The changes the above makes are found in COLL Chapter 5 and became effective from 23rd July 2008.

4.3 Markets in Financial Instruments Directive (MiFID)

> **LEARNING OBJECTIVES**
>
> 2.3.1 Know the purpose of the following EU directives: undertakings of Collective Investment in Transferable Securities Directive (UCITS); Eligible Assets Directive (EAD); Markets in Financial Instruments Directive (MiFID); Capital Requirements Directive (CRD); Distance Marketing Directive (DMD); Market Abuse Directive (MAD); European Savings Directive (EUSD)

Formerly the Investment Services Directive (ISD) set out a common set of standards for, and criteria to be met by firms involved in the provision of certain types of financial services. This has been replaced by the Markets in Financial Instruments Directive (MiFID) which became effective from 1 November 2007. It extends the previous directive to reflect the developments in financial services and markets since the ISD was implemented. It is about passporting financial services across the EEA. Where the UCITS Directive enables a **product** to be passported, the MiFID enables a **firm** to be a passported. The term '**passported**' means that once approval has been given in one EEA country it is valid in another, although subject to certain conditions set down by the Regulatory Authority in that other country. Thus a firm authorised in Germany may set up business in the UK without having to apply to the FSA for a separate permission by virtue of the single passport route. If the German firm wanted to operate as a trustee of property funds in the UK, the firm would be supervised by the German authorities in relation to the capital adequacy and by the FSA in relation to the conduct of its UK business activities.

The new Directive sets out detailed requirements governing the organisation and conduct of business of investment firms, and how regulated markets operate. There are new pre- and post-trade transparency requirements (ie, disclosure requirements) for equity markets and more extensive transaction reporting requirements.

The main investments covered are transferable securities. These include shares, bonds, units in collective investment schemes, money market instruments, and futures and options contracts. This latest directive extends the scope of the passport to cover commodity derivatives, credit derivatives and financial contracts for differences for the first time.

The FSA is continuing to simplify its handbook in line with its move towards more principles-based regulation. It has also replaced its Conduct of Business sourcebook with a shorter, simpler one (See Chapter 2, Section 1.1).

4.4 Capital Requirements Directive (CRD)

> **LEARNING OBJECTIVES**
>
> 2.3.1 Know the purpose of the following EU directives: undertakings of Collective Investment in Transferable Securities Directive (UCITS); Eligible Assets Directive (EAD); Markets in Financial Instruments Directive (MiFID); Capital Requirements Directive (CRD); Distance Marketing Directive (DMD); Market Abuse Directive (MAD); European Savings Directive (EUSD)

Firms that are authorised within the requirements of the MiFID are obliged to maintain resources in accordance with the Capital Requirements Directive (CRD) which came into force on 1 January 2007. It replaces the Capital Adequacy Directive. As with other directives that affect the UK financial services industry, the FSA has incorporated these requirements into its own rules. The CRD is reflected within the FSA's Prudential Sourcebook for Banks, Building Societies and Investment Firms (BIPRU). The rules relating to operators of collective investment schemes, and trustees can be found in UPRU (Prudential Requirements for UCITS Firms Sourcebook). This sourcebook sets out the detailed financial resources and prudential standards that the FSA applies to certain firms.

The framework consists of three 'pillars':

- **Pillar 1** of the new standards sets out the minimum capital requirements firms have to meet for credit, market and operational risk.
- Under **Pillar 2** firms and supervisors have to take a view on whether a firm should hold additional capital against risks not covered in Pillar 1.
- The aim of **Pillar 3** is to improve market discipline by requiring firms to publish certain details of their risks, capital and risk management.

The Directive requires disclosure of financial resources. This is to ensure that each organisation subject to the rules has adequate financial resources and that the regulator is sufficiently informed about the capital structure of an organisation. The regulator can then assess whether that organisation is adequately capitalised and, if not, what further measures are needed to ensure investors and other parties involved are adequately protected.

The basic requirement is that a firm must ensure at all times that its financial resources are not less than its financial resource requirement, calculated in accordance with detailed rules contained in the IPRU (INV).

How are the financial resources of organisations engaged in financial activities measured?

There are a number of categories but a bank, building society or full scope investment firm would have to consider the liabilities against its assets and then carry out a calculation of capital resources: eligible assets less foreseeable liabilities. Having calculated its assets it would then subtract borrowings and intangible assets and inadmissible assets to calculate its capital resources.

To illustrate this the FSA has published an example.

Example

Liabilities	£	Assets	£
Borrowings	100	Admissible assets	350
Ordinary shares	200	Intangible assets	100
Profit & Loss			
Account and other reserves	100	Other inadmissible assets	100
Perpetual subordinated debt	150		
Total	**550**	**Total**	**550**

Calculation of **capital resources** eligible assets less foreseeable liabilities

Total assets	550
Less intangible assets	(100)
Less inadmissible assets	(100)
Less liabilities (borrowings)	(100)
Sub total	**250**

Calculation of **capital resources**: components of capital

Ordinary shares	200
Profit & Loss account and other reserves	100
Perpetual subordinated debt	150
Less intangible assets	(100)
Less inadmissible assets	(100)
Capital resources	**250**

This example shows that the company has a clear £250 of free resources after taking into account liabilities.

4.5 Distance Marketing Directive (DMD)

> **LEARNING OBJECTIVES**
>
> 2.3.1 Know the purpose of the following EU directives: undertakings of Collective Investment in Transferable Securities Directive (UCITS); Eligible Assets Directive (EAD); Markets in Financial Instruments Directive (MiFID); Capital Requirements Directive (CRD); Distance Marketing Directive (DMD); Market Abuse Directive (MAD); European Savings Directive (EUSD)

The Distance Marketing of Consumer Financial Services Directive (known as the Distance Marketing Directive, or DMD) seeks to ensure that retail customers within the EU receive sufficient information before contracting at a distance for any financial product or service. As the definition of **financial service** includes effecting payments, the effect of this EU Directive is wider than FSA-regulated business.

In 2004 the FSA revised various COBs rules to reflect the requirements of the DMD. These relate to a retail customer acting at a distance (via a telephone, post, or internet service) to enter into a financial contract, such as investing in a CIS. The product provider must ensure that an internet investor has received the necessary information, such as the Key Features Document, before entering into a binding contract. For postal investors this information can be issued immediately after the deal is placed, though the product provider need not provide a copy of the Key Features Document if it knows the investor has already received a copy of the current information.

An investor can make an investment by telephone without first receiving the Key Features Document, but the product provider must ensure that the investor is willing to deal on the basis of **limited information**. Otherwise the deal should be refused as it might be found legally unenforceable.

Whilst investors receiving advice have cancellation rights there are no mandatory cancellation rights applying to distance deals in collective investment schemes, though a product provider can independently choose to provide cancellation rights.

4.6 Market Abuse Directive (MAD)

The Market Abuse Directive (MAD) came into force on 1 July 2005. It is a law that aims to fight cross-border market abuse by establishing a common approach among EU member states.

What is Market Abuse?

There are seven types of market abuse.

1. Insider dealing – the MAD defines inside information as information that is precise, non-public and likely to have a significant impact on the price of a financial instrument (eg, if an employee finds out his company is about to become the target of a takeover bid and he buys shares before the information becomes public).
2. Improper disclosure – so in the above example he discloses the information to a friend.
3. Misuse of Information – behaviour based on information that is not generally available but would affect an investor's decision about the terms on which to deal.

4. Manipulating transactions – trading or placing orders to trade that gives a false or misleading impression of the supply of, or demand for, one or more investments, raising the price of the investment to an abnormal or artificial level.

5. Manipulating devices – trading/placing orders to trade, which employs fictitious devices or any other form of deception or contrivance (eg, spreading misleading information/rumours designed to increase the cost of shares).

6. Dissemination – giving out information that conveys a false or misleading impression about an investment or the issuer where the person doing this knows the information to be false or misleading.

7. Distortion and misleading behaviour – behaviour that gives a false or misleading impression of either the supply of, or demand for, an investment; or behaviour that otherwise distorts the market in an investment.

The FSA has introduced a code of practice for those involved in authorised firms. It works alongside criminal law but will apply to a wider range of activities. If the FSA is able to prove market abuse it can impose an unlimited fine. The existing criminal offences of insider dealing and market manipulation will remain and continue to carry very stiff penalties – up to seven years in jail. For a number of years we had seen very few successful cases brought by the FSA but more recently it has brought a number of successful cases.

5. UNIT/SHAREHOLDER RIGHTS AND PROTECTION

One of the four statutory objectives of the FSA is to secure the appropriate degree of protection for consumers. The risks that investors face range from the financial failure of institutions through to financial crime, misconduct, and inadequate understanding of the products and services that they use. As a result, the FSA objective of protecting consumers is a common theme applied throughout the FSA Handbook.

Protection for unit/shareholders in a CIS is provided in a number of different ways. The following helps to explain some of the ways in which such holders are protected. These include:

- the provision of rules to regulate the financial services industry;
- the provision of dispute resolution and compensation arrangements; ensuring that the promotion of schemes is not misleading and that investors have the right if they have received advice to change their minds and cancel investments; and
- requiring fund managers to seek approval for significant changes to the operation of a unit trust or OEIC.

5.1 The FSA Rules

FSMA requires the FSA to "maintain arrangements designed to enable it to determine whether persons on whom requirements are imposed by or under this Act are complying with them". Organisations wishing to be involved in the financial services industry must comply with FSA rules.

These must be set out in writing and include:

- establishment of procedures to ensure company representatives are competent to act, are trained and behave in a reasonable manner, when dealing with private customers;
- the maintenance of records and allowing access and inspection by FSA officers and co-operation with inspectors; and
- compliance with S.56 FSMA 2000, which seeks to ensure that individuals who are unfit to be involved in investment business are not engaged by the organisation.

It should be understood that all AFMs and trustees/depositaries are regulated and have to be considered fit and proper. Adequate arrangements must be in place to ensure all employees engaged in regulatory activity are suitable, sufficiently trained and, if appropriate, properly supervised. This would cover recruitment procedures, including the vetting of applicants for employment and taking up of references.

Officers, employees, and representatives must all be made aware of their obligations under the regulatory system and comply with them. Clearly, anyone guilty of serious breaches of the regulations is unlikely to be able to continue working in financial services in a key role.

5.2 How the FSA ensures Organisations are Compliant

Each firm is required to appoint senior individuals to be responsible for controlled functions and to have appropriate systems and controls. The FSA's regulatory approach aims to focus and reinforce the responsibility of the management of each firm, in order to ensure that it takes reasonable care to organise and control the affairs of the firm responsibly and effectively, developing and maintaining adequate risk management systems. It is the responsibility of the management to ensure that the firm acts in compliance with the regulatory requirements.

The FSA's relationship with authorised firms includes baseline monitoring which is designed to ensure that firms comply, on a continuing basis, with the regulatory requirements that apply to them. The FSA has responsibility for gathering information about firms and the products they offer, primarily receiving this information from either regular reporting by firms or notification of specific events. For example, a firm must notify the FSA immediately it becomes aware of any matter which could have a significant adverse impact on its reputation, or any matter that could affect its ability to continue to provide adequate services to its customers. Regular reports include financial reporting, eg, monthly, quarterly and annual returns.

Students should note that the reporting requirements tend to focus on the AFM as AUTs are exempt and OEICs are largely exempt from those rules relating to supervision of firms, such as the reporting and notification requirements and the Conduct of Business rules. The FSA does, however, require regular quarterly reports from the trustee/depositary of the scheme covering areas such as notifiable breaches relating to pricing errors and negative boxes.

Authorised firms are required to appoint a person to be responsible for the compliance oversight function, known as the compliance officer. This is a key person and must be of suitable status: a partner or senior manager who has significant authority within an organisation to see that compliance with the rules is maintained.

Further details about the nature of the FSA's relationship with firms, and the role of its personnel in assessing, supervising and carrying out enforcement responsibilities, can be found in the FSA's handbook and the *IAQ FSA Financial Regulation* workbook.

The FSA has a range of regulatory tools available to meet its statutory objectives. It has powers to take disciplinary action (such as issuing a public censure), vary a firm's permission, and levy financial penalties. There are four circumstances in which the FSA may impose a financial penalty, three of which are potentially relevant to AFMs. These are:

- on a firm where the FSA considers that the firm has breached requirements laid down by, or under, FSMA;
- on an approved person who is guilty of misconduct through failure to comply with the FSA principles, or knowingly involved in a contravention of a requirement of FSMA; or
- on any person who is found to have engaged in market abuse (such as insider dealing).

The principal purpose of financial penalties is to promote high standards of regulatory conduct by deterring firms and approved persons who have breached regulations from committing further breaches, and generally to encourage firms and individuals to act in a compliant manner.

5.3 How this Helps Investors

Each AFM must keep adequate records of transactions with investors, compliance monitoring, complaints by customers, and any disciplinary action taken against officers/employees of the organisation involved. The significance of this becomes more apparent if an investor considers that his rights have been infringed and makes a complaint against a firm.

Providing good customer service is vital for AFMs in today's competitive environment, and endeavouring to resolve all investor complaints made to them is a very important part of that service. Responsibility for attempting to resolve a complaint must rest, in the first instance, with the firm itself. It is in the interests of both firms and consumers that complaints should be resolved at the earliest possible stage.

The FSA has issued a sourcebook to detail the regulatory requirements for Dispute Resolution: Complaints. This sourcebook is known as DISP and provides detailed requirements for handling complaints and the Financial Ombudsman Service (FOS) arrangements.

5.4 Treating Customers Fairly (TCF)

> **LEARNING OBJECTIVES**
>
> 2.4.1 Know the outcome arising from the FSA's principles-based approach to treating customers fairly (TCF)

As part of its drive towards Principle Based Regulation (PBR), the FSA has for some time been working on ensuring that firms are treating customers fairly. This initiative aims to deliver six improved outcomes for retail consumers. Firms should be making TCF an integral part of their business culture and it should be a continuing process. It is important that senior management should be both aware and ensuring that TCF is fully implemented. The FSA expected that firms should have at least reached the implementation stage by March 2007. In 2008, the FSA started to measure the change in outcomes for consumers and this will in time be brought about by enforcement action if not implemented satisfactorily. The FSA is providing training and targeted communications to help firms implement TCF.

If TCF is implemented successfully it should lead to:
- customers being confident they are dealing with firms where fair treatment of customers is central to corporate culture;
- products and services marketed and sold in the retail market being designed to meet the needs of identified consumer groups and being targeted accordingly;
- consumers being provided with clear information and being kept informed before, during and after point of sale;
- consumers receiving advice which is suitable and takes account of their circumstances;
- consumers being provided with products that perform as firms have led them to expect, and the associated service being both of an acceptable standard and as they have been led to expect;
- consumers not facing unreasonable post-sale barriers imposed by firms to change products, switch provider, submit a claim or make a complaint.

You may ask why TCF is necessary when all firms are subject to the FSA Principles for Business, including Principle 6 which states a firm must pay due regard to the interests of its customers and treat them fairly. It is obvious, however, that there are still a significant number of complaints by retail customers buying financial products who are confused over what they have purchased or who get poor after-service. Most of the daily newspapers have a readers' queries page each week dealing with financial queries over the service provided, though most of these are not relating to CISs.

5.5 The FSA Requirements for Complaints Handling

LEARNING OBJECTIVES
2.4.2 Know the regulatory procedures for handling customer complaints

All CIS operators are required to:
- provide the FSA with details of persons within the firm responsible for dealing with complaints;
- have in place an appropriate written complaints procedure;
- publish their complaints handling procedures and make them easily available to consumers;
- publicise availability of the internal complaints handling procedures and membership of the FOS at the initial point of sale and send complainants a copy of this when a complaint is first made;
- have effective internal complaints procedures;
- notify the complainant within five days of the receipt of a complaint, giving the name or job title of the person handling the complaint (together with details of the firm's internal complaint handling procedures);
- keep records of complaints for a minimum of three years from the date of their receipt (to align with the requirements of the Conduct of Business Sourcebook);
- advise the complainant that, where the dispute is not settled, the matter can be referred to the FOS. A copy of their leaflet describing the procedure should be forwarded. The complainant has six months from the time that the final notice is sent to take action;
- make return of complaints to the FSA twice-yearly.

5.6 Dealing with Complaints

> **LEARNING OBJECTIVES**
>
> 2.4.3 Know the role of the Financial Ombudsman Service (FOS)

The following diagram details the timetable for the handling of a complaint relating to a CIS.

Complaints Handling Arrangements – General Action to be Taken

COMPLAINANT	CIS Manager	TIME
Written complaint submitted →		
	Complaint acknowledged by letter giving name/job title of person handling. Plus details of internal handling process	Issued promptly: eg within 5 days of receipt of complaint

Complaint to be investigated promptly and complainant to be kept informed of progress

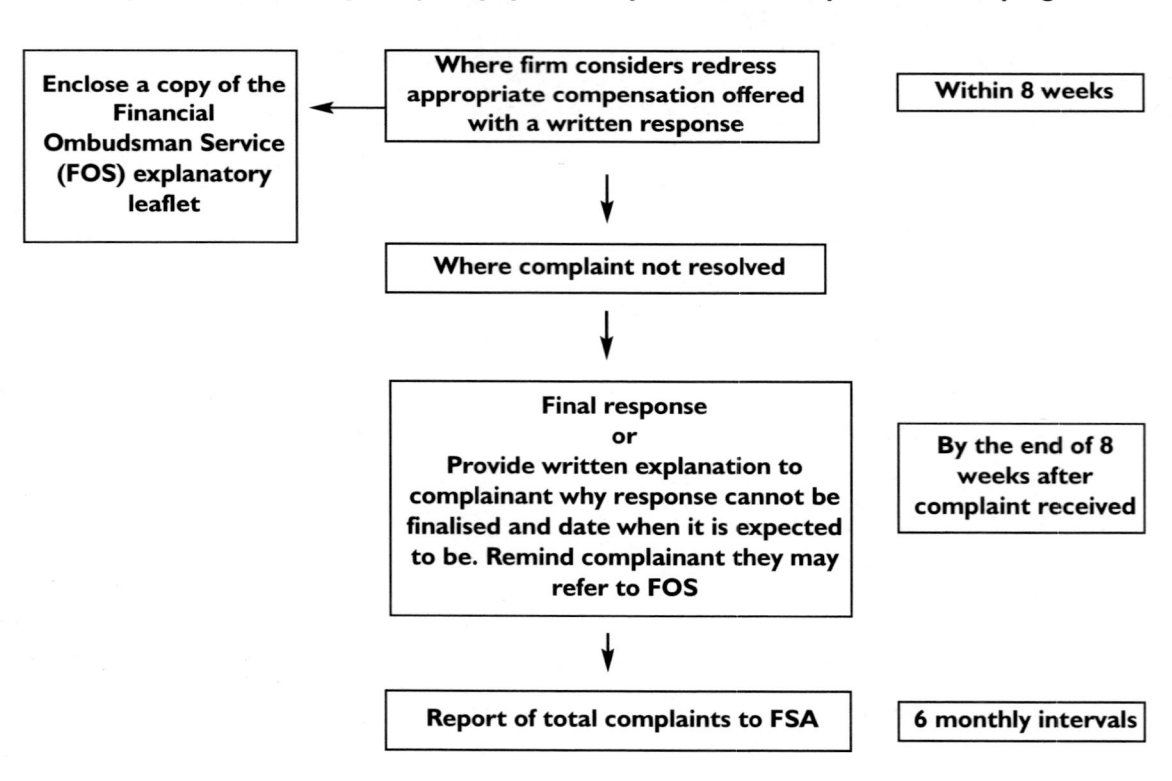

COMPLAINANT	CIS Manager	TIME
← Enclose a copy of the Financial Ombudsman Service (FOS) explanatory leaflet	Where firm considers redress appropriate compensation offered with a written response	Within 8 weeks
	↓ Where complaint not resolved ↓	
	Final response or Provide written explanation to complainant why response cannot be finalised and date when it is expected to be. Remind complainant they may refer to FOS	By the end of 8 weeks after complaint received
	↓ Report of total complaints to FSA	6 monthly intervals

The main stages to complaint resolution are:

1. Stage 1

    The complaint should be taken up by the investor (or the IFA) with the person within the organisation handling the complaint. Most problems will be resolved at this stage.

2. Stage 2

    Within eight weeks of receiving complaint, the complainant should be sent a:
    - final response; and
    - an explanation that will consider the complaint resolved if the complainant does not reply within eight weeks.

3. Stage 3

    At the end of eight weeks after the receipt of a complaint the firm must send a:
    - final response; or
    - response which;
        i. explains why it has not been able to finalise the response and gives an indication when the firm expects to give a final response; and
        ii. informs the complainant of their right if he remains dissatisfied with the response to refer the complaint to the FOS within six months from the date of the final response.

What are the time limits for referral?

The FOS will not entertain a complaint if the complainant refers:

- *less* than eight weeks after the receipt of the complaint by the firm, unless the firm has already sent their final response;
- *more* than six months after the date on which the complainant is advised of the firm's final response and that he may refer the complaint to the FOS; or
- *more* than six years after the event complained of, or (if later) more than three years from the date on which he became aware that he had cause for complaint.

How does the FOS determine claims?

The FOS may reject claims out of hand if it considers them frivolous or vexatious, or that the complaint clearly does not have any reasonable prospect of success, or that a fair and reasonable offer of compensation has already been made. There are several reasons why a more suitable method may be used or the claim may not be within their jurisdiction. However, the FOS will consider what is fair and reasonable in all the circumstances of the case in determining a complaint. It will take into account relevant law and codes of practice.

How much will the FOS award?

If the FOS finds in favour of the customer, it can make an award of up to £100,000, plus costs. If it feels a higher award would be appropriate, it can recommend to a firm that it pays the higher figure, but cannot force it to do so. In line with the nature of complaints that it can consider, the award could be for actual financial loss, pain and suffering, distress or inconvenience, or damage to reputation. Any decision reached is binding on the firm but not on the customer who would still try to explore other avenues of redress. The Ombudsman also has the power to make any decision it sees fit, instructing the firm to take appropriate steps in relation to the claimant.

To summarise, as provided under S.229 FSMA 2000, if an award is determined in favour of the complainant the determination may include:

- a money award against the firm of such amount as the FOS considers fair compensation for financial loss or damage; or
- a decision that a firm takes such steps in relation to the complainant as the FOS considers just and appropriate; or
- both of the above.

5.7 Financial Services Compensation Scheme (FSCS)

LEARNING OBJECTIVES

2.4.4 Understand the circumstances under which the Financial Services Compensation Scheme pays compensation and know the compensation payable

Payment of Compensation

FSMA established a Financial Services Compensation Scheme (FSCS) that provides a single compensation scheme for aspects of financial services regulated by the FSA. This provides for those cases where an authorised firm is unable to meet its liabilities. An example would be if an AFM were unable to pay an award made against them by the FSA in favour of an investor.

The compensation scheme is a final safety net for consumers when a financial services firm goes out of business and it provides a key part of the FSA framework to provide appropriate protection for consumers. The scheme seeks to provide a reasonable level of compensation to individual consumers and small businesses that have lost money through the collapse of a bank, building society, insurance company or investment firm.

The compensation limits for the scheme are shown in the following table:

Protected Deposits	Absolute maximum £50,000 per person for firms declared in default from 7 October 2008
Protected Investments	Absolute maximum £48,000 (100% of first £30,000 and 90% of next £20,000)
Protected Insurance (long term, eg, pensions and life assurance)	100% of first £2,000 plus 90% of the remainder of the claim
Insurance General: Compulsory	100% of valid claim/unexpired premiums
Insurance General: Non-compulsory	100% of first £2,000 of valid claim and unexpired premium plus 90% of remainder of claim
Mortgage advice and arranging	Absolute maximum £48,000 (for business conducted on or after 31 October 2004) (100% of the first £30,000 and 90% of the next £20,000)

Further details can be found at www.fscs.org.uk

6. FINANCIAL PROMOTION RULES

Chapter 3 of the Conduct of Business Sourcebook contains the FSA's rules on Financial Promotions. These rules reflect two of the FSA's principles for business: Principle 6 (Customers' Interests, which states that a firm must pay due regard to the interests of its customers and treat them fairly) and Principle 7 (Communications with Clients, which states that a firm must pay due regard to the information needs of its clients and communicate information to them in a way which is clear, fair and not misleading).

6.1 Financial Promotion

The term **financial promotion** is broader and more encompassing than simply advertising. A definition of the term is "an invitation to or inducement to engage in investment activity". There is no restriction on the method of communication applying to financial promotions. Thus, the following are covered:

- product brochures;
- general advertising in magazines, newspapers, radio and TV programmes, and websites;
- mailshots (post, fax, or email);
- telemarketing activities;
- written correspondence, telephone calls, and face-to-face discussions;
- sales aids;
- presentations to groups of individuals;
- tip sheets and other publications, which may contain non-personal recommendation as to the acquisition, retention, or disposal of investments of any description.

The Rules distinguish between **real time financial promotions** and **non-real time financial promotions**. A real time financial promotion is one that is communicated in the course of a personal visit, telephone conversation, or other interactive dialogue. Non-real time promotions include all other methods, for example, those promotions made by letter, email, or contained in a newspaper, journal, or magazine.

6.2 Confirmation of Compliance and Approval

Firms must arrange for an individual or individuals with **appropriate expertise** to confirm the compliance of non-real time financial promotions. In most companies this may be undertaken by the compliance officer, although what constitutes **appropriate expertise** will vary depending on the complexity of the financial promotion. A firm may arrange for a third party to carry out the confirmation exercise on the firm's behalf, but the responsibility for the financial promotion remains with the firm.

If a firm becomes aware that a financial promotion no longer complies with the financial promotion rules it must ensure that it is withdrawn as soon as reasonably practicable. The FSA will expect a firm to monitor its relevant financial promotions as part of the firm's routine compliance monitoring programme. If at any time the firm becomes aware that investors may have been misled by a financial promotion, it should consider whether those investors who responded should be contacted with a view to explaining the position and offering any appropriate form of redress to those who have suffered financial loss.

The firm must keep appropriate records to show its compliance with the financial promotion rules, particularly concerning the form and content of such promotions. If a CIS issues a direct offer promotion then the promotion must contain key features in the same order as a key features document, and an adequate explanation of the charging structure, including whether all or part of the scheme expenses will be taken out of capital or income, together with the likely long-term effect on capital or income. The FSA has indicated that it does not want to see risk warnings in the small print at the bottom of advertisements. The print size should be no smaller than in the main text of the financial promotion.

In the case of real time financial promotions, the firm must take reasonable steps to ensure that the individual delivering that promotion on the firm's behalf does so in a way which is clear, fair and not misleading; does not make any untrue claims; makes clear the purpose of the promotion and identifies both himself and the firm he represents. In addition, where the date and time of the communication was not previously agreed with the customer, he must check that the customer is happy to proceed and, if not, terminate the contact. He must also respect the customer's right to end the communication at any time or refuse to make another appointment. Promotional telephone calls must not be made at unsocial hours, and no calls should be made to those who are ex-directory (unless they have previously consented).

7. CANCELLATION OF AN INVESTMENT

LEARNING OBJECTIVES

2.4.5 Know the circumstances under which cancellation rights are available to investors including under the EU Distance Marketing Directive

7.1 An Investor's Right to Change his Mind

Once a contract has been issued an investor can sometimes change his mind and cancel within a short period after placing the investment (normally 14 days). There are, however, a number of situations where the contract is binding and the investor does not have the right to change his mind. Such circumstances are set out in Section 15 of the Conduct of Business Sourcebook (COBS).

Cancellation rights enable a person who has entered into, or has offered to enter into, an investment agreement with an authorised person, as a result of advice, to rescind the agreement or withdraw the offer. The rules are applicable to all authorised persons who are either product providers (eg, operators of collective investment schemes) or intermediaries selling units/shares as principal.

The purpose behind these rights is to protect the investor from a salesperson or intermediary selling them something they do not need and may not be able to afford. In most cases, any refund is subject to a deduction in respect of the loss that the authorised person would otherwise suffer as a result of a fall in the market price of the investment (this deduction is referred to as **shortfall**).

7.2   Firms Give Notice of an Investor's Right to Cancel

Firms are no longer required to provide prescribed notices of cancellation, although they may continue to use forms previously prescribed under the original cancellation rules issued in 1989. Cancellation rights may be communicated by providing:

- a summary of cancellation rights pre-sale, eg, in marketing material;
- full details of those rights post-sale, eg, in a letter or brochure, together with a form in which the investor may give instructions to cancel;
- an example of a cancellation notice, see opposite.

Example of a Cancellation Notice

XYZ LIMITED
XYZ HOUSE, FUND STREET, LONDON, AB1 2CD
Registered Office: Registered in England (No. 00000)
Telephone: (000) 0000 Fax: (000) 0000 Telex: 00000
                       Email: XYZ@server.co.uk

CANCELLATION FORM
To be returned only if you wish to cancel the agreement.

To: XYZ Limited, as Authorised Corporate Director of The UK Growth Investment Fund (an investment company with variable capital)

I hereby give notice that I have decided not to proceed with this agreement; and I require the return of any money paid to you or your agent in connection with it which I am entitled to have returned.

| [   ]   Signed: |
| [   ]   Date: |

This notice relates to contract reference

IMPORTANT! YOU SHOULD READ THIS CAREFULLY
YOUR RIGHT TO CHANGE YOUR MIND

YOU HAVE ENTERED INTO THE ABOVE CONTRACT WITH XYZ LIMITED.
You have a legal right to consider the matter again and change your mind if you wish.

Points you should consider

Before you decide whether you want to change your mind, ask yourself:
- If you received personal advice on your investment, are you clear whether the advice was given by an independent adviser working on your behalf or by someone representing us, the company?
- In most cases you should have received a Terms of Business Letter, telling you about your adviser and what to expect in the way of advice and information.
- Have you received all the information you want in order to understand your investment? You should have received Key Features describing the important features of your investment.
- Are you satisfied that the investment is suitable for your needs?

Do you, for example:
- Understand how much you will have to pay now and in the future?
- Understand the charges, expenses and risks which will affect the value of the investment?

If the answer to any of these questions is No you should consult your adviser or the Authorised Corporate Director as quickly as possible. There is no extension to the cancellation period if you ask for further information or if the reply is delayed.

Your right to withdraw from the transaction

If you wish to go ahead with the transaction you should do nothing with the attached cancellation form. If you wish to withdraw, you should send the cancellation form to XYZ Limited, XYZ House, Fund Street, London, AB1 2CD and you must post it on or before the 14th day after the day on which you received this notice.

Financial consequences of withdrawal

If you withdraw, you are entitled to have repaid to you any money you have paid the company subject to a deduction of the amount (if any) by which the value of your investment has fallen at the time at which your cancellation form is received by the company. You will, of course, have to repay any amounts already paid to you under the contract.

7.3 Issue of a Cancellation Notice

If an AFM wishes to apply shortfall, the post-sale notice must be issued within eight days of the investment being made. The notice, explaining the investor's right to cancel, must be sent by post direct to the investor and not via the intermediary. An investor may exercise that right and obtain a refund up to 14 days after they have received the notice. Usually, a slip is provided for the investor to sign and return to the AFM. This slip must be posted to the AFM not later than the last day of the 14 day period.

If an AFM does not intend to apply shortfall, then the issue of the notice, in any other case, should be within 14 days of the investment being made.

7.4 What is the Position if Shortfall Occurs?

LEARNING OBJECTIVES

2.4.6 Be able to calculate cancellation proceeds including shortfall when applicable

Where units/shares are purchased or sold at a single price, eg, in the case of OEICs, any shortfall is simply the difference between the purchase consideration paid by the investor and the sale proceeds. The latter will be based on the price at the valuation point after receipt of the cancellation notice by the AFM.

In the case of a dual-priced CIS, the shortfall on cancellation is calculated on an offer to offer basis. For example, if 1,000 units/shares are purchased at 209p, and the offer price is 196p at the time when the firm receives the notice from the investor that he wishes to cancel, the shortfall is calculated as:

$$(209 - 196) = 13 \times 1000 = £130$$

The AFM has the right to charge shortfall unless:

- the firm fails to provide pre-sale cancellation rights information;
- there is no mention of shortfall in the pre- or post-sale notice of cancellation rights;
- the firm fails to send a post-sale notice within the timetable mentioned above.

8. STAKEHOLDER PRODUCTS

LEARNING OBJECTIVES
2.4.7 Understand the protection provided by stakeholder products

8.1 Development of a Simplified Products Regime (Stakeholder Products)

During 2003/04 the government consulted the industry, consumer groups and others on proposals for the launch of a series of simple, low-cost, risk-controlled savings and investment products. These products were recommended by a report commissioned by the government (the Sandler Report). The main aim of the Sandler Report was to find ways of improving financial inclusion, ie, encouraging individuals and families, many of whom do not have bank accounts or savings, to start or increase saving. A good many of these cases will involve low-income families and others who simply do not understand financial products and are concerned about the risks.

Apart from financial inclusion, the government is seeking to reduce the burden on the state by encouraging people to save for retirement; it was also conscious of the need to promote confidence in the UK financial services industry following a number of high profile failures, such as the Maxwell affair and the problems experienced by policyholders in Equitable Life.

8.2 Savings and Investment Products Regulations 2004

As indicated above, these products have been dubbed **Stakeholder Products**. The Treasury issued the Stakeholder Savings and Investment Products Regulations in November 2004 in time for a planned launch of the products in April 2005.

The regulations provide for the issue of products which cover the range of financial services. They include:

- a cash deposit account on which the rate of interest must be within 1% of the Bank of England base rate;
- medium-term products, such as unit trusts and OEICs. Such products must be single-priced, subject to an annual management charge cap of no more than 1.5% per annum and contribution can be invested in a limited range of fund types which are perceived to be lower risk;
- pension products, ie, stakeholder pensions, with similar rules around providing investors with simple pensions with clear charges (a single charge) which are capped and reduce risk through relevant asset classes.

The success of these products will depend, to a large extent, on the willingness of product providers such as AFMs to provide products which meet the regulations. At this stage it is too early to say whether these products will be successful.

9. MEETINGS OF UNIT/SHAREHOLDERS

LEARNING OBJECTIVES

2.4.8 Understand the rights of unit/shareholders in relation to changes to the fund and the protection afforded by meetings

A formal meeting of unit/shareholders is a method of allowing holders to participate in the decisions on key issues concerning the collective investment scheme involved. Meetings of shareholders in listed public companies, for example, are commonplace; such companies may have extraordinary general meetings (EGMs) for special purposes in addition to annual general meetings (AGMs) as required under company law. It is an early court case which provides the definition for meetings as "an assembly of people for a lawful purpose" or "the coming together of at least two persons for any lawful purpose" (Sharp v Dawes 1876).

The FSA (COLL) sourcebooks provide for meetings of unit/shareholders as part of the investor protection framework put in place by the FSA. Until recently, OEICs, because they are companies, were required to hold AGMs but this is no longer a requirement for newly launched OEICs and existing OEICs can choose to dispense with AGMs subject to shareholder notice being given. The reason is twofold. Firstly, AGMs tend to cover only routine matters like re-appointment of auditors and, secondly, very few shareholders in practice attend the meetings.

Under the COLL sourcebook only fundamental changes which the AFM proposes to make will require a meeting to be held. The following diagram provides an overview of the requirements for treating proposed changes:

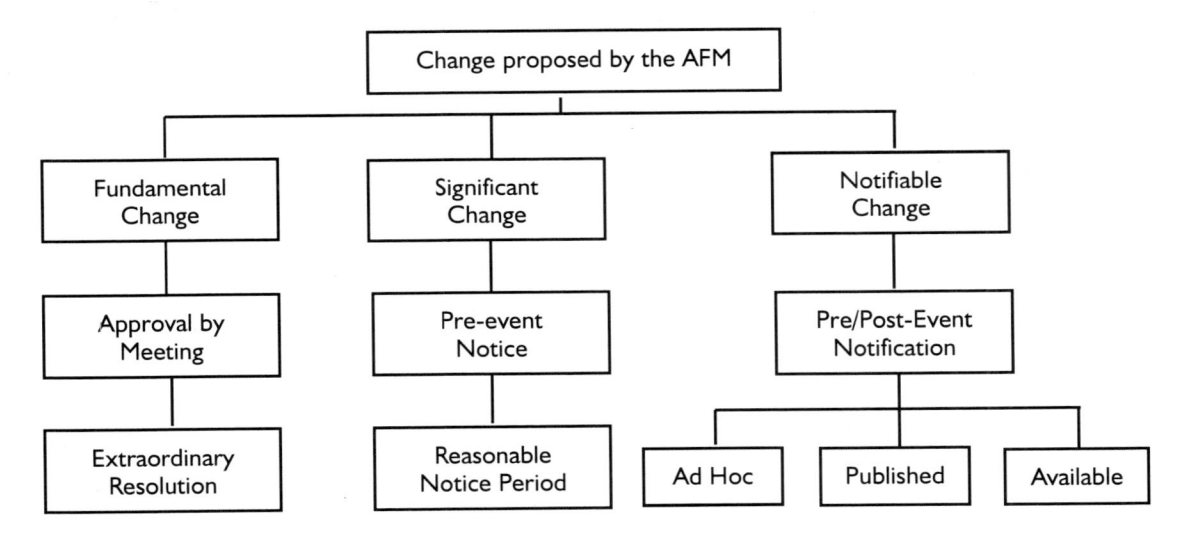

```
                    Change proposed by the AFM
                              |
        ┌─────────────────────┼─────────────────────┐
   Fundamental           Significant            Notifiable
     Change                Change                Change
        |                    |                     |
   Approval by            Pre-event           Pre/Post-Event
    Meeting                Notice              Notification
        |                    |                     |
                                          ┌────────┼────────┐
  Extraordinary          Reasonable      Ad Hoc  Published  Available
   Resolution           Notice Period
```

An example of a significant change is a change in any operational policy such as dilution policy or an increase in the AFM's initial charge where units/shares are purchased through a group savings plan. The AFM must issue a notice of such changes using a reasonable period (at least 60 days) prior to the change taking effect.

An example of a notifiable change is a change in the time of the valuation point. The manner and timescale of notification would depend on the nature of the change but could involve:

- sending an immediate communication to unit/shareholders;
- publishing the information on a website; or
- including notice in the next Manager's Report and Accounts.

Fundamental changes are covered below.

9.1 Why Meetings of Unit/Shareholders in CIS are held

The FSA (COLL sourcebook) requires unit/shareholders to be given notice to attend a meeting for their agreement to a fundamental change. The AFM must determine, in each case, whether a change is fundamental. Examples of such changes are:

- modification of the instrument of constitution, eg, trust deed (subject to defined exceptions);
- a change of investment objectives or policy, eg, from investing in one country to another;
- reconstruction of a scheme whereby part or all of the property of a unit trust scheme becomes the property of another scheme or schemes, eg, mergers of CISs;
- removal of the manager of a CIS;
- a change in investment policy to allow the CIS to invest in derivatives as an investment strategy which increases volatility.

These changes must be approved by extraordinary resolution.

9.2 Who may Convene a Meeting of Unit/Shareholders in a CIS?

To convene a meeting is to call a valid meeting with the required notice and in the form stated by the regulations. A meeting may be convened by:

- the trustee/depositary, manager or ACD; or
- the trustee/depositary or manager, on the request in writing of registered unit/shareholders holding not less than one-tenth (or any lesser proportion than one-tenth specified for this purpose in the instrument of constitution) in value of the units/shares in issue. In practice, this power is little used.

If unit/shareholders requisition a meeting, the regulations require the trustee/depositary or manager to convene a meeting within eight weeks. In the unlikely event that they fail to do so, the unit/shareholders would have a right to take up the matter with the FSA which allows for powers of intervention.

9.3 The Notice Required and how it is Given

In the case of unit/shareholders, at least 14 days' notice must be given to all those who hold units/shares before the notice is given. Unless a unit or share is a **participating security**, the AFM can select a cut-off point for holders on the register which is a reasonable time before notices are sent out.

The notice period is at least 14 days, inclusive of the day on which the notice is first served and the day of the meeting. Notice is considered given on the second business day following the day of posting. An example is shown in Appendix 2. The notice must specify the place, day and time of the meeting, and the wording of the motions which are to be resolved.

The accidental omission to give notice, or the non-receipt of notice by any of the unit/shareholders, does not invalidate a meeting. This, of course, does not validate the meeting if a unit/shareholder, who might not agree to a change, is deliberately excluded.

9.4 Those Entitled to Attend a Meeting

The following have the right to attend:

- the AFM (and other directors, if any);
- trustee/depositary;
- all registered unit/shareholders (and any bearer holders);
- persons appointed as proxies by registered unit/shareholders;
- auditors, in the case of a CIS.

Additional people may be entitled to attend as non-associated beneficial owners. These might include a bank acting on behalf of others by holding units/shares in a nominee name. In the case of a CIS, the Instrument of Incorporation may include other categories of person or organisation that are entitled to attend (but not vote) at the meetings.

9.5 Who Conducts the Meeting?

A chairman, who is nominated by the trustee/depositary, is required at every meeting. In the case of a CIS, the Instrument of Incorporation will usually provide that the chairman will be the duly authorised representative of the AFM who will preside at every meeting. If no such person is nominated to be chairman, or if at any meeting the person nominated is not present after a reasonable time of the appointed time of the meeting, the unit/shareholders must choose one of them to be chairman.

The chairman's main function is to ensure that the meeting is conducted according to the notice and agenda, unless the meeting consents to a variation in the order. The chairman may decide points of order and other incidental matters which require a decision at the time.

9.6 The Quorum

A quorum is the minimum number of persons entitled to be present at a meeting (or their proxies) for it to be valid.

In a CIS, the number of unit/shareholders required to constitute a quorum at a meeting is two, present in person or by proxy or, in the case of a corporation (company), by a duly authorised representative.

The requisite quorum must be present at the commencement of the business, otherwise any business transacted is invalid. If after a reasonable time from the time appointed for the meeting, a quorum is not present, the meeting does not continue. If the meeting was convened on the requisition of unit/shareholders in a CIS it is dissolved. In any other case the meeting shall stand adjourned to such a day and time, not being less than seven days after the day and time of the meeting and a place to be appointed by the chairman.

Generally, few people attend, but the regulations allow that, where at an adjourned meeting, a quorum is not present after a reasonable time from the time of the meeting, one person entitled to be counted towards a quorum present at the meeting shall constitute a quorum. The notice of the adjourned meeting warns unit/shareholders that those attending will form a quorum. The chairman may adjourn the meeting to another time and/or place with the consent of the quorum present, and may do so if so directed by the meeting. No business can take place at any adjourned meeting except that which might have taken place at the meeting from which the adjournment took place. The chairman may adjourn because of disorder among those present. He may also adjourn if more attend than the accommodation can cope with. However, adjournments for these reasons are not very common.

10. VOTING AT MEETINGS

LEARNING OBJECTIVES

2.4.8 Understand the rights of unit/shareholders in relation to changes to the fund and the protection afforded by meetings

Except where an extraordinary resolution is required or permitted under the Instrument of Incorporation, any resolution of unit/shareholders is passed by a simple majority of the votes cast. After each item on the agenda has been considered by those present, the chairman must dispose of each item in some way; usually this means that a vote is taken. A motion is put to the meeting and is resolved as an extraordinary resolution by vote on a show of hands unless, either before or on a declaration of the result of a show of hands, a vote by poll is demanded by any of the following parties:

- the chairman;
- trustee/depositary; or
- at least two unit/shareholders (including proxies for unit/shareholders).

In the case of equality of votes cast in respect of a resolution put to a general meeting, any chairman appointed is entitled to a casting vote in addition to any other vote he may have.

It must be noted that as unit trusts have converted to the COLL sourcebook they have amended their scheme documentation in respect of meetings to be more aligned with the OEIC model. One reason for this is the ability within COLL for a unit trust to issue multiple unit classes.

10.1 How Voting by Poll Differs from a Show of Hands

The important difference between a poll and a show of hands is that whereas on a show of hands each person present gets one vote, in a poll each unit/shareholder shall have voting rights according to the value of his unit/shares as a proportion of the value of all the units/shares in issue at the cut-off date selected by the AFM prior to the service of the notice of the meeting.

An extraordinary resolution requires, whether on a show of hands or on a poll, a majority consisting of 75% of the total number of votes cast for and against such resolution. Votes do not all have to be cast the same way, eg, a nominee company may vote for or against as instructed by the beneficial owner.

Note: The term 'proxy' is also the name given to a person who can be appointed to attend and vote on behalf of a unit/shareholder at a meeting. The authority vested in a proxy may be valid for up to 12 months and the proxy may or may not be a unit/shareholder. No manager or director of a CIS shall be entitled to be counted in the quorum of or be entitled to vote at any meeting of the trust/company in respect of units/shares held in the manager's box. Similarly, an associate of the manager/director(s) who may hold units/shares (eg, of an associate of a life company or of a discretionary investment management company) may not vote, although they could count towards a quorum. This prohibition does not apply to any units/shares held on behalf, or jointly with, a person who, if he were the registration holder, would be allowed to vote and from whom the director, manager or its associate have received voting instructions.

10.2 Class Meetings

Some CISs may have multiple unit/share classes. Some unit/share classes may have different rights to other unit/share classes. To be fair to the unit/shareholders of each class, the trustee/depositary may require separate class meetings to be held when there may be a conflict of interest between the classes of holders. In these circumstances, only if the unit/shareholders at each separate meeting duly pass the same extraordinary motion is the resolution considered passed.

10.3 Keeping Records of Meetings

Minutes must be made at every meeting of unit/shareholders and are defined as a written record of the business transacted, including all resolutions and proceedings. The AFM is responsible for the expense of keeping and recording the minutes.

When the minutes of meetings are completed they are signed by the chairman as conclusive evidence of the matters stated in the minutes. The meeting shall be deemed to have been duly held, and convened and all resolutions passed to have been duly passed until the contrary is proved.

END OF CHAPTER QUESTIONS

Think of an answer for each question and refer to the appropriate section for confirmation.

Question		Answer Reference
1.	In a sentence, describe what the Financial Services and Markets Act 2000 represents in connection with financial services.	Section 1
2.	What are the two objectives that the FSA Handbook seeks to achieve?	Section 1.1
3.	Outline the structure of the FSA Sourcebook.	Section 1.2
4.	What are the main aims of the FSA Sourcebook?	Section 1.2
5.	Why has the CIS (COLL) Sourcebook: a) introduced the concept of mixed funds? and b) what benefit is this to AFMs?	Section 1.2
6.	What are the distinctive features of qualified investor schemes funds?	Section 1.3
7.	Name four rules under the Data Protection Act, for the computerised storage of clients' personal information.	Section 2
8.	What are the three stages of money laundering?	Section 3.2
9.	How can collective investment scheme operators be confident of complying with the Prevention of Money Laundering Regulations?	Section 3.3
10.	What is the reporting procedure if a collective investment scheme operator is suspicious about potential money laundering and to which body should he report it?	Section 3.4
11.	What European Union legislation provides for the co-ordination of regulations applying to collective investment schemes?	Section 4.1
12.	What is the purpose of the MiFID?	Section 4.3
13.	Under the Capital Requirements Directive distinguish between what are an authorised firm's own funds and liquid capital.	Section 4.4
14.	Under the Capital Requirements Directive what are the four categories of investment firm?	Section 4.4
15.	Explain the purpose and principal features of the Distance Marketing Directive.	Section 4.5

Question	Answer Reference
16. What are the FSA requirements for complaints handling?	Section 5.5
17. What are the limits for financial compensation under the Financial Services Compensation Scheme?	Section 5.7
18. Under what circumstances has an investor the right to change his mind and cancel his investment?	Section 7.1
19. Explain what shortfall is in connection with the purchase of units/shares in a collective investment scheme.	Section 7.4
20. Who may convene a meeting of unit/shareholders?	Section 9.2
21. Who is responsible for the conduct of a meeting of unit/shareholders?	Section 9.5
22. What is: a) a Quorum b) a Quorum for a meeting of unit/shareholders?	Section 9.6
23. Who may: a) adjourn meetings of unit/shareholders? b) on what grounds?	Section 9.6
24. How is voting at such meetings carried out?	Section 10
25. Following a vote on a show of hands at a meeting of unit/shareholders, who may demand a vote by poll?	Section 10
26. How may: a) a person vote at a meeting, yet not attend? and b) what are the rules involved?	Section 10.1
27. What majority of a vote is required for passing of an extraordinary resolution?	Section 10.1
28. When would separate meetings be held of holders of income units and holders of accumulation units in a unit trust?	Section 10.2
29. Who is responsible for taking the minutes of a meeting of unit/shareholders?	Section 10.3

CONSTITUTION 3

1.	ESTABLISHMENT OF A SCHEME – ALTERNATIVE STRUCTURES	67
2.	INSTRUMENT OF INCORPORATION – PURPOSE AND CONTENT	69
3.	SCHEME STRUCTURE	72
4.	ISSUE AND CANCELLATION OF UNITS/SHARES – AFTER THE LAUNCH ENDS	73
5.	THE LAUNCH OF A COLLECTIVE INVESTMENT SCHEME	75
6.	ARE THERE ANY OTHER WAYS A CIS CAN BE SET UP?	78
7.	HOW IS A CIS WOUND-UP?	79

This syllabus area will provide approximately 3 of the 50 examination questions

1. ESTABLISHMENT OF A SCHEME – ALTERNATIVE STRUCTURES

LEARNING OBJECTIVES

3.1.1 Know the alternative constitutional structures of authorised Collective Investment Schemes

1.1 Introduction

As we saw in Chapter 2, there are three broad levels of regulation of collective investment schemes in the UK. These are summarised as European, HM Government and the FSA. They should be viewed as a hierarchy of rules that, at each level, deals with more specific aspects of collective investment scheme regulation. To recap, the three levels are:

Level 1	European – UCITS Directive
Level 2	Government Legislation:
	i. Financial Services and Markets Act 2000 (FSMA); and
	ii. OEIC Regulations 2001 (as amended).
Level 3	FSA Regulations – Collective Investment Schemes Sourcebook (COLL).

If a UK scheme complies with the provisions of the UCITS Directive it is a UCITS scheme and, subject to local registration requirements, can be promoted throughout the EEA. Not all regulated schemes are UCITS schemes but are, nevertheless, permitted to be established under HM Government legislation and FSA regulations.

The two types of retail scheme authorised by the FSA are unit trusts and open-ended investment companies (OEICs, also known as investment companies with variable capital, or ICVCs). From a legal standpoint, authorised unit trusts (AUTs) will be established under FSMA whilst OEICs will be established under the OEIC regulations.

1.2 Authorised Unit Trusts (AUTs)

Under Section 237 of FSMA, a unit trust scheme is a collective investment scheme under which the property is held in trust for the participants by the trustee. An AUT is constituted by a **Trust Deed**, entered into by the fund manager and the trustee who must be independent of each other. The fund manager and the trustee are authorised persons under FSMA. The trustee is charged with safeguarding the assets of the trust for the benefit of the unit holders. The unit holders have a direct beneficial interest in the unit trust's portfolio of investments. The AUT does not have a separate legal personality and cannot, therefore, sue or be sued in its own name – everything is done on its behalf by the trustee or AFM.

1.3 Open-Ended Investment Companies (OEICs)

Section 262 of FSMA empowers the Treasury to make regulations that enable the establishment of open-ended investment companies (the OEIC Regulations). The OEIC is constituted by an **Instrument of Incorporation**, ie, it is a corporate body, and Regulation 15(4) of the OEIC Regulations requires such a company to have at least one director; if the company has only one director then it must be a corporate director authorised under FSMA and is referred to as an authorised corporate director (ACD). A corporate director is a company with limited liability. The OEIC will appoint a depositary to hold the scheme's assets and provide oversight of the operation of the scheme. In contrast to investors in a unit trust, the shareholders in an OEIC will have no direct beneficial interest in the schemes underlying portfolio but, through their shareholdings in the OEIC, will have an indirect beneficial interest. Again, in contrast to a unit trust, the OEIC as a corporate body has its own legal personality and can sue or be sued.

1.4 Application and Authorisation

> **LEARNING OBJECTIVES**
>
> 3.1.2 Understand the process and requirements of authorisation
>
> 3.1.3 Know the purpose of the following documents: instrument of incorporation (OEIC); trust deed (Unit Trust); prospectus and simplified prospectus; key features/ key facts; marketing plan; FSA application form and solicitor's certificate

While the regulations governing applications are provided under FSMA for AUTs and under the OEIC Regulations and FSMA for OEICs, the requirements are similar. Application forms are available from the FSA. As appropriate, the fund manager and trustee or the ACD and depositary, who must be duly authorised persons, are required to:

- Submit a joint application giving details of themselves and the scheme.
- Be independent of each other.
- Provide a copy of the draft trust deed (for AUTs) or instrument of incorporation (for OEICs).
- Provide a three year business plan.
- Provide a solicitor's certificate stating that the trust deed or instrument of incorporation complies with the relevant rules under the FSMA (for AUTs) and the OEIC Regulations (for OEICs).
- Submit a copy of the draft prospectus and simplified prospectus.
- A checklist for the contents of the prospectus.

The name of the scheme must not be undesirable or misleading. Examples here would be to adopt the same name as another existing scheme or to have a name that implied the fund or fund manager has merits or qualities that may not be justified. Other examples would be if the name were inconsistent with the investment objectives of the fund, or suggested that the return to investors was guaranteed when it did not meet all the requirements for such a guarantee.

The completed application form and draft documents are sent to the FSA's Collective Investment Schemes and Mutuals Department, accompanied by the relevant application fee. The FSA has up to six months in which to consider a completed application following its receipt and must inform the applicants of its decision within that timescale. In practice, the FSA aims to process a completed application relating to a UCITS scheme within six weeks. If the FSA is satisfied with the application an authorisation order is issued.

2. INSTRUMENT OF INCORPORATION – PURPOSE AND CONTENT

LEARNING OBJECTIVES

3.1.3 Know the purpose of the following documents: instrument of incorporation (OEIC); trust deed (Unit Trust); prospectus and simplified prospectus; key features/key facts; marketing plan; FSA application form and solicitor's certificate

2.1 Instruments of Constitution – Trust Deeds and Instruments of Incorporation

The Trust Deed for an AUT and Instrument of Incorporation for an OEIC are similar in that they set out the terms of the scheme's constitution, its name, location and investment objectives, and contain rules about the internal management of the scheme. In each case the purposes of the document are to protect consumers and to ensure that holders of different classes of units or shares are treated equally; both are key from a regulatory perspective. Further detailed rules about the management of the scheme will be included in the prospectus (see Section 2.3 of this chapter).

The FSA COLL sourcebook (Chapter 3) sets out requirements that are:

- common to both types of collective investment scheme; and
- specific to the type of scheme.

The OEIC regulations (Schedule 2) sets out requirements that:

- are required for OEICs; and
- have some commonality with the FSA COLL sourcebook but also include some additional requirements.

Thus several of the matters set out in the COLL sourcebook are required to be included under the OEIC regulations or as a consequence of relevant trust law.

Further statements are required if the scheme or the fund manager are to take advantage of the powers under the rules in the sourcebook. In other words, some of the matters covered by the rules are not mandatory but permissive; for example, if the manager wishes to issue more than one class of unit or share then appropriate provisions must be included in the document.

Additional matters that are not specified in the COLL sourcebook may be required to be included in order to comply with the OEIC regulations and for the purposes of making the scheme eligible under relevant tax, pensions or charities legislation.

The Investment Management Association (IMA) has prepared a model Trust Deed and a model Instrument of Incorporation as guides for the industry. In the case of the Instrument of Incorporation, this document is broadly similar to the Memorandum and Articles of Association of a company set up under the Companies Act.

In both cases the document sets out the powers and limitations of the scheme and serves as a guide to all those involved, whether investors, the fund managers, the depositary, auditors or regulators. The document will show how the scheme will be managed and provides a benchmark for those with oversight responsibilities to ensure the AFM operates the scheme as intended.

2.2 COLL Requirements common to Trust Deeds and Instruments of Incorporation

There are some basic requirements that apply to the relationship between the instrument constituting the scheme (the *document*) and the COLL rules. The document must not contain any provision that:

- conflicts with any rule in COLL;
- prevents units or shares in the scheme being marketed in the UK;
- is unfairly prejudicial to the interests of the holders generally or to the holders of any class of units/shares.

Where a power is conferred by the rules then exercise of that power is subject to any restriction that may be included in the document. So, for example, where the investment and borrowing powers of the scheme are subject to restrictions in the COLL sourcebook the scheme operators can put in place more restrictive provisions in the document if they wish.

Instruments relating to UCITS Schemes and Marketing in Europe

Where the fund is a UCITS scheme then the instrument of constitution may not be amended, once the fund has been launched, in such a way that it ceases to be a UCITS scheme. There is nothing to prevent a non-UCITS scheme being converted to a UCITS scheme subject to it meeting all the UCITS requirements. If an AFM wishes to market a UCITS fund in any EEA state other than the UK, the manager must notify the FSA of its proposal, specifying the EEA state concerned. The FSA is required to be notified no later than the notification to regulatory authorities in the other EEA state concerned.

2.3 Prospectus

The COLL rules require that the authorised fund manager must draw up a detailed prospectus to provide information for investors. This information must be up to date and available and free of charge, to help investors and their advisers make a balanced and informed decision as to any investment prior to purchase. It does, therefore, contain details on the fund's constitution, investment objectives, operation and the persons responsible; it will also contain details about the fund's investment policy, investment and borrowing restrictions, eligible markets, valuation and pricing policies, what expenses are deductible from the scheme property and any dilution levy/adjustments arrangements. A copy of the original prospectus and any alterations must be sent to the FSA. The detailed requirements for publishing are:

- A prospectus must be drawn up in English and published as a document by the authorised fund manager and, for an OEIC, it must be approved by the director(s).
- The authorised fund manager must ensure that the prospectus:
  - contains the comprehensive information required by the COLL sourcebook (see list below);
  - does not contain any provision which is unfairly prejudicial to the interests of unit/shareholders generally or to the unit/shareholders of any class of units/shares;
  - does not contain any provision that conflicts with any rule in the sourcebook; and
  - is kept up to date and that revisions are made to it, whenever appropriate.

2.4 Simplified Prospectus, Key Features Documents and Key Facts

> **LEARNING OBJECTIVES**
>
> 3.1.3 Know the purpose of the following documents: instrument of incorporation (OEIC); trust deed (Unit Trust); prospectus and simplified prospectus; key features/key facts; marketing plan; FSA application form and solicitor's certificate

Although fund managers are obliged to publish and make available the detailed prospectus, in practice few investors have the time or inclination to read such documents. In order to improve the provision (disclosure) of information to investors the regulators, prior to the FSA, introduced a document called key features which was intended to provide potential investors with more focused information about the products.

The EU has also sought to introduce a Simplified Prospectus (SP) designed to provide investors with key information about a UCITS fund. The requirement to issue an SP was included in the UCITS directive and, following consultation, the FSA has recently introduced new rules to implement this document.

As the name 'Key Features' suggests, the information in this document is important for investors and their advisers to use in deciding whether to invest in a fund. Whilst the prospectus must be available, on request, there is no requirement to issue it to investors automatically. In contrast, the FSA requires all potential investors to be supplied with a copy of the Key Features Document (KFD). An example is shown in Appendix 3.

It is a requirement that, whether printed in hard copy or in an electronic format, KFDs must be produced and presented to at least the same quality and standard as the associated sales or marketing material; if KFDs are produced as part of sales material for a CIS then the KFDs have to be given appropriate prominence in the document.

Key Facts was originally intended to be a document that gave a very short description of an investment or fund, along with certain information about the adviser where financial advice was sought or provided. The purpose of this document is currently focused on information about the financial adviser, advice provided and the costs of advice; information about a fund is contained in the KFD.

Meanwhile, documents with more detailed point-of-sale information will continue to be provided to investors. The content of such documents must comply with the new SP rules. In practice, the content requirements are far from simple and there is a growing recognition that the aim of a simplified prospectus which investors would read has not yet been achieved.

The Total Expense Ratio (TER) has been a common method of disclosing the costs of investment in collective investment schemes outside of the UK and, in particular, in Europe. In the UK, the FSA has previously favoured a method whereby fund managers show an impact of charges tables to illustrate to investors the effect of charges on an investment through a reduction in yield (RIY) over different time periods. Following the implementation of the UCITS Directive on Simplified Prospectus the FSA has decided, at least for the time being, to require fund managers to display both a TER and RIY for funds which are distributed within the UK. For those UK funds distributed in other European states, the fund manager may omit the RIY from the Simplified Prospectus produced for those states. An example of the impact of charges table is shown in the Key Features Document in Appendix 3.

3. SCHEME STRUCTURE

LEARNING OBJECTIVES
3.2.1 Know the differences between single fund and umbrella schemes

As we saw in Chapter 1, a CIS can typically be established as an umbrella scheme. A fund manager may establish such a scheme with a single fund initially and then add additional funds later; each fund is then referred to as a 'sub-fund'. Each sub-fund will generally be treated under the FSA rules as if it were a single fund, although being part of the same CIS. One of the major benefits of umbrella schemes is that they are not necessary to establish a new legal entity each time a new fund is launched. It is, therefore, easier, quicker and cheaper for a fund manager to add new funds.

3.1 Share Classes

LEARNING OBJECTIVES
3.2.2 Know the permissible share and unit classes issued by schemes

What unit/share classes may a Collective Investment Scheme Issue?

Under the COLL sourcebook a number of different classes of shares in the scheme can be issued or in the case of an umbrella CIS, in any sub-fund. The classes do not have to be the same for each sub-fund.

Under the COLL sourcebook the rules enable AFMs to propose any type of unit/share class, providing that it is fair to all holders and can be explained in terms of its nature and operation to prospective investors.

4. ISSUE AND CANCELLATION OF UNITS/SHARES – AFTER THE LAUNCH ENDS

LEARNING OBJECTIVES

3.2.3 Know the following characteristics of scheme constitution: issue and cancellation (on a continuing basis); limited issue; limited redemption; guaranteed

4.1 Those Responsible for the Issue and Cancellation of Units/Shares

Reflecting the open-ended nature of a CIS, the prospectus will include particulars of the procedures, dealing periods and the circumstances in which the AFM will effect the sale and redemption of units/shares and arrange the issue or cancellation of units/shares.

Once a fund has been launched, and any initial period during which units/shares have been offered for sale has finished, there will be a continuing need to value the fund on a regular basis. This valuation will then be used to allow existing investors in the fund to redeem their units/shares or to purchase additional units/shares; it will also be used to allow new investors to join through purchasing units/shares.

Where existing investors sell their units/shares back to the AFM he may decide to keep them if he operates what is called a 'manager's box'. These units/shares may then be sold by the AFM to new investors or other existing investors who wish to add to their holding.

If the AFM has insufficient units/shares in his box to satisfy purchase orders he has received, or he does not operate a box, he will arrange for additional units/shares to be issued to satisfy the orders. In the case of an OEIC, the AFM, as the ACD, will issue the shares on behalf of the company, while in the case of a unit trust the AFM will request the trustee to issue the units. The total number of units/shares in issue will increase accordingly.

Where investors sell back to the AFM more units/shares than he wishes to hold in his box or needs to meet purchase orders, or if the AFM does not operate a box, he will arrange for the units/shares to be cancelled on behalf of the company, in the case of an OEIC, or by the trustee in the case of a unit trust. The total number of units/shares in issue will decrease accordingly.

The regulations permit the AFM to deal as principal, ie, for his own account, with appropriate rules to ensure that he treats the CIS fairly when units/shares are issued or cancelled and treats investors fairly when they buy or redeem units/shares.

Although unusual, the AFM can act as an agent, rather than as principal, and arrange for units/shares to be issued or cancelled directly by the trustee of a unit trust or by the OEIC. The AFM may require this, subject to agreement with the depositary/trustee, or may permit it on the request of the investor. The instrument constituting the scheme, however, must provide for this and the prospectus must provide details of the procedures to be followed.

The COLL sourcebook requires AFMs to have appropriate controls over the issue and cancellation of units/shares to prevent any conflict of interest; these controls include agreeing with the trustee/depositary a period of time during which the AFM will give instructions to issue or cancel units/shares. This is dealt with in more detail in Chapter 6 of this workbook.

4.2   Limited Issue, Guaranteed and Protected Funds

A fund manager is obliged to issue and redeem units/shares at the written request of an investor. However, the FSA now considers it appropriate to allow AFMs to limit dealings, and to allow and control the use of words such as **guaranteed** or **capital protected**. It acknowledges that the retail investment market has evolved and that there is now a desire for limited issue and guaranteed products – demand is largely being met in the UK by other investment vehicles more often than not from another EU member state.

Limited Issue Funds

Limited issue funds have the ability to restrict the issue of units/shares and limit the size of the fund. A limited issue is dealt with by way of introducing a new class of units, rather than a new category of scheme. AFMs are able to limit the issue of units/shares by allowing a single issue at launch or a series of issues from time to time. The issue can be limited by number or value. Importantly, a second or subsequent issue must not dilute the rights of existing investors or compromise the investment objective of a fund. AFMs are required to provide full details of single or multiple issues in the Trust Deed or Instrument of Incorporation.

Use of limited issue to manage the size of the fund should in theory make it easier and more cost effective for the fund manager to devise a capital protection method for investors.

Limited Redemption

The investments made by certain NURS funds might make it difficult for the fund to retain sufficient liquidity to meet frequent redemption instructions from investors. Therefore, NURS that invest substantially in physical property can apply 'limited redemption' arrangements. The arrangements must be recorded in the fund's constituting documentation, and the scheme must enable redemptions at least once in any six-month period. Different classes within a scheme can adopt different redemption arrangements.

Guaranteed Funds

The FSA now allows a fund to include the unqualified expression such as **guaranteed** in its name, provided that the following conditions are satisfied:

- the capital value of the investment is unconditionally guaranteed as a minimum return at a specified point in the future;
- the guarantee is provided by a regulated third party, through a legally enforceable agreement;
- the guarantee applies to all investors.

It is also possible to use the term in a qualified sense, eg, '90% guaranteed', where the promise is to return less than 100% of the investment.

Capital Protected Funds

Capital protection can be achieved, subject to a fund's objective, by using derivatives or by a separate insurance policy. A fund may be described as **capital protected** or **protected** where no guarantee exists but where the fund adopts investment policies to provide protection. Any change in the investment policy would require the approval of holders.

Additionally, if names are used which imply some degree of capital security, rather than a full guarantee, they will only be permitted if the degree of capital security implied fairly reflects the nature of the underlying arrangements for providing that security. The FSA will assess each application for authorisation of such funds on a case by case basis.

The new rules also include new disclosure requirements to ensure that investors are given clear information about any restrictions on the issue, sale or redemption of any class of limited issue share, and/or any guarantee or similar arrangement.

5. THE LAUNCH OF A COLLECTIVE INVESTMENT SCHEME

LEARNING OBJECTIVES

3.2.4 Understand the treatment of the following in respect to the initial offer period: share and unit issue; large market movement; pricing; settlement

5.1 Initial Offer Period and Pricing

Under the COLL sourcebook providing the valuation of the assets has not moved by more than 2%, the offer must be kept open to investors for the whole period of the initial offer. This means that, in the normal course of events, the company cannot close the offer prematurely. An initial offer of units/shares may also be made for any sub-fund which is added subsequently. This will obviously apply if the scheme is an umbrella scheme.

The price paid by investors during an initial offer period is a fixed price, set by the AFMs, and notified in writing to the depositary/trustee before the start of the initial offer period.

The COLL sourcebook requires that the length of an initial offer period should not be unreasonable when considered alongside the characteristics of the fund. For example, the initial offer for a scheme operating limited issue or limited redemption arrangements, or intending to invest in illiquid assets, may be longer than one for a scheme that does not have these features. Nevertheless, the initial offer period would still come to an end before the date/time stipulated by the AFM in the prospectus if he reasonably believes the value of the scheme's investments had changed by more than 2% from the initial price.

5.2 Units/Shares are Issued during the Initial Offer

Units/shares are treated as issued during the initial offer period once the AFM has, prior to the close of the offer:

- agreed to sell the units/shares; or
- has received an order, whether by written application, or other means such as telephone, email, fax or via internet website.

This applies even if the AFM accepts the applications during the offer period but does not issue the units/shares until shortly afterwards. Clearly, if the issue is a popular one, it may take a few days for the registrars to process all the applications and enter unit/shareholder and transaction details on the register.

5.3 Settlement during Initial Offer Period

During an initial offer the AFM is required to:

- pay over to the trustee/depositary the price of the units/shares issued, although it can retain any preliminary or initial charge made by it; and
- make payment to the trustee/depositary by the close of business on the fourth business day after the AFM has received the agreed price from the investor.

In practice, most initial offers will be based on applications made by investors, accompanied by payment (eg, cheque), sometimes referred to as **cash with order**.

In the normal course of business, the AFM is required to pay over to the trustee/depositary the price of units/shares within four business days of the units/shares being issued, whether or not the investor has paid the AFM for those units/shares. However, during an initial offer the AFM must, as soon as practicable after the investor has paid for the units/shares, pay the monies over to the trustee/depositary as long as this is no later than four business days after the end of the initial offer period.

5.4 Making an Initial Offer Overseas

Initial offers may be made outside the UK. The initial price of units/shares must be expressed in the base currency of the company or, if separate currency classes are available, the currency of designation for that class. Additionally, the AFM is permitted to sell and arrange the issue of units/shares in any other currency providing that the price in that currency, compared to the fixed initial price, is not detrimental to the interests of the unit/shareholders or potential unit/shareholders. In other words, taking into account exchange rates, the value received for units/shares during the initial offer should be consistent irrespective of the country in which they are sold.

Initial offers overseas may be subject to additional costs. These costs may include duties or taxes levied by each country in which the offer is made, in respect of the issue of units/shares. There may also be some costs involved in remitting the money taken from foreign investors back to the UK. Where these costs arise, the AFM is permitted to add to the initial price, paid by investors in the country concerned, an amount sufficient to cover such costs. Investors in such countries will, therefore, pay a little more for the shares but the net proceeds received for investment by the company will be consistent with the proceeds received from other investors.

All this makes it possible for UK-based CISs to be truly international investment vehicles with an initial offer being made in several countries at the same time. For example, in theory, an initial offer made in several EU countries at the same time is now feasible. The UK CIS market is still in an early state of development and, perhaps understandably, thus far the companies have been very much UK-focused. It will be interesting to see, as the market's use of these new investment vehicles develops, to what extent UK CISs are promoted overseas. The promotion of CISs authorised in one EU jurisdiction into other jurisdictions is subject to relevant notification/registration requirements (see Chapter 2).

5.5 The Impact of Large Market Movements on an Initial Offer

Large market movements can lead to an early termination of the initial offer.

As money is received from investors during an initial offer it may be invested by the CIS. If the AFM believes that the chosen market in which the company is investing has been subject to a significant movement then it may be necessary to bring the initial offer period to an end and stop offering units/shares at the initial price.

For example, the UK stock market experiences a sudden rise in value during the initial offer period of a CIS investing in that market. If the AFM reasonably believes that, on the basis of a valuation of the CIS's assets, a calculated price for the units/shares being offered would be more than 2% above the fixed initial price then the initial offer period comes to an end. The AFM must stop accepting applications and issuing units/shares at the initial price, although orders already accepted can be met. AFMs generally keep assets in near-cash or cash during the initial offer period to avoid the problems mentioned.

The same requirements apply if the market has fallen and the calculated price of the units/shares is more than 2% below the initial price.

From a regulatory point of view, it will presumably be a question of fact as to whether the AFM had reason to believe that failure to act in such circumstances and bring the initial offer period to an end would be a serious matter and might lead to disciplinary action against the AFM by the regulatory authorities.

6. ARE THERE ANY OTHER WAYS A CIS CAN BE SET UP?

LEARNING OBJECTIVES

3.3.1 Know the process and relevant regulatory requirements in relation to: termination; conversion; amalgamation; reconstruction

An **initial offer**, often accompanied by a significant advertising campaign, is a common method of launching a new unit trust or OEIC. However, funds may also be launched to provide a vehicle for investors who have invested in an existing product which is coming to the end of its life. This process in addition to offering a continuing investment opportunity can, subject to approval by HM Revenue & Customs, offer tax advantages by allowing investors to roll-over capital gains made in the first vehicle into the new fund.

An example would be for an investment trust, which is always a public company, and which may have a fixed life of 10 or 15 years, to decide to convert into a CIS. Section 110 Insolvency Act 1986 allows a scheme of reconstruction whereby such a company, not necessarily one within the meaning of the Companies Act, may reorganise into a CIS.

How this can be effected

Shareholders in the investment trust would be required to approve the scheme by passing an extraordinary resolution in a general meeting. The company would have to be put into liquidation but shareholders in the existing investment trust would receive units/shares in the CIS in proportion to the value of those held in the investment trust.

There are provisions to safeguard dissentients but the liquidator would probably purchase their shares. The approval of the FSA would still be required.

6.1 How Existing Unit Trusts can Convert to OEICs

Unitholders approval is required by way of an extraordinary resolution to be passed by a majority of not less than three-quarters (75%) of the votes cast (whether on a show of hands or on a poll) in favour of the resolution.

Conversions must be approved at a meeting of unitholders held in accordance with the regulations laid down within the FSA COLL sourcebook Chapter 7.

Following authorisation of the OEIC, the timetable would probably be:
- **Month 1** – advance notice mailings to all clients, with copies to IFAs and advisers;
- **Month 2** – conversion circulars to unitholders and advisers. Unit/shareholder meetings held;
- **Month 3** – conversion of unit trust to OEIC undertaken.

6.2 Amalgamations and Reconstructions of CISs

An amalgamation or reconstruction of a CIS or a sub-fund of a CIS has to be approved by the FSA. It also requires approval by extraordinary resolution in a general meeting of relevant classes of unit/shareholder affected.

If the unit/shareholders of a continuing fund or sub-fund of a CIS are receiving the portfolio of another fund then if the director(s) or manager and trustee (of a unit trust) are reasonably satisfied that the inclusion of the portfolio:

a. is not likely to result in any material prejudice to the interests of the current unit/shareholders of the company;

b. is consistent with the objectives of the continuing fund; and

c. would not breach any investment and borrowing powers;

then no unit/shareholders' meeting is necessary.

7. HOW IS A CIS WOUND-UP?

LEARNING OBJECTIVES

3.3.1 Know the process and relevant regulatory requirements in relation to: termination; conversion; amalgamation; reconstruction

7.1 Winding up of an OEIC or Termination of a Sub-Fund

This will depend on whether the OEIC is solvent (ie, able to pay all its debts) or insolvent. If the OEIC is solvent, the procedure is set out in the FSA COLL sourcebook Chapter 7 and provides that the ACD and other directors (if applicable) must satisfy themselves that the company can meet all its liabilities within the following 12 months. Winding up is carried out by the ACD who will instruct the depositary how to distribute assets of the fund.

The OEIC Regulations 2001 state that, in the case of an insolvent OEIC, the provisions of the Insolvency Act 1986 in relation to an unregistered company apply, subject to certain amendments, eg, the FSA will be entitled to receive and be heard on a petition to windup.

Guidance on Winding-up or Termination

Summary of the main steps in winding up a solvent OEIC or terminating a sub-fund under FSA rules, assuming FSA approval.

Notes: N =   notice to be given to the FSA under regulation 21 of OEIC Regulations
E =   commencement of winding up or termination
W/U =   winding-up
FAP =   final accounting period (COLL 7.3.8R(4))

Step number	Explanation	When	COLL rule (unless stated otherwise)
1.	Commence preparation of solvency statement	N – 28 days	7.3.5 (2)
2.	Send audited solvency statement to the FSA with copy to depositary	By N + 21 days	7.3.5 (4) and (5)
3.	Receive FSA approval	N + one month	Regulation 21 of OEIC Regulations
4.	Normal business ceases; publish notices	E	7.3.6
5.	Realise proceeds, wind up, instruct depositary accordingly	ASAP after E	7.3.7
6.	Prepare final account or termination account and have account audited	On completion of W/U or termination	7.3.8
7.	Send final account or termination account auditor's report to the FSA and unit/shareholders	Within 2 months of FAP	7.3.8 (6)
8.	Request FSA to revoke relevant authorisation order	On completion of W/U	7.3.7 (9)

7.2 Winding up of a Unit Trust

The COLL sourcebook allows the ACD and/or trustee to request the FSA to revoke the authorisation order for the fund. Changes to the Trust Deed and Prospectus will need to be made and, following FSA approval, a scheme of arrangement will be put to a meeting of unitholders for passing of an extraordinary resolution. On termination, the unitholders will receive their respective share of the proceeds of the fund or entitlement to receive units in another regulated CIS in exchange for their units.

For an authorised unit trust which is a relevant pension scheme, payments must not be made to unitholders; the realisation proceeds are paid by the trustee in accordance with the Trust Deed.

END OF CHAPTER QUESTIONS

Think of an answer for each question and refer to the appropriate section for confirmation.

Question		Answer Reference
1.	Explain the hierarchy of levels of regulation of CISs in the UK.	Section 1.1
2.	Explain the purpose and content of the Instrument of Incorporation.	Section 2.1
3.	Set out the main purpose of a CIS Prospectus.	Section 2.3
4.	What are the differences between a Prospectus and a Simplified Prospectus of a CIS?	Section 2.4
5.	What are the permissible share and unit classes issued by a CIS?	Section 3.1
6.	Who is responsible for the issue and cancellation of units/shares in a CIS?	Section 4.1
7.	What should happen if an AFM makes an error in the number of units/shares cancelled?	Section 4.1
8.	Explain why a fund might offer a limited issue of units/shares?	Section 4.2
9.	What is the difference between a capital protected fund and a guaranteed fund?	Section 4.2
10.	When a new CIS is launched can an initial offer be made overseas?	Section 5.4
11.	What impact can large market movements have on initial offers of units to investors?	Section 5.5
12.	How can existing unit trusts convert to OEICs?	Section 6.1
13.	What are the main steps in winding up a solvent OEIC?	Section 7.1

ROLES AND RESPONSIBILITIES 4

1.	THE ROLE OF THE AUTHORISED FUND MANAGER	85
2.	HOW IS AN AUTHORISED UNIT TRUST MANAGED?	86
3.	HOW IS AN OEIC MANAGED?	87
4.	THE ROLE AND RESPONSIBILITY OF THE TRUSTEE/DEPOSITARY	91
5.	AUDITORS	94

This syllabus area will provide approximately 3 of the 50 examination questions

INTRODUCTION

This chapter covers the duties, obligations and responsibilities of those who manage and those who carry out oversight of management and custody functions for a collective investment scheme. While brief mention has previously been made of the respective duties of the authorised fund manager (AFM – a term used to describe either the manager of an AUT or the ACD of an OEIC, as appropriate) and the trustee/depositary, a fuller explanation is necessary to show their legal and regulatory responsibilities. This chapter identifies various items specific to either AUT or OEIC management, though some common items are described in relation to the AFM. The position, duties and rights of auditors are also included.

1. THE ROLE OF THE AUTHORISED FUND MANAGER

LEARNING OBJECTIVES

4.1.1 Know the role of the AFM in relation to the following: making investment decisions; box management; investor transactions (AFM as agent or principal); maintaining register of holders; maintaining other client and scheme records; valuation and pricing; distribution of income; voting; issuing reports; compliance with investment and borrowing regulations; marketing the fund

The AFM's specific responsibilities include:

- investment management of the scheme property (although more usually the appointed investment adviser makes the necessary day-to-day investment decisions);
- directing the trustee/depositary on the exercise of voting rights attached to the scheme property;
- valuation pricing of units/shares and rectifying any breach of pricing regulations facilitating the issue and redemption of units/shares;
- managing the issue, cancellation, sale and redemption of units/shares (investor transactions) and, if applicable, the manager's box (see Chapter 6 of this workbook);
- ensuring the scheme does not breach investment and borrowing regulations;
- calculation of the scheme's income and arranging for the trustee/depositary to make a distribution in respect of income units/shares;
- maintenance of the scheme's accounting and other records required by regulations, including the register of holders;
- ensuring that the AFM and the scheme complies with the relevant regulations in maintenance of the register of unit/shareholders;
- issuing of half-yearly and annual report and accounts to unit/shareholders;
- execution of any agreements required to be signed or sealed by, or on behalf of, the scheme.

In practice, the AFM will often undertake the marketing or promotion of the unit trust/OEIC, but is under no obligation to do so. In fact, many of the responsibilities listed above can be delegated to other firms – either in the same group as the AFM or in a separate company.

2. HOW IS AN AUTHORISED UNIT TRUST MANAGED?

2.1 Appointment of the Manager of an Authorised Unit Trust

In the case of an authorised unit trust the operator of the scheme is known as the 'manager' and must satisfy the requirements of S.243 of FSMA 2000, ie:

- be an authorised firm with permission to act as a manager;
- be a corporate body incorporated in the UK or another EEA state;
- have its affairs administered in the country in which it is incorporated;
- have a place of business in the UK; and
- be independent of the trustee.

The directors and officers of the manager, as an authorised firm, must be fit and proper persons and approved persons under S.59 FSMA 2000. This means they have been approved by the FSA.

The manager is named in, and derives his authority from, the trust deed constituting the unit trust.

2.2 Restrictions on the AUT Manager

The manager must operate the scheme within the provisions of the:

1. Instrument of Constitution/Trust Deed;
2. FSA Sourcebook; and
3. most recently published Prospectus.

These requirements include those designed to ensure that each fund has a sufficiently diversified spread of risk once it has operated for six months. **Investment and Borrowing Powers** regulations are considered in detail in Chapter 5.

2.3 Replacement and Retirement of the AUT Manager

Managers can be replaced or may retire.

The manager is subject to removal by written notice given by the trustee. There are a number of reasons why the trustee might remove a manager. Examples include where the manager is in the process of being wound up as a result of insolvency, where the trustee reasonably believes in his opinion that it is in the interests of unitholders, or unitholders of 75% in value of the units in issue make a request to the trustee to remove the manager. All of these examples are extremely rare.

On receipt of the notice from the trustee the manager ceases to be the manager and the trustee, by means of a Supplemental Trust Deed, must appoint another manager who meets the requirements under FSMA 2000.

The manager of a unit trust has the right to retire in favour of another manager eligible under FSMA 2000, subject to the new manager being approved by the trustee. Again, appropriate Supplemental Trust Deeds will be completed to give effect to the retirement and new appointment.

3. HOW IS AN OEIC MANAGED?

3.1 The Authorised Corporate Director (ACD)

As part of work undertaken to draft the OEIC Regulations, it was considered that an OEIC should be managed by several directors, as with investment trusts and companies generally. This would be in line with general thinking about corporate governance whereby responsibility is sub-divided and independent external parties, ie, non-executive directors, are introduced to oversee some aspects of management.

Following representations from the financial services industry, this requirement was withdrawn. As a result, an OEIC must have an authorised corporate director (ACD) and may have additional directors. The OEIC's Instrument of Incorporation will specify whether that OEIC only has an ACD or if it is required to have other directors in addition. In most OEICs, the main responsibility will probably rest with the ACD alone, with the independent depositary safekeeping the OEIC's property. This is broadly similar to the roles of the manager and trustee in an AUT.

In many instances it is likely that there will be a sole director, the ACD. Where other directors are appointed they do not have the power to undertake the management functions that the FSA regulations state are to be carried out by the ACD. Thus the ACD must manage the OEIC in much the same way as a manager of a unit trust (see Section 2.2 of this chapter), although he is also subject to the OEIC Regulations 2001.

3.2 The Appointment and Removal of Directors

As indicated in Chapter 3, the details of the first director(s) must be submitted to the FSA prior to incorporation. The ACD will be a corporate body who must be authorised by the FSA. Existing unit trust managers are eligible to be ACDs, subject to approval by the FSA.

The FSA must be notified, in writing, of any changes to the board and the ACD may not cease to hold office without a replacement ACD being appointed prior to its resignation. Such a replacement must be approved by the FSA. As the ACD is a body corporate it would be most unusual for the OEIC to be left without a director. If this were to happen, the depositary's powers are temporarily extended to cover this eventuality and to appoint another body corporate to be the ACD, subject to their being qualified to act as such.

An OEIC's Instrument of Incorporation will include provisions as to the procedure for the appointment, retirement or removal of directors. While the total number of directors may not exceed the maximum laid down in the Instrument of Incorporation, the ACD shall have power, at any time, and from time-to-time, to appoint any person to be a director of the company, as an addition to existing directors. The ACD will also determine the length of appointment of any additional director.

Other OEIC directors can now be co-opted to provide the ACD with assistance. In practice, OEICs invariably do not have other directors. However, such directors are removable if 10% of shareholders by value successfully call for an extraordinary general meeting (EGM) which approves an ordinary resolution to that effect.

A shareholder who is duly qualified to attend and vote at an EGM may nominate a person to be elected a director of the company. They must, not less than seven and not more than 42 days before the date appointed for the EGM, give notice, in writing, to the head office of the OEIC of the intention to propose a person as director, together with notice, in writing, signed by the nominee, of his willingness to be elected. It is unlikely that this provision would be exercised.

An OEIC is itself a legal entity, unlike an AUT. Under Schedule 5 Paragraph 1(3) of FSMA it is an authorised person for the purposes of the Act, with permission to carry on operation of the scheme and any activity in connection with, or for the purposes of, the scheme. As the OEIC is an authorised person the directors of the OEIC must qualify as fit and proper and if there are two or more directors, their combined knowledge and expertise must be appropriate.

The FSA sourcebook provides that the office of ACD shall be vacated in the following circumstances:

- upon ceasing to be a director; or
- notification of termination of that appointment as ACD, the terms of which have been agreed by resolution of the board of directors, as given to the ACD; or
- the ACD goes into compulsory liquidation; or
- a receiver is appointed of the undertaking of the ACD; or
- an administration order is made in relation to the ACD under Section 8 Insolvency Act 1986.

In addition to the above, the following provisions are in the IMA's Model Instrument of Incorporation for the removal of a director, namely that a director:

- becomes prohibited by law or regulation, eg, is no longer an authorised person; or
- becomes bankrupt, compounds with creditors or, being a body corporate, a receiver or liquidator is appointed for the winding up of the company; or
- becomes mentally incapable; or
- is absent from meetings of directors (or committees of directors) for six months without the sanction of the directors and they resolve that his office be vacated; or
- has a period stated in his agreement with the company and this comes to an end or such agreement is summarily terminated; or
- may by ordinary resolution in general meeting, be removed before the expiration of his period of office.

It is not possible for a director to assign his office or appoint an alternate in his stead. This would conflict with the need for the FSA to approve all director appointments and to adjudge as to being fit and proper.

In the unlikely event of the OEIC being without an ACD, the depositary may manage the company pending the appointment of a new ACD, or the winding up of the OEIC. The depositary may also retain the services of another authorised person to carry out the ACD role.

3.3 The Duties of the other Directors

Any directors appointed in addition to the ACD are responsible for seeing that the ACD is carrying out its functions in a competent manner. They will be entitled to, and must receive information from, the ACD as to how duties are being carried out. This would probably take the form of accounts, details of contracts etc. that would be considered at regular board meetings.

3.4 The Duties an AFM can Delegate

> **LEARNING OBJECTIVES**
>
> 4.1.2 Know the scope for delegation by the AFM of: investment management; fund accounting; registration and client administration

Under the FSA sourcebook, the AFM may retain the services of third parties, including the depositary, to assist them in the performance of their duties. For example, investment management, pricing of the units/shares, their issue and redemption, fund accounting and registration/investor record keeping may be delegated to a third party. This may result in considerable cost savings and, therefore, be a sensible arrangement. In these circumstances, the AFM will, however, retain full regulatory responsibility for any errors or losses incurred by the third party.

Functions are delegated for various business reasons, but the decision to outsource an activity would require consideration of factors such as:

- expertise requirements for specific functions;
- technology costs (small firms can avoid having to invest in expensive systems by outsourcing to specialist firms with economies of scale);
- staff costs (for example, a firm in London could outsource to a less expensive geographical location); and
- premises costs (particularly as a firm grows and might otherwise require additional premises).

Although the AFM retains regulatory responsibility, it is possible through contractual terms to place financial responsibility to the extent agreed on the third party service provider. Delegation or outsourcing can, therefore, reduce some risks.

It is likely that the Instrument of Incorporation will limit the exemption directors can obtain from liability, but insurance can be taken out to indemnify directors against personal loss in certain circumstances.

3.4.1 FSA Requirements

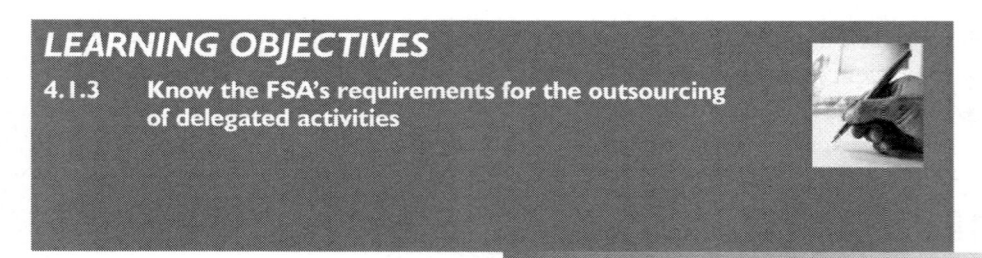

> **LEARNING OBJECTIVES**
>
> 4.1.3 Know the FSA's requirements for the outsourcing of delegated activities

The FSA's requirements for outsourcing of delegated activities are contained in the Senior Management Systems and Controls (SYSC) Sourcebook, Chapter 8.

3.5 The Legal Position of Directors of an OEIC

Any act of a director is binding on the company, even if it is discovered subsequently that there was a defect in his appointment or that the director has acted beyond the powers conferred in the Instrument of Incorporation. This is to protect outside bodies and persons who would not be aware of the defect and it does not require them to consult public documents such as the Instrument of Incorporation before dealing with the OEIC. This is similar to S.40 Companies Act 2006, relating to companies, though someone who was aware of the defect would not be able to enforce the contract.

If a director or his associate does enter into a contract on behalf of the OEIC which is ultra vires (beyond the powers of) the company, then the transaction is voidable by the OEIC and the director who authorised the transaction must account to the company for any gain he has made, and indemnify the company for any loss or damage resulting from the transaction.

It is possible for any ultra vires act of directors to be remedied by the shareholders passing a resolution in a general meeting (ie, EGM) rectifying the situation in the case of an OEIC. This is not possible, however, if restitution of any money or other assets, which were the subject matter of the transaction cannot be made.

Similarly, any AUT manager and any director of an AUT manager is bound by the terms of the trust deed, prospectus etc, when acting on behalf of the trust. If the manager acts ultra vires he would similarly become liable to the trust for any loss or damage the trust incurs. If an appointed director of an AUT manager were found to have acted ultra vires in respect of the AUT, the manager would seek guidance from the trustee.

Every OEIC must keep either written copies of the contracts of service for each director or, if not in writing, a memorandum setting out the terms. All copies and memoranda must be kept in the same place and are open to inspection by any shareholder (but not by members of the public). The OEIC may keep these documents at any of the following places:

- head office of the OEIC;
- the place where the register of shareholders is kept;
- where the Instrument of Incorporation designates a body corporate as a director, the registered or principal office of that director.

In addition, the contract or memorandum must be open for inspection by any shareholder. In practice it may be that the OEIC only has one director, the ACD, and the contract will include length of service, remuneration, duties etc, which will also include responsibilities as laid down by the FSA Sourcebook.

For an AUT, the main agreement/contract is in the form of a Trust Deed, entered into between the manager and trustee. Again, this document must be available for inspection by unitholders.

4. THE ROLE AND RESPONSIBILITY OF THE TRUSTEE/DEPOSITARY

LEARNING OBJECTIVES

4.2.1 Know the role and responsibilities of the depositary or trustee in relation to the following: protecting investors; oversight of the AFM in relation to scheme management; custody of the funds' assets; registers and sub-registers; delegation; issuing and cancelling units; valuation; accuracy of prices; breach reporting

4.1 Independent Oversight

Every CIS is legally obliged to have a separate institution as trustee/depositary to act as an independent arbiter, safeguard the assets within the scheme, and ensure that the scheme is managed according to the terms of the FSA sourcebook scheme documentation (trust deed and scheme particulars, or Instrument of Incorporation and Prospectus – as appropriate) and the investment objective and investment restrictions of the scheme. It is in this particular area that there is scope for different interpretations of the trustee's/depositary's role in protecting the interests of the investors.

The trustee of an AUT will be appointed as a result of entering into the trust deed with the AFM and derives their authority from that document. The depositary of an OEIC will be appointed under contract by the ACD on behalf of the OEIC.

Each trustee/depositary must be:

- a body corporate in the UK or an EU state;
- an authorised person under FSMA 2000;
- independent of the OEIC and its directors, and managers in the case of AUTs; and
- act solely in the interests of the unitholders/shareholders.

The unit/shareholder deals directly with the AFM while the trustee/depositary usually has little contact with the unit/shareholder. There is, however, a close relationship between the AFM and the trustee/depositary.

- A trustee/depositary is invariably part of a large financial institution. They must be authorised and regulated by the FSA whose regulations require that their gross capital should be at least £4m.
- The trustee/depositary must take all reasonable steps to ensure that the AFM is complying with FSA regulations.
- If the trustee/depositary suspects that the AFM is not acting in the unit/shareholder's interests, he has the power ultimately to replace him.
- In order to fulfill these obligations, the trustee/depositary carries out regular compliance audits of the AFM's operations.
- Where any power has been delegated to a third party (examples being unit dealing or pricing functions) the trustee/depositary will make similar inspection visits to review the operations of the relevant third party administration (TPA) firms.

The trustee/depositary must take reasonable care to ensure that the scheme is managed in accordance with the FSA sourcebook and the requirements of the scheme documentation (trust deed or Instrument of Incorporation, as applicable) and the prospectus. In particular, the trustee/depositary will review:

- initial offer, issue, cancellation, sale, and redemption of units/shares;
- pricing of shares;
- any use of a dilution levy;
- valuation of the scheme property;
- accounting periods;
- calculation of income available for allocation;
- allocation, payment or retention of income;
- unclaimed distributions; and
- investment and borrowing limits.

On appointment, the trustee/depositary will examine and satisfy itself as to the AFM's control systems and other procedures, including record keeping. At least annually the trustee/depositary will review the AFM's valuation procedures, also reviewing controls whenever major changes are made to existing procedures. These reviews will include visits to the AFM's offices and preparation of written reports detailing any findings that require a formal response from the AFM. Such responses will state the proposed action and timescales involved in remedying any weaknesses.

The trustee/depositary has a responsibility for safe custody of a fund's/company's assets. All the assets are held in the trustee's/depositary's name on behalf of the scheme. Regulations allow the trustee/depositary to entrust custody of any of the scheme property to a third party, but the trustee/depositary remains liable to the scheme for any loss or damage caused by that third party.

The trustee/depositary must prepare a report to shareholders/unitholders for inclusion in the annual report and accounts. Examples of such reports can be seen in Appendix 4.

The trustee/depositary should notify to the FSA matters which include, but are not limited to, any circumstances that they become aware of whilst undertaking functions or duties that the FSA would view as significant.

The trustee/depositary should report any breach of the rules in COLL 6.3 immediately to the FSA in instances which it considers to be material.

Any instance of incorrect pricing should be reported to the FSA immediately, where the error is 0.5% or more of the price of a unit, where a depositary believes reimbursement or payment is inappropriate and should not be paid by the AFM.

In accordance with SUP 16.6.8.R a depositary/trustee should make a return to the FSA on a quarterly basis which summarises the number of instances of incorrect pricing during a particular period.

4.2 Monitoring of Prices

An important part of the trustee/depositary role is to monitor the valuation of the fund and to calculate unit/share prices. Accurate valuations and pricing are vital. Further details on the pricing of unit/shares can be found in Chapter 6.

4.3 The Special Rights of the Depositary

Schedule 1 to the OEIC Regulations 2001 gives the depositary the rights to:
- require from the company's officers such information and explanations as it thinks necessary for the performance of its functions as depositary, eg, to ensure investment limits are complied with;
- have access to all books, reports, statements etc, which are to be considered at any meeting of directors or shareholders in so far as they concern them as depositary;
- receive the same notices as shareholders in relation to OEIC's general meetings;
- to attend and be heard at any general meeting of the OEIC which concerns it as depositary; and
- convene a general meeting of the OEIC when it sees fit.

While the above applies to depositaries under the regulations as stated, similar rights attach to trustees of AUTs.

4.4 Trustee's/Depositary's Fees

Regulations enable the trustee's/depositary's fees (and, as a separate trustee/depositary expense, registrar's fees) to be paid as a charge on the fund. In some cases, such as stakeholder products, these fees may be paid out of the AFM's annual management charge. Where the trustee's/depositary's fees are charged to the fund, the amount involved should represent a very small percentage of total assets and should not, therefore, significantly affect performance.

5. AUDITORS

> **LEARNING OBJECTIVES**
>
> 4.3.1 Know the requirements for appointment of auditors
>
> 4.3.2 Know the auditors' rights, obligations and responsibilities: conducting an audit; reporting to the FSA; reporting to shareholders/unit holders

In addition to the controlling function of the trustee/depositary, each scheme must have an auditor who is required to be qualified as eligible to audit the accounts of companies governed by the Companies Acts. The auditor cannot also be an officer or employee of the scheme or company being audited, or a partnership of which the scheme or company is a partner and, therefore, must be independent.

It is the ACD's responsibility to appoint, re-appoint each year and remove, where appropriate, the auditors of the OEIC. Failure to appoint allows the FSA the right to so appoint.

AUTs are required to appoint auditors to audit the reports and accounts for each fund (see Chapter 9). The FSA sourcebook requires the manager, with the approval of the trustee, to appoint an auditor at the outset of an AUT and upon any vacancy. The auditor may be any person qualified as auditor of an authorised person, ie, a person authorised to carry on regulated activities under FSMA.

The audit fees of the auditor are determined by the manager with the approval of the trustee.

5.1 The Rights, Obligations and Responsibilities of the Auditor

In relation to OEICs, the auditor's rights are specifically provided for under the OEIC Regulations 2001 and include the following:

- access at all times to the company's books, accounts vouchers etc. and to require from the company's officers such information and explanations as they think necessary for performance of their duties;
- to receive all notices of general meetings of the company as shareholders are entitled to;
- to attend any general meetings of the company and be heard at such meetings on any part of the business of the meetings which concerns them as auditors; and
- remuneration to be fixed by the ACD.

Auditor rights in relation to AUTs are similar, although not specifically provided for in legislation.

Report of the Auditor

The authorised fund manager must ensure that the report of the auditor to the unit/shareholders includes a statement on:

- whether, in the auditor's opinion, the accounts have been properly prepared in accordance with the IMA SORP, the rules in the FSA sourcebook, and the instrument constituting the scheme;

- whether, in the auditor's opinion, the accounts give a true and fair view of the net income and the net gains or losses of the scheme property of the authorised fund (or, as the case may be, the scheme property attributable to the sub-fund) for the annual accounting period in question and the financial position of the authorised fund or sub-fund as at the end of that period;

- whether the auditor is of the opinion that proper accounting records for the authorised fund (or, as the case may be, sub-fund) have not been kept, or whether the accounts are not in agreement with those records;

- whether the auditor has been given all the information and explanations which, to the best of his knowledge and belief, are necessary for the purposes of his audit; and

- whether the auditor is of the opinion that the information given in the report of the directors or in the report of the authorised fund manager for that period is consistent with the accounts.

END OF CHAPTER QUESTIONS

Think of an answer for each question and refer to the appropriate section for confirmation.

Question		Answer Reference
1.	List the main duties of an Authorised Fund Manager.	Section 1
2.	What are the requirements for the appointment of the manager of an AUT?	Section 2.1
3.	What is the position if an OEIC is left without a director?	Section 3.2
4.	On what grounds do the regulations provide that the office of ACD shall be vacated?	Section 3.2
5.	Is it possible for a director of an OEIC to assign his office to another person?	Section 3.2
6.	For what reasons may an AFM delegate duties to third parties?	Section 3.4
7.	What is the legal position of an act performed by a director that is ultra vires an OEIC?	Section 3.5
8.	What special rights does the depositary of an OEIC have?	Section 4.3
9.	From where are trustee/depositaries normally paid?	Section 4.4
10.	Who is responsible for appointing auditors to an authorised unit trust?	Section 5
11.	Describe the contents of the auditor's report to unit/shareholders.	Section 5.1
12.	Describe the rights, obligations and responsibilities of an auditor of an OEIC.	Section 5.1

INVESTMENT & BORROWING POWERS (IBP)

5

1.	INTRODUCTION	99
2.	PERMITTED INVESTMENTS: UCITS SCHEMES	101
3.	PERMITTED INVESTMENTS: NON-UCITS RETAIL SCHEMES (NURS)	108
4.	SUMMARY OF IBP LIMITS FOR COLL RETAIL SCHEMES	110
5.	NON-REGULATORY RESTRICTIONS ON INVESTMENT AND BORROWING POWERS (ALL SCHEMES)	111
6.	WHAT ARE THE RULES RELATING TO STOCK LENDING?	112
7.	CAN A COLLECTIVE INVESTMENT SCHEME BORROW MONEY?	113

This syllabus area will provide approximately 4 of the 50 examination questions

1. INTRODUCTION

> **LEARNING OBJECTIVES**
>
> 5.1.1 Understand the requirement for a prudent spread of risk and the principles of investment and borrowing powers
>
> 5.1.2 Know the basis for investment or borrowing limits, the factors used in and obligations attached to valuing scheme property

This chapter details the main regulatory limits imposed on a scheme in relation to the assets it purchases with investors' money and the borrowing it enters into to raise additional liquid funds, although there are different sets of limits that apply to different classifications of schemes, ie, whether they are UCITS or non-UCITS retail schemes (NURS).

As has been noted earlier in this workbook, the current regulatory restrictions on investment and borrowing powers arise from two sources: the evolution of an EU standard for collective investment products; and the desire of fund managers to devise collective investment products to meet specific investor needs.

The regulatory limits are designed to ensure a sufficient spread of risk through diversification of the investment portfolio. Maximum limits are set for various classes of investment asset, such as:

- transferable securities;
- holdings in other collective investments;
- cash, etc;

and these limits are generally set as a **percentage of the scheme property**. The scheme property relates to the net asset value of the scheme, ie, the whole valuation of the scheme including the liabilities of the fund, as determined at each valuation point. The amount of income awaiting distribution is therefore included within the calculation. The percentage represented by a single holding is the value of that holding divided by the net asset value at the last pricing point. For a single-priced scheme, there is only one net asset value (based on the mid-values of investments) and for a dual-priced scheme the bid valuation is used to determine percentage exposure.

1.1 EU Standard: the Impact of UCITS on FSA IBP Limits

EU directives have an impact upon FSA regulation, and the ratification of amending directives also requires changes to existing UK requirements. The original European Directive relating to collective investment schemes came into effect in 1989 and permitted schemes that satisfied the Directive's requirements to be sold cross-border providing that they were, generally speaking, invested in transferable securities (essentially in equities or bonds). This UCITS (Undertakings for Collective Investment in Transferable Securities) Directive was useful in setting a standard across Europe, but two main problems arose:

- The AFM of a UCITS scheme could not provide other investment services, but was restricted to management of collective investment schemes or activities ancillary to that purpose.
- Secondly, the Directive was too restrictive in terms of allowable asset types. Domestic legislation in EU countries (including the UK) has allowed UCITS collective investment schemes to invest in a wider range of financial instruments since 1989.

To resolve these concerns, two amending directives (the Product Directive and the Management Directive) were approved in January 2002, with member states required to implement the provisions by 13 August 2003. The Product Directive extends the investment powers of UCITS schemes and was implemented by the FSA, following consultation, on 1 November 2002. The details of the Management Directive are covered in Chapter 2.

1.2 Product Directive

The Product Directive extended the investment powers of UCITS schemes, which now operates under the FSA sourcebook.

The main purpose of the Product Directive is to:

- extend the investment powers of UCITS schemes to allow them to invest in a wider range of investments such as transferable securities, money market instruments, units in collective investment schemes, deposits and derivatives and forward transactions;
- introduce a regime for schemes that aim to replicate an index (ie, tracker funds).

At the same time the FSA implemented proposals to:

- allow AFMs to limit the issue of shares (so called limited issue funds); and
- establish circumstances in which the word 'guaranteed' or other terms that imply a degree of capital security can be used in the name of a UK collective investment scheme.

1.3 Fund Managers seeking to meet Specific Needs

While the FSA was required to update its regulations to reflect the new UCITS standard, it also chose within the FSA sourcebook, to give fund managers wider freedom for those funds that are not designed to meet the UCITS standard.

Non-UCITS Retail Schemes (NURS) will enable fund managers to invest scheme property into a wider range of assets than previously possible in a UK-authorised CIS.

This chapter will first outline the investments that are available to UCITS funds, before commenting on the additional investments that can be made by NURS. Finally, this chapter will consider various measures that can apply on a fund level – where the AFM has documented the item in the scheme documentation.

2. PERMITTED INVESTMENTS: UCITS SCHEMES

LEARNING OBJECTIVES

5.2.2 Know the specific limits applying to: UCITS funds; Non-UCITS retail funds; Qualified Investor Schemes (QIS)/Qualifying Money Market schemes (QMM)

There are various types of asset that can be held within a UCITS scheme. Here we look at various key categories, together with the regulatory limits on the size of positions taken. These limits ensure that there is an appropriate spread of investment between different issues/companies in order that any negative effect of market failure by a specific company is diluted within the fund. The rules also ensure that the investments held can be accurately valued and readily disposed of. These regulations can be found in Chapter 5 of the FSA Sourcebook.

These spread regulations do not apply until six months after the scheme has been authorised or the start of an initial offer period provided a prudent spread of risk is maintained.

2.1 Transferable Securities

LEARNING OBJECTIVES

5.2.1 Know the definitions of: eligible markets; transferable securities; approved securities; derivatives; approved derivatives; off-exchange derivatives

A transferable security is essentially an equity or a bond issue or another asset directly representing an equity or a bond (such as a warrant or depositary receipt). It is a security with transferable title, ie, the current holder can exchange it for its current value and no longer be the owner of the asset.

The regulations divide transferable securities into two groups – though the scheme documentation is important in determining where a particular security falls for a given scheme.

CESR's UCITS eligible assets guidelines introduced in July 2008 further defined a transferable security. A UCITS may only invest in a transferable security if the following criteria are fulfilled:

- the potential loss is limited to the amount paid for it;
- its liquidity must not compromise the AFM's ability to redeem units;
- a reliable valuation must be available for it.

Approved Securities

Approved securities are transferable securities listed on particular stock markets throughout the world markets which the AFM has decided are key to the scheme being able to satisfy its investment objective and policy. A list of **Eligible Markets** is stated in the scheme prospectus. For example, a US growth fund will tend to name the main US markets as **eligible** (New York, NASDAQ, Philadelphia, etc), while a Far East growth fund might specify the main market from a lager number of countries (such as Tokyo, Kuala Lumpur, Hong Kong, Singapore, etc).

The regulations permit any market in an EEA State to be declared as eligible as a result of EU free movement of goods and services – providing that it is regulated, operates regularly, and is open to the public. Additionally, any other market can be named as eligible providing that it satisfies the following list of requirements:

- the market must be regulated;
- it must operate regularly;
- it must be recognised by an overseas regulator;
- it must be open to the public;
- it must be adequately liquid; and
- it must have adequate arrangements for the transmission of income and capital to and for investors.

The list of eligible markets is compiled by the AFM, though the trustee/depositary must be satisfied that each meets the FSA's requirements. The AFM's documentation to demonstrate the appropriateness of eligible markets is known as the **Market Due Diligence** review. The trustee/depositary must also be satisfied that it can provide safe custody of any assets purchased in the market.

There is no limit to the aggregated investment a fund can make in approved securities, though there are limits over the percentage of fund value that can be represented by any single body. The general rule is that approved securities and money market instruments issued by a single body should not be valued at more than 5% of the total scheme property, although this limit can be increased to 10% per body provided the aggregate value of such holdings over 5% does not exceed 40% of fund value.

This regulation has caused some problems in recent years for AFMs operating funds that aim to track the performance of a specific market index, such as the FTSE. At times, some companies have exceeded 10% of the value of the index, and so tracker funds (that track an index) seeking to replicate the index have found themselves in breach of the 10% limit. The latest amendment to the UCITS Directive, as reflected in the FSA Sourcebook, makes a special provision for **schemes replicating an index**. For such schemes the 10% maximum limit on approved securities issued by a single body can be increased to 20%, and up to 35% for a single body at any time where exceptional circumstances arise, but these increased limits are only available if the level of investment matches the proportion of the index that security represents.

Unapproved Securities

The regulations enable a scheme to make investments in securities that are not traded on eligible markets. A maximum of 10% of the scheme value can be invested in unapproved securities, though individual holdings are also subject to the 5% maximum limit to ensure an appropriate spread of investment.

2.2 Government and Public Securities (GAPS)

As government debt is generally considered to be less risky than other market-listed securities, it is subject to a separate limit (and so is excluded from the 5%/10%/40% limits noted above). Providing that a fund does not invest more than 35% of the scheme property in debt issued by (or guaranteed by) any single government there is no spread limit, ie, a scheme could invest 33% of its assets in a single UK gilt issue (providing it was in keeping with the scheme's investment objective). The definition of GAPS includes not only local and national governments, but also international bodies of which any EU member state is a member.

Where a scheme's investment in issues from a single government does exceed 35%, no individual position can exceed 30% of scheme property, and the fund must hold at least six GAPS issues in total (issued by any issuer). However, the AFM must ensure that the scheme documentation (both the instrument incorporating the scheme and the current prospectus) names the states, local authorities, or issuing bodies in whose issues the fund will invest more than 35% of the scheme property.

If an AFM wishes to invest more than 35% in value of the scheme's investments in issues by a single body, he must consult with the depositary/trustee and, as a result, consider the issuer is one which is appropriate in accordance with the scheme's investment objectives.

The regulations consider that any issue guaranteed by a particular government, local authority or international body should be treated as if it was issued by that government, local authority or international body.

2.3 Units/Shares in Regulated Collective Investments

A UCITS scheme can only invest in another scheme (the **second scheme**) if the following three requirements are met:

- the second scheme satisfies the conditions necessary for it to enjoy the rights conferred by the UCITS Directive;
- where the second scheme itself invests in schemes operated by the same firm, the first scheme must disclose the fact in its prospectus, ensuring that the first scheme is treated appropriately by the AFM of the second scheme;
- the second scheme must be prohibited from investing more than 10% of its value in collective investment vehicles – ensuring that pricing always relates to assets that are held, rather than schemes that mutually invest in each other but hold no underlying investments (a form of pyramid selling).

No more than 20% of the scheme property can be invested in any single CIS. There is also a limit on the aggregated holding of CISs, though holdings in UCITS schemes are excluded. A UCITS scheme cannot invest more than 30% of its property in:

- schemes recognised by the FSA under Section 270 of the FSMA;
- Non-UCITS Retail Schemes that meet the requirements of Article 19(1)(c) of the UCITS Directive; and
- schemes authorised in another EEA state that meets the requirements of Article 19(1)(c) of the UCITS Directive.

This prevents a NURS that invests in assets not permitted by the UCITS Directive (such as gold or real estate) from being held by a UCITS scheme.

2.4 Warrants and Shares Not Fully Paid

UCITS schemes can invest in warrants (securities with rights that can subsequently be exercised and converted into equity). There is no specific limit on the amount of the scheme that can be invested in warrants, although as warrants are a sub-set of transferable securities the spread requirements noted above apply. Also, the AFM must ensure that no breach of any other limit would arise if the warrants were all to be exercised into the related security.

> **Example**
>
> A scheme might hold 8% of its value in Vodafone and a further 1% of value in a Vodafone warrant. The total current exposure to Vodafone is 9% - but the exercise terms of the warrant must also be considered, as these will tend to increase the value of the asset. If exercise of the warrants results in new shares worth 3% of the scheme the total proportion of the scheme property invested in Vodafone would be 11%. This would be acceptable if the scheme is an index-replicating scheme and Vodafone represents 11% of the respective index. However, if the scheme is not an index-replicating scheme, or if Vodafone represents only 9% of the respective index, holding the warrants and shares would be a breach of the regulations – even though the unconverted combined total of the current holdings is only 9%.

Nil paid and partly paid securities produce a contingent liability on a scheme, a payment that will be required (or *called*) at a future date. Schemes may invest in such securities providing that such calls could be paid from the scheme and without any breach of the IBP limits.

2.5 Deposits

A scheme is able to make deposits with an approved bank, providing that it can be withdrawn on demand and matures in no more than 12 months. In order to ensure a spread of investments, not more than 20% of the scheme property may be deposited with a single body.

Approved Money Market Instruments

An approved money market instrument is an instrument which is normally dealt on the money market, is liquid and has a value which can be accurately determined at any time.

A money market instrument is regarded as normally dealt in on the money market if it:

- has a maturity at issue of up to 397 days;
- has a residual maturity of up to 397 days;
- undergoes regular yield adjustments at least every 397 days;
- has a risk profile (including credit and interest rate risk) corresponding to that of an instrument which has a maturity of up to 397 days.

2.6 Derivatives

A UCITS scheme may use derivatives (the generic term for futures contracts, options contracts, and contracts for differences such as forward currency transactions) for the purpose of hedging its exposure to a certain investment/asset/market – but the FSA sourcebook also permits derivatives to be used for investment purposes, as well as protection strategies. The derivative must be appropriate to the scheme's stated investment objective. Derivative positions will be either approved (where performed on an Eligible Derivatives Market named in the prospectus – following a due diligence review similar to that for eligible securities markets) or Over-The-Counter, also known as OTC (an off-exchange transaction subject to tighter restrictions within the FSA Sourcebook).

There is a limit of 5% of the scheme property on the total exposure to a single market counterparty for OTC derivative transactions, though this limit is increased to 10% where the counterparty is an approved bank.

Hedging

Hedging is a process by which the investment manager protects the overall fund from a loss of value of a certain asset or assets. There are two broad risks that give the potential for such loss: loss of value of the asset itself, or a change in a currency exchange rate that reduces the sterling value of the asset for valuation purposes, even if the asset itself is increasing in value.

The means used to protect the scheme's position will depend upon the risk and the breadth of cover required. Where a scheme holds assets overseas and the investment manager is concerned that the exchange rate will go against the scheme, he would perform a foreign currency transaction with a settlement date far in the future (common periods being three months, six months, or one year). The transaction would **sell forward** the currency being protected. When the settlement date approaches, the investment manager has two main options on behalf of the scheme:

- **Allow the deal to settle** (paying away the currency he sold, and receiving a pre-determined amount of sterling) – useful if the sterling he will receive is worth more than the current rate.
- **Close the exposure**. This involves performing an opposing transaction to cancel out the currency figure. The sterling equivalent will be different from the original forward transaction, creating a profit/loss that will be exchanged with the broker concerned.

Financial futures and options are forms of investment contract that reflect the market prices of the underlying securities. The process is similar: the scheme takes a position that has an expiry date and, based upon the market position near the end of that period, can either settle or close the position. (For more information about futures and options refer to the IAQ Introduction to Securities and Investment workbook.)

Collective Investment Schemes Administration

Therefore, a UK growth fund might hedge some or all of its portfolio against the FTSE index (using a financial future or option contract); a Japan growth fund (or other internationally invested fund) might use forward currency transactions to reduce the potential that a change in the exchange rate would affect the fund value.

For a UCITS scheme, the amount of the hedge must not exceed the exposure created by the underlying asset or assets, ie, any derivative position is covered by the value of related underlying assets in the scheme. Therefore, if a Japan growth fund with 600m Yen of securities is to be protected against foreign exchange loss, the hedge should not exceed the value of those assets. Similarly, a UK fund with £30m wishes to protect that value against a general fall in the FTSE, the future or option contract should not exceed this figure. However, due to the increased flexibility provided by the FSA sourcebook, cover is only required on a global basis. The AFM need not ensure that a UK derivative position is covered solely by UK assets.

The Risk Management Process

One change that resulted from the UCITS Amending Directive is that, where the AFM wishes to use derivatives, the regulations require it to establish a risk management process to monitor and measure all open positions and the effect on the scheme's overall risk profile. Certain details of the risk management process must be notified to the FSA prior to any derivative transactions being performed. These include the methods for estimating the risks involved, and the types of derivatives to be employed. Guidance in the regulations indicates that the risk management process should enable analysis of open positions and the associated risks to be performed at least daily. The risk management process should also be reviewed by the trustee/depositary.

Following the introduction of these requirements (which also apply to both UCITS and NURS various industry bodies and participants recognised the need for fund managers to have more detailed guidelines to assist them in the production of a risk management process. The Investment Management Association (IMA), the Depositary and Trustee Association (DATA), and the Futures and Options Association (FOA) established a joint working party to draft guidelines to assist fund managers in developing appropriate mechanisms for managing the various risks generated by the use of derivatives. The FSA has supported this industry led initiative and have provided input that has been incorporated into the guidelines.

The IMA, DATA and FOA guidelines propose that:

- Each AFM nominates one or more senior individuals (referred to as a **Committee**), who maintain a significant degree of independence from the AFM, to be responsible for overseeing the AFM's use of derivatives.
- The AFM must ensure that the Committee understands derivative instruments.

The Committee should report regularly to the fund manager's board on derivative positions and exposures.

- Use of derivatives to be monitored and reviewed regularly by persons independent of those involved in managing derivatives and that these activities comply with the FSA's sourcebook.
- Qualifications and experience of senior managers are to be examined by the Committee and that undue reliance is not placed on too few people.
- Where appropriate the Committee should seek additional professional advice and/or support from external specialists.

- Staff responsible for controlling risks and administrating transactions should be independent of those initiating the transactions. They are required to have the skills and experience to enable them to challenge the initiators effectively if necessary.
- As well as ensuring procedures are adequately documented, and that there are contingency plans to cover staff leaving, there should be links with both internal and external audit processes.
- The FSA must be notified by the fund manager of details of the risk management process, in particular, methods and use of estimating risks in derivative transactions. Details of this process must be discussed with the depositary.
- As a result of the Eligible Assets Directive, the requirement to have a risk management process in place has been extended to include all investments, not just derivatives. An AFM is expected to demonstrate more sophistication in its risk management process for a scheme with a complex risk profile than one with a simple risk profile. Only a risk management process relating to derivatives requires notification to the FSA.

2.7 Cash/Near Cash

It is necessary for a scheme to hold cash or near cash (such as a current account or other forms of highly liquid asset, eg, Treasury Bills) in order to enable dealing within the fund. Income received but not yet distributed is also held in the form of cash. While there is no stated limit to the amount of cash that can be held, the nature of a CIS requires that it is invested in line with its investment objective. As such, the levels of cash should not be excessive when compared with the investment objective and the short-term need for cash.

2.8 Limits relating to Control of Voting Shares of Companies

Concentration

Public companies are aware of the importance of cultivating good investor relations and are often prepared to listen to, or indeed seek, the views of the investing institutions such as AFMs. These institutions provide much of a company's capital requirements and have considerable experience of other companies. In practice, as a result of a close professional relationship through working together with similar, if not the same, long-term objectives, an AFM may influence a company in which it has invested.

Such influence, however, is normally of a participative style rather than confrontational; as a result, in many cases, if a takeover bid arises, the incumbent management of the target company will be supported or, if additional capital is required, the proposal for and the subsequent offer of a rights issue may be supported. Exceptions can arise where perhaps, through mismanagement, a company falls into difficulties and several different investing institutions are like-minded about the need to influence the company in order to safeguard their investors' interests. Occasionally, situations can become confrontational and naturally attract media attention, but these are rare.

The regulations ensure that a UCITS scheme would not be in a position to affect the running of any company in which it invests. A UCITS scheme may not hold more than:

- 25% of the units/shares of any collective investment scheme;
- 10% of the debt securities issued by a single body;Ss
- 10% of the money market instruments issued by a single body; or
- 10% of the voting shares of a company.

It must also be noted that a UCITS scheme is not permitted to purchase equities that do not carry voting rights.

Significant Influence

In addition to the concentration limits relating to a UCITS scheme, each OEIC and the manager of an AUT are subject on a corporate level to **significant influence** regulations.

The manager of an AUT must aggregate all positions held in all trusts and ensure that he does not control more than 20% in total of the voting shares. For OEICs (which may have sub-funds within the single OEIC company) this 20% limit is applied to the OEIC as a whole.

3. PERMITTED INVESTMENTS: NON-UCITS RETAIL SCHEMES (NURS)

> **LEARNING OBJECTIVES**
>
> 5.2.2 Know the specific limits applying to: UCITS funds; Non-UCITS retail funds; Qualified Investor Schemes (QIS)/Qualifying Money Market schemes(QMM)

Various regulations noted above for UCITS schemes do not apply to NURS. While the permitted categories of investment, and aggregated limits on the various categories, are broadly the same, the FSA sourcebook does provide slightly different requirements for NURS. This permits greater flexibility to funds that, while being retail in nature, are not seeking the UCITS capability to be marketed across the EU.

Unlike for UCITS schemes, the regulations do not specify the period of time before which the investment limits of the NURS must apply. Instead, the regulations provide for a reasonably practical period. Also, a NURS is not subject to any regulatory concentration/significant influence regulations (though a scheme might choose to apply a limit within its scheme documentation).

This section draws out the main IBP regulations applicable to NURS, concluding with a table to summarise the limits for different asset classes for both types of COLL fund.

3.1 Transferable Securities

The maximum holding in transferable securities or money market instruments issued by any single body remains at 10%, with the ability to increase it to 20% for schemes that replicate an index. However, there is no ability to increase this figure to higher levels in the event of exceptional circumstances. The total aggregated value of unapproved securities is 20% for NURSs (compared with 10% for UCITS schemes).

3.2 Units/Shares in Regulated Collective Investments

A NURS is enabled to invest up to 35% in the units/shares of another scheme.

3.3 Units/Shares in Unregulated Schemes

A NURS is able to invest in unregulated schemes, but any such schemes are viewed as unapproved securities and, therefore, included in the aggregated limit of 20% of scheme property.

3.4 Real Property

A NURS is able to invest in real property – with no upper aggregated limit. A maximum of 15% may be invested in any single property, though this figure can increase to 25% of the scheme once the property has been purchased. Investment limits generally apply at the point of purchase and subsequently, which can result in the AFM incurring a breach position either by accidentally purchasing too many shares (this is known as an **advertent breach**) or by subsequent movements of stock market prices increasing the value of one holding relative to the rest of the portfolio and so increasing the percentage of the scheme represented by that asset (known as an **inadvertent breach** if an IBP limit is breached as a result). Due to the price movements of immovable property, the regulations permit the proportionate value of a single asset to increase significantly without incurring an inadvertent breach.

Not more than 20% of the scheme may be invested in mortgaged immovables, with no mortgage exceeding 100% of the independent valuer's valuation. Not more than 50% of the scheme property can consist of immovable property that is unoccupied or currently under development, redevelopment, or refurbishment.

Any property must be subject to an independent valuation, reviewed at least monthly.

3.5 Gold

While CISs have previously invested in the mining and precious metal/gem exploration sector, it has not been possible to hold gold (other than a small number of 'Futures and Options Funds' regulated under the CIS sourcebook). A NURS can invest up to 10% of scheme property in gold, but would need to ensure that the trustee/depositary can arrange for safe custody – though this can sometimes be arranged via gold depositaries.

3.6 Deposits

A maximum of 20% of the scheme property can be deposited with any single body.

3.7 Borrowing

A NURS is bound by the same 10% limit on borrowing, but (unlike a UCITS scheme) this borrowing need not be temporary in nature. This permits a small level of gearing in the fund's operation.

3.8 Significant Influence/Concentration

The regulations noted above in relation to concentration and significant influence do not apply to NURS, though the manager of an AUT would still be subject to the requirements where any of their schemes are UCITS schemes.

3.9 Derivatives

The total exposure arising from OTC derivative transactions in respect of any single counterparty may not exceed 10% of the scheme property. The requirement for a risk management process is essentially unchanged from the UCITS scheme, requiring analysis at least daily, but also noting a requirement for increased sophistication in the approach as the risk profile of the NURS increases.

4. SUMMARY OF IBP LIMITS FOR COLL RETAIL SCHEMES

The following table summarises the permitted categories of asset and any limits that apply to the aggregated positions held.

Scheme investments / techniques	Limits for UCITS Schemes		Limits for Non-UCITS Schemes	
	Permitted?	Max. Limit	Permitted?	Max. Limit
Approved securities	Yes	None	Yes	None
Transferable securities that are not approved securities	Yes	10%	Yes	20%
Government and Public Securities	Yes	None	Yes	None
Regulated schemes	Yes	None	Yes	None
Unregulated schemes	No	N/A	Yes	20%
Warrants	Yes	None	Yes	None
Investment trusts	Yes	None	Yes	None
Deposits	Yes	None	Yes	None
Derivatives	Yes	None	Yes	None
Immovables (i.e, real property)	No	N/A	Yes	None
Gold	No	N/A	Yes	10%
Hedging	Yes	None	Yes	None
Stock lending	Yes	None	Yes	None
Underwriting	Yes	None	Yes	None
Borrowing	Yes	10% (temporary)	Yes	10%
Cash and Near cash	Yes	None	Yes	None

Source: COLL Sourcebook

5. NON-REGULATORY RESTRICTIONS ON INVESTMENT AND BORROWING POWERS (ALL SCHEMES)

LEARNING OBJECTIVES

5.1.2 Know the basis for investment or borrowing limits, the factors used in and obligations attached to valuing scheme property

Restrictions additional to those set out in the sourcebook can be included in the Trust Deed/Instrument of Incorporation and/or the Prospectus. Such additional limits are generally included to support the needs of a particular target market, or to differentiate the fund from competitors, and may include:

- the kind of investments in which the fund invests;
- the proportion of the capital which may be invested in assets of any description;
- descriptions of transactions permitted; and
- the borrowing powers of the fund.

Any additional restrictions included in a company's Trust Deed/Instrument of Incorporation or Prospectus have the same power as if they were included in the regulations, as the fund is under a regulatory obligation to operate according to the scheme documentation.

Qualified Investor Schemes (QIS)

This is particularly important for Qualified Investor Schemes. As such schemes are not retail by nature the FSA has not imposed such extensive restrictions on their behaviour. The approach of a given QIS will be primarily set out in its scheme documentation.

Qualifying Money Market Funds (QMMFs)

QMMFs are not subject to limits as such – they are a different type of fund designed to offer a constant share price by taking daily calculation of income/expense out of the fund valuation (though possibly only paid to investors less frequently).

6. WHAT ARE THE RULES RELATING TO STOCK LENDING?

LEARNING OBJECTIVES
5.3.1 Know the definitions, uses and restrictions of stock lending

The regulations allow schemes to use stock lending, when it appears to be reasonably economically appropriate to do so with a view to generating additional income for the scheme with either no risk or an acceptable degree of risk.

Stock lending is not a loan, but a disposal of the relevant securities in return for an obligation to transfer back securities of the same kind and amount at a later date. The borrower is also required to provide and transfer collateral to the fund to cover the scheme against the risk that the transfer back of shares may not be completed.

The AFM or the trustee/depositary (at the request of the scheme) will enter into such a transaction on behalf of the scheme if:

1. it is of the kind described in S263B of the Taxation of Chargeable Gains Act 1992;
2. the agreement and the collateral are acceptable to the trustee/depositary;
3. the counterparty is an authorised person (or included on the relevant Bank of England list of money market institutions) and approved by HM Revenue & Customs (HMRC) under the ICTA.

For the collateral to be acceptable, it must be:

1. at least equal in value to the shares or securities 'lent' at the time of transfer of the collateral;
2. transferred to the trustee/depositary or its agent;
3. the subject of an agreement which states that once the security loaned has been returned to the lender, the trustee/depositary will repay the collateral to the borrower;
4. in the form of certain liquid assets, eg, cash, near cash, gilts, certificates of deposits, a letter of credit or securities transferred in CREST by means of the **delivery by value (DBV)** system.

There is no limit on the value of property that may be used for stock lending.

7. CAN A COLLECTIVE INVESTMENT SCHEME BORROW MONEY?

LEARNING OBJECTIVES

5.3.2 Know the restrictions and powers relating to cash, borrowing, stock lending and the exceptions applying

Subject to the obligations of the trust/company to comply with any restriction in the Trust Deed/Instrument of Incorporation and/or Prospectus particulars, a scheme (UCITS or NURS) may borrow money for its own use from an eligible institution, on terms that repayment will be made from the property of the scheme.

Any borrowing for a UCITS scheme must be temporary – for no longer than three months, unless the prior consent of the trustee/depositary is obtained. This consent may be given only on such conditions as appear to the trustee/depositary appropriate to ensure that the borrowing does not cease to be on a temporary basis only.

Any borrowing must not exceed 10% of the value of the fund in one business day. This regulation does not apply to 'back to back' borrowing. (ie, foreign exchange hedging transactions).

A scheme is not permitted to lend money (though it is able to lend securities providing the **stocklending** requirements noted above are satisfied).

END OF CHAPTER QUESTIONS

Think of an answer for each question and refer to the appropriate section for confirmation.

	Question	Answer Reference
1.	Two UCITS amending directives were agreed by the EC in January 2002. They are referred to as the Productive Directive and the Management Directive. What is the purpose of these amending directives?	Section 1.1
2.	The spread regulations for CIS schemes do not apply until the expiry of a length of time. What is the time period?	Section 2
3.	How do AFMs determine the eligibility of markets to invest in?	Section 2.1
4.	Securities companies can only invest up to how much in any one company (or sub-fund) in transferable securities that are not approved securities?	Section 2.1
5.	Distinguish between a transferable security and an approved security.	Section 2.1
6.	With whom must the AFM consult over the eligibility of Government and Public Securities if the aggregated position invested with a single issuer is to exceed 35% of the scheme property?	Section 2.2
7.	What is: a) hedging used for by AFMs in relation to funds under their control?; and b) what is the limit on AFMs for CIS schemes?	Section 2.6
8.	It is necessary for an AFM to enable dealing within a fund to hold cash or near cash. Give two examples of near cash.	Section 2.7
9.	Explain the limits on a UCITS scheme regarding the maximum percentage holdings of units/shares, debts securities and voting shares that may be held.	Section 2.8
10.	Where can the rules relating to the investment and borrowing powers of a Non-UCITS Retail Scheme be found?	Section 3
11.	In a NURS there are limits on the holding of real property. Set out these limits.	Section 3.4

12. The Regulations allow stock lending by a scheme.
    a) Define this term; and
    b) Set out what the borrower is required to provide.   Section 6

13. In what circumstances can a scheme borrow money?   Section 7

14. Can a scheme lend money out of the property of the scheme?   Section 7

BUYING AND SELLING UNITS/SHARES

6

1.	OVERVIEW OF SINGLE- AND DUAL-PRICING	120
2.	DUAL-PRICING	121
3.	SINGLE-PRICING	127
4.	PRICING BASIS	130
5.	ERRORS IN THE PRICING OF A SCHEME	131
6.	THE DEALING PROCESS	135
7.	THE LAUNCH PERIOD	137
8.	ONGOING CREATION AND CANCELLATION OF UNITS/SHARES	138
9.	BOX MANAGEMENT ERRORS	140
10.	INVESTING THROUGH INTERMEDIARIES	141
11.	PRODUCT AND COMMISSION DISCLOSURE FOR NON-LIFE PRODUCTS	146

This syllabus area will provide approximately 9 of the 50 examination questions

Collective Investment Schemes Administration

INTRODUCTION

LEARNING OBJECTIVES

6.2.1 Know how and when valuations are made including frequency

6.2.2 Be able to calculate the price of units and shares using the different methods permitted by the FSA

6.2.6 Know the requirements for price publication

This chapter covers the buying and selling of units/shares, together with the procedures governing the calculation of prices and the creation and cancellation of units/shares. The investor's cancellation rights are also covered.

Each unit/share in a collective investment scheme represents a proportional part of the property of the scheme. Therefore, the price of each unit/share is the corresponding proportion of the value of the whole scheme. This is important as it removes any supply/demand effect from the price of a scheme on any day.

In broad terms, the price of a unit/share is obtained by valuing the property of the scheme and dividing that value by the number of units/shares in existence. While that sounds straight forward, the calculation of unit/share prices for an operational scheme is complex. The AFM must establish a valuation at a specific point in time, including all assets held within the scheme. It may also include adjustments to ensure that investors entering and leaving the scheme meet the costs that may be incurred when purchasing/selling underlying investments of the scheme resulting from such investment/disinvestment by investors (such as brokerage fees for underlying security purchases).

There are various pricing methods available for the AFM. Whichever method is selected must be recorded in the scheme prospectus to ensure that investors and potential investors are aware of how the price of units/shares will be determined. At all stages the fundamental aim of scheme pricing is to ensure that investors deal at a price that truly reflects the value of the scheme property.

Once the calculation is completed the regulations require that a price be quoted to four significant figures. The first non-zero digit is the first significant figure; subsequent digits are the second, third, etc, significant figures – including zeros and decimals where required. Any remaining places prior to the decimal point would be shown as zero. For example, here are some numbers expressed to four significant places:

Number	To 4 significant figures
12345	12350 (rounded up)
10001	10000
9.8765	9.877 (rounded up)
0.013579	0.01358

The important point to note is that significant figures are not the same as decimal places. In terms of unit/share prices, the key point is that a figure of 56.3458 pence per unit would be quoted as 56.35p per unit.

Most authorised funds are valued on a daily basis and details of the valuation point and the frequency of valuations will be found in the scheme's prospectus. Under the COLL rules an authorised fund must not have fewer than two valuations per month and if they do have only two valuations then they must be at least two weeks apart.

There are some exceptions to the minimum two valuations per month rule. If a fund has limited redemption arrangements then valuations could be up to six months apart. The AFM in these cases is still required to publish the prices at least once a month.

Other exceptions are higher volatility funds and Qualifying Money Market funds which must have at least one valuation point per business day. No valuation points are required during the initial offer period for any new fund as all units or shares will be issued at the initial offer price.

The official prices must then be published to enable investors and potential investors to assess the performance of each scheme over time. COLL includes a requirement to ensure that the prices are made public in an appropriate manner. While some AFMs will continue to use national newspapers, others have established telephone numbers or use their internet sites to provide prices to investors. The IMA has included a section on its website where any member firm can publish its prices.

An appropriate manner of making prices public means that:

- an investor can obtain prices at a reasonable cost;
- prices are available at reasonable times;
- publication is consistent with the manner and frequency at which units are dealt in, eg, using a daily newspaper to publish the prices of funds that offer daily dealing;
- the manner of publication is disclosed to investors in the prospectus;
- prices are published in a consistent manner, eg, in the same daily newspaper if published in that way and this allows the assessment of performance over time.

The AFM should also make previous prices available to any investor. Generally, these prices will be available on request direct from the AFM.

1. OVERVIEW OF SINGLE- AND DUAL-PRICING

Following the introduction of COLL in 2007 all authorised collective investment schemes have the choice of single- or dual-pricing. The rules can be applied separately to each sub-fund of a scheme which is an umbrella and, if appropriate, the currency of a sub-fund may be used instead of the base currency of the umbrella. Consequently, different methods of pricing units may be applied by an AFM to different sub-funds of an umbrella scheme. The AFM must, however, use the same method of pricing for each class of units in an authorised fund or in a sub-fund of an umbrella.

Accordingly AUTs which operated on a dual-pricing basis prior to COLL have been able to continue using this method post 12 February 2007 as the COLL Sourcebook applies to all funds.

It is possible for a dual-priced unit trust scheme to change to a single-pricing approach, though this requires notification to unitholders, including:

- the AFM's reason for the change;
- the date the change is intended to take effect;
- an explanation of the main features of the single-pricing system;
- an outline of the main differences between single- and dual-pricing;
- dilution: what it is, how it will affect investors, and the manager's policy on imposing a dilution levy or making a dilution adjustment;
- an indication of the implications of a change from single- to dual-pricing for investors, taking into account the particular circumstances of the scheme concerned (eg, if the fund is currently on a bid basis, the price at which units are redeemed will be higher – assuming no change in the value of assets – than under the previous system);
- an explanation of the major differences in the valuation of the property of the scheme; and
- any other material facts which the manager feels a unit holder should be aware of in order to understand the implications of the intended transition.

2. DUAL-PRICING

LEARNING OBJECTIVES

6.2.2 Be able to calculate the price of units and shares using the different methods permitted by the FSA

6.2.3 Understand how prices are calculated for funds with multiple share classes

6.2.4 Know the charges that may be made by the AFM

6.3.6 Be able to calculate purchase consideration and redemption proceeds using the different methods permitted by the FSA

2.1 Introduction

Dual-pricing was historically the standard method of pricing unit trusts and remains common for these types of scheme. The regulations now permit an OEIC to use this method too although most use a single-price method.

In various stock markets around the globe an investor purchasing a security pays a higher price than an investor selling that same security. There is a spread between the cost of buying and the proceeds of selling. As a collective investment scheme's value should at all times reflect the value of the underlying assets, it was historically the case that two portfolio values were calculated: one representing the cost of purchasing the entire portfolio (known as the offer side), and another representing the proceeds of selling the entire portfolio (known as the bid side).

The AFM must, therefore, obtain a bid and offer price for each asset held. In some cases the relevant stock market might use the same price for both buying and selling, in which case the CIS will value that asset by using that price on both the bid and offer sides of the valuation.

Cash and any income received will be included at par value. Such assets are, therefore, given the same value on the bid and offer sides of the valuation.

Likewise, the number of units in existence is the same on both sides of the valuation, leading to the following example:

Example – Unit Trust		Bid		Offer	
Asset		Price per share (£)	Value (£)	Price per share (£)	Value (£)
Portfolio					
1,000	ABC Ltd	1.50	1,500	1.55	1,550
1,500	XYZ Ltd.	1.80	2,700	1.85	2,775
2,000	HAL Ltd.	1.45	2,900	1.50	3,000
Total Portfolio value		7,100		7,325	
Cash		300		300	
Total Capital Assets		**7,400**		**7,625**	
Income for distribution		1,000		1,000	
Total Asset Value		**8,400**		**8,625**	

Assuming there are 10,000 units in existence the bid price per unit would be 84.00p and the offer price per unit would be 86.25p.

The above example is useful, though there are a number of items not included. The following sections will explain these in detail.

2.2 Notional Broking Charges

We noted above that the pricing regulations ensure that existing investors are not disadvantaged by new investors or those exiting the fund. Suppose that one investor holds 2,000 of the units in the above example and wishes to redeem these units. The bid price would be used (the AFM buys units at bid), so the fund would need to pay the investor £1,680 to redeem his holding, but this exceeds the level of cash available. The scheme will generally, therefore, be required to sell underlying investments to raise the necessary funds (assuming that the AFM is not able to resell these units to new investors and, therefore, cancels them).

Shares are bought and sold through stockbrokers and such transactions incur a charge. For UK equity-based transactions this might be 0.2% of the bid value and 0.7% of the offer value (the difference being due to stamp duty). It seems unfair that the costs of buying or selling shares due to one investor's investment should not be paid for by that investor, and so the regulations enable a dual-priced fund to add a **notional broking charge** (though other names are sometimes used) to its price calculation. The notional broking charge is the theoretical average cost that the fund would suffer if the portfolio was either rebuilt from no holdings (an offer calculation, as it involves the purchase of securities) or sold if the scheme were to be wound up (sale of securities being a bid figure). As every investor's deal includes the notional broking charge calculated that day, each investor receives fair treatment both buying and selling.

For example, to consider the bid side first, the AFM has established that it suffers 0.2% when it sells UK equities. Assuming that all the shares held in the example fund above are UK equities the AFM knows that selling all holdings would, therefore, cost £14.20 (being 0.2% of £7,100). Therefore, the effective value of those shares is not £7,100 but £7,085.80. The notional broking charge on the bid side reduces the value of the portfolio.

What of the offer side? The AFM has established the average charge to be 0.7% on purchases of UK equities, and the current value is £7,325. Therefore, to buy this portfolio from cash would incur a dealing charge of £51.28 (rounding up to the nearest penny) – meaning that to purchase the full portfolio would actually cost the fund £7,376.28 (the cost of the investments plus the broking fee). The notional broking charge on the offer side increases the value of the portfolio.

Our example valuation now looks like this:

Example Asset		Bid		Offer	
		Price per share (£)	Value (£)	Price per share (£)	Value (£)
Portfolio					
1,000	ABC Ltd	1.50	1,500.00	1.55	1,550.00
1,500	XYZ Ltd.	1.80	2,700.00	1.85	2,775.00
2,000	HAL Ltd.	1.45	2,900.00	1.50	3,000.00
Total Portfolio value			7,100.00		7,325.00
Notional Broking Charge					
UK equities		0.2%	-14.20	0.7%	51.28
Cash			300.00		300.00
Total Capital Assets			7,385.80		7,676.28
Income for distribution			1,000.00		1,000.00
Total Asset Value			8,385.80		8,676.28

The bid price is now 83.86p and the offer price 86.76p. Notional broking charges have the effect of increasing the spread between prices.

2.3 Initial Charge

The other item to be added to the valuation is the AFM's initial charge. The initial charge is unique in that it is applied only to one side of the valuation. It is only relevant to investors buying units, so will it affect the bid or offer price?

Hopefully you recognised that the AFM sells units at the offer price (the investor buys at the higher price). Suppose the initial charge is 5%. Adding this to our example valuation gives the following result:

Example – Unit Trust							
Asset		**Bid**			**Offer**		
		Price per share (£)	Value (£)	ppu*	Price per share (£)	Value (£)	ppu*
Portfolio							
1,000	ABC Ltd	1.50	1,500.00		1.55	1,550.00	
1,500	XYZ Ltd.	1.80	2,700.00		1.85	2,775.00	
2,000	HAL Ltd.	1.45	2,900.00		1.50	3,000.00	
Total Portfolio value			7,100.00			7,325.00	
Notional Broking Charge							
UK equities		0.2%	-14.20		0.7%	51.28	
Cash			300.00			300.00	
Total Capital Assets			7,385.80			7,676.28	
Income for distribution			1,000.00			1,000.00	
Total Asset Value			8,385.80	83.86		8,676.28	86.76
Initial Charge					5%	433.81	
Scheme Value			8.385.80	83.86		9,110.09	91.10

* ppu = pence per unit

The bid price is, therefore, unchanged at 83.86p whilst the maximum offer price increases to 91.10p.

The initial charge, sometimes referred to as the **initial service charge**, which the AFM is entitled to add to the price when he sells a unit, is designed to cover promotional expenses, commissions to agents, such as independent financial advisers, and the actual cost of putting new unitholders on the register.

2.4 Creation and Cancellation Prices

The prices at which units are created and cancelled in a dual-priced fund are determined by the calculation above. In order to ensure that the creation and cancellation of units has no impact upon any investor these prices are not subject to any initial charge or other variation. The creation and cancellation prices are the figures shown as **Total Asset Value** in the above example. Units will be cancelled at 83.86p and units will be created at 86.76p. The AFM has no power to vary these figures.

2.5 Dealing Spread: the Pricing Basis

> **LEARNING OBJECTIVES**
> 6.2.5 Understand the AFM's discretion in setting dealing prices under single and dual pricing

While the AFM is obliged under the regulations to always use the creation and cancellation prices for the purpose of increasing and reducing the number of units in issue calculated, there is some flexibility in the bid and offer prices for the purpose of selling and redeeming units.

Referring back to our worked example, the bid and offer prices shown have a total dealing spread of 8.6% – meaning that the fund value would need to rise by 8.6% before the investor could sell his units without losing money.

Many investors would be discouraged by this and so the AFM is able to vary these prices, within certain limits. Where the AFM intends to employ such flexibility he will state, in the scheme documentation the spread that will be used on the fund. Let us consider that the AFM wants to set the spread at 7%, and see how this affects the prices in our calculation.

Where the AFM has received net redemption instructions during a given dealing day (more sellers of units than buyers), the AFM is likely to make a cancellation instruction. The cancellation price is fixed and the AFM will not wish to lose money on performing the cancellation, so the AFM will want to pay redeeming unitholders the same price to investors as he receives from the trustee for the cancellation of units.

The AFM will, therefore, set the **quoted bid price** (ie, the price paid to redeeming unitholders) to the lowest allowable price, which is the cancellation price (ie, the price determined on the bid side of the valuation). The AFM is not permitted to make the quoted bid price less than the cancellation price. He could then reduce the calculated maximum offer price (the one including the full initial charge) until the difference between the prices is 7% – the stated spread.

Collective Investment Schemes Administration

This is known as quoting the fund on a bid basis. The four prices for our fund when quoted on a bid basis are:

- Cancellation   83.86
- Quoted bid   83.86
- Creation   86.76
- Quoted offer   89.73 (being 1.07 x the quoted bid)

No deals are performed at the calculated maximum offer price of 91.10p. The AFM is essentially sacrificing just over 1p per unit of the available initial charge in order to reduce the price differential. While the AFM, therefore, does not collect the maximum initial charge on those units he sells, it is preferable to losing money on each unit redeemed (as the bid basis is used when the AFM is a net redeemer of units).

The offer basis is used when the AFM is a net seller of units. In order to gain the maximum possible initial charge the AFM will set the quoted offer price at the maximum offer price (91.10p). The creation and cancellation prices are unchanged by the basis as these cannot be varied. The quoted bid price will, therefore, be fixed at a level so that 1.07 x the quoted bid will equal the quoted offer price.

Therefore, if our example fund were quoted on an offer basis the prices would be as follows:

- Cancellation   83.86
- Quoted bid   85.14 (being the quoted offer price divided by 1.07)
- Creation   86.76
- Quoted offer   91.10 (being the maximum offer price calculated)

While the AFM essentially makes a small loss on each unit redeemed, the gain made by receiving the full initial charge is sufficient to cover that loss. The AFM will, therefore, use the offer basis when he is a net seller of units. In practice the units redeemed are most likely to be resold to new investors at the quoted offer price and, therefore, the AFM makes a gain which is the difference between the quoted bid price and the quoted offer price.

The third pricing basis is called the full or maximum spread. It is used when the AFM has not specified a dealing spread, or where the prices calculated lie within the spread.

Suppose that the AFM of our example fund was operating a spread of 9%. The prices would be set as follows:

- Cancellation   83.86
- Quoted bid   83.86 (the calculated minimum redemption price)
- Creation   86.76
- Quoted offer   91.10 (the calculated maximum offer price)

As the difference between the bid and offer prices does not exceed the maximum spread of the scheme, the AFM can set the prices as wide as the calculation will permit.

Whichever basis is used, all four prices must be notified to the trustee in order that they can confirm any creation/cancellation required by the AFM, and also for subsequent use in testing the AFM's unit dealing records as part of its oversight responsibilities.

3. SINGLE-PRICING

LEARNING OBJECTIVES

- **6.2.2** Be able to calculate the price of units and shares using the different methods permitted by the FSA
- **6.2.4** Know the charges that may be made by the AFM
- **6.2.5** Understand the AFM's discretion in setting dealing prices under single and dual pricing
- **6.2.8** Know the definitions, uses and requirements of forward and historic pricing
- **6.3.5** Understand the AFM's discretion in relation to: large redemptions; in specie transactions; dilution levy/dilution adjustment; Stamp Duty Reserve Tax
- **6.3.6** Be able to calculate purchase consideration and redemption proceeds using the different methods permitted by the FSA

3.1 Introduction

The **dual-pricing** system outlined above has both good and bad aspects. Investors pay an appropriate price for their investment, the AFM is limited in his use of the bid/offer spread, but the two prices appear confusing to investors and in many markets (particularly continental Europe) the dual-priced model is not used. AFMs seeking to market their schemes abroad needed a simpler pricing mechanism, which led to the **single-pricing** method being introduced.

A **single-pricing** method means that the AFM calculates one price at each valuation point. This price will be used for both creation and cancellation, and that an investor buying units/shares will do so at the same core price as another investor who sells units at the same time (though we will see that initial charges remain and affect the single price).

3.2 How Single-Pricing differs from Dual-Pricing

The cause of the dealing spread in a dual-priced fund is the spread on the underlying portfolio of investments, the dealing costs on those investments, and the initial charge.

Rather than using the bid and offer prices of the underlying securities, a single-pricing fund will use a single price for each asset. Some securities markets quote only a single price for equities (the New York Stock Exchange being one example), and where bid and offer prices are quoted for an asset the AFM will use an arithmetic average of the two prices. Single-pricing is, therefore, sometimes referred to as 'using the mid-price'.

Notional broking charges also affect the spread (albeit slightly) and so another means of reflecting these in the dealings with investors must be used.

The regulations permit two methods by which the cost of dealing in underlying investments can be appropriately factored into the price. These are the **Dilution Levy** and the **Dilution Adjustment**: a fund may apply either of these, but not both.

Unlike the bid/offer spread on underlying investments and the notional broking charge (which were part of the price calculation for dual pricing) the dilution levy is an adjustment which may be made to each investor's transaction. The AFM will determine the conditions in which a dilution levy will apply – generally based on the size of the deal (a figure of £15,000 is commonly used) – and will calculate an appropriate rate for the dilution levy. The policy on charging is set out in the prospectus. The trustee/depositary will review these calculations (as with the calculations of the notional broking charge percentages) to ensure that the AFM's rates are appropriate to the fund's investments and the actual brokerage charges suffered.

Therefore, where a dilution levy is applied, the investor's contract note will detail the transaction based on the single price, but with an additional levy charged to the investor. While there is officially a single price, one investor subject to the levy will effectively pay a different price to an investor whose transaction is small enough not to require the levy. The dilution levy method is, therefore, able to distinguish between larger and smaller investors. The AFM's initial charge does not form part of the price (as is the case for dual-priced funds) and will, therefore, be shown as a separate charge for investors purchasing units/shares.

The dilution adjustment is more subtle. Here, the AFM determines the expected net effect of the dealing activity during the day and establishes an approximate cost of underlying transactions. The single price is then adjusted (ie, the quoted single price is the calculated single price amended to reflect the dilution adjustment). Each investor deals at the same price at each valuation point, as the quoted price already reflects the necessary dilution adjustment.

Amending our earlier example, calculation of dual-pricing provides the following example for a single-priced fund prior to dilution:

Example				
Asset		**Mid**		
		Price per share (£)	Value (£)	Pence per unit
Portfolio				
1,000	ABC Ltd	1.525	1,525.00	
1,500	XYZ Ltd.	1.825	2,737.50	
2,000	HAL Ltd.	1.475	2,950.00	
Total Portfolio Value			**7,212.50**	
Cash			300.00	
Total Capital Assets			**7,512.50**	
Income for distribution			1,000.00	
Total Net Asset Value			**8,512.50**	**85.13**

In the above example, the price on the valuation date is 85.13p per unit (compared to the creation and cancellation prices of 86.76p and 83.86p, respectively). A levy for dilution might be applied on particular deals. Alternatively, the AFM may adopt the dilution adjustment pricing method and adjust the single price in line with the aggregated dealing position of the AFM. The dilution adjustment approach is still new to the industry and it is possibly too soon to tell whether this method will gain widespread support.

Again, the finalised price under any single-pricing method must be notified to the trustee/depositary.

Note that while the examples shown in this section do not include an exit charge, the regulations do provide for an AFM to levy such a charge on redemptions. Very few AFMs have introduced such a charge, but the most frequent use of this ability is to apply a charge that decreases the longer the units/shares are held. For example, redemptions within the first year may suffer a 5% charge, reducing to 4% in the second year, and so on. After five years no exit charge would be payable.

Those AFMs applying an exit charge will probably not apply an initial charge, enabling an investor to avoid both initial and exit charges by retaining their units/shares for the necessary period, though the AFM will collect their annual management charge during that time.

An AFM may, providing it is stated in the prospectus, make a charge to provide for Stamp Duty Reserve Tax (SDRT). Where charged, the AFM will require the:

- payment of an SDRT provision for the issue or sale of units/shares; or
- deduction of an SDRT provision for the redemption or cancellation of units/shares.

In practice, any SDRT liability is often met by the fund although the AFM may, as part of the policy set out in the prospectus, reserve the right to charge investors. More details of the SDRT regime for collective investment schemes can be found in Chapter 10.

3.3 Classes of Units/Shares

LEARNING OBJECTIVES

6.3.1 Understand how different classes are used for different types of investor

OEICs and unit trusts regulated under the COLL sourcebook are able to issue multiple classes of unit/share. These would be designed by the AFM to meet the different requirements of investors. For example, a retail class unit/share might have a low initial investment level as retail investors may have smaller sums available. An institutional class of share may have a higher initial investment requirement, though would probably benefit from a lower rate of charges.

This creates an important distinction in the calculation on the scheme price. Capital assets are allocated in proportion to the investments made in each class of unit/share. However, the net income and expense accrued since the previous valuation point is apportioned in accordance with the rules for each class. The ratio for apportionment between different classes, therefore, changes at every valuation point.

This is in contrast to those CISs with only income and accumulation units, where the accumulation factor reflects the income previously retained within the scheme. Such a factor is only changed at an accounting date where a distribution is payable.

4. PRICING BASIS

> **LEARNING OBJECTIVES**
>
> 6.2.8 Know the definitions, uses and requirements of forward and historic pricing
>
> 6.3.6 Be able to calculate purchase consideration and redemption proceeds using the different methods permitted by the FSA

Regardless of whether a single- or dual-pricing method is used, schemes may be priced for dealing on either a forward or historic basis.

4.1 Forward Pricing

A forward basis means that orders (to buy or sell) taken from investors will be dealt at the prices determined at the next valuation point. This can be off-putting for the investor because he is dealing blind – he does not know the actual price he is dealing at until after the next valuation point, and the published prices available to him offer only a guide.

Within the UK market, forward pricing with a 12 noon valuation point is a popular choice. For example, an investor who phones at 9.30am on Monday receives the price determined after the noon valuation the same day. An investor who phones at 3.30pm on Monday has his deal priced after the valuation at noon the next business day. Forward pricing is helpful in protecting continuing unit/shareholders particularly where the fund is subject to higher market volatility. Forward pricing is now the method used by the vast majority of funds.

4.2 Historic Pricing

The alternative is to deal on historic prices, ie, those calculated at the previous valuation point. Few AFM groups still do this, the main benefit being that the investor knows the price at which he is dealing. However, this knowledge can enable investors to take advantage of subsequent market movements – particularly institutional investors with large holdings.

Consider an investor holding 100,000 shares in a 12 noon historic-priced OEIC. The price struck at noon is 100p, but in the afternoon and evening the US market falls. The UK market opens and share prices start to fall. Historic pricing would enable the investor to sell his holding at the known price of 100p. If the price falls to 95p by the next valuation point he could then buy the units/shares back at the reduced price and collect £5,000 – essentially a cost borne by the other investors in the scheme. This is a very simple example and ignores other charges such as initial/exit charges, pricing spreads and dilution levy/adjustment.

To protect investors against such actions the regulations specify circumstances where the AFM of a historic-priced scheme must use forward prices (until the next valuation point). These circumstances include:

- where the AFM believes the fund value has moved (up or down) by 2% or more; or
- where the investor requests a forward price.

5. ERRORS IN THE PRICING OF A SCHEME

LEARNING OBJECTIVES

6.2.9 Know what constitutes a pricing error, the consequences and the action to be taken by the AFM and trustee/depositary

The valuation example shown earlier in this chapter is simple but, in practice, the number and complexity of different investments which may be held can present problems in ensuring accurate price information and so make valuation more complicated. Incorrect pricing of investments happens and cannot be avoided completely – the regulations provide guidance on the actions to be taken when these complex calculations are found to be incorrect. They also outline various controls that the AFM should have in place in order to minimise the impact of pricing errors.

The regulatory provisions covering these problems can be found in COLL 6.3. These specific regulations give the trustee/depositary wide discretion to determine whether or not compensation is required. Subject to the AFM and trustee/depositary having appropriate controls in place to prevent incorrect pricing, it is necessary only to carry out the detailed investigation if an incorrect unit price is different from the correct price by plus or minus 0.5% (known as the **de minimis** level). The regulations cover the following areas:

- pricing controls by the AFM;
- review of the AFM's systems and controls for pricing by the trustee/depositary;
- the regulatory position of the AFM; and
- any action required if incorrect prices are found.

5.1 Valuation and Pricing Controls of the AFM

The AFM is required by regulations to exercise due diligence in connection with valuation and pricing, and to show that he has complied with the minimum control requirements set out by the FSA. It will be difficult for an AFM to demonstrate that he has met the requirements if:

- persistent or repetitive errors occur; or
- errors occur which are consistently in the manager's favour.

The following sets out examples of the checks that an AFM should carry out in relation to valuation and pricing of a CIS:

1. Investments should be valued using a reputable source. The reliability of the source of prices should be kept under regular review, with doubtful prices investigated. As we know already the valuation of a single-priced authorised fund should reflect the mid-market value of the fund's investments while a dual-priced fund will reflect both the offer and bid prices of the investments.

2. For Qualifying Money Market (QMM) schemes, the money market instruments in which they invest should be valued on an amortised basis with regular comparisons, at least weekly, to the market price to ensure they are broadly in line. The FSA provides guidance on appropriate action where the prices vary significantly.

3. If valuation is delegated to a third party administration company or an associate company, the AFM must be satisfied that the third party's system is robust and will produce accurate results. The AFM is required to ensure that at all times it can monitor effectively any relevant outsourced activity. Typically, the AFM should review the outputs from the system at least annually and on any significant system change.

4. Unless the valuation and record keeping systems are integrated, the valuation output should be agreed with the AFM's records of the scheme at each valuation point. The AFM's records should be agreed with the trustee's/depositary's records at least monthly and any differences in this reconciliation followed up promptly. This check should include the reviewing of debtors for recoverability.

5. Checks to ensure all securities deals should be confirmed in writing as quickly as possible to the AFM (or relevant third party company) by fax, email or telex, if necessary. As far as practicable, all deals entered into prior to a valuation should be included in the valuation. Industry practice (reflecting earlier, more detailed FSA rules) suggests an hour before the valuation as the cut-off point, but it is important to have accurate cut-off procedures to ensure that deals are not omitted or duplicated.

6. A record should be maintained of the source and basis for the value placed on any investment if the price is obtained other than from the main pricing source (eg, unquoted, suspended or illiquid stocks).

7. Checks to ensure that investment and borrowing powers (see Chapter 5) are not breached and, if breaches occur, that they are identified promptly.

8. Checks to ensure dividends, interest and expenses are all accounted for at the appropriate time (eg, a dividend at the stock's XD date) unless it is prudent to account for them on receipt.

9. A review, at least quarterly, of the full tax position of the fund.

10. A review, at least quarterly, of the justification of the figures for dealing expenses and commissions included in the pricing process (whether notional broking or dilution).

11. Fixed percentages or absolute limits should be set for key elements of the valuation and any movement outside these limits must be investigated (such as any security price moving more than 3% from the previous day).

12. The investigation and outcome should be documented and signed. The key elements include:

    a. the overall price of the fund against relevant markets;
    b. the movement in price of individual investments;
    c. changes in currency rate;
    d. the accrual figures for income and expenses; and
    e. tax.

13. Prices that are unchanged for a period of time (eg, four days) should be investigated.
14. Cash should be reconciled to the bank account regularly, with any discrepancies investigated and a full reconciliation sent to the trustee/depositary monthly.
15. There should be controls to ensure that the correct number of units/shares in issue is recorded at each valuation point and reconciled with the register at least monthly.
16. The investment manager (either an individual fund manager or the team responsible for managing the investments) should receive a copy of the valuation at least weekly and should check that the correct securities are recorded.

Fair Value Price

Circumstances may arise where the AFM is unable to obtain a reliable price for a security at a valuation point or the most recent price available does not reflect the AFM's best estimate of the value of a security at the valuation point. Such circumstances include, for example, where no recent trade in the security has taken place or a significant event takes place after the close of a market where the price of the security is taken. In such circumstances the AFM should value an investment at a price which, in its opinion, reflects a fair and reasonable price for that investment (the fair value price). Such fair value pricing must be clearly documented and applied consistently. AFMs will normally have a Fair Value Committee, with written terms of reference and policies, who will meet when such circumstances arise. The methodology used and rationale for fair value decisions will be reviewed by the trustee/depositary. If subsequent information comes to light that indicates the actual price was different from the fair value price, the latter will not normally be regarded as an incorrect price.

5.2 Pricing Checks a Trustee/Depositary Should Make

The following sets out the types of checks that the FSA expects the trustee/depositary to perform to satisfy itself that the AFM's pricing operation is adequately controlled and the risk of incorrect prices is minimised.

1. A thorough review and analysis of the manager's pricing system and controls should be made to ensure they are satisfactory and to assess their reliability. This review should be conducted when the trustee/depositary is appointed and thereafter when appropriate, given its knowledge of the robustness and stability of the systems and controls and their operation, eg, on any major change in the manager's system, or where a series of minor changes could have a significant effect on accuracy.
2. If the manager's controls are found to be satisfactory, further review of these controls should be carried out at least annually.
3. At least annually, a check of the valuation of each fund should be made. All assets, liabilities and accruals should be checked on a sample basis if the fund portfolio is very large, together with units/shares in issue and any accumulation factor or currency conversion factor. Also, in particular, a check of the prices of unapproved securities and the basis for the valuation of unquoted securities.
4. Checks will need to be increased if:
    a. the manager's systems are manual, new and unproven, or otherwise regarded as weak; or
    b. a number of occurrences of incorrect pricing have been identified.
5. Any issues which are identified must be properly followed up and resolved.

5.3 How the AFM and Trustee/Depositary deal with Incorrect Prices

An AFM has a professional duty to ensure that prices used to value the investments are correct. The AFM also has a duty, if incorrect pricing has taken place, to take action to rectify the valuation. As has been noted above, the regulations require a price to be quoted to four significant figures. Many errors will be so minor as to not change the fourth significant figure. For instance, the single pricing example earlier in this chapter calculated a fund value of £8,512.50 (and a price of 85.13p per unit). If the cash at bank figure of £300 was incorrectly calculated, adding 50p to the figure, the total fund value would have been stated as £8,513.00, still resulting in a price of 85.13p per unit.

Where the fourth significant figure is not affected, no pricing breach is recorded.

However, suppose the error had increased the cash figure from £300 to £320. The fund value would have been calculated as £8,537.50 (a price of 85.38p per unit). The fourth significant figure is changed and so the event is recorded as a pricing error. You will note that the error was large enough to also affect the third significant figure of the price, but the important feature in assessing a pricing error is the percentage by which the calculated figure differs from the correct figure.

Where the magnitude of the error is less than 0.5% the error is described as being below 'de minimis' (the minimum level at which the AFM is required to recalculate all deals performed). The error here is £20 divided by £8,512.50 – being 0.23% and so this error would be below de minimis.

Where the magnitude is greater than 0.5% the error is above de minimis and all deals performed on that valuation point must be recalculated. This extends to either reimbursing or compensating any investor or former investor, and to the AFM reimbursing the scheme (or receiving compensation) for any benefit incorrectly gained. All these steps are taken with the agreement of the trustee/depositary.

However, the regulations grant some flexibility to the trustee/depositary to judge an event appropriately. If the trustee/depositary is satisfied that the incorrect pricing is of minimal significance, the valuation must still be corrected but reimbursement need not be made. Equally, where the trustee/depositary considers that an investor who dealt during a below de minimis error has suffered material loss, it can require the AFM to compensate the investor. If the trustee/depositary considers the reimbursement or payment made by the AFM to be inappropriate it should report the matter to the FSA, together with its recommendation and justification.

The requirements can be summarised as follows:

- On discovery, incorrect prices (to the fourth significant figure) must be recorded by the AFM.
- The errors should also be reported to the trustee/depositary.
- Action should be taken to avoid repetition of the breach.
- Any pricing errors exceeding the de minimis limit (ie, incorrect pricing of plus/minus 0.5% or more of the price of a unit/share) must be reported by the trustee/depositary in a quarterly return to the FSA.
- Unit/share deals must be corrected in line with the following table. Correction is required even if the correct price would have been within the maximum and minimum prices permitted by the regulations.

Example		
Compensation Decisions	Prices Correct By	
	Less than 0.5%	More than 0.5%
1. Dealings between fund and manager		
Fund Gains (creation – too high or cancellation – too low)	Normally no action	Trustee to compensate AFM from fund
Fund Losses (creation – too low or cancellation – too high)	Normally no action (1)	Trustee directs AFM to compensate fund
2. Dealings between Unit Holders and Manager		
Incoming Unit Holder Gains (offer price – too low)	No action	See (2)
Incoming Unit Holder Loses (offer price – too high)	Normally no action (1)	AFM to compensate incoming unit/shareholders
Outgoing Unit Holder Gains (bid price – too high)	No action	See (2)
Outgoing Unit Holder Loses (bid price – too low)	Normally no action (1)	AFM to compensate outgoing unit/shareholders

Notes

1. In any of these cases the trustee could, if he felt it appropriate, require the AFM to pay compensation, but this would be unlikely.
2. It may not be practical or even legally permissible for the AFM to seek compensation from the unit/shareholders if they have benefited from an incorrect price. The AFM needs to consider his legal position and commercial implications when deciding whether to seek compensation.

6. THE DEALING PROCESS

LEARNING OBJECTIVES

6.2.7 Know the requirements for notification to the depositary/trustee

6.1 Introduction

Having established how the price has been calculated it is time to consider how an investor actually places his money in, or removes it from, a scheme. The following sections consider various aspects of dealing.

6.2 The Manager's Box

The AFM issues units/shares to any individual (or company) who applies to buy them at the price fixed by the AFM in line with the regulations. AFMs often hold a box (the **Manager's Box**) of units/shares to aid their work as market makers – buying units/shares from holders wishing to sell and selling them to new investors. On any given dealing day the AFM might find that his box does not hold sufficient units/shares to meet the investment deals he has accepted. In such cases the AFM will instruct the trustee/depositary to create a specified number of new units/shares. The AFM will be required to pay the trustee/depositary the correct value for these units/shares, which are added to the manager's box. Purchasers of units/shares, therefore, may receive either units/shares that have just been created, or ones that have previously been issued and bought back by the AFM. However, this has no impact on the investor.

If the AFM considers that he has excessive units/shares in his box he can instruct the trustee/depositary to cancel a given number. In this case the trustee/depositary will pay the appropriate sum to the AFM on the settlement date. The regulations only place one restriction on the AFM in relation to the size of the box: at each valuation point, having established the net investment and redemption deals performed, the AFM must ensure he holds sufficient units/shares to meet all outstanding orders. This can include any units/shares already held in the box, plus any additional units/shares being created by the trustee. Where the AFM does not hold sufficient units/shares in his box he is said to have a **negative box position**, and it is a serious breach if an AFM does not instruct the creation of sufficient units/shares to cover this.

6.3 How Investor Deals

There are many methods by which an investor may place a deal – either investing or redeeming. The investor would often contact the AFM directly, though various intermediaries exist in the financial services market. An investor who is working with a stockbroker or independent financial adviser might use them to perform deals on his behalf.

Upon receipt of an appropriate instruction the AFM places the deal. For a scheme using historic prices the AFM can immediately advise the investor of the price he will pay for the units/shares, but if the scheme uses forward prices he would only be able to state the previous price calculated.

Terms for the purchase of units/shares by investors may require cash with order, or may typically require that payment is made within four business days of the transaction being placed. In many cases an investor would include a cheque with his investment deal – especially on his first investment, where he may be required to complete an application form. Various AFMs accept payment by debit card. In either of these cases the AFM will already be in the process of collecting the investor's payment, but the units/shares are not considered to be owned by the investor until payment has been received by the AFM (see Chapter 7 for more detail of the settlement and registration process).

The investor will be sent a contract note detailing the transaction performed (price, units/shares, and total consideration, including any additional items such as dilution levy payable). An example contract note can be seen in Appendix 5.

An investor wishing to purchase units/shares might use any of the following options (providing that the specific AFM enables dealing by these channels). The investor may:

- complete an application form, which may have appeared in newspapers or been sent to the investor by a mail shot, and send it by post to the AFM (including share exchange);
- deal with the AFM by telephone;
- use an intermediary to place the deal on their behalf;
- make regular investments using direct debit or direct credit; or
- subscribe to a monthly investment scheme.

For redemptions, investors may give instructions in the same way (ie, by post or telephone, or via an intermediary). Whatever route is used, investors must normally complete a **Form of Renunciation**, renouncing their interest in the units/shares being sold. The completed form is effectively a transfer of units/shares back to the AFM, used by the AFM to ensure that it has received a genuine instruction from the holder of the units/shares. These forms can usually be found on the reverse of unit/share certificates (where issued) or may be issued with the contract note at the time of purchase or sale (see Appendix 6).

In some cases an investor invests in an Individual Savings Account (ISA), with the ISA being invested in one or more CISs. In such cases the investor's contract is with the ISA manager, and the units/shares are purchased by the ISA manager. The individual investor would not be a unit/shareholder of the collective investment scheme, but is rather transacting on the basis of the ISA manager's terms and conditions.

To encourage investors AFMs may from time to time offer discounts. The discount may be applied for lump sums and might have a closing date. In all cases the discount will be applied to the AFM's initial charge and not to the unit/share creation price. For dual-priced funds the discount will be reflected in the offer price while for single-priced funds a reduced initial charge will be shown separately.

AFMs also pay commission to agents, such as IFAs, who introduce business. Typically, AFMs will pay 3% commission to agents on initial purchase and may pay a trail or renewal commission of, say, 0.5% per annum to the agent providing the that investor retains the investment. These commissions are paid out of the AFM's own income (ie, from the Initial Charge and the Periodic or Annual Management Charge). Disclosure of these payments will be shown in the contract note and/or statements issued to the investor. The actual rates of commission may vary.

7. THE LAUNCH PERIOD

When a CIS is launched (ie, first made available to investors) the offer price is fixed by the AFM – typically, units/shares would be issued at prices such as 50p or £1 per unit/share. The price is fixed for the period of the launch or initial offer period which may, for example, be 21 days. The period of the offer and the initial price, which is agreed by the AFM and the trustee/depositary, are stated in the prospectus.

The initial price is a fixed price, including any AFM's initial charge, that may be paid by an investor to the AFM for units/shares bought during an initial offer. The AFM may decide to have units/shares created on a day-to-day basis during the offer period, or create all units/shares at the end of the offer period. The AFM must pay the initial price over to the trustee/depositary as soon as practicable and no later than four business days after the end of the initial offer period.

The launch of a new CIS is usually heralded by publicity and a discount may be offered during the initial offer period (such as a reduction in the AFM's initial charge). For example, the manager may offer a discount (typically 1% or 2%) for certain amounts and for a limited period.

The initial offer period will come to an end if the AFM reasonably believes the price that would reflect the current value of the fund would vary by more than 2% from the initial price.

8. ONGOING CREATION AND CANCELLATION OF UNITS/SHARES

8.1 Creation and Cancellation

Once the initial offer or unitisation is over, units/shares are created and cancelled by reference to regular valuations of the scheme. The regulations for the creation and cancellation of units/shares are found in the FSA COLL sourcebook.

Creations and cancellations are instructed by the AFM to the trustee/depositary to ensure that sufficient units/shares are available so that the AFM can meet all outstanding unit/share transactions, with the desired number of units/shares remaining in the manager's box.

When the AFM holds insufficient units/shares in the box to meet all orders received at the valuation point, he must give instructions for the creation of at least the relevant number of units/shares to meet this shortfall. Under the FSA COLL sourcebook regulations it is left for the AFM and trustee/depositary to agree an appropriate period for this to be effected. FSA guidance suggests that where the AFM operates a box with the principal aim of making a profit, this period will be short (eg, two hours); otherwise a longer period (eg, up to the next valuation point but in all cases within 24 hours) may be acceptable, providing that controls to manage any conflict of interest and treat customers fairly are established.

The purpose of these regulations is to try to ensure that the AFM never has a short position or negative box, ie, he never sells more shares than he has available. The reason for this is to prevent an AFM from manipulating share orders and making hidden profits from selling more shares at one price in the expectation that he will be able to buy back sufficient shares before the next valuation point.

As the unit/share price of a forward pricing fund is unknown during this period, the AFM is unable to provide a full instruction to the trustee/depositary (recording the number of units/shares, price, and cash concerned). The notification will generally allow an estimate of the total net creation/cancellation to be performed, with the trustee/depositary ensuring that the finalised figure does not differ significantly.

Once the pricing process is completed the creation and cancellation prices will be known and the AFM can send a final notification to the trustee/depositary. The AFM is obliged to pay for units/shares created by the trustee/depositary by the close of business on the fourth business day following his instruction. Similarly, where a cancellation is instructed, the trustee/depositary must pay the proceeds to the AFM on the fourth business day, subject to the trustee/depositary receiving such evidence of transfer of legal title as they may require. Thus, strictly speaking, settlement does not become due and payable until four business days after the valuation point or the receipt of properly completed documentation, whichever is later. The documentation in this respect may be completed forms of renunciation or stock transfer forms signed by the unit/shareholder, or a certification and undertakings by the AFM to deliver such documentation if called to do so by the trustee/depositary.

Thus, an AFM may decide to arrange for the CIS to cancel units/shares if there are more sellers than buyers, taking into account all orders received before the relevant valuation point. The AFM is prevented from cancelling units/shares if to do so would leave him an insufficient number to fulfil all the orders he had received for the purchase of units/shares. On first consideration this seems simple common sense, but again the regulations are framed in such a way as to prevent the AFM from manipulating the buying and selling of units/shares and taking a short position in expectation of a fall in the market.

An exception to the four-day settlement requirement is where the unit/shareholder requires payment in a currency for which the scheme holds insufficient cash or has insufficient facility to borrow in that currency to meet the redemption. In such circumstances the settlement period is extended until the shortage of currency is rectified.

8.2 In Specie Deals

> **LEARNING OBJECTIVES**
> 6.3.5 Understand the AFMs' discretion in relation to: large redemptions; in specie transactions; dilution levy/dilution adjustment and Stamp Duty Reserve Tax

Due to the costs of investing large sums of cash within a collective investment scheme the regulations permit an investor to pay for his units/shares by providing assets rather than cash. Similarly, where a large redemption is placed (normally considered to be 5% of the scheme value), the AFM may require that the investor receives a proportionate share of all assets held by the scheme. Such deals are referred to as in specie, and the assets exchanged with the investor are also used to settle the resulting creation/cancellation.

The position of an investor settling his deal in specie is discussed in Chapter 7 (Registration and Settlement).

The prospectus may also have provision for large deals to be carried out at a higher sale price or a lower redemption price than those published, providing that they do not exceed the relevant maximum and minimum parameters. A typical level for determining whether a deal is large is £15,000 or more; the purpose is to ensure that any SDRT provision or dilution caused by the large deal is covered.

8.3 When the Trustee/Depositary can Refuse to Create or Cancel Units/Shares

If the trustee/depositary believes that it is not in the best interests of participants to create or cancel units/shares (or to do so in the number requested by the AFM) he can refuse to do so. The trustee/depositary has to give notice to the AFM to be relieved of the duty to create or cancel units/shares. It is difficult to envisage a trustee/depositary taking this very serious step unless the AFM seriously breached regulations, the terms of the scheme documentation, or FSA's Conduct of Business rules.

9. BOX MANAGEMENT ERRORS

LEARNING OBJECTIVES

6.2.9 Know what constitutes a pricing error, the consequences and the action to be taken by the AF and trustee/depositary

9.1 Requirements for the Correction of Box Management Errors

There are occasions when the AFM will make an error in calculating the box position. The FSA regulations permit that, providing that an effective control system is in place and with the agreement of the trustee/depositary, an isolated error in calculating the box may be corrected without paying compensation.

A common reason for box management errors is the tight deadlines on the AFM to notify the trustee/depositary of creations or cancellations; these deadlines are intended to protect investors from unscrupulous AFMs taking advantage of market movements. The guidance provided by the FSA:

- requires the AFM to be able to demonstrate that it has effective controls over its calculations of what units it owns and that it can comply with requirements to prevent a negative box;

- requires AFMs to record all negative box errors as soon as they are discovered and to report the fact to the trustee/depositary, together with details of corrective action to avoid repetition.

To take advantage of these rules, the AFM must demonstrate to the trustee/depositary that it has effective controls. Any error must be an isolated one and, except in exceptional circumstances, the adjustment to correct the original creation or cancellation instructions must be given to the trustee/depositary by the end of the next business day following the relevant valuation point. For example, if the valuation point is noon on Monday, any adjustment must be given to the trustee by the close of business on Tuesday.

As a result of an error in the box calculation an AFM may effect a late creation settlement. In such cases the AFM must reimburse the fund for any lost interest unless the trustee/depositary agrees the amount is not material.

10. INVESTING THROUGH INTERMEDIARIES

LEARNING OBJECTIVES

6.4.1 Know the methods by which investor transactions are executed

6.4.3 Understand how commissions and discounts affect investor transactions

6.4.4 Know the definition, role and function of intermediaries

6.4.6 Understand the difference between investing direct with the AFM or via an intermediary

Many investors choose to take professional advice in their financial affairs; others simply find it convenient to have an intermediary firm place instructions on their behalf. In either case a significant amount of investment activity comes to AFMs via UK-regulated intermediaries. Generally, the intermediary is granted the power to act in accordance with his client's instructions (ie, the investor's instructions), and the AFM will perform transactions based on the intermediary's instruction to him. It is essentially an agency arrangement, so intermediaries are commonly referred to as **agents**.

Normally an agent will simply place orders and instructions on behalf of a specific client, with the AFM recording that client's holding in the register. Such instructions are normally placed via fax, telephone or internet. However, there are two alternative approaches which have become more important to the activities of agents within the UK.

10.1 Commissions and Discounts

Typically an IFA will receive commission from fund managers as remuneration for providing advice to their clients and/or organising execution of the investment. They may also provide on going services such as regular valuations and financial advice/annual reviews.

The commission as a result may take two forms. Initial commission (typically 3%) for the investment of funds and trail or renewal commission (typically 0.5%) to cover on going services.

A small but growing number of IFAs are paid on a fee basis by the client rather than through commission paid by the AFM. In these circumstances, the IFAs will often request the AFM to reinvest any commission which might be due either by way of a discount to the issue price or the purchase of additional units for the client.

Direct investors, ie, those who purchase units direct from the AFM do not enjoy such discounts unless the AFM offers a promotional period. Such promotions often are for a limited period and a limited range of funds. Direct investors are attracted via direct marketing campaigns which can be more expensive for AFMs than selling through intermediaries.

Collective Investment Schemes Administration

10.2 Use of Fund Platforms by Investors and IFAs

The fund supermarket is an idea that started in the USA and, in its basic form, it is a one-stop shop for investors in CISs. The idea has also been developed successfully in South Africa.

In the UK, a fund supermarket typically offers schemes either wrapped within an ISA or as direct investments (though, for the purposes of this examination, we will focus on direct investments). The main difference is that the supermarket offers schemes from a range of different AFMs, acting as a consolidator/distributor for investments placed with various AFM firms.

The investor (via his IFA or direct with the fund supermarket) chooses the schemes in which they wish to invest. The supermarket handles all the administration: contacting and placing deals with each AFM; keeping a consolidated record of the investments; offering a single statement to the investor, and consolidating commission payments for the IFA.

Fund supermarkets are taking advantage of the development of new electronic means of investing through the internet, although the more flexible versions also handle paper-based applications.

The fund supermarket aggregates orders to buy and sell shares so that a smaller number of contracts will be placed with each AFM. Shares are registered with the fund managers in a single nominee company name while the supermarket maintains records of each underlying investor and deals with queries and other correspondence with investors and their advisers. In this respect the position is similar to that of an ISA: the units/shares are held by a firm who is responsible for recording the respective number of units/shares it holds for each of its clients.

Distributions of income, and other rights, are received by the fund supermarket from the fund managers and are split (**disaggregated**) into the appropriate size for each underlying investor. Certain rights, such as voting rights, may not be passed on to the investors and these will be governed by the terms and conditions between the investor and fund supermarket provider.

Before the supermarket was created each investor/IFA needed to establish their own communication channel with each AFM with whom they placed investments. The position can be shown by this diagram:

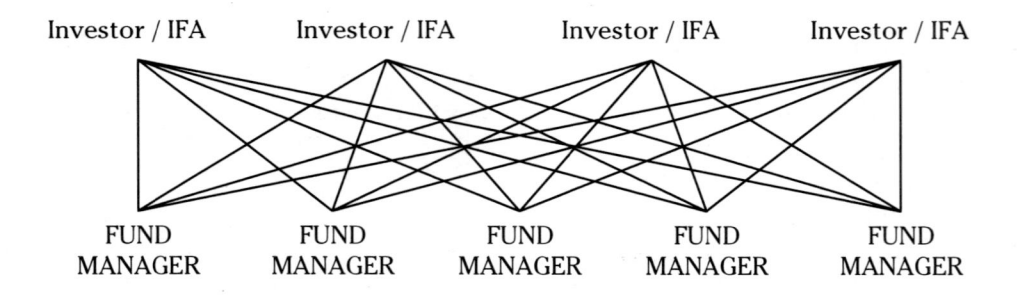

However, a fund supermarket sits between the investor/IFA on one hand and the AFM on the other, reducing the number of communication contacts required to achieve the investments.

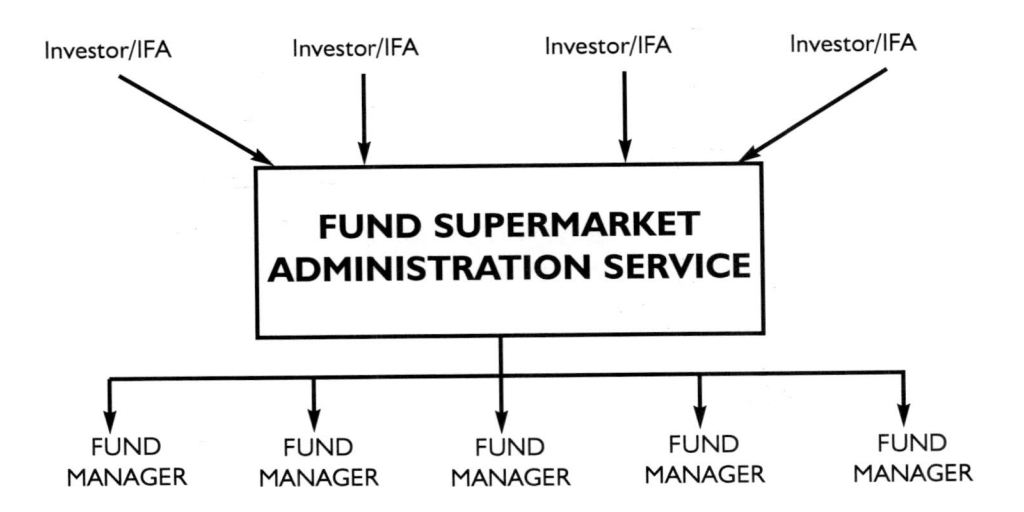

```
Investor/IFA    Investor/IFA    Investor/IFA    Investor/IFA
     \               |                |              /
      \              |                |             /
       v             v                v            v
       ┌─────────────────────────────────────────┐
       │        FUND SUPERMARKET                  │
       │        ADMINISTRATION SERVICE            │
       └─────────────────────────────────────────┘
         |         |          |         |         |
         v         v          v         v         v
       FUND      FUND       FUND      FUND      FUND
      MANAGER  MANAGER    MANAGER   MANAGER   MANAGER
```

What are the benefits to the investor?

- a broad range of funds are available;
- less paperwork – a single statement gives information on all holdings on request;
- a single ISA with the fund supermarket can hold funds from various AFMs;
- increased flexibility to switch schemes within an ISA; and
- no need to transfer the plan to a different plan manager.

What are the benefits to the IFA?

- simplified administration;
- efficient buying and selling of investments on behalf of clients;
- increased time to spend advising clients and achieving sales;
- reduced time spent building a portfolio from the schemes of various AFMs;
- simplified switching between schemes and different AFMs – using a fund supermarket reduces the time when the client is out of the market, and reduces the IFA's costs;
- in most cases the IFA can continue to receive the same level of remuneration as negotiated direct with the AFMs;
- renewal commission can be obtained on a consistent basis (eg, monthly on a regular date);
- a single commission statement is also helpful for reconciliation purposes.

What are the benefits to the AFM?

- administration costs can be reduced significantly;
- only one account is maintained on the register, in the name of the fund supermarket's nominee company;
- reduced maintenance tasks, the amount of correspondence and telephone queries;
- fewer contracts will have to be processed and much less paper handled;
- only one distribution payment is made;
- the fund supermarket can produce significant economies of scale. This means the fund manager can afford to share the initial and annual management charges with the fund supermarket;

- the supermarket can help to obtain new funds under management and retention of funds because an investor does not have to transfer the entire holding.

Beyond this, some fund supermarkets are beginning to develop other services for clients, such as execution-only stockbroking. More products are likely to be introduced, including stakeholder pensions and the offering of advice. The UK is also likely to be a springboard for fund supermarkets to launch into Europe. Firms offering a broader range of supplier products and ancillary services are sometimes referred to as platforms because they bring together the investor record keeping in a single place and often use a co-ordinated or single technology platform/system.

The regulators are watching the development of supermarkets closely to ensure investor protection is maintained. In particular, security surrounding the use of the internet to process transactions is an area to which the regulators will pay a good deal of attention.

Fund supermarkets are likely to prove a major development for the UK investment fund industry.

10.3 Electronic Message Exchange (EMX)

Since the mid 1990s the internet and e-commerce have gained considerable momentum. The rapid developments present opportunities to make it easier for consumers to deal with suppliers and for improving efficiency and reducing costs in businesses everywhere. These changes are particularly relevant to the fund management industry where there is a need to modernise and streamline the way in which unit trusts and other investment funds are traded.

It is against this background that in late 1999 the Association of Unit Trust and Investment Fund Managers (AUTIF) co-ordinated the design and development of the EMX Message System and created an electronic, paper-free environment for the dealing, settlement and valuation of investment funds. The aim was to automate the fund industry, thus eliminating the administrative inefficiencies and delays associated with it.

The EMX Message System is an electronic message exchange providing a means through which distributors and fund providers communicate purchases, sales and valuations for investment funds, including retail, institutional and hedge funds.

A new company (EMXCo) was formed to supervise the setting up and running of the EMX Message System. EMXCo is responsible for agreeing how the service operates and for setting and monitoring standards. However, EMXCo has evolved to operate for profit to enable it to be independent and generate sufficient levels of shareholder return, as well as profitability, to ensure investment in the development of the EMX Message System.

The EMX Message System is open to all CIS and investment fund companies to allow them to offer a fast, paperless, efficient and error-free service to IFAs, stockbrokers and other distributors.

The benefits of the EMX Message System to the industry include:

- a set of common standards across the whole industry;
- increased dealing capacity with no extra staff;
- lower costs for transactions and payment processing;
- high service standards for transactions, statements and valuations;
- a reduction of duplicated effort/rework through automation;
- greater accuracy, with less time spent sorting out errors;
- improved cash flow, with the ability to settle transactions electronically;
- access to both nominee and own account information held on the register to facilitate reconciliations.

Participants in the system are able to place buy or sell instructions through the EMX Message System. When issuing a buy or sell instruction, information about the IFA, the client, the trade transaction and settlement instructions are required and are provided in a single common format. All products available via the EMX Message System are required to be in this standardised format. It is a requirement that full registration information is provided by the IFA within the trading instruction sent via the EMX Message System.

Upon receipt of the trading instruction, the AFM either accepts or rejects the transaction request and informs the intermediary of this outcome electronically, within a turnaround time set by EMXCo as a standard. When the transaction has been accepted and priced by the AFM, contract details are returned, via the EMX Message System, to the intermediary within a set response time.

There is also a Cash Settlement Message which allows participants to agree settlement details.

The EMX Message System is now acknowledged as a standard for fund messaging and is estimated to be routing more than 40% of all UK fund trades.

The EMX Message System was launched in June 2000. Participants can either interface with the EMXCo computer hub via their own computer systems or use the web-based interface provided by EMXCo. The hub connection integrates directly with the end user's IT systems and enables data to be entered into their proprietary/in-house systems without any interference with normal routine. The hub then automatically receives the required data through its interface with their systems.

The data carried by the EMX Message System can be classified under the following headings:

- account openings;
- orders for purchase or sale of products (including settlement instructions);
- responses to orders including details of prices;
- requests for reconciliations and valuations of client holdings;
- responses to requests for reconciliations and valuations; and
- remittance advice.

In addition to providing these gateway communication services, EMXCo offers access for its end users to its database of historical transaction data and appropriate client information and fund referencing data. EMXCo acts, therefore, as both a message and transactional data exchange.

EMXCo handles domestic messages (ie, UK distributor to UK fund provider) as well as cross-border messages (where either the fund provider or distributor is non-UK). Cross-border messages account for approximately 15% of total message volume.

The system can handle requests for valuations at either an individual, account or agency level. The EMX Message System also has the facility to run regular reconciliations to aid those FSA-regulated intermediaries who have a requirement to reconcile their nominee account holdings on a regular basis. This reconciliation will take the form of a register enquiry against individual providers (such as AFMs).

11. PRODUCT AND COMMISSION DISCLOSURE FOR NON-LIFE PRODUCTS

LEARNING OBJECTIVES

6.1.1 Know the AFM's responsibilities to make available and/or supply the following: prospectus; simplified prospectus; key features/key facts; report and accounts (including short reports); Trust Deed/Instrument of Incorporation

6.4.2 Know the documentation required in relation to the execution of investor transactions

Product and commission disclosure requirements for what are referred to as non-life packaged products have been recently revised because of EU directives. The Distance Marketing Directive required the FSA to change its rules on the provision of pre-contractual information to investors who place deals at a distance (such as by post, telephone or electronic means).

The UCITS Management Directive introduced the concept of a **Simplified Prospectus** which is required to be made available for each fund or sub-fund. The FSA responding to industry requirements also allows the issue of a composite simplified prospectus covering a range of funds. This is broadly in line with Key Features Documents (KFDs) which are discussed below. The FSAs New Conduct of Business Sourcebook (COBS) contains detailed requirements in Chapter 13 for KFDs.

11.1 What is the Purpose of Disclosure?

Disclosure requirements enable investors to compare the different products across the industry. The information available to them includes key features such as:

- the investment objectives or aims;
- any special risks involved;
- any cost for advice given to the investor (when dealing with an IFA for example);
- details of the charges made to the scheme;
- the effect of those charges on what the investor may get back after having held the investment for various periods.

Further details can be seen in Appendix 3.

11.2 Those Responsible for making Disclosure

Disclosure is required depending on the circumstances either pre-sale (ie, before the investment is made) or post-sale. Responsibility for making the disclosure to the investor will depend on who is involved and the channel through which the investment is made. Where an IFA introduces business the IFA has primary responsibility for disclosure, while in other cases it will be the product provider/AFM. In practice product providers make available material on their products in order that IFAs can meet their obligations (for example, by preparing Key Feature Documents (KFD) or a simplified prospectus with key features which the IFA can hand to his clients).

The necessary material is also available electronically in many cases. The Exchange (an IFA industry network), the internet (ie, product providers' web-sites) and CD-ROMs are all being used to provide key features. Such methods should help to save a few trees and avoid the IFA having to keep large stocks of key feature documents which may have to be destroyed when they become out of date.

Since the implementation of the Distance Marketing of Consumer Financial Services Directive (known as the Distance Marketing Directive, or DMD) the product provider must ensure that an internet investor has received the necessary information, such as the Key Features Document (KFD), before entering into a binding contract. Where the investor's deal is placed following advice from an IFA, the regulations place this requirement on the IFA rather than the AFM (though some AFMs will opt to send this or similar material in a welcome pack to new investors regardless of the lack of a regulatory requirement).

The following sections will consider these disclosure requirements in more detail.

11.3 When an AFM must provide Key Features

Most AFMs conduct their business on an execution only basis and/or via IFAs. An AFM must incorporate key features in each direct offer advertisement (that is an advertisement that includes contact details to enable dealing, such as a telephone dealing number) whether it be a direct mail or newspaper advertisement.

If an investor has used an application form from a direct offer advertisement which itself incorporated Key Features, or where he has already been sent key features which incorporate up-to-date disclosure information, it is not necessary for the AFM to send key features again. Many AFMs include an application form in the key features document, using a code or reference number to enable dealing staff to determine whether an investor has seen the relevant key features (rather than an old and out-dated version).

Where a retail investor telephones to invest and the AFM cannot verify that they have received a copy of the relevant key features, the AFM is enabled to take the deal – but only if certain conditions are met. The AFM must undertake to provide limited information to the caller, sufficient information to ensure that the investor is purchasing the product that they intended to purchase, laid down in the FSA regulations, and the caller must agree to proceed on this basis. After the completion of any such deal, the key features document must be sent immediately to the investor. Alternatively, the investor might not agree to proceed on the basis of limited information, in which case the AFM will send full key features for them to review prior to investing.

For internet dealing services, the AFM should ensure that the investor has accessed the key features document before accepting any transaction from them. This is sometimes achieved by including a tick box on the site in which the investor will confirm that he has read the key features.

As the DMD ensures that investors received the necessary information to make their investment decision prior to placing a deal, it has reduced the cases in which cancellation rights apply to transactions. A direct investor acting at a distance has no regulatory cancellation rights – though some AFMs offer such rights on a voluntary basis. However, cancellation rights still apply to any investments made on the advice of an IFA – providing protection if the IFA has failed to provide the investor with the necessary information.

11.4 When an IFA must provide Key Features

When the investor deals with an AFM through an intermediary, it is the responsibility of that intermediary to deliver key features before dealing (ie, pre-sale) unless:

- the transaction is execution-only; or
- the transaction is a conversion of unit/share type, ie, accumulation to income or vice versa, and the investor has already seen key features.

To help IFAs, most AFMs provide sales literature incorporating key features. When an AFM provides financial advice he will have a similar responsibility as an IFA to deliver key features.

In the normal course of events an AFM will not send key features to an IFA investor unless the IFA requests post-sale disclosure. The AFM will, however, as part of the contract note or on a separate statement, disclose the commission payable to the IFA.

11.5 The Form Key Features must Take

Each AFM is under an obligation to prepare key features, for issue to investors in the UK, covering each authorised CIS and investment trust savings scheme it offers to investors. In addition, any of these products sold within an ISA constitutes a separate scheme.

Key features have a prescribed format, as set out in COB 6, and may be prepared either as a stand alone document for each scheme (such as when included in the AFM's report) or, alternatively, on a composite basis covering more than one scheme (eg, a product handbook). They are not client-specific. If a publication covers more than one scheme, the format may be varied if this would improve the investor's understanding of the information. The important thing to emphasise is the need for clarity, with particular emphasis on the aims and the risks.

The document, or part of the document constituting key features, must be designed and presented to a standard that is consistent with the remainder of the document. It is, however, permissible to deliver key features by fax if speed is important. In addition, it is permissible to transmit these electronically.

The key features must be amended whenever any significant change takes place and must, in any event, be reviewed at least once a year.

It should be clear that the content is time-sensitive, and that it is important to check the current position if an investor is intending to invest based on the figures given. This is particularly relevant to yields for corporate bond funds, as these may change significantly and KFDs can quickly become out of date.

11.6 Commission Disclosure (Hard Disclosure)

IFAs are responsible for making hard disclosure of their commission entitlement on a pre-sale basis. This means that they must tell their clients how much initial commission they will receive, in pounds and pence, from a fund manager. They must also indicate how much they would receive in those cases where renewal commission applies; they should use the initial investment value and a doubling of the investment's value to illustrate their potential remuneration from such commission. Fund managers will in most cases facilitate post-sale disclosure by including hard disclosure on contract notes, acknowledgements and, if necessary, on regular statements.

An investor is entitled to request a written statement of the commission paid in respect of a transaction. If this happens, the fund manager must send such a statement to the investor within five business days.

11.7 The Simplified Prospectus and Key Facts

The FSA implemented in 2005 rules for a new document. This document, known as the Simplified Prospectus, replaced the former key features document for UCITS funds. Unfortunately, the document was anything but simplified and contains so much detail that most retail investors are likely to be daunted by the amount of information provided.

Following research and consultation the FSA are proposing to seek improvements to the key features and Simplified Prospectus documents. This includes the use of the FSA's 'Key Facts' logo on product information to help consumers to identify important information more easily. It is hoped the changes proposed will make the Simplified Prospectus a more consumer-focused document, suitable for use in any EU jurisdiction. This will be of particular benefit to AFMs of UCITS schemes that seek to use the passport to sell units/shares in other EU member states.

The Committee of European Securities Regulators ('CESR') is considering potential changes to the Simplified Prospectus and the introduction of shorter and more focused documents aimed at providing investors with appropriate information; these documents are being referred to as Key Information Documents or 'KIDs'.

END OF CHAPTER QUESTIONS

Think of an answer for each question and refer to the appropriate section for confirmation.

Question		Answer Reference
1.	Explain what dual-pricing is.	Section 2
2.	How is a CIS valued?	Introduction & Sections 2 & 3
3.	Explain what single-pricing is.	Section 3.1
4.	Who determines the conditions under which a dilution levy will apply?	Section 3.2
5.	Explain what is meant by dilution adjustment pricing.	Section 3.2
6.	What is: a) forward-pricing? b) historic-pricing?	Sections 4.1 and 4.2
7.	In what circumstances would a scheme be required to move from historic to forward-pricing?	Section 4.2
8.	What is the FSA's objective in providing guidance on incorrect pricing?	Section 5
9.	a) What are the key elements of a valuation to be investigated? b) What triggers the investigation?	Section 5.1
10.	By how much does the price need to be incorrect for a manager to pay compensation to unit holders? a) plus or minus 1% b) plus or minus 0.5% c) plus or minus 0.05%?	Section 5.3
11.	Name three routes by which investors may buy and sell units/shares.	Section 6.3
12.	What is the typical initial offer period on the launch of a fund?	Section 7
13.	How do units in a trust come into existence?	Sections 7 and 8
14.	What must an AFM do if he cannot meet all orders received at valuation point?	Section 8.1

Collective Investment Schemes Administration

Question	Answer Reference
15. How is the creation price calculated?	Section 8.1
16. What procedure is involved in the cancellation of units/shares?	Section 8.1
17. How and when are creation and cancellation instructions settled?	Section 8.1
18. Describe the operation of a fund supermarket and identify the advantages for: a) the investor; b) an independent financial adviser; c) the AFM.	Section 10.2
19. What are the benefits to the CIS industry of using EMX?	Section 10.3
20. Who is responsible for the making of product and commission disclosure for non-life products?	Section 11
21. When must an AFM provide key features?	Section 11.3
22. How often must key features be reviewed?	Section 11.5
23. In what way do key features assist a potential investor in understanding how changes and expenses affect their investment?	Sections 11.3 and 11.5

REGISTRATION AND SETTLEMENT

1.	WHAT RULES COVER THE REGISTRATION OF UNIT TRUST/ OEIC SHAREHOLDINGS?	155
2.	THE REGISTER AND EVIDENCE OF TITLE	157
3.	ARE UNITS/SHARES TRANSFERABLE?	159
4.	THE CHANGE OF NAME OR ADDRESS OF A UNIT/SHAREHOLDER	162
5.	THE RIGHTS OF BEARER UNIT/SHAREHOLDERS	162
6.	CONVERSION BETWEEN INCOME AND ACCUMULATION UNITS/SHARES	163
7.	EXCHANGE OF UNITS/SHARES	164
8.	SUB-DIVISION AND CONSOLIDATION OF UNITS/SHARES	165
9.	SUB-REGISTERS FOR SAVINGS PLANS AND ISAS	166
10.	SETTLEMENT	167

This syllabus area will provide approximately 7 of the 50 examination questions

INTRODUCTION

To denote the entitlement to ownership of units in a unit trust, or ownership of shares in an OEIC, some form of registration is required. This is similar in many ways to the registration requirements for shares in companies registered under the Companies Acts that enable legal ownership of shares (but not third party rights) to be recognised by the company. This chapter will examine the requirements to establish and maintain a register, and also outline the procedure for the exchange of shares.

1. WHAT RULES COVER THE REGISTRATION OF UNIT TRUST/OEIC SHAREHOLDINGS?

LEARNING OBJECTIVES

7.1.1 Know the requirements for the establishment, maintenance and contents of a Register

The duty of companies to maintain registers of shareholders is contained within the Companies Acts 2006, but the duty concerning the register of holders in unit trusts is set out in the COLL sourcebook. In areas not covered by these rules, the legal principles that apply to companies generally apply to CISs. Schedule 3 of the OEIC Regulations 2001 requires an OEIC to keep and maintain a Register of Shareholders with title to shares (other than bearer shares) evidenced by such an entry.

1.1 Who is Responsible for the Register?

Title and registers is the subject of Section 6.4 of the COLL Sourcebook. It places responsibility on either the AFM or the trustee of an AUT (as nominated in the trust deed) to establish and maintain a register of unitholders as a document.

The ACD of an OEIC is seen as responsible for the register of shareholders under Schedule 3 of the OEIC Regulations 2001.

In practice, the registrar function, even where the trustee is nominated in the trust deed, is usually delegated to the AFM or to a third party registrar company and so the difference in responsibility is outlined within the service contract entered into by the different parties.

As part of its own oversight responsibility, the trustee/depositary will carry out periodic (usually half-yearly) inspections of the registers to ensure that the registers and their maintenance comply with the FSA's requirements and OEIC regulations. Where the function is delegated, the ACD (on behalf of the OEIC) will be responsible for ensuring that a third party administrator, appointed to carry out the registration and/or other functions, does so in a compliant manner (though the depositary will also review these in order to oversee the ACD's controls).

For both AUTs and OEICs there is the duty to maintain in legible form at all times a register of unit/shareholders. In practice, the register is kept on a computer system with facilities to produce a printed copy when required. The systems employed vary between the firms due to variables such as product type and the size and number of funds.

1.2 The Duties of the Registrar

The registrar has a duty to ensure that the register is maintained to show the correct number of units/shares held by each investor. This duty extends to registered units/shares and does not apply to any bearer shares issued by the scheme. The entries on the registers must contain the following:

- the name and address of each holder – up to four names may be registered per holding, as with property generally under English law and as specified under the OEIC Regulations 2001;
- the date each unit/shareholder's name was entered on the register;
- number of units/shares (including fractions of units or smaller denomination shares, where applicable) of each type held by each holder. This should also reflect any different denominations of unit/share issued, and must be updated regularly, normally daily;
- the number of units/shares of each type in issue and represented by bearer certificates and the numbers of those certificates;
- dates of change of unit/shareholdings;
- date(s) of cessation of the unit/shareholding.

Any units/shares held in the manager's box must also be recorded.

In practice, little use is made of the provisions permitting bearer units/shares to be issued, though bearer securities are popular in Europe. The register of shareholders of an OEIC scheme must be kept at head office unless it is held elsewhere (ie, either at another office of the AFM or at the office of a third party registrar engaged for the purpose), in which case it may be kept there. In the case of AUTs and OEICs the COLL rules specify that the register must be available to holders free of charge in the UK.

The Registrar (which may be the AFM, trustee/depositary, or some other regulated firm) must ensure that the information contained in the register is always complete and up to date. It is the AFM's specific responsibility to obtain the registration details and advise the registrar of any information he receives relating to the accuracy of, or any change to, an entry on the register. For example, the AFM must obtain the necessary details to enable the entry of newcomers on to the register. This usually means sending a registration details form, with the contract note, for completion and return to the registrar within a reasonable period.

Part of the registrar's duty is to ensure that the total number of units/shares recorded on the register reconciles with the number of units/shares in issue. These reconciliations should, as a matter of good practice, be carried out at least monthly. If the registrar function is delegated, the trustee/depositary is likely to expect the registrar to report satisfactory completion of these reconciliations.

1.3 The Position if an Error is Found in the Register?

The registrar has a duty to ensure that the register is maintained in a complete and accurate manner. Where an error is found the data must be corrected to ensure the register is again accurate. Such corrections can require units/shares to be created or cancelled, which requires an instruction from the AFM.

While the AFM will generally absorb such a correction into the creation/cancellation instructed at the next valuation point there is an option for the AFM to modify the previous creation/cancellation instruction, though this requires the approval of the trustee/depositary. The trustee/depositary must be satisfied that the purpose of modification is to rectify the consequence of an error, and that the AFM's control systems are unlikely to allow this to happen again.

The AFM should, therefore, ensure that it has established a proper internal checking/audit system for registering entries and changes.

1.4 Third Party Administrators as Registrars

The industry includes a number of third party administrators who provide registration and/or other services (eg, pricing) to AFMs. It is important to note that while the fund manager and trustee may delegate administration functions to third parties, they cannot delegate responsibility. Consequently, the trustee or AFM will remain responsible for ensuring that a third party administrator it has contracted to carry out the registration of holdings does so in a compliant manner.

2. THE REGISTER AND EVIDENCE OF TITLE

LEARNING OBJECTIVES
- 7.1.2 Understand who can be registered as a holder of units/shares
- 7.1.3 Know the status of the Register as proof of ownership
- 7.1.4 Know the process for rectification of registration errors
- 7.1.5 Understand the registration treatment of third party interests
- 7.1.6 Understand the entitlement to inspection

With units in an AUT or shares in an OEIC it is the entry in the register that provides conclusive evidence of the persons entitled to the units entered in it. Certificates, where issued to the holders, are regarded as prima facie evidence but not conclusive.

2.1 Who can be Registered as a Holder of Units/Shares?

No notice of any trust (express, implied or constructive) is binding on the AFM and trustee and, although such notice may be entered on unit trust registers, such practice is prohibited in the case of a company register and most unit trust registrars adopt the same approach. This means that the registrar can only look to the registered holder(s) for authority to deal with the units/shares. The registrar is unable to act on documents such as Deeds of Appointment where the holders may be trustees of a private trust and the trustees are changing. In this situation the registrar requires a completed common stock transfer form, signed by the existing registered holders.

Registrars need to be certain as to who has authority to deal with a holding of units/shares and, consequently, the style of the registration of units is limited to legally recognised persons, including individuals and corporate bodies. Examples are John Robert Smith, John Smith Limited and John Smith Plc. There are some unusual corporate bodies which are also acceptable, such as NHS Trusts which, despite the name, are in fact corporate bodies, normally incorporated by a specific Act of Parliament, and certain government bodies such as The Public Trustee and The Treasury Solicitor who both generally execute documents under Seal.

Partnerships, unincorporated bodies such as clubs and official capacities such as 'The Trustees of ...' or 'The Treasurer and Secretary of...' would all normally not be accepted for registration. Limited partnerships (ie, those registered with the Register of Companies) are acceptable.

Holdings of units/shares may be designated for the convenience of the holders, but normally such designations are limited to an eight digit alpha/numeric format (eg, 'ABC Account' or '123 Account'). Names are not permitted because of the possibility of an implied trust and the problems arising from confusion with the registered holder(s).

The register, however, does not necessarily reflect all entitlement to units/shares as those held for the manager or for anyone holding bearer certificates may not be recorded except at specific times, eg, for distribution.

The regulations do not expressly enable an aggrieved investor to seek rectification of the register, whereas such provision does exist under the Companies Act 2006, Section 125 for shareholders of limited companies. However, the FSA regulations require firms to act with due skill, care and diligence in relation to investors' accounts so this distinction does not have significant effect on investors.

Another important difference is that a scheme's register must be available for inspection by the holders (or any party bearing their legal authority, such as an agent) but, unlike other share registers, it is not available to the public generally (ie, to non-investors). The register does not have to be available abroad even if a scheme is promoted overseas (eg, other EU member states), though holders overseas may, like UK resident holders, request a copy of the entry relating to them specifically.

Under the OEIC Regulations 2001, Part III Section 50, an OEIC may, on giving notice in a national newspaper circulating in all countries in which shares are sold, close the register for up to 30 days in each year. In a similar manner under the COLL regulations AUTs may also close the register for up to 30 days in each year.

2.2 Do Certificates have to be Issued?

There is no longer any requirement to issue certificates, although the manager and trustee/depositary can agree to do so. However, if certificates continue to be issued, the procedures are to be agreed between the manager and trustee/depositary and must comply with the form permitted by the Trust Deed/Instrument of Incorporation.

2.3 Holder Reconciliation Requests

Those holders who are authorised persons under FSMA 2000 (such as stockbrokers) may have to meet requirements under the regulation of their business to reconcile their holdings of CISs as shown in their records with those of the registrar. They typically carry out a reconciliation monthly.

Such holders may reconcile their position using the last statement or tax voucher issued to them by the registrar with records of contract notes issued subsequently and their own record of dealing.

The FSA has confirmed that it is not necessary for registrars to issue monthly statements. In some cases, however, if the authorised firm has difficulty in concluding the required reconciliation, the firm may need to request from the registrar a current statement of his account(s) as shown on the register. The registrar is required to supply to a holder or his authorised representative, at his request and free of charge, a copy in print of the entries on the register relating to that holder. For non-MiFID firms they are required to carry out reconciliations no less than every six months and in the case of MiFID firms, as often as necessary. The latter is an example of more principles based regulation and the firm will need to be able to justify the frequency with which it carries out reconciliations.

3. ARE UNITS/SHARES TRANSFERABLE?

LEARNING OBJECTIVES

7.2.1 Understand the processes and information requirements relating to transfers by the holder, in favour of the AFM, and by the operation of law

7.2.2 Know the difference between transfers: by the holder; to the AFM; to third parties; by operation of law

As a registered security, title to units/shares is transferable either by the holders or by what is called **operation of law**, such as following the death of the holder.

3.1 Transfers by the Holder

There are two types of transfer. Units/shares may be transferred by completing a Stock Transfer Form, in accordance with the Stock Transfer Act 1963, which is sent to the registrar and accompanied by the unit/share certificate (where issued). Provided the transfer is completed correctly, and any appropriate stamp duty paid, the register will be updated and a new certificate (where issued) is issued in the name of the transferee(s).

The second common type of transfer is where the unit/shareholder sells his units/shares back to the AFM. In this case he completes a form of renunciation; this form may appear on the reverse of the certificate or may be sent to him with his contract note. This form is approved by the AFM/trustee to the fund. An example of this type of form appears in Appendix 6. Some AFMs do not require a specific form of renunciation to be completed, but will require a written confirmation from the investor.

Both types of form must be signed by the person transferring the holding (or any person legally acting on their behalf, such as under a Power of Attorney). This person is known as the transferor. In the case of a joint holding, registered in the names of two or more holders, all holders must sign. If the holder is a corporate body, the transfer may be executed either under seal or signed by authorised officials of the company. It is normal for two signatures to be required in such cases, either two directors or one director and the company secretary.

If a transfer is signed on behalf of the holder, the registrar may require proof of authority of the transfer. For example, if a power of attorney has not previously been registered, the original, or an appropriately certified copy, needs to be forwarded with the transfer. Similarly, if a transfer is signed on behalf of a company by **authorised signatories** who are not officials, the registrar will normally require to see a copy of the **board resolution** (certified by the company secretary) appointing them as authorised signatories. The copy resolution should be accompanied by specimen signatures.

All instruments of transfer must be retained in original or non-documentary form (eg, microfilm or computer image) for a period of six years from the date of registration. Providing that the system used for taking/recording images is documented, and certain other requirements are met (including the recording of destruction of the originals), the images are acceptable by the courts and the regulatory authorities under best evidence rules.

3.1.1 Stock Transfer Form for AUTs and OEICs

> **LEARNING OBJECTIVES**
>
> 7.1.7 Know the requirements for the collection of beneficial holder details

Historically the common Stock Transfer Form used to effect a transfer of company shares or stock has also been used for UK unit trusts and OEICs. From 15 December 2007, however, new money laundering regulations imposed a requirement on fund managers to verify the identity of all registered holders of their funds and any underlying beneficial owners or controllers. For this reason it was necessary to introduce a bespoke form for UK funds. An example and guidance notes on this form are shown in Appendix 6A. Other provisions relating to the transfer of legal title between registered unit holders continue to be as set out in the Stock Transfer Act 1963.

3.2 Transfers in Favour of the Manager

Upon the registration of a transfer in favour of the AFM, any certificate issued is cancelled and the name of the holder removed from the register. The name of the AFM does not have to be entered on the register, nor is a certificate issued. The units/shares will be added to the manager's box for future reselling, unless the AFM decides to cancel the units/shares.

3.3 Transfers by Operation of Law

In the case of a joint holding of units/shares, on the death of one of the holders the surviving holder(s) is (are) recognised as having title to the units/shares. The registrar needs to see a death certificate, together with unit/share certificates (if in issue). The death is then registered and the certificates enfaced or new certificates in the survivors' names issued.

If either a sole holder or the last surviving holder dies, authority to deal with the holding rests with the executors or administrators of the deceased holder. The registrar must see the **Grant of Probate** or **Letters of Administration** in such cases to establish title. The executors or administrators can complete a simple **Letter of Request** form to have the holding placed in their names as unit holders, without reference to the deceased. Alternatively, they may transfer the units/shares to beneficiaries by means of the usual stock transfer form or, of course, sell the units/shares back to the AFM.

This type of transfer may also take place in the event of bankruptcy or, in the case of corporate holders, liquidation. The registrar needs to see satisfactory evidence of the appointment of the person claiming title to the units/shares, such as a receiver, before registering any transfer.

Until the units/shares have been transferred into the name(s) of the new holder(s), the legal representatives, such as executors, are not entitled to receive notices or attend or vote at any meeting of unit/shareholders.

If a unit/shareholder wishes to transfer only part of his holding to several parties, he will notify the company in writing and complete the appropriate transfer. A certification is made by the AFM if the instrument of transfer bears the words **certificate lodged** and is signed by someone within the organisation with relevant authority. The certificate (where issued) must also be lodged. The certificate is retained by the organisation and then transfers are subsequently lodged for registration in due course.

3.4 Transfers using the CREST System

LEARNING OBJECTIVES

7.2.3 Understand the objectives of introducing electronic transfer of title for Collective Investment Schemes

Regulations are in place for units/shares to be admitted to dealing on the Stock Exchange, using the paperless CREST system for settlement and registration. Unit trusts have not generally sought a listing in the past and few OEICs have adopted this facility – both because of the additional cost involved and due to the fact that the ACD will act as market maker for the shares, providing the liquidity otherwise given by a listing. However, where the scheme is admitted to CREST, it is possible for the transfer of units/shares to be performed within CREST.

For more details of the CREST system, see Section 10.2 of this chapter.

The Treasury consulted in May 2007 on proposals to amend the effect of the Law of Property Act 1925 and Open-Ended Investment Companies Regulations 2001 to permit AFMs/registrars of authorised funds to act on transfer instructions and renunciations of title to units that are received by electronic means. In January 2008, the FSA consulted on corresponding revisions to its COLL sourcebook (as well as other changes designed to facilitate full delivery versus payment (DvP) settlement in CREST.

The revised legislation and FSA rules will permit the acceptance of electronic communications for transfer and renunciation of title where the person responsible for the register (the AFM or trustee of a unit trust, depending on its constitution, or in the case of an OEIC the company itself) takes 'reasonable steps' to ensure the authenticity of the instruction. Those steps will not be prescribed in the legislation or regulations, but will instead be left to FSA-confirmed industry guidance prepared by the IMA. It is anticipated that the relevant regulations will be laid before Parliament in the Autumn of 2008 and the FSA will issue an update to the COLL rules shortly thereafter.

The objective, ultimately, is to:

- permit more automated and efficient processing for investors; while
- providing adequate protection to the AFM and to investors against fraud.

It means that investors will have a choice as to whether they use physical documents, such as a stock transfer form or form of renunciation, or an electronic means to authorise the transfer of title. A properly appointed agent will also have the ability to use an electronic means to transfer title.

4. THE CHANGE OF NAME OR ADDRESS OF A UNIT/SHAREHOLDER

LEARNING OBJECTIVES

7.1.1 Know the requirements for the establishment, maintenance and contents of a Register

The register is updated with the changes notified in writing by the unit/shareholder, providing that the registrar is satisfied with the validity of the instruction. Evidence of the change of name may be requested and any certificate will be either endorsed or cancelled and a new one issued.

Some registrars accept written instructions from IFAs to change their client's registered address. In such circumstances it is normal as a security measure for the registrar to send an acknowledgement direct to the unit/shareholder at the former and present addresses. This is designed to give the holder the opportunity to reverse the instruction if incorrect.

5. THE RIGHTS OF BEARER UNIT/SHAREHOLDERS

OEICs and unit trusts are permitted to issue bearer units/shares. However, while bearer units/shares are found in continental Europe, it is unlikely they would be issued in the UK because there is no history or culture of bearer instruments with this type of investment. In addition, as the security passes from hand to hand without the need for formal registration, they could be used to circumvent the money laundering regulations.

The unit/shareholder's name is not placed in the register of unit/shareholders because physical possession rather than registration is evidence of ownership. The terms of issue would be shown on the reverse of the certificate itself and the CIS would communicate details about distributions and meetings of unit/shareholders by notice in national newspapers.

6. CONVERSION BETWEEN INCOME AND ACCUMULATION UNITS/SHARES

LEARNING OBJECTIVES

7.3.1 Know the Capital Gains Tax implications of conversions on a value-for-value basis

6.3.2 Know the difference between an exchange and a conversion

6.3.4 Be able to calculate the number of units following conversion

The COLL sourcebook regulations relating to CIS allow the conversion between income and accumulation units/shares providing that there are appropriate provisions in the prospectus.

For example, in the case of a unit trust only a simple letter or request form is required. The conversion is determined by the managers and trustees based on the conversion factor, reflecting how much income has been earned by the fund and reinvested in respect of each accumulation unit. This factor increases at each ex-distribution date where an income distribution is payable. Thus, if a holder of accumulation units converts to income, he receives more income units than he had accumulation and the reverse applies if converting from income to accumulation units. The registrar will normally issue a confirmation letter giving the details of the conversion and the number of new units.

Generally, such conversions are on a value-for-value basis so that the value of units held before it is the same as the value of units held immediately after. Because there has been no change in the assets held in terms of the undivided shares in the property of the scheme, conversions are not regarded by HM Revenue & Customs as a disposal and acquisition for capital gains tax (CGT), and no stamp duty is payable. Units are categorised either Group 1 or Group 2 for equalisation purposes – see Chapter 8, Section 3 for explanations of equalisation. Where a conversion takes place the conversion will carry over the same group holding, eg, if the units/shares were Group 1 before the conversion they would be Group 1 after the conversion.

Example – Unit Trust

A unit holder wished to convert his 400 accumulation units of the XYZ dividend fund to income units. The conversion factor at the last ex-distribution date for the fund was 2.1250.

To establish the number of income units to be allocated multiply the number of accumulation units by the conversion factor:–

400 x 2.1250 = 850 income units

To complete a conversion from income units to accumulation units, the income units are simply divided by the conversion factor to produce the number of accumulation units to be allocated.

7. EXCHANGE OF UNITS/SHARES

LEARNING OBJECTIVES

7.3.1 Know the Capital Gains Tax implications of conversions on a value-for-value basis

6.3.2 Know the difference between an exchange and a conversion

6.3.3 Be able to apply the IMA's suggested formula to ensure proper and fair exchange of shares/units

The COLL sourcebook permits units/shares of CISs to be issued in a number of different classes, but the CISs Instrument of Incorporation or Trust Deed, will need to specify what they are. Under current rules such exchanges are not subject to CGT. A unit/shareholder wishing to exchange his holding from one class to another will be able to obtain from the AFM a form in which to give his instructions.

On receipt of a completed form the AFM will arrange for the scheme to cancel the original units/shares (or hold them in the manager's box). To ensure that a proper and fair exchange is used between units/shares of different classes, the following formula is suggested in the model instrument to be applied to work out the number of units/shares to be issued:

$$N = O \times \frac{(CP \times ER)}{SP}$$

Where:

N is the number of new units/shares to be issued or sold (rounded down to nearest whole number of smaller denomination shares);

O is the number of original units/shares specified (or deemed to be specified) in the exchange – notice the units/shares that the holder has requested to exchange;

CP is the price at which a single original unit/share may be cancelled or redeemed as at the valuation point applicable to the cancellation or redemption as the case may be;

ER is 1 if the original units/shares and the new units/shares are designated in the same currency and, in any other case, is the exchange rate determined by the AFM in its absolute discretion (subject to FSA regulations). This represents the effective rate of exchange between two relevant currencies, as at the date the exchange notice is received by the scheme, having adjusted such rate to reflect costs incurred by the scheme making any transfer of assets as may be required; and

SP is the price at which a single new unit/share may be issued or sold as at the valuation point applicable to the cancellation or redemption as the case may be. The AFM may adjust the number of new units/shares to be issued or sold to reflect the imposition of an exchange charge or other levies to cover the costs involved. After the above has been completed, the appropriate alteration to the register will be made.

Details of the arrangements for exchange or conversion of units/shares will be included in the prospectus/trust deed.

8. SUB-DIVISION AND CONSOLIDATION OF UNITS/SHARES

LEARNING OBJECTIVES

7.3.2 Know the AFM's procedures for sub dividing or consolidating units/shares

The AFM can, unless the scheme documentation forbids it, with the approval of the trustee/depositary, decide either to:

- sub-divide each unit/share into two or more units/shares (rather like a scrip issue for an equity); or
- consolidate two or more units/shares into a single unit.

Appropriate notice has to be given to the holders of such an event and either new certificates are issued (in respect of the additional units/shares issued) or the old ones are submitted for endorsement. The latter course is impractical in terms of the administrative resources that would be required, and is of little practical value.

Sub-divisions may be undertaken when the price of units/shares has increased and, for example, appears relatively expensive per unit/share, eg, a price of £60. Using this price, a regular contribution of £50 per month would buy less than one unit. Sub-division has no impact on the underlying value of the fund but, from a marketing point of view, it may be more reassuring to investors to receive a larger number of units. Similarly, consolidation may be used where the price of a unit/share is considered to be light or low. The investor's perception of a unit/share price of 1p may be that the fund is a poor investment. However, consolidation could allow the penny-share image to be removed. Thus a 50:1 or 100:1 consolidation would produce a unit/share price of 50p or £1.00 Once again, the underlying value of the investment has not changed.

If the AFM carries out a sub-division or consolidation then, in addition to appropriate notice being given to holders, disclosure would also be made in the fund Report and Accounts.

9. SUB-REGISTERS FOR SAVINGS PLANS AND ISAs

LEARNING OBJECTIVES

7.4.1　Know the requirements governing the sub-registers for savings plans and ISAs

7.4.2　Know the rights of holders on sub-registers

7.4.3　Know who has responsibility for sub-registers

Where an investor places money in a savings plan or ISA, the plan manager places an aggregated deal with the underlying collective investment scheme. The scheme's register does not, therefore, record units/shares as being held by the various individual investors – it shows a single position for the plan manager (usually using a corporate nominee as the registered holder). The plan manager must keep a sub-register that enables it to evidence how many units/shares held by the nominee company are actually held on behalf of each plan investor.

In December 1997 the FSA amended the regulations to permit the cost of maintaining savings plan sub-registers operated by the AFM or registrar to be paid out of the property of the scheme, though 60 days' notice must be given to holders of any proposal to establish such a sub-register (due to the increase in chargeable costs that may arise). The regulations for costs regarding plan registers are now contained in Section 6.4 of the COLL Sourcebook.

As a result of these changes, if the cost of maintaining the sub-registers is charged to the CIS fund, the plan holders must be afforded the same rights as those holders who hold units/shares directly on the register (ie, not through a plan). This includes receipt of the fund manager's reports and the right to attend and vote at unit/shareholder meetings.

The changes also mean that such sub-registers become the responsibility of the trustee or AFM and will be included in their monitoring programme if responsibility is delegated to the fund managers or third party administrators, as registrars. Consequently, the trustee/depositary will require that periodic reconciliations are performed, matching the units/shares on the sub-registers against the holding(s) on the main register, and will generally review such items during regular monitoring visits.

10. SETTLEMENT

LEARNING OBJECTIVES

7.5.1 Know the regulatory requirements for settlement

7.5.2 Understand the different methods of settling investor transactions

10.1 Traditional Methods of Settlement

Once a person has entered into a contract to buy or sell units/shares the next stage is for the contract to be settled. This requires the amount of money due under the contract to be paid and the legal title to the units/shares to be transferred (see Section 3).

The AFM must describe the arrangements for the sale and redemption of units/shares in the prospectus. This will normally include the terms on which settlement of transactions takes place.

The regulations require redemptions to be settled on the fourth business day following the trade (known as T+4) or once the AFM has received all the duly executed instruments and authorisations to effect the transfer of title to the units/shares back to the AFM, for example, a form of renunciation signed by the unit/shareholders.

For redemptions, the AFM must ensure that it remits the proceeds to the investor (who is no longer shown as owner of the units/shares that have been sold), as failure to make payment would be a breach. For sale transactions (units/shares purchased by the investor), the period of settlement is not specified by the regulations but may be cash with order or, typically, where telephone dealing takes place, on the same T+4 basis. The AFM will normally chase the investor for payment if the funds are not received by T+4. If payment remains outstanding, the AFM is entitled to cancel the transaction as the investor has failed to satisfy his requirement under the contract. The units/shares are removed from the registered holding of the investor and returned to the manager's box on the date the transaction was cancelled.

The traditional methods of payment are for the cash to be paid by the buyer of the units/shares using a cheque or a telegraphic transfer. In the case of regular purchases through a savings plan, the investor may pay via direct debit claimed by the fund managers, using the Bankers Automated Clearing Service (BACS).

As a result of more business being done over the telephone, and the introduction of websites facilitating the purchasing of units/shares via the internet, a number of AFM groups accept payment by means of debit cards. The investor simply provides his debit card number at the time of dealing.

Faster Payments Service

The Association for Payment Clearing Services (APACS) is the UK payments association and in May 2008 introduced a new system for institutions to deliver payment services to customers. It is known as the Faster Payments Service and is the first new payment service to be introduced in the UK for more than 20 years by the major banks and some building societies. The system will enable payments to be made and cleared within a couple of hours, providing that it is a bank working day and that the payment is up to £10,000 rather better than the traditional three days. The service will operate 24 hours a day, seven days a week. For AFMs it means they can receive and pay out cleared funds from/to investors much quicker.

10.2 The Settlement of CISs through CREST

Another method of making payment, particularly for institutions, is to use the CREST system. In 1999, CRESTCo introduced new functionality to facilitate the settlement of CISs via CREST, using a process referred to as a 'residual settlement transaction'. This provides secure delivery of physical stock and the use of CREST's assured payment mechanism.

These proposals were welcomed by CREST members and fund managers.

CREST settlement of CIS investments follows a different process to settlement of securities through CREST's central settlement system. CIS investment deals are described within CREST as 'residual'. With residual securities, the unit/share certificate and stock transfer form are passed from the seller to buyer (normally via their brokers), either inter-office or through the CREST Courier and Sorting Services (CCSS).

Residual settlement of CIS investment differs from residual settlement of corporate securities because in the normal course one of the parties to a residual CIS transaction will always be the AFM. This means that settlement risk can be reduced, since the AFM can ensure that transfer of title is co-ordinated with payment.

There are a number of benefits to be gained by CREST members and AFMs. These include:

- the system complements the electronic trading system EMX introduced in 2000;
- the CIS industry is able to use infrastructure that is already proven and very firmly established;
- CREST settlement ensures the secure and efficient delivery of stock and payment of cash, reducing the elements of settlement risk in existing procedures (ie, it speeds up delivery of cleared funds for purchases and redemptions);
- CREST members are already significant investors in collective schemes and have indicated that their transaction volumes will increase as a consequence of the efficiencies described above. As an example, the cost of settlement of unit trust transactions is expected to reduce;
- residual settlement is the first phase. Further developments are taking place to enable the integration of automated cash settlement of AUTs and OEICs in CREST's settlement system. A facility to allow the extraction of an electronic deal instruction from the EMX system and permit the automated settlement in CREST has been introduced. The anticipated development of electronic transfer of title should also help to provide even further efficiencies.

10.3 In Specie Issues of Units/Shares

Occasionally, an investor may wish to settle his investment by transferring investments (rather than cash) to the scheme. This is termed an in specie transfer. Under the regulations, the trustee/depositary may issue units/shares in exchange for assets other than money, subject to the following:

- any SDRT liability on issue of the units/shares is satisfied; and
- existing and potential unit/shareholders are unlikely to be materially prejudiced by the assets acquired, ie, the assets are consistent with the objectives of the scheme.

On the issue of the units/shares the AFM must ensure transfer of the assets to the trustee/depositary. This may entail, initially, the transfer of beneficial ownership by the date of the issue of the units/shares, followed by the legal transfer of ownership. The first requires an agreement while the legal transfer will in the normal course be completed by means of a stock transfer (in paper form or via CREST) into the name of the trustee's nominee company. This nominee company holds the assets on behalf of the scheme.

10.4 In Specie Cancellation (Redemption) of Units/Shares

Similarly, subject to a provision in the Trust Deed or Instrument of Incorporation, where a unit/shareholder decides to redeem units/shares representing typically 5% or more of the scheme value, he may receive assets rather than cash in settlement of his redemption. Such a transfer may be either:

- at the choice of the AFM, subject to giving the holder notice; or
- requested by the unit/shareholder (providing the scheme documentation permits such requests).

The AFM might decide to make such a transfer where, for example, the fund is invested in securities, the market for which is limited, and the sale of a large part of the portfolio could materially affect the performance of the fund. The AFM must give the holder notice, no later than two days after receipt of the holder's request, to redeem his units/shares. When he receives the notice the holder may elect for the AFM to sell the assets being allocated to him and to send him the net proceeds of the sale in cash instead. This still has the desired effect of protecting the fund from the dilutionary charges arising from broking fees when selling the underlying securities. The risk of a poor price being achieved on the sale of the assets is borne by the redeeming investor.

The assets transferred to the redeeming investor will be either a:

- proportionate share of the assets held by the fund; or
- reasonable selection from the assets held by the fund chosen by the trustee, in consultation with the AFM.

Where the first option is used, the in specie cancellation will not be liable to SDRT.

Once the AFM has confirmed that the title to the units/shares has been surrendered, the trustee/depositary will cancel the appropriate number of units/shares and complete the in specie transfer to the former unit/shareholder.

END OF CHAPTER QUESTIONS

Think of an answer for each question and refer to the appropriate section for confirmation.

Question	Answer Reference
1. In which set of rules would you find the requirements for: a) registration of details of unit holders in a unit trust? b) keeping and maintenance of the Register of Shareholders for a CIS?	Section 1
2. What details of a unit/shareholder must be entered on the register?	Section 1.2
3. a) What is the maximum number of persons who may be registered as joint holders? b) Why is a maximum set?	Section 1.2
4. What is the position if an error is found in the register?	Section 1.3
5. What does entry on the register indicate with regard to proof of ownership?	Section 2
6. "Third party rights cannot be entered on an OEIC register of shareholders." What does this statement mean?	Section 2.1
7. Which of the following are acceptable registration styles? a) John Smith b) Smith & Co c) J. Smith Limited d) The Trustees of J. Smith deceased	Section 2.1
8. Do unit/shareholders have to be issued with certificates when entered on the register?	Section 2.2
9. From whom are holder reconciliation requests likely to be received in respect of the register of unit/shareholders?	Section 2.3
10. Name the two ways a unit/shareholder may transfer his holding.	Section 3.1
11. What is required from the executors of a holder before such executors may have units/shares transferred into their own names?	Section 3.3
12. Why are bearer shares unlikely to be issued by a CIS in the UK?	Section 5
13. Explain the formula for an exchange of unit/share classes.	Section 7
14. What must an AFM/ACD do prior to sub-dividing units?	Section 8

Collective Investment Schemes Administration

Question	Answer Reference
15. If the cost of maintaining savings plan sub-registers is to be paid out of scheme property what period of notification must be given by the AFM to holders on such registers prior to implementation?	Section 9
16. What are the benefits to the CIS industry of using CREST?	Section 10.2

DISTRIBUTION OF INCOME   8

1.	THE INCOME A CIS RECEIVES	175
2.	HOW ARE INCOME DISTRIBUTIONS PAID TO UNIT/SHAREHOLDERS?	182
3.	EQUALISATION	186

This syllabus area will provide approximately 5 of the 50 examination questions

INTRODUCTION

LEARNING OBJECTIVES

6.4.5 Understand the treatment of distributions of income and other rights

This chapter covers the calculation and distribution of income received by authorised schemes, the different types of distribution that may be made, how and when distributions are made, income equalisation, and the provision of distribution statements and tax vouchers.

1. THE INCOME A CIS RECEIVES

LEARNING OBJECTIVES

8.1.1 Know the sources of income

The income of a scheme usually comprises of dividends and/or interest from investments held on behalf of the fund/company or sub-fund. Further income may include underwriting fees or interest on cash deposits. This total income, less expenses, is paid out regularly to the unit/shareholders or reinvested on their behalf; reinvestment is reflected either in the price of accumulation units/shares (if these are issued) or by the purchase of additional income units/shares. Furthermore, if stock is taken in lieu of income, a transfer from capital to income may be made. This income is not generally subject to corporation tax. For further details on how various types of income are treated for taxation purposes see Chapter 10, Taxation of Collective Investment Schemes.

1.1 Income Payment

LEARNING OBJECTIVES

8.1.2 Understand the different treatment of income for income and accumulation shares/units

8.1.3 Be able to apply the timetable for distribution of income

While income may be paid annually, quarterly or even monthly, the most common payment interval is half-yearly. Under the FSA regulations (COLL 6.8 for retail funds) each fund must have an annual and half-yearly accounting period and may have additional interim accounting periods each year. The AFM calculates the amount of income received during an accounting period, while the trustee/depositary, in conjunction with the registrar, distributes the income to the unit/shareholders or allocates it to accumulation unit/shares in proportion to their respective interest in the property of the fund. Thus income unit/shareholders will normally receive a payment of the income and accumulation unit/shareholders will have their income reinvested in the fund automatically; such income will be reflected in the price of units/shares.

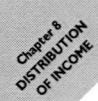

The trustee/depositary arranges for an amount, calculated by the AFM, to be transferred from the fund's income account to a distribution account. The registrar prepares and dispatches the payments and tax vouchers; payment is normally in the form of a warrant (similar to a company dividend warrant) drawn on the distribution account, though electronic payments by direct credit via the Bankers Automated Clearing Services (BACS) are also an option.

The income is calculated on the last day of each annual accounting period; this is referred to as the **accounting reference date**. The amount of income per unit/share is established and the unit/share price is quoted ex-distribution until the payment date. A CIS may also have one or more interim income allocation dates and interim accounting periods.

The payment or allocation of income must be within four months after the relevant accounting reference date or end of the relevant interim accounting period. If a fund makes one or more interim distributions, ie, within an annual accounting period, the prospectus must specify the payment date(s) (referred to as the **interim allocation date(s)**). The income will be calculated on the last day of the interim accounting period and generally treated in the same way as if it were an annual income allocation.

One difference with interim distributions is that not all income at the interim accounting dates needs to be distributed, but all income at the annual accounting reference date must be distributed.

The sub-funds of an umbrella-type CIS will all have the same annual accounting reference date and, in the normal course, the same annual income allocation date. If several unit trusts are converted to form sub-funds of a single CIS, often there will be a change to the payment date(s) but the frequency of payments may remain the same.

1.2 Action Taken if the Income Available is Small

Some funds may earn very little income. For example, growth funds that have capital growth as an objective may ignore income considerations. Once the expenses of the fund have been deducted there may be no, or very little, income to distribute; in the latter case the trustee/depositary may, on the AFM's request, either carry the income forward to the next accounting period or credit the income to the capital account.

The COLL rules enable the AFM to agree with the trustee/depositary the figure (known as de minimis) below which the distribution will not be paid. This would, for example, enable a fund offering an institutional class of unit/share to set a far higher figure before the income would be distributed. It is not yet known to what extent AFMs will choose to apply this flexibility.

The reason for this regulatory provision is to allow the AFM to avoid making income payments that are simply not economic given the cost incurred (such as the preparation and mailing of distribution warrants and tax vouchers).

The policy relating to de minimis will be laid down in the scheme prospectus.

1.3 How to Calculate the Available Income

LEARNING OBJECTIVES

8.1.4 Be able to calculate the available income

The calculation is completed as in the following example:

Example

Income Available for Distribution: 1 May 20XX to 30 April 20XX

	£000
Income brought forward (note 3)	200
Gross income (received or receivable during the period) – including franked investment income (eg, dividends received, and stock dividends) and unfranked income (such as interest on debt securities, bank deposit interest, and underwriting commission)	3,800
Equalisation: add the amount received on shares issued during the period (note 1)	100
	4,100
Deduct:	
Charges and expenses of the company paid or payable out of income (note 2) This may include the AFM's periodic charge, registrar's and depositary's fees, safe custody fees, etc	(1,000)
Equalisation: deduct the amount paid on shares cancelled during the period (note 1)	(10)
Taxation (tax credits, corporation tax, withholding tax)	(600)
Income carried forward: any income it is agreed should be carried forward to a subsequent accounting period (note 3)	(300)
Amount available for distribution (note 4)	2,190

---

1. Equalisation is the proportion of the price received or paid for units/shares that are related to income. It is included only if provision for equalisation is included in the Trust Deed/Instrument of Incorporation.

2. The charges and expenses must also be covered in the prospectus if they are to be taken out of the income or capital property of the trust/company. Certain charges and expenses may be charged to the fund's capital account. If the objectives of the fund are to provide income or a balance between income and growth the AFM's periodic charge can be treated as a charge against capital. Taking this charge from income to capital increases the amount available for distribution, but could have an adverse impact on capital. The prospectus must state which charges are taken from income or capital and, if capital, it must include appropriate risk warnings on the effect of this on capital.

3. This may include income that is unlikely to be received until 12 months after the income allocation date.

4. This includes any amount to be transferred to the capital account in respect of accumulation units/shares.

1.4 Types of Distribution

> **LEARNING OBJECTIVES**
>
> 8.1.6 Know the difference between dividend, interest and property income distributions and the relevant criteria

Dividend and Interest Distributions

CISs can pay the following types of distributions:

- a **dividend distribution** resulting from investment by the fund in shares generally; or
- an **interest distribution**: funds invested 60% or more throughout the accounting period in gilts, UK or overseas bonds and/or money market deposit, ie, interest bearing assets may pay an interest distribution instead of a dividend distribution.

The tax credit on dividend distributions is currently 10%. The income tax deducted from interest distributions is 20%. Further details on taxation of distributions can be found in Chapter 10, Section 3.

Property Income Distributions (PIDs)

A Property AIF is a form of Authorised Investment Fund whose investment portfolio comprises predominantly real property or shares in UK Real Estate Investment Trusts (UK REITs) and certain other similar entities.

The intention of the Property AIF regime is to tax investors in a similar way to those that invest directly in the underlying assets and to remove tax barriers in the way of collective investment in rental property. So, the regime exempts property income and gains from corporation tax, similarly to the way the UK REITs regime exempts property income gains from corporation tax for companies that are not collectives. This then allows an open-ended fund to be exempt from corporation tax on property income and gains in a similar way to that achieved for UK REITs.

As Property AIFs may have a mix of income (they are only required to derive 60% of their net income from the property income business), it is necessary to ring-fence property income as it passes through the fund to ensure that it remains identifiable. This income is tax-exempt in the hands of the fund. It is treated for UK tax purposes, once the expenses of managing the property have been paid, as property income. The investor then pays tax on the amount received as if it were the profits of UK property business (irrespective of whether the property income is derived from the UK or overseas).

The other main form of taxable income likely to be received by a Property AIF is interest on funds invested while awaiting opportunities within the property investment business or to provide a convenient buffer for expected redemptions. This category of income also includes foreign dividends, except in cases where these count as property income. This income will be within the charge to corporation tax, but the Property AIF will be able to get a deduction for tax purposes when it is distributed. It is treated for tax purposes in the same way as other savings income (such as interest from a bank account).

Finally, the Property AIF may also receive dividends from UK companies which are not chargeable to corporation tax. Again, this income is treated for UK tax purposes as if it is UK dividends.

In general, investors will pay approximately the same level of tax as if they had invested directly in the underlying assets. In order to achieve this, the fund must make distributions to investors in a way that enables the investor to identify the amount attributable to the different types of income, and to pay tax on them accordingly.

This means that the fund's total income will fall into one of the following three pools:
- property income (including property income from UK REITS and foreign equivalents);
- other taxable income (primarily interest and non-UK dividends); and
- UK dividend income;

so that investors will receive three different types of income.

1.5 Calculation of Effective Yield

LEARNING OBJECTIVES

8.1.5 Know the requirements for calculation of the effective yield

During 2007 there have been changes to the way in which bond income is accounted for and distributed from authorised funds (unit trusts and OEICs). For most funds, there will be little difference in what investors receive over time; however, information must be provided to investors on the accounting change and any consequent change in the fund's distribution basis, and managers will likely make that information available more widely (eg, on their websites). The IMA has provided a guidance note on the changes and this section follows that guidance.

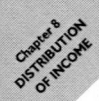

Specifically, funds will need to decide whether to distribute on the new accounting basis ('effective yield' – explained below) or to continue to distribute coupon income, as previously. In practice, only those funds whose investment objective is to provide high income are expected to continue to distribute on a coupon basis.

For authorised funds, bond income used to be accounted for, and distributed, on the basis of coupon income receivable for most bonds. However, following changes in accounting rules, for periods beginning on or after 1 January 2007 funds are required to account for income from bonds on an effective yield basis.

Effective yield takes account of all expected cash flows from a bond over its lifetime. This differs from the coupon basis because expected cash flows include, in addition to coupons, any differences which exist between the purchase cost of a bond and its final redemption amount (as shown below).

In light of this change in accounting rules, and in order to allow high income funds to continue to distribute coupon income notwithstanding the change in accounting, the FSA has clarified its rules. From 23 March 2007, the rules allow managers of authorised funds to choose to distribute income from bonds on the newly introduced effective yield basis (as shown in the fund's accounts) or on a coupon basis. Coupon distributions are permitted only if these are at least equal to the amount of the income calculated on an effective yield basis.

Funds will have to declare whether they are distributing on a coupon or effective yield basis. Many funds will choose to keep distributions in line with accounting income, and will distribute effective yield income. Some funds, particularly those whose objective is to produce regular income for investors (such as high income bond funds), will continue to distribute coupons. Funds that distribute on a coupon basis may have a higher risk of capital erosion or constrained future growth. However, it is important to note that other factors, such as changes in interest rates, may impact the value of bonds held by a fund, no matter what its distribution policy.

1.5.1 Effective Yield and Coupon Bases Compared

In order to illustrate the differences between effective yield and coupon-based accounting and distribution two simple examples are set out below.

In reality, a fund will hold a portfolio of investments and may not hold them to maturity. The distribution which an investor receives will depend on the net income from the entire portfolio. For the purpose of these examples, however, the impact of a fund's distribution policy is illustrated on the assumption that the fund holds only one bond and that it holds it to maturity. In example A, a fund purchases a bond at a premium to its redemption value. In example B, a bond is purchased at a discount.

> **Example A**
>
> A fund buys a bond for £102. The bond is due to redeem in one year's time for £100 and pays an annual coupon of £8. The total return on holding this bond over the year is, therefore, £6 (that is, £8 of coupon minus the £2 loss when the bond is redeemed). The coupon and effective yield basis of calculating income (ignoring any investor tax) can be compared as follows:
>
> 1. The fund's income on a coupon basis for the coming year is £8; if income is accounted for on a coupon basis, the fund in this example will make a capital loss of £2 as the amount receivable on redemption is less than the purchase cost.
>
> 2. The fund's income on an effective yield basis is £6; if income is accounted for on an effective yield basis, the fund in this example will make no capital loss or gain as the £2 premium paid on purchase of the bond is brought into the income calculation.

In this example, an investor in the fund would in the past typically have received a distribution of £8, being the amount of the coupon income. In future, the fund may choose either to continue to distribute on a coupon basis or to distribute on an effective yield basis:

1. Distribution on a **coupon** basis will enable investors to continue to receive distributions as they have done in the past, with potential impact on the capital value of their investment, in this case, £8.

2. Where a fund distributes on an **effective yield** basis, investors may notice a change in the amount of distributions compared with previous years. In this case, the investor would receive a distribution of £6 compared with the £8 received in the past, but the capital value of their investment is not reduced as it is taken into account when the income is calculated.

> **Example B**
>
> A fund buys a bond for £98. The bond is due to redeem in one year's time for £100 and pays an annual coupon of £4. The total return on holding this bond over the year is, therefore, £6 (that is, £4 of coupon plus the £2 gain when the bond is redeemed).

In this example, the fund's income on a coupon basis for the coming year is £4 and the accounting income on an effective yield basis is £6. The fund is not permitted to distribute on a coupon basis as this is less than the amount of the fund's income calculated on an effective yield basis.

An investor in this fund would, in the past, typically have received a distribution of £4, being the amount of the coupon income.

When the fund changes to distribute on an effective yield basis, investors may notice a change in the amount of distributions compared with previous years. In this case the investor would receive a distribution of £6 compared with the £4 received in the past as the redemption amount is taken into account when the income is calculated.

Examples A and B above are summarised in the following table:

	Example A £	Example B £
Bond details		
Cost of bond	102	98
Redemption amount	100	100
Annual coupon	8	4
Total return	6	6
Coupon basis		
Coupon income	8	4
Capital gain/(loss)	(2)	2
Effective yield basis		
Effective yield income	6	6
Capital gain/(loss)	0	0

It is important to note that these examples relate to only one bond with only one year to maturity; funds will have a mix of bonds in their portfolio, all of which, taken together, will determine an investor's net income. In practice, therefore, for a number of funds effective yield income will be little different from coupon income for the portfolio as a whole. It is only those funds whose portfolios predominantly contain either high coupon bonds or low coupon bonds where the difference may be material. Typically, high income bond funds will be heavily invested in bonds bought at a premium and/or with high coupons. For these funds, coupon income will generally be above effective yield, so are more likely to choose to distribute on a coupon basis.

2. HOW ARE INCOME DISTRIBUTIONS PAID TO UNIT/SHAREHOLDERS?

LEARNING OBJECTIVES

8.1.7 Know the customary payment processes and their associated requirements for the following: tax vouchers; BACS; distribution warrants

Distributions may be paid by crossed cheque or warrant. In respect of units/shares represented by a bearer certificate, the warrant is paid to the person entitled to that distribution, and is sent to the address disclosed by that person to the trustee/registrar.

If the units/shares are held in registered form, the warrant is drawn in favour of the sole or first-named holder and sent to that holder's registered address by post, either on or just before the distribution payment date. Examples of distribution warrants/tax vouchers are shown in Appendices 8-11. Any income due to the AFM (ie, in respect of units/shares held in the manager's box) is paid to the AFM, along with the associated tax credit.

2.1 Alternative Payment Methods

If the units/shares in issue include income units/shares on or before each annual income date the AFM is required to give the trustee/depositary timely instructions to enable him to distribute the income. The actual method of payment, however, is left to the AFM and trustee/depositary to determine, or may be provided for in the Instrument of Incorporation.

Unit/shareholders can authorise for income distributions to be paid in some other way. This authority may be in favour of:

- a third party (ie, someone other than the unit/shareholder, such as a beneficiary); or
- a bank, building society or firm (eg, solicitors).

Authority needs to be given in writing and signed by the holder (or, in the case of joint holders, by all of them). Although written instructions are accepted, most registrars provide a form, referred to as a **distribution payment request** or **distribution mandate form** (see Appendix 11), in which the instructions may be given.

Distributions paid via Bankers Automated Clearing Services (BACS)

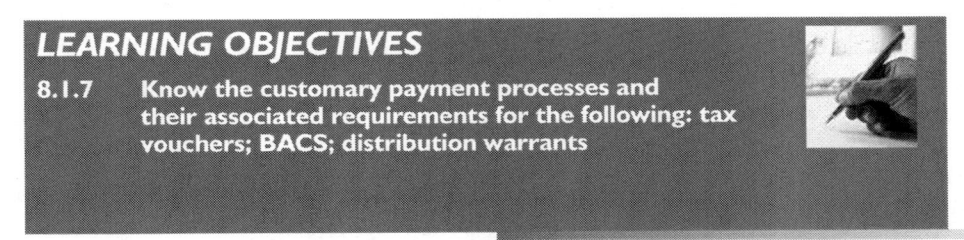

> **LEARNING OBJECTIVES**
>
> 8.1.7   Know the customary payment processes and their associated requirements for the following: tax vouchers; BACS; distribution warrants

If instructions are given in favour of a bank (and certain building societies) it is now common for payment to be made via BACS. Instead of printing warrants and sending them by post, details of each distribution payment are downloaded to BACS via a telecommunications link (BACSTEL) a few days before the actual payment date.

The data is processed and the unit/shareholder's bank account automatically credited on the payment date with the amount due. On the same day the scheme's distribution account is debited. The advantages of the BACS system are:

For the holder:

- no risk of a warrant being delayed or lost in the post;
- income is credited as cleared money on the due date, ie, there is no three-day cheque-clearing delay;
- there is no need to visit the bank or building society to pay in the warrant;
- the tax voucher can still be sent direct by post to inform the unit/shareholder of the amount credited to the bank account.

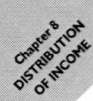

For the registrar/CIS:

- paper handling is reduced;
- reconciliation problems are reduced;
- costs are reduced significantly.

Most registrars encourage holders to have payments made direct to their bank account because of the benefits to both parties. The administration involved in preparing distribution warrants, handling the aftermath of each distribution, reconciling the paid warrants with the distribution account, dealing with those returned undelivered by the post office and the issue of duplicates if the originals have been lost or destroyed, can be enormous. However, there are data management and maintenance costs attached to operating direct credits.

Minimal Risks in Payment by Direct Credit

The risks associated with payment by direct credit are minimal. The registrar is responsible for the payment to the bank, but he has no control over the account to be credited once the payment passes to the bank. For example, an account may be closed and a new one opened through merger or transfer to another branch, resulting in the distribution being credited to a different account. This is dealt with by the provision of indemnities given by the banks and some building societies to registrars (for further details of these indemnities reference should be made to the UK Registrars Group of the Institute of Chartered Secretaries and Administrators). It is necessary for a completed distribution mandate to be lodged via the bank branch with the bank's sort code, account details and branch stamp inserted in the boxes provided (see the notes at the foot of the form in Appendix 11). However, since there are few problems associated with this method of payment, some registrars record instructions given in the mandate form, even if it is lodged direct by the unit/shareholder and has not been stamped by the branch bank.

2.2   The Presentation of Distribution Warrants

LEARNING OBJECTIVES

8.1.7   Know the customary payment processes and their associated requirements for the following: tax vouchers; BACS; distribution warrants

8.1.8   Know the treatment of unclaimed distributions

Distribution warrants are normally valid for six months from the payment date. Those not presented for payment by this deadline must be returned to the registrar for re-dating. Often the amount outstanding on the distribution account after six months is transferred (following reconciliation against the paid warrants) to an unclaimed distribution account where it should earn interest for the benefit of all unit/shareholders in the fund.

Any distribution payment remaining unclaimed six years after the payment date is transferred to, and becomes part of, the capital property and neither the unit/shareholder nor payee, if different (or their executors), can reclaim the income.

2.3 Distribution Information for Unit/Shareholders

LEARNING OBJECTIVES

8.2.1 Know the contents of tax vouchers in relation to distributions, including requirements for corporate investors

8.2.4 Know how equalisation is shown on tax vouchers

8.2.5 Understand the alternative methods of delivering tax voucher information: single tax vouchers; composite tax vouchers; electronic tax vouchers

When a distribution of income is made, or income reinvested, the registrar sends a statement and tax voucher to the unit/shareholder (or the first-named in a joint holding) on or just before the payment date. Although the regulations refer to the statement and tax voucher (or tax certificate) separately, in practice the two are combined in one document. Some AFMs send consolidated, or composite, tax vouchers representing multiple payments; a good example where an AFM may issue composite vouchers is a monthly payment high interest corporate bond fund.

The document shows the following:

- the amount of income to which the holder is entitled (whether paid out or reinvested);
- how much of the amount to which the holder is entitled represents income equalisation, if applicable (see below for details on equalisation); and
- a tax credit or, in the case of an interest distribution, the amount of income tax deducted.

Examples of the different types of distribution statement and tax voucher are shown in Appendices 7 to 10. Information about a fund's income and distribution account can also be found in the manager's report. Further details are given in Chapter 9. Students should review the contents of the vouchers shown in the appendices.

2.4 Electronic Dispatch of Distribution Information

LEARNING OBJECTIVES

8.2.5 Understand the alternative methods of delivering tax voucher information: single tax vouchers; composite tax vouchers; electronic tax vouchers

The Income and Corporation Taxes (Electronic Certificates of Deduction of Tax and Tax Credit) Regulations 2003 allow information about distributions to be made by payers to investors, including CIS shareholders and unit trust holders, electronically rather than by post. Before this can be done the following must be carried out:

- the payer (eg, CIS) must have indicated to the shareholder/unit trust holder that he intends to use electronic communications;
- the proposed recipient has consented to information being delivered by the sender in this way, and that consent has not been withdrawn; and
- the electronic statement format allows it to be stored and permits a copy to be printed, but does not allow alteration of the contents.

While this facility became available to AFMs in January 2004, various investors might not have access to a computer. It is unlikely at this time that many firms will change their processes and procedures.

3. EQUALISATION

LEARNING OBJECTIVES
8.2.2 Know the definition of equalisation and its treatment in respect to investor's tax liability

8.2.3 Understand the equalisation rate calculation

A CIS typically receives income spread throughout the accounting period. The unit/share price reflects this income as it is accrued until the next accounting date. The first valuation after the accounting date is known as the **ex-distribution date** (or **XD date**) as investors buying units/shares on or after that date will not receive the distribution payment relevant to the accounting period just ended. As the accrued income is stripped out of the price on XD date, the unit/share price tends to fall, and the fund's income cycle begins again.

Therefore, when most investors first purchase units/shares, the price normally includes an element of income. Obviously, those units/shares purchased at the beginning of the period will have less income included in the price than those purchased towards the end of the period. Equalisation is the element of income included into the price of units/shares purchased by investors during the accounting period, and is paid out to these investors as a return of capital at the end of the accounting period.

It is deemed by HM Revenue & Customs to be a return of capital, not income, and as such is not liable to income tax and is deducted by investors from the purchase cost of those units for CGT purposes. The amount of income equalisation may be the actual amount of income included in the price of units/shares purchased or as is the case more commonly, it is an average amount, calculated as follows:

$$\frac{\text{The aggregate of the amounts of income included in the creation issue price of the unit/shares issued or re-issued in the accounting period}}{\text{The total number of unit/shares purchased by investors during the period}}$$

The resultant average rate is applied to each of the units/shares purchased in question – hence the term **equalisation**. The average rate is referred to as the **equalisation rate**. Units/shares purchased during the distribution period are referred to as Group 2 units/shares, whereas units held at the beginning of the period are referred to as Group 1 units/shares. Any distribution statement/voucher shows the breakdown between Group 1 and 2 units held and, usually, in the case of Group 2 units/shares, the amount of equalisation applicable to those units/shares.

It is possible, however, in the case of a fund of funds, that Group 1 units may be allocated an equalisation rate. This is because the underlying investments include the purchase of new investments, and either the unit trust fund or the fund of funds is required to pass on the equalisation to all its holders.

Equalisation periods are not always accounting periods. The Trust Deed/Instrument of Incorporation will specify if grouping is allowed for periods within an accounting period and, if so, what those periods should be. For example, fortnightly equalisation periods could be used but, because of the accounting complications, these are rare.

In the case of a unit trust, in order to apply equalisation, the manager's policy and a provision for grouping must be included in the Trust Deed. It is optional for managers to apply equalisation. If they do not wish to do so, reference in the Trust Deed will be omitted.

A simplified example:

An investor has 100,000 units/shares @ 50p each invested in a fund holding fixed interest securities earning 12%pa. No capital appreciation is assumed. A new investor purchases 10,000 shares on the last day of month 2, and a second new investor purchases 10,000 shares on the last day of month 4. Equalisation would be calculated as follows:

End of Month	Group 1 Shares	Group 2 Shares	Income Group 1	Income Group 2	Price (p)	Equalisation	Capital (£)
0	100,000				0.500		50,000
1	100,000		500		0.505		
Purchase		10,000			0.510	100	5,000
2	100,000	10,000	500		0.510		
3	100,000	10,000	500	50	0.515		
Purchase		10,000			0.520	200	5,000
4	100,000	20,000	500	50	0.520		
5	100,000	20,000	500	100	0.525		
6	100,000	20,000	500	100	0.530		
			3,000	300	0.530	300	60,000
Distribution			-3,000	-300	-0.030	-300	0
			0	0	0.500	0	60,000

The distribution is payable to 120,000 units/shares at a rate of 3p per unit/share. This equals £3,600 as shown:

Group 1 income	3,000
Group 2 income	300
Equalisation	300
	3,600

For Group 1 units/shares the whole distribution of 3p is income.

For Group 2 units/shares:

- In theory:
  - 1st investor: 2p is income and 1p is equalisation.
  - 2nd investor: 1p is income and 2p is equalisation.
- In practice:
  - Due to averaging, for both investors half the distribution is income and half is equalisation.

For learning objective 8.2.5 students should also refer to Appendices 8 to 11.

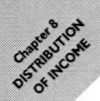

END OF CHAPTER QUESTIONS

Think of an answer for each question and refer to the appropriate section for confirmation.

Question		Answer Reference
1.	Name four types of income a CIS may receive.	Section 1
2.	Who is responsible for calculating the amount of income received by a CIS during an accounting period?	Section 1.1
3.	When must income be distributed by?	Section 1.1
4.	What are the different types of distribution that may be paid by a CIS?	Section 1.4
5.	How is income distributed by a CIS?	Section 2
6.	What is the name of the system used to distribute payments to unit/shareholders by direct credit via the banking system?	Section 2.1
7.	What alternative payment arrangements can be made other than crossed cheque or warrant, in respect of CIS distributions?	Section 2.1
8.	What advantages are there to a unit/shareholder in having his distribution paid direct to a bank or building society?	Section 2.1
9.	a) For how long is a distribution warrant valid if not presented for payment? b) What is the position of the warrant at the end of this period of time?	Section 2.2
10.	What will be shown on the statement and tax voucher (or the certificate) sent to the unit/shareholder?	Section 2.3
11.	Explain: a) what is equalisation? b) how is it calculated?	Section 3

INVESTOR COMMUNICATIONS

9

1.	THE COLL SOURCEBOOK	193
2.	THE SORP – FORMAT AND CONTENTS OF THE FINANCIAL STATEMENTS	198
3.	THE TRUSTEE'S/DEPOSITARY'S REPORT	202
4.	THE AUDITOR'S REPORT	203
5.	WHAT SHOULD INVESTORS LOOK FOR IN THE REPORT AND ACCOUNTS?	204
6.	FSA COMPARATIVE TABLES	206
7.	SCHEME CHANGES – UNITHOLDER MEETINGS, NOTIFICATION AND CIRCULARS	209

This syllabus area will provide approximately 3 of the 50 examination questions

INTRODUCTION

This chapter looks at the regulatory requirements for the AFM to provide annual and interim reports to investors. The regulations for investor relations concerning COLL retail schemes can be found in COLL Chapter 4 (with COLL 4.5 dealing specifically with Reports and Accounts).

This chapter will also consider the application of the Statement of Recommended Practice (or SORP). This document, maintained by the IMA, details the presentation of accounting data in the report and accounts. Apart from the legal requirement, the report enables both existing and potential investors, and their financial advisers, to obtain a regular update on the financial position of the scheme. This chapter will also note some items that investors should look for in the report and accounts.

The AFM must publish the annual report and accounts within four months after the end of each annual accounting period. The interim or half-yearly report and accounts must be published within two months after the interim accounting date. Copies of the report and accounts, where they are required to be issued, must be sent free of charge to each unit/shareholder, and must also be available free of charge upon request to any member of the public. A copy must also be provided to the FSA.

1. THE COLL SOURCEBOOK

LEARNING OBJECTIVES

9.1.1 Know the FSA requirements in relation to the reports and accounts

9.1.2 Understand the purpose and benefits of short reports

9.1.3 Know the difference in content between short reports and long form report and accounts

1.1 Introduction

The AFM of a COLL retail scheme is required to prepare reports and accounts in the manner prescribed by the SORP. This detailed document, termed the **Long Report**, must be available to any unit/shareholder who requests a copy.

Each investor of a COLL retail scheme must be sent a copy of the **Short Report**, intended to be a briefer and more user-friendly document. The short report is not subject to any SORP standard as it contains far less accounting data.

The AFM must, for each annual and interim accounting period, prepare both a short report and long report for a scheme. For an umbrella scheme, the AFM must prepare a short report for each sub-fund, but this is not required for the umbrella as a whole.

Where the period from a scheme's launch to its first annual accounting reference date is less than 12 months, that scheme need not prepare an interim report.

1.2 The Long Report

> **LEARNING OBJECTIVES**
>
> 9.1.5 Know the main differences between interim and final reports and accounts

The **Annual Long Report** must contain the following items:

- the audited full financial accounts, for the annual accounting period, prepared in accordance with the SORP;
- the AFM's report;
- a comparative table;
- the trustee's/depositary's report, detailing that the scheme has been operated in line with the regulations; and
- the auditor's report, giving the auditor's opinion of the financial accounts.

For an umbrella scheme the long report must include the separate accounts of each sub-fund, together with an aggregated set of accounts.

The **Interim Long Report** contains less data. It need not contain a comparative table or a trustee's/depositary's report and, as the interim accounts are not subject to audit, no auditor's report will be included.

1.3 The Authorised Fund Manager's Report

The AFM's report must specify the following:

- confirmation of the names and addresses of the main parties (the AFM, trustee/depositary, registrar, investment adviser, auditor, and any standing independent valuer for a scheme investing in immovable property);
- for an OEIC the names of any directors other than the ACD;
- a statement of the scheme's authorised status;
- the investment objectives of the scheme and its policy for meeting those objectives;
- a review of the investment activities during the reporting period;
- details of any fundamental or significant changes to the scheme's operations made since the last report; and
- any other information necessary to enable investors to make an informed judgement on the activities of the scheme during the period, and the results as at the end of the period.

Other requirements apply to certain types of fund. A CIS must name any directors appointed in addition to the AFM, and state that investors are not liable for the debts of the scheme. For a UCITS scheme that invests in other schemes the report must include a statement detailing the maximum proportion of management fees charged to the scheme itself and to the schemes in which it invests. For an umbrella scheme the report must provide the above information in respect of each sub-fund and also clarify that, as the sub-funds are not legal entities, any shortfall in one sub-fund might be met from the assets of other sub-funds.

1.4 The Comparative Table

This table must set out the following for each of the last five calendar years (or the full period of the scheme's existence, where less than five years):

- the highest and lowest price for each unit/share class in issue during each year;
- the net income distributed or allocated to each class of unit/share in each year.

The following data should be provided for the last three annual accounting periods (or each annual period where the scheme is less than three years old):

- the total net asset value at the year end;
- the Net Asset Value (NAV) per unit/share for each class; and
- the number of units/shares of each class in existence/issue.

The table should also record any event during the period shown that has a material impact upon the size of the fund (such as a merger) or any change to the scheme's investment objectives.

The examples on the following pages illustrate the comparative tables.

Comparative Table: Highest and Lowest Prices

Example Fund Statistics

		Prices			
	Calendar year	Income shares		Accumulation shares	
		Highest	Lowest	Highest	Lowest
Sterling		P	P	P	P
Class 'A'	2002*	77.24	52.36	171.90	116.88
	2003	76.98	51.83	173.74	116.06
	2004	98.47	76.79	224.52	173.96
	2005+	109.01	97.87	249.66	223.66
Class 'X'	2002**	58.60	52.38	130.80	116.91
	2003	76.90	51.95	172.91	115.95
	2004	98.35	76.90	222.40	173.13
	2005+	108.93	97.95	246.82	221.53

* From 11 March 2002 (the date the first share was available) to 31 December 2002.
+ To 1 July 2005.
** From 1 October 2002 (the launch date of the share class) to 31 December 2002.

Comparative Table: Net Income Distributed/Reinvested

Example Fund Statistics

Distribution Dates	
The ex-distribution dates for the coming year will fall on the dates listed and the payment dates will fall on or before the dates listed:	
xd	**payment**
Interim 03.01.06	28.02.06
Final 03.07.06	31.08.06

		Income			
	Calendar year	Interim	Distributed Final	Total	Re-invested
Sterling (net)		P	P	P	P
Class 'A'	2002	n/a	0.1970	0.1970	0.8625
	2003	0.1900	0.5100	0.7000	1.1421
	2004	0.2920	0.5530	0.8450	1.9118
	2005+	0.2330	0.3860	0.6190	1.4134
Class 'X'	2002	n/a	n/a	n/a	nil
	2003	nil	0.4840	0.4840	1.0803
	2004	0.1010	0.3750	0.4760	1.0714
	2005+	0.0220	0.1940	0.2160	0.4885

\+   Up to final: ex-distribution date 1 July 2005; payment date 31 August 2005.

Comparative Table: Net Asset Value per Share

Example Fund Statistics

		Net Asset Value per Share			
	Period ended	Value per share		Number of shares	
		Inc	Acc	Inc	Acc
Sterling		P	P		
Class 'A'	Jun 2003	65.56	147.96	138,611,540	13,105,372
	Jun 2004	85.96	195.98	128,387,600	12,276,323
	Jun 2005	108.63	249.14	136,931,551	12,642,772
Class 'X'	Jun 2003	65.66	147.64	36,604	1,365
	Jun 2004	86.08	194.64	12,499	25,469
	Jun 2005	108.71	246.31	79,568	176,842

Total net asset value of Sub-fund		
Period ended	£	€8/*
Jun 2003	110,291,000	159,392,000
Jun 2004	134,480,000	200,373,000
Jun 2005	180,768,000	268,900,000

* Based on the midday exchange rate on the last business date of each financial year.

Significant Fund Information

Immediately after 3 September 2004 the M&G Innovator Fund merged with the M&G Smaller Companies Fund.

1.5 The Short Report

The short report must contain various pieces of information, and the AFM must ensure that the report is written in a manner that enables the average investor to understand it. The short report must be a separate document with no additional information added, though a single short report is permitted to include details of more than one sub-fund of an umbrella. The AFM must also ensure that all information in the short report is consistent with the long report.

The following items must be included, either in relation to the scheme or each sub-fund of an umbrella scheme:

- details of the scheme/sub-fund (name, investment objective and policy, a brief assessment of its risk profile, and the AFM's name and address);
- a review of investment activities and performance during the period;
- a comparative table (see above);
- sufficient information to inform the investor on the portfolio at the end of the period, and the extent to which it has changed over the period;
- any further significant information the investor would require to make an informed judgement of the scheme's activities, and the results of those activities.

You may wonder why both long and short reports are required to be prepared by AFMs. If you obtain a copy of both for a CIS you will see that the long report is much more detailed and many private investors will probably not trouble to read them. The average investor needs to have some details on which to assess how well their investment is performing so the short report is quite adequate for the purpose. The long report is, of course, available to investors free of charge if requested. This is similar to the accounts of companies governed under the Companies Acts, where both simplified and full accounts are available to shareholders.

The main benefit to AFMs is the considerable cost saving on producing shorter and therefore less costly documents and saving on the costs of postage.

2. THE SORP – FORMAT AND CONTENTS OF THE FINANCIAL STATEMENTS

LEARNING OBJECTIVES

9.1.4 Know the requirements of the Statement of Recommended Practice (SORP) in relation to the content of the long form annual and half-yearly reports and accounts: the statement of total return; the statement of movement in unit/shareholders' funds; the balance sheet; the portfolio statement; summary of material portfolio changes; notes to the accounts; distribution tables

The Investment Management Association (IMA) is the SORP-making body for authorised funds. The IMA formed a working group, made up of people who prepare and use accounts, and independent outsiders who represent the wider public interest, and has produced a combined SORP for authorised funds. This SORP came into effect for all schemes whose annual accounting periods commenced on or after 1 December 2003. A revised SORP was issued by the IMA in December 2005.

The COLL sourcebook requires the SORP requirements be applied to all long reports prepared.

The SORP specifies that the financial statements for an annual and interim reporting period must include the following items:

- statement of total return;
- statement of movements in unit/shareholders' funds;
- portfolio statement;
- balance sheet;
- summary of material portfolio changes;
- statement of the material accounting policies used in preparing the financial statements;
- further details in notes to the financial statements;
- distribution table.

Brief comments on all of these items follows, though the SORP itself contains detailed comments on how various assets and receipts should be shown in the accounts.

Comparative figures should be given for all items in the statement of total return, statement of movements in unit/shareholders' funds and the balance sheet, and the notes to each, and for sector percentage totals in the portfolio statement.

An example of a set of financial statements is shown as Appendix 4. The SORP also includes a **Typical Unit Trust Annual Report and Financial Statements**, which more or less prescribes the format of financial statements for authorised unit trusts.

The SORP reflects the COLL requirement for the AFM or ACD (and, in the case of an OEIC, one other director, where other directors in addition to the ACD are appointed) as appropriate to sign the report.

2.1 Statement of Total Return

This statement summarises the net investment gains or losses, together with the income earned after tax and expenses. It identifies that part of the total return that is to be distributed in accordance with the regulations.

The statement of total return must show:

- net gains/losses on investments during the period;
- other gains/losses (eg, currency gains/losses);
- net income/expenses after taxation for the period, showing, separately, gross income, total expenses and the tax charge;
- total return for the period;
- distributions;
- net increase/decrease in unit/shareholders' funds from investment activities.

The statement of total return must also include comparative figures for the equivalent period last year.

2.2 Statement of Movement in Unit/Shareholders' Funds

The statement of movements in unit/shareholders' funds should summarise the movements in the total value of the fund. This statement reconciles the changes in net assets during the period in summary form. It draws on the statement of total return for the net increase/decrease in assets attributable to the investment activities and shows the extent to which the fund has grown or contracted as a result of the creation or cancellation of units/shares.

The statement of movements in unit/shareholders' funds should be presented on the same page as the financial statement of total return, thereby providing unit/shareholders with a summary of the principal features of the scheme's results for the period. It should also include comparative figures for the previous period, ie, the previous report figures whether final or interim.

2.3 Statement of Assets and Liabilities (or Portfolio Statement)

This statement essentially lists all the investments of the scheme, reconciling the total to the total net asset value of the scheme as per the statement of movement in unit/shareholders' funds and the balance sheet. It must show the portfolio according to the different sectors which comprise the assets (eg, by country or by industrial/market sectors such as **retail, pharmaceuticals, manufacturing**, etc).

The statement must show the following:

- the number, quantity, description and value of each asset;
- the percentage of value of property of the scheme each holding represents;
- any instruments relating to indebtedness;
- the net current assets of the scheme; and
- the total value of all assets in the scheme.

The portfolio statement should detail, and distinguish between, assets that are approved or unapproved securities, and also distinguish those that are admitted to official stock exchange listing. It is considered that a geographical analysis of the portfolio would give an adequate indication of the official stock exchanges on which the securities are listed, provided any individual securities traded on a different exchange (or not listed) are clearly indicated.

The portfolio statement must include comparative figures for each sector as at the end of the previous report period, though need not provide comparative figures for each security.

2.4 Balance Sheet

The balance sheet provides a consolidated statement of the scheme's assets and liabilities, including:

- total investments valued at mid-market price;
- cash and bank balances;
- amounts payable/receivable to/from brokers for buying/selling securities; and
- any other sundry debtors and creditors (amounts due or payable).

2.5 Summary of Material Portfolio Changes

Significant changes in the disposition of the assets of the scheme should be provided. The summary of material portfolio changes should identify the value of purchases or sales of a security exceeding 2% of the net assets of the scheme at the start of the period. In any event, a minimum of the 20 largest purchases and 20 largest sales must be shown. To provide information about the extent of investment activity, the total cost of purchases and net proceeds from sales of investments during the period should also be disclosed.

2.6 Notes to the Financial Statements

The notes should include any other information required by the OEIC regulations or the FSA COLL sourcebook, together with the accounting policies used, and any information that is required for the accounts to give a true and fair view.

The typical open-ended investment company annual report and financial statements included in the SORP gives details of what should typically be included (items such as the distribution policy, treatment of income, application of equalisation, etc).

Disclosure should also be made of the aggregate underwriting commitments at the balance sheet date. The aggregate commitment on partly paid shares, nil paid shares and warrants should be disclosed.

2.7 Distribution Table

The financial statements include a table detailing the distribution payable or allocated for both Group 1 and Group 2 units/shares of each unit/share class in issue. The table shows the following items in pence per unit/share:

- gross income (for interest distributions);
- income tax (for interest distributions);
- net income;
- equalisation;
- distribution payable; and
- distribution paid in the equivalent period (annual or interim) 12 months earlier.

If there is a significant difference between net income shown in the statement of total return and the amount distributed, managers may wish to include an explanation of the difference in the notes, but this is not compulsory.

3. THE TRUSTEE'S/DEPOSITARY'S REPORT

> **LEARNING OBJECTIVES**
>
> 9.1.1 Know the FSA requirements in relation to reports and accounts

The trustee's/depositary's report (only required for an annual accounting period) should state whether, in their opinion, the AFM has managed the scheme during the period in accordance with:

- the investment and borrowing restrictions applicable to the CIS scheme; and
- otherwise in accordance with the provisions of the Trust Deed, Instrument of Incorporation, prospectus and the appropriate COLL sourcebook.

The trustee/depositary signs the report. If the trustee/depositary cannot confirm that the scheme has been managed in accordance with the conditions above he must describe any material failures and state what steps he has taken as a result of those failures.

It is unlikely that an AFM will make serious breaches of regulations. However, if such a breach is discovered, the trustee/depositary has a duty to take certain actions. He must ensure that the breach is rectified in such a way that neither the fund nor any investor is materially prejudiced. This requirement arises because the role of the trustee/depositary is to protect the interests of investors – not only those affected by the breach (such as if the wrong price is used for dealing units/shares) but also those investors that remain in the fund (and would otherwise bear the cost for correcting an excessive holding in a particular security, breaching an investment and borrowing powers limit). This requirement is regulatory, though for the trustee of a unit trust it also applies because of trust law.

It is the trustee's/depositary's duty to report the circumstances of certain breaches to the FSA. These include negative positions in the manager's box and any pricing errors where the trustee/depositary considers the circumstances or scale of the error to be sufficiently significant to notify the FSA. The FSA may discipline the AFM if the breaches are found proven, though disciplinary action does not tend to follow a single incident. In extreme cases, the FSA may require the trustee/depositary or manager to arrange for the scheme to be wound-up. A result of such circumstances might be that dealing in units/shares is suspended with no immediate chance of being reintroduced.

4. THE AUDITOR'S REPORT

LEARNING OBJECTIVES
9.1.1 Know the FSA requirements in relation to reports and accounts

The auditor is the independent financial watchdog for the investors and will be a registered firm of accountants. Their report includes the basis of their opinion (how they reached their decision), and confirms that they have received sufficient evidence that accounts are accurate. The report to members will state:

- whether, in the auditor's opinion, the accounts for that period have been properly prepared in accordance with generally accepted accounting principles, the SORP, the regulations, and the Trust Deed or Instrument of Incorporation;
- any material departure from the standard expected above, detailing any such departure and the reasons for it; and
- whether, in the auditor's opinion, the accounts give a true and fair view of:
  - the net income and the net gains or losses on the property of the scheme for the period; and
  - the financial position of the scheme at the end of that period.

The auditor signs the report. An audit report is only required to be included with the annual report. The interim or half-yearly financial statements are not required to be audited.

If the auditor is of the opinion that:

- proper accounting records for the scheme have not been kept by the AFM; or
- the accounts are not in agreement with the AFM's records; or
- they have not received all the information and explanations necessary to complete the audit satisfactorily; or
- the information given in the report of the AFM for that period is inconsistent with the accounts;

then the auditor must report these facts in its report.

5. WHAT SHOULD INVESTORS LOOK FOR IN THE REPORT AND ACCOUNTS?

LEARNING OBJECTIVES

9.1.6 Understand what investors should look for in the reports and accounts

9.1.7 Know the different methods by which reports may be delivered to investors

The AFM must send a copy of the Short Report to:

- each unitholder or to the first named of joint holders;
- to each holder of bearer units at his request; and
- to any other person free of charge on request whether they are a holder or not.

Normally the reports will be sent through the post but the COLL rules are not specific about the method. Consequently, providing that the unitholder consents, copies may be issued, for example, electronically either via a website (with e-mail notification to the holder) or directly via e-mail.

Long reports need not be sent automatically but must be sent to any person on request. In addition, they must be available in English, for inspection by the public free of charge at an office nominated by the AFM; and for a UCITS scheme at a place in each EEA state other than the UK in which units of the fund are marketed, again in English but also in at least one of that EEA state's other official languages. Finally, a copy must be sent to the FSA.

Here are some important questions a potential investor should address before investing:

- What is the growth record of the fund?
- Are the objectives of the fund the same as those of the potential investor? For example, an older investor is often looking for income rather than growth.
- Are the aims of the fund being met?
- How successful has management been in achieving performance?
- What are the management charges?
- Although not required in the contents of the AFM's report, are there any other benefits or features (such as share exchange) available?

As noted previously, the regulations require that certain basic information is included in the report. However, managers usually present additional information to clarify the fund's performance. This information may be quite useful in helping to answer some of the above questions.

From time-to-time the trustee/depositary or auditor of a scheme changes, and the report is required to name the parties so any such change would be visible. However, any such change that takes place without an explanation being offered should be investigated.

An example of an extract from a AFM's/ACD's report is shown opposite.

> **Example**
>
> **Authorised Corporate Director's Report**
>
> ### Objective of the M&G Smaller Companies Fund
>
> The Fund invests in smaller companies, where a good management can have most impact on earnings. Investment in such shares can offer prospects of above average capital growth. Income is not a major factor and the yield can be expected to be less than that of the FTSE All-Share Index.
>
> ### Policy for achieving objective
>
> The M&G Smaller Companies Funds uses a bottom-up approach in order to capture the superior long-term growth that can be found in smaller organisations. Company meetings are key to this approach, as the strength of management is crucial to the success of a small company. Further to the meetings, the fund manager uses financial analysis and valuation methods to assess the company's potential.
>
> Several additional buy criteria are applied: competitive edge (strong market position, strong brand, proprietary technology or barriers to entry etc); financial strengths (high return on capital and strong balance sheet) and high incentivisation (management should own shares in their own companies).
>
> Generally, shares will be held for the long term as companies that meet the required criteria often outperform over a longer period. However, shares will generally be sold when a company is significantly overvalued, is taken over or if the original reasons for buying no longer apply.
>
> ### Investment Activities Over The Report Period
> ### As at 1 July 2008, for the year ended 30 June 2008
>
> Notable additions to the Fund during the year under review included Carter & Carter, a car mechanic training company that is flourishing after its listing on the London Stock Exchange this February; information technology solutions firm Anite Group, where the business is turning around after extensive restructuring; and BSS Group, a plumbing equipment distributor, where sales have been boosted by its government contracts linked to the increased investment in schools, hospitals and subsidised housing. New holdings were funded by the disposal of successful holdings such as Topps Tiles, waste disposal company Shanks Group and aerospace engineer Meggitt. At the same time, we secured some profits by trimming our exposure to a number of stocks that had performed well over the year, including housebuilder Westbury, support services group Interserve, as well as Restaurant Group, the owner of Caffe Uno and Garfunkel's chains. Funds were reinvested in a number of existing holdings that have great potential for further growth, such as engineering company Charter, digital inkjet manufacturer Xaar and home insurance specialist Homeserve.
>
> Please note that the views expressed in this Report should not be taken as a recommendation or advice as to how the M&G Smaller Companies Fund or any holding mentioned in the Report is likely to perform. If you wish to obtain financial advice as to whether an investment is suitable for your needs, you should consult a Financial Adviser.

The review by the manager over the reporting period (note: the investment review in interim reports should cover the past six months; those in final reports should cover the past year) is included in all reports and the investor should check whether predictions have been fulfilled, and if the change is reflected in the state of the fund.

Good predictions and performance are usually treated with some prominence, whereas bad predictions may be dealt with briefly. Comparison should be made with the relevant stock market indices in the same sectors covering the same period. The income and distributions statements should be read in connection with the accompanying explanatory notes. Comparison with previous period figures is useful and instructive.

The price and distribution records are important and a statement usually illustrates whether the managers have increased the level of income during the life of the trust, taking inflation into account.

It is possible for the AFM's annual charge to be paid out of the capital of the fund, if the objective is to provide income or a balance between income and capital growth. This increases the distributable 'income', though at the risk of capital under-performance (or even capital erosion). This policy has adverse tax consequences in that investors, who are not liable to pay CGT, are converting tax-free capital gain into taxable income. If this policy is adopted there is a requirement for disclosures to current and prospective investors.

The fund portfolio should also be examined to see the spread of holdings. The holdings may, in part, have been sold since the report was made, but the number of holdings gives an indication of the concentration of the fund. Usually a greater rather than a smaller spread of holdings is desirable because of the risks involved.

6. FSA COMPARATIVE TABLES

LEARNING OBJECTIVES
9.1.6 Understand what investors should look for in the reports and accounts

In October 2001, the FSA introduced comparative tables to help consumers compare similar investment products available from various providers and make an informed choice. These tables are available on their website at www.fsa.gov.uk/tables

6.1 Products Covered

The tables provide a snapshot of products currently available, providing consumers with accessible, independent information to help them shop around and make better-informed decisions. CISs, ISAs, personal pensions and stakeholder products are available on the tables, together with investment bonuses, savings and mortgage endowments.

The ISA tables include the whole of the UK All Companies sector, and five new fund sectors. An ethical filter for sorting the UK All Companies sector has also been added.

6.2 How Consumers use the Tables

Consumers are able to compare products on a like-with-like basis and draw up a shortlist that can be explored in more detail, either by consulting a financial adviser or contacting the product provider. consumers access the tables via the internet.

Consumers using the FSA's Unit Trust & OEIC ISA table are able to make comparisons between more than 100 UK growth funds using key indicators such as:

- the effect of charges and deductions on the value of a fund over a 10- or 25-year period;
- where the product is available – through IFAs, other advisers, or direct from the product provider;
- the number of other funds available in the ISA;
- the impact of charges if the ISA is closed by the investor in the first three years.

A series of click-through options provides further details about individual products and links to the provider's own website. There are also useful links to other sources of information, such as industry bodies.

6.3 Do the FSA Recommend Funds?

It is important for consumers to be aware that the tables do not represent FSA best buys or recommendations. All providers have been asked to provide data. Products are not ranked as such, though consumers can choose to sort their results in alphabetical order or accordingly to the expected charges. However, consumers can use various options (such as tracker or non-tracker or ISAs) to filter the products using their own criteria to create a shortlist.

The FSA provided the following example on the launch:

As an example, the tables show that charges on an investment of £100 a month in an equity fund ISA over a 10-year period would come out at less than £400 for some of the cheaper funds compared with over £2,500 for the most expensive fund. Understandably, tracker funds tend towards the lower end of charges whereas actively managed tend to be more expensive. This does not mean that the more expensive funds are not worth buying but that they will typically have to outperform the cheapest fund by more than 2% compound over 10 years simply to eliminate the effect of the higher charges.

An extract from an FSA comparative table for ISAs using the UK Corporate Bond Sector is shown on the next page (full tables are available from www.fsa.gov.uk/tables).

Chapter 9
INVESTOR COMMUNICATIONS

FSA Comparative Tables from the Financial Services Authority

Unit trust and OEIC ISAs

You chose to compare unit trust and OEIC ISAs from the UK Corporate Bond IMA sector, based on a single payment of £5,000.00 over 5 years.

Your table shows 61 products.

Your table is sorted by provider name.

Some funds in this table may now be unclassified by the IMA and no longer in the sector chosen. This is because the providers have not given monthly updates on fund holdings. Check this information with the provider or a financial adviser

This table contains a large number of entries. Try using the filter to reduce the table to a more manageable size.

These products are not FSA recommendations. Always confirm the product details with the provider or an adviser.

Short-listed	Provider	Product name	Illustrated fund	Available from	Charges & deductions £	Charges in early years £	Transfers in	Transfers out	Stake-holder	Number of funds	Number of free switches	Minimum withdrawal £	Minimum balance £
	Abbey	Investments ISA	High Income Bond Unit Trust	S	586	397	Standard charges	Free	No	6	All	250	500
	Abbey	Investments ISA	Multi-Manager Bond Monthly Income (Inc)	S	612	424	Standard charges	Free	No	6	All	250	500
	Abbey	Investments ISA	Multi-Manager Cautious Accumulation (Acc)	S	852	566	Standard charges	Free	No	6	All	250	500
	AEGON	ISA	Ethical Income Fund - A	D, WOM	694	476	Standard charges	Free	No	11	5	100	250
	AEGON	ISA	Extra Income Fund - A	D, WOM	683	470	Standard charges	Free	No	11	5	100	250
	Allianz Global Investors	Investment Funds Maxi ISA	UK Corporate	D, WOM	614	416	Standard charges	Free	No	15	Most	1,000	500

Collective Investment Schemes Administration

7. SCHEME CHANGES – UNITHOLDER MEETINGS, NOTIFICATION AND CIRCULARS

Section 9 of Chapter 2 covers the details relating to COLL requirements for:

- notifying unitholders of changes to a scheme; and
- where necessary, holding meetings of unitholders.

AFMs will normally use regular communications with holders to update them on minor changes to the scheme; for example, giving notification post-event in the six-monthly short reports. Where the AFM needs to give notification prior to a change, separate circulars will be issued.

Where the change is a fundamental one, unitholders will need to pass a resolution at a meeting of holders; the AFM will, therefore, need to give holders the necessary notice of the meeting and issue a detailed circular setting out the changes proposed. Examples of such fundamental changes will be a change in the fund's investment objectives, or perhaps the merger of the fund with another.

END OF CHAPTER QUESTIONS

Think of an answer for each question and refer to the appropriate section for confirmation.

Question		Answer Reference
1.	To whom apart from unit/shareholders, must a fund manager make available a copy of his report?	Introduction
2.	a) How often must reports be made? b) What is the timescale involved?	Introduction and Section 1
3.	What are the essential differences between: • an annual long form report and accounts; • an interim or half-yearly report; and • short report?	Introduction and Section 1
4.	Under SORP requirements for financial statements, what does the statement of total return contain?	Section 2.1
5.	The financial statements contain a portfolio statement. What does this contain?	Section 2.3
6.	In preparing financial statements under the regulations, with what must these financial statements comply?	Section 3
7.	What does the auditor's report to unit/shareholders state?	Section 4
8.	Of what significance is the review of the AFM in the report to potential investors?	Section 5
9.	How do investors access the FSA Comparative Tables?	Section 6

10

TAXATION OF COLLECTIVE INVESTMENT SCHEMES

1.	CORPORATION TAX AND INCOME TAX	213
2.	OTHER TAXES	218
3.	WHAT ARE THE TAXATION IMPLICATIONS FOR INVESTORS IN CISS?	226
4.	REPORTING OF INVESTOR INFORMATION TO HMRC	233

This syllabus area will provide approximately 5 of the 50 examination questions

INTRODUCTION

This chapter provides an introduction to the complex subject of taxation as it relates to collective investment schemes (CISs) and to investors in such schemes. It is not intended to provide a comprehensive guide to relevant taxation. For more detailed information on taxation, students should refer to *Collective Investment Schemes: The Law and Practice* by MacFarlanes (Thomson/Sweet & Maxwell) or other appropriate tax guides.

Provisions covering the taxation of AUTs are included in the Income and Corporation Taxes Act 1988 and the Taxation of Capital Gains Act 1992.

The tax legislation was extended to cover OEICs in 1997. These regulations are referred to as the Open Ended Investment Companies (Tax) Regulations 1997 (the *Tax Regulations*).

Statutory references, unless otherwise specified, are to the Income and Corporation Taxes Act 1988 (the 1988 *Tax Act*).

1. CORPORATION TAX AND INCOME TAX

1.1 The Basis on Which Collective Investment Schemes (CISs) are Taxed?

LEARNING OBJECTIVES

10.1.1 Understand the basis on which authorised Collective Investment Schemes are taxed:
(see syllabus learning map for details)

The Open-Ended Investment Companies (Tax) Regulations 1997 provide, subject to certain modifications and exceptions, that OEICs should be taxed in the same way as authorised unit trusts under the 1988 Tax Act and the Taxation of Capital Gains Act 1992 (TCGA).

Accordingly, each type of CIS (OEIC and AUT) is taxed, as set out in S468(1) of the 1988 Act, as if:
- it is an ordinary company (formed under the Companies Act) resident in the UK; and
- the rights of the unit/shareholders are as shareholders in such an ordinary company.

If the scheme is an umbrella-type scheme (which has two or more sub-funds), each sub-fund is treated, for tax purposes, as if it were a separate scheme and the umbrella company is not considered as a separate taxable entity.

Unlike unit trusts where the trustee is seen as the tax payer, the depositary to an OEIC is not. It is the OEIC which is the tax payer; the ACD is responsible for the completion and submission of all tax returns to HM Revenue & Customs (HMRC) on behalf of the OEIC.

1.2 Applicable Tax Rates

> **LEARNING OBJECTIVES**
> 10.1.2 Know the tax treatment of different types of income distribution

Under the Finance Act 1994, authorised CISs are divided into two categories for tax purposes, distinguished by the nature of their investments. At present both categories are subject to corporation tax of 20% on their taxable profit. The tax treatment of distribution of income to investors is different, however.

Category of CIS	Tax treatment of income distributions
a) less than 60% of property in interest bearing assets (eg, gilts)	If (a) applies at any point during the distribution period, the CIS must opt to pay a dividend distribution. Such a distribution carries a 10% tax credit.
b) 60% or more of property in interest bearing assets	If (b) applies throughout the distribution period, the CIS may opt to pay an interest distribution. Such a distribution is subject to income tax at the lower rate of 20%.

There is a general obligation on the payer of the yearly interest to deduct at source income tax at the appropriate rate (20%) on the gross amount payable. This requirement does not apply to interest distributions paid to non-resident unit/shareholders who have completed the appropriate declaration and the income is permitted to be paid gross. Completion of a declaration may not be required if the fund issues a gross share class which is only marketed to non-UK investors. Interest can also be paid gross to corporate investors and certain other exempt investors listed in Section 349A of the Tax Act and as amended by the Finance Act 2002 paragraph 94. An example would be to an ISA manager.

When is Tax Paid?

When an interest distribution is paid, income tax has to be accounted for to HMRC at the end of the quarter in which the distribution was paid.

There is a requirement to estimate the tax liability of large companies, including CISs, (ie, companies whose taxable profit plus Franked Investment Income (FII – see below for an explanation of FII) is greater than £1,500,000) and account for a proportion of the total tax due 6, 9, 12, and 15 months from the start of the CIS's year. Any under- or over-paid tax is subject to interest, either payable to or receivable from HMRC.

1.3 Taxable Income

> **LEARNING OBJECTIVES**
>
> 10.1.1 Understand the basis on which authorised Collective Investment Schemes are taxed: (see syllabus learning map for details)
>
> 10.1.2 Know the tax treatment of different types of income distribution

A CIS's taxable profit is calculated by deducting the chargeable expenses from the taxable income. The treatment of taxation of income earned by the CIS depends on its source.

Dividend income received from UK-resident companies is tax-free, when received by other UK-resident companies, including CIS. This is because the paying company has already paid tax out of the sum available to pay the dividend. This type of income, along with the attributable tax credit, is termed 'franked investment income' or 'FII'. Similarly, the franked part of distributions from other CISs is tax-free, when received by a CIS.

If the CIS receives other forms of income, referred to as 'unfranked investment income', in the absence of any relief or credit, it is subject to corporation tax. A CIS taxable profit is determined by calculating the total amount of unfranked income, received from the fund's investments, less any allowable expenses, eg, AFMs Annual Management Charge. Examples of unfranked income include:

- interest on debt securities;
- bank deposit interest;
- underwriting fees;
- foreign income.

CISs are exempt from capital gains tax (CGT, see Section 2.1 of this chapter) on gains on their investments. If, however, HMRC finds their activities constitute dealing or trading in securities, rather than investment, then any gains from these activities may be taxed as income and thus are not protected by CIS CGT exemption. Where active investment becomes trading is a matter of opinion and HMRC's position is not entirely clear.

The rate of turnover (ie, the percentage or number of times the assets of the fund are bought and sold in a year), while an indication of whether there is active trading, is not conclusive and the only real determinant is the intention of the AFM. Assuming the CIS is not considered to be dealing in securities, it is taxed as an investment company on the income it receives.

An increasing number of funds are using derivatives as part of their core investment portfolio. The inclusion of gains or losses from derivative products in net gains or losses on investments or in net income before taxation will depend upon the nature of the transaction. Where positions are undertaken to protect or enhance capital return, the gains or losses should be dealt with in gains or losses on investments; where they are for generating or protecting income, the costs or income should be dealt with in net income before taxation. Accordingly, both motives and circumstances in the use of derivatives are important in determining whether items should be treated as income or capital.

A brief guide to Property Authorised Investment Funds (PAIFs) is included in Chapter 8.

1.4 Chargeable Expenses

LEARNING OBJECTIVES

10.1.1 Understand the basis on which authorised Collective Investment Schemes are taxed:
(see syllabus learning map for details)

The CIS's liability to corporation tax is calculated on the balance of taxable income after the deduction of chargeable expenses. Chargeable expenses are shown below.

Chargeable Expenses	Non-chargeable Expenses
AFM fees	Stockbroker's fees
Trustee's/depositary's fees	Interest payable (eg, overdraft)
Safe custody fees	Foreign exchange losses
FSA fees	
Auditor's fees	
Interest expenses*	
Registration fees	
Interest distributions	
ACD fees	

* Relief can be obtained providing the borrowing is within that permitted under the FSA regulations.

Any management expenses not utilised, ie, management expenses exceeding the unfranked income, may be carried forward and treated as management expenses of subsequent periods.

1.5 FSA: Charging the AFM's Periodic Charge to Capital

In certain circumstances, in accordance with the FSA regulations, all or part of the AFM's annual management fee (periodic charge) can be levied against the capital account of those funds which place a high priority on the generation of income, or express equal emphasis on income and capital growth.

This provides the AFM with greater flexibility when maintaining improved distributions of income in line with CIS objectives. It also benefits investors for whom income from their investment is most important, eg, those living on retirement pensions. There is a risk, however, that the capital performance of the fund could be affected and, in the long term, this could be detrimental to income growth as well.

What administrative arrangements are needed?

The following arrangements need to be made:

- the trustee's/depositary's agreement must be obtained;
- the charge must first be levied against the income account, with a subsequent transfer to the capital account in accordance with the SORP;
- the prospectus must include information:
  - concerning the higher or equal emphasis on the generation of income and that this may constrain capital growth;
  - disclosing the fact that the AFM's fee is charged to the capital account and the details of the actual or maximum that may be treated in that way;

If the AFM wishes to change from charging the fee to income, to charging it to capital:

- the changes to the prospectus can be made without approval of unit/shareholders if:
  - the CIS investment objectives already give a clear priority to the generation of income or equal emphasis between income generation and capital growth;
  - 60 days' written notice is given of the intention to charge the AFM's fee to the capital account.

What are the tax implications of this provision in the rules?

The amount of the AFM's periodic charge transferred to the capital account is still available to be offset as an expense to the CIS corporation tax liability. In theory, the transfer should be made net of tax relief.

AFMs should compare the tax position of the CIS, if there is a transfer of the AFM's charge to the capital account, with the position of the fund had there been no such transfer. If no tax benefit arises in respect of the transfer, the AFM's charge should be transferred gross as there is no attributable tax relief. In circumstances where the AFM wishes to take advantage of this rule, it should consult with both the depositary and the auditor in advance, to agree the proposal.

1.5.1 Other Charges to Capital

Under the COLL sourcebook any payment as a result of effecting transactions for the fund should be made from the capital of the scheme. All other payments must be made from income in the first instance but may be transferred to capital subject to appropriate disclosure in the prospectus. Any change to the allocation of payments will need the relevant approval/notification.

1.6 How the is Tax Calculated

The following is a simple example of a tax calculation in respect of a CIS paying an interest distribution.

Tax calculation if a CIS has suffered no overseas tax

	£(000s)	£(000s)
Unfranked income:		
Interest on debt securities	20	
Bank deposit interest	80	
Underwriting commission	20	120
Less expenses:		
AFM's fee	(10)	
Depositary's fee	(5)	
Safe custody charges	(5)	(20)
Income before taxation		100
Corporation tax at 20%		(20)
Net distributable income		80

2. OTHER TAXES

LEARNING OBJECTIVES

10.2.1 Know the types of overseas taxes on income received in the UK from an overseas company and the treatment of such taxes as they affect the income available for distribution

Typically, income (ie, dividends or interest) received by a CIS in the UK from an overseas company suffers two types of local tax:

- **underlying tax**: the local equivalent of corporation tax which reduces the profits available for distribution by the company; and
- **withholding tax**: the foreign tax paid directly as a result of remitting the interest or dividend, overseas.

The UK system of Double Taxation Relief (DTR) is set out in the Taxes Act 1988 (Part XVIII). This authorises the UK government to enter into agreements with foreign governments for the purpose of preventing double taxation in respect of the same income. These are referred to as Double Taxation Agreements (DTAs). A further objective of these agreements is to render reciprocal assistance in the prevention of tax evasion.

CISs are unlikely to obtain UK tax relief for underlying tax paid unless the unit/shareholder owns more than 10% of the voting share capital of the dividend-paying company. They can, however, obtain relief from withholding tax.

Under the UK DTR system, income which would have been doubly taxed may be relieved by:

- exemption of income from UK taxes;
- deduction of foreign tax from the income liable to UK tax;
- credit of foreign tax suffered against the UK tax on the income.

Most DTAs restrict the relief from withholding tax to a certain rate (say 15%) and anything above this rate has to be recovered from the tax authority in the foreign country concerned. The AFM in the case of an OEIC or the trustee of an AUT undertakes such claims on behalf of the CIS. In some countries (eg, Italy) there have been problems in obtaining repayment under the DTAs. The outcome here is that instead of including a withholding tax refund as income arising (ie, on an accruals basis, in anticipation of its receipt) in an accounting period, it has to be included on a received basis.

2.1 Capital Gains Tax (CGT)

LEARNING OBJECTIVES

10.1.1 Understand the basis on which authorised Collective Investment Schemes are taxed:
(see syllabus learning map for details)

Capital gains made by CISs on investment transactions are not chargeable and are thus exempt from tax (Taxation of Capital Gains Act 1992 S.100[1]). This important exemption means that investors investing in CISs are not subject to an additional layer of tax on realised capital profits.

In view of this exemption, the distinction between capital gains and income is extremely important for AFMs and holders of CISs. Gains accruing on disposals of some categories of investment are, by statute, taxed as income. The position regarding trading or dealing in securities has already been covered in Section 1.3.

The exemption from tax on chargeable gains relates to UK tax only. A CIS scheme invested in overseas securities may be liable to overseas capital gains tax, if the local law so provides, and, subject to any double taxation agreement with the UK, to local tax on gains realised on the disposal of securities.

2.2 Value Added Tax (VAT)

> **LEARNING OBJECTIVES**
>
> 10.2.2 Know the treatment of VAT on schemes

A CIS may be subject to VAT on services provided to it (known as 'supplies'). Thus depositaries' and auditors' fees are subject to VAT which may be paid out of the property of the scheme and are, therefore, borne by the unit/shareholders. However, fund management and fund administration services have been the subject of a recent legal decision which has led to some changes.

HMRC's policy has been to apply the exemption of VAT to fund management in a strict sense, ie, where it involves the assessment of financial risk, the making of investment decisions as to both the selection and disposal of assets under management and a direct involvement in the transactions concerning the assets of the fund, mainly in securities. Services not comprising such investment management functions, such as fund accounting and administration services, were regarded as taxable. In the recent case of Abbey National plc vs Inscape Investment Fund an appeal was made to the European Court of Justice on HMRC's interpretation of what constitutes 'management'.

The Court found that the services of trustees or depositaries by reference to the UCITS Directive are not covered by the concept of management and are therefore excluded from exemption. For fund accounting and administration services the Court found that they would qualify as management of special investment funds for the purpose of the VAT exemption if, 'viewed broadly, they form a distinct whole and are specific to, and essential for, the management of those funds'.

Again by reference to the UCITS Directive, the Court viewed that tasks, such as those set out in the Directive under the heading 'Administration', and which are functions specific, to special investment funds, are capable of coming within the scope of the exemption. Under this heading are:

- legal and fund management accounting services;
- customer enquiries;
- valuation and pricing (including tax returns);
- regulatory compliance monitoring;
- maintenance of a unitholder register;
- distribution of income;
- unit issues and redemptions;
- contract settlements (including certificate dispatch);
- record keeping.

To be exempt, it is necessary for the service to be distinct as a fund administration service. This 'distinctiveness' is normally attained by the bundling, into a single supply, of numerous operations that are typical of the administrative management of, eg, an OEIC. In deciding whether the overall service is distinct as fund administration, both the number of specific operations and their individual characteristics need to be taken into account. For example, the daily valuation of assets is of particular importance and relevance to CISs in determining the price of shares or units and so this, together with related accounting and reporting functions would be sufficiently distinctive as a fund administration service.

It should be noted that the maintenance of a register of shareholders does not, in isolation, represent a fund administration service. However, if the service is combined with the issue and redemption of the units or shares and collating the number of shares in issue for the purpose of establishing the daily price of the units, such a package takes on the distinct characteristics of fund administration and will be exempt.

Any substantial UK organisation whose activities relate directly or indirectly to managing a CIS is likely to be registered for VAT. Registration is required if the value of taxable supplies exceeds the limits prescribed by statute (and revised from time to time by the Chancellor). Many CISs and their depositaries are not registered. This is because the CIS is not making sufficient taxable supplies to register for VAT, and is accordingly treated as the ultimate consumer of services, rather than the supplier.

The expenditure incurred in managing a scheme is one of two types:
- items paid by the trustee/depositary on behalf of the scheme, including its own fee;
- items paid by the AFM and listed in the FSA regulations.

This distinction is important in respect of the VAT implications of such expenditure incurred by persons registered for VAT (eg, AFM), if the recipient of the supply is able to obtain relief from tax.

2.3 Stamp Duty and Stamp Duty Reserve Tax (SDRT)

LEARNING OBJECTIVES

10.2.3 Know the situations in which UK Stamp Duties are likely to arise

10.2.4 Understand the treatment of Collective Investment Schemes for Stamp Duty Reserve Tax (SDRT) and exemptions: basic treatment; in specie contributions and redemptions; fund reconstructions and mergers

Stamp duty is collected on the transfer of title to property. SDRT is a charge which applies to agreements for the sale of property if the transfer of ownership does not require a stock transfer form or other stampable instrument. SDRT only applies to the transfer of chargeable securities, including stocks, shares and similar equity rights, where generally no form is used, but not those securities which are exempt from stamp duty. The current rate of SDRT is 0.5% of the value of the securities sold.

Stamp duties arise in the following situations involving CISs.

Investment Transactions within the Fund – Basic Treatment

CISs are normally subject to stamp duty on transfers when purchasing UK-registered stocks and securities, except, for example, gilts and loan stocks. The duty is payable at the rate of 50p per £100 or part thereof of the stock or security value.

A SDRT regime was introduced with effect from 6 February 2000 for transactions in the units/shares of CISs (see below).

In Specie Cancellation (Redemption) of Units/Shares

If underlying securities are transferred in specie from a CIS to a withdrawing holder, there is no transfer of cash. In these cases if the in specie transfer is not part of a winding-up of the fund, the stamp office believes that stamp duty of 0.5% of the value of the securities transferred should be payable, as opposed to the nominal stamp duty charge of £5.00 per transfer. However, if a CIS is terminated and the underlying investments are transferred to all the holders pro rata to their holdings of units/shares, there is no change in beneficial ownership and, therefore, nominal stamp duty is payable, ie, £5.00 per transfer.

Fund Reconstructions and Mergers

In a proposed merger of two or more CISs, liability to stamp duty or SDRT must be considered if there will be a:

- conveyance on sale (ie, transfer) of the units/shares in one or both of the schemes;
- transfer of the underlying property held by the schemes.

The Treasury announced the temporary exemption of AUTs to OEIC conversions from the 0.5% stamp duty. Provisions were included in the 1997 Finance Act and, originally, there was a two year window of opportunity for exempt conversions to take place. If AUTs were converted and/or amalgamated with an OEIC (eg, six unit trusts are converted to create three sub-funds) before 30 June 1999, the exemption from stamp duty applied.

The temporary exemption was then extended to 30 November 2002, ie, a year after the Regulations putting in place the framework to allow a broader range of OEICs to be formed. In October 2002 HM Revenue & Customs announced that, following discussions with AFMs, this temporary exemption would be extended indefinitely beyond the end of November 2002.

Transfer of Units/Shares by Shareholders

CISs units/shares are registered securities which can be transferred by unit/shareholders using a common stock transfer form; such transfers, prior to 6 February 2000 were liable to stamp duty unless the transfer fell within either an exempt or nominal category, as shown in one of the two certificates on the reverse of the stock transfer form. Since 6 February 2000, transfers for value of units or shares in CISs are no longer subject to stamp duty, but are subject to SDRT. The most common transfers are gifts between husband and wife and those between nominee companies and beneficiaries which are exempt from duty. This regime is explained below.

Why is SDRT applied to CISs?

The government, in the Finance Act 1999, introduced legislation relating to unit trusts and OEICs. Section 122 and Schedule 19 of the Finance Act 1999 introduced, with effect from 6 February 2000, a new SDRT regime for surrenders and other transfers of units of unit trusts in place of the existing stamp duty charges. Corresponding changes were made to the SDRT regime for transactions in shares in OEICs using regulatory powers introduced in the same section.

Calculation of Stamp Duty Reserve Tax (SDRT)

The first major difference is that SDRT is a transaction tax, unlike stamp duty which is a tax attached to documents. With effect from 6 February 2000, SDRT became chargeable at 0.5% on the value of surrendered units of a unit trust or shares in an OEIC, although this figure can be reduced by two ratios. These are if the fund concerned:

- is contracting and there are more units/shares surrendered than issued over a two week period;
- has investments in exempt assets such as overseas securities and/or bonds.

The calculation is based on the relative levels of issues and redemptions of units/shares during a rolling two-week period, multiplied by the value of surrenders in the first week of the period. The new tax ignores the concept of cancellation, or that the AFM may have revolved units/shares and is purely concerned with the number of units/shares that the AFM has issued and redeemed over a two-week period.

Thus, if more units/shares are redeemed than issued during a two week period, the liability to SDRT is reduced by multiplying the value of the shares surrendered in the first week by the fraction I/S, where I and S are the numbers of units/shares issued and surrendered, respectively, in the relevant two week period.

The basic calculation is as follows:

SDRT liability =

Value of Surrenders in week 1 @ 0.5% x $\dfrac{\text{No of units/shares issued in weeks 1–2}}{\text{No of units/shares surrendered in weeks 1–2}}$

Therefore, if the value of units/shares redeemed in week one is £450,000, and the number of units/shares issued and redeemed over a two week period is 50,000 units/shares and 76,200 units/shares, respectively, the calculation would look like this:

SDRT liability = (£450,000 x 0.5% = £2,250) x $\dfrac{50,000 \text{ units/shares}}{76,200 \text{ units/shares}}$ = £1,476

The above figures are calculated on the assumption that all the securities held in the fund are subject to stamp duty. A notional or base unit/share is used for SDRT calculations where multiple unit/share classes exist.

In practice, the underlying rationale for charging SDRT is that a fund should only be liable in the same proportion that it would have been subject to stamp duty. For example, a fund holding only overseas equities and/or bonds would not be subject to SDRT as its assets are generally exempt from stamp duty. Consequently, the charge will mainly fall on funds holding UK equities and other assets held which are subject to stamp duty.

If a fund has investments in exempt assets, eg, gilts, overseas/foreign registered securities, the liability to SDRT is further reduced by multiplying it by the fraction $N/(N+E)$ where N and E are the average market values of the non-exempt and exempt assets, respectively, of the fund over the two week period.

HM Revenue & Customs does not lay down a rule for averaging these values. Any of the following are considered acceptable:

1. an average over all the valuation points falling within the two week period; or
2. an average from a valuation point at an equivalent time in each of the two weeks concerned; or
3. an average from the values on the last business day of month one and month two; or
4. another specifically agreed valuation method.

HM Revenue & Customs requires AFMs to inform it of the approach chosen and for it to remain consistent. If an AFM needs to change the way in which the valuation is done the reason must be given on the first return following the change.

Thus, if the UK assets constitute a smaller part of the overall valuation of a fund, say of an international fund, the amount payable is further reduced. For example, if the UK assets chargeable to stamp duty are 25% of the fund, the example figure of £1,476 would be reduced to £369 (£1,476 x 25%). The ability to distinguish between exempt assets and assets subject to stamp duty is very important.

Third party transfers, lodged for registration with the AFMs, generally fall within the scope of this regime but exemptions are available in some cases; in particular, the categories which could previously be certified as exempt or attracting fixed duty on the reverse of a stock transfer form, eg, change of nominee, gifts, death etc. Fuller details can be found in Schedule 19 Finance Act 1999 and the Guidance Notes.

What Information does HMRC Require?

LEARNING OBJECTIVES
10.2.5 Know HM Revenue & Customs' information requirements, timetable for returns and payments, and penalties, in relation to SDRT

A monthly return is required on or before the **accountable date**. The accountable date is the 14th day of the month following the month in which the relevant two week period ends. Hence, a return for periods which end during the month of April should be accounted for by 14 May at the latest.

A return will cover a month during which four or five two week periods will end. Hence, the return will consist of four or five subsidiary calculations. An example spreadsheet is shown as Appendix 13. This sets out the information required and the calculations needed to arrive at an SDRT figure for the month. If returns are submitted after the accountable date, or if they prove to be incorrect, then they will be subject to an interest charge and penalty.

The return must also contain a declaration relating to the number of shares for pro-rata in specie redemptions and exempt transactions, although these do not form part of the calculation for SDRT purposes.

If relevant, the certification on the reverse of a stock transfer form will be deemed as acceptable evidence of the exemption from SDRT by the Stamp Office.

Detailed checks are carried out by HM Revenue & Customs' SDRT Operations Unit of all CIS returns submitted to ensure validity. In addition, the AFM is, upon request, required to provide supporting material (on a small random selection of funds) as a means of substantiating the figures recorded on the monthly return. These checks include SDRT exemption categories, such as exempt third party transfers and pro-rata inspecie redemptions/cancellations.

Who Pays SDRT?

> **LEARNING OBJECTIVES**
>
> 10.2.6 Know AFMs' options in making an SDRT provision

In the case of a unit trust, the trustee on behalf of the fund is liable under the Finance Act 1999 for the payment of SDRT to HM Revenue & Customs and the AFM is accountable. In the case of an OEIC, it is the company itself which is liable. The FSA has, however, amended the CIS regulations to provide a means to recoup the tax.

The regulations permit SDRT to be charged to incoming/outgoing investors. It is recognised that the amount of tax cannot be calculated at the time of dealing so the regulations permit an AFM to require a separate payment or deduction as a provision against SDRT when shares are bought or sold by an investor. Any such provision paid by the investor must be paid over by the AFM to the depositary and becomes part of the property of the fund. Thus, in dealing with investors, the choices facing AFMs are to charge:

- SDRT to the fund and make no separate charge to investors;
- investors a provision on entry to the fund, ie, when they purchase units/shares;
- investors a provision on exiting the fund, ie, when redeeming units/shares;
- SDRT to the fund and express the right to charge a provision to the investor, eg, in the event of a large transaction.

In the case of a third party transfer for value, ie, a transfer which attracts SDRT, the registrar would be entitled to refuse to register the transfer until the amount of SDRT (currently 0.5% of the value of the units/shares) is paid by the person lodging the transfer. The rate of charge must be agreed between the AFM and the trustee/depositary. The actual rate of SDRT paid by the fund may be less than 0.5%, depending on the pattern of dealings. Alternatively, the AFM may simply choose to charge SDRT to the fund and make no charge on the person lodging the transfer.

How are investors informed of SDRT charges?

The FSA requires AFMs to advise investors:

- where they may be subject to a separate charge as a provision against SDRT; and
- about the circumstances in which an AFM may impose such a charge.

AFMs may send a separate notice to all investors or include such notice in the fund's half-yearly or annual report before an SDRT provision is charged. Such provision cannot be charged until the required notice has been given.

The policy on charging SDRT provision must be disclosed in the key features document. If simply charged to the fund then it can be treated as dealing costs and reflected in the effect of charges calculation shown in key features. If a separate SDRT provision is to be made on the issue or redemption of units/shares this must be disclosed as indicated above.

Relevant details about SDRT and the AFM's policy on any charge to investors must be included in the prospectus.

If a separate SDRT provision is made contract notes will need to show the amount of the provision.

3. WHAT ARE THE TAXATION IMPLICATIONS FOR INVESTORS IN CISs?

The taxation of investors falls into two areas: income and capital. The position of different types of investor (non-taxpayer, higher rate taxpayer, etc) is covered, along with the position of the non-resident holder in the following sections.

3.1 Taxes on Income

> **LEARNING OBJECTIVES**
>
> 10.3.1 Know the income tax, corporation tax and capital gains tax implications for the following investors: corporate (including other Collective Investment Schemes); individuals (tax payers, non-tax payers, and ISA investors)

Shareholders are subject to tax on distributions of income. As explained in Chapter 8 of this workbook, the Finance Act 1994 introduced different types of income distribution which may be paid. These are:

- dividend distributions;
- interest distributions; and
- property income distributions ('PIDs').

Dividend and income distributions are dealt with in more detail below; a brief guide to PIDs is given in Chapter 8.

Units/shares in a CIS are deemed to be shares in a UK-resident company under S.468(1). However, the taxation of distributions from an authorised CIS depends on the character of the distribution.

3.2 Dividend Distributions

LEARNING OBJECTIVES

10.3.2 know the taxation treatment of dividend and interest distributions

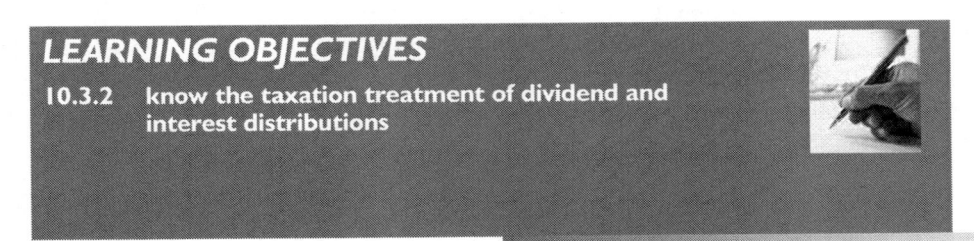

A dividend distribution is paid to a holder, together with an associated tax credit equal to 10% of the sum of the distribution and tax credit (this sum is referred to as the grossed-up value of the dividend distribution).

Tax Credit	Dividend Distribution Payable	Grossed-up Value
£8.89	£80	£88.89

For individual holders, the £88.89 is subject to income tax, with the tax credit satisfying a UK resident unit/shareholder's liability for basic rate income tax (even though calculated at the 10% rate). Basic and lower rate taxpayers have nothing further to pay. Higher rate taxpayers will, generally, have a further liability of 22.5% of the grossed-up value. This means they will retain £60 from a gross distribution of £88.89. A UK non-taxpayer can no longer reclaim the tax credit, ie, on distributions paid on or after 6 April 1999. ISA holders also can no longer reclaim the tax credit on dividend distributions but higher rate tax payers will not have any further liability.

This taxation is identical to the taxation of ordinary dividends paid by a UK resident company.

A holder of accumulation units/shares, where the income is automatically reinvested and reflected in the price of the units/shares, is also treated as receiving a dividend equal to that income and the associated tax credit, even though the income is not distributed.

For UK corporate shareholders, including other collective investment schemes investing in a CIS, it is necessary to show the distribution in terms of the percentages that FII and unfranked investment income represent of the total distribution. The reason is that while corporate holders receive franked investment income tax-free, they generally have a further liability to tax on the unfranked portion. This arises because CISs which pay dividend distributions, ie, equity-type funds, are subject to corporation tax at the lower rate of 20% whereas, unless the small companies' rates apply, UK corporate holders are subject to corporation tax at a higher rate of 30% for the year 2001/02 and subsequent tax years. A note explaining the streaming of FII and unfranked investment income with the relevant percentages appears in the notes to tax credit vouchers issued by CISs (see Appendix 11).

From 6 April 1999 rules apply which mean that the unfranked portion of the dividend is grossed-up using a 20% tax rate instead of the 10% shown on the tax voucher. This tax can be offset against a UK corporate unit/shareholder's liability to corporation tax, or if corporation tax is paid by the underlying fund, some or all of this may be recoverable. Again this information is disclosed in the notes to the tax credit vouchers (see Appendix 11).

3.3 Interest Distributions

LEARNING OBJECTIVES

10.3.1 Know the income tax, corporation tax and capital gains tax implications for the following investors: corporate (including other Collective Investment Schemes); individuals (tax payers, non-tax payers, and ISA investors)

10.3.2 Know the taxation treatment of dividend and interest distributions

10.3.3 Know the main types of investor eligible for gross payment of interest distributions: (see syllabus learning map for details)

CISs which are predominantly invested in gilts, corporate bonds and cash deposits may pay interest distributions under the provisions of the Finance Act 1994 which introduced this type of distribution.

Prior to the 1995/96 tax year, unit trusts would have paid a dividend distribution with a 20% tax credit. Since 1995/96, qualifying unit trusts and, since their launch, qualifying OEICs, have paid interest distributions with income tax deducted at source. Thus these funds will pay investors interest distributions net of a 20% income tax deduction. The interest payment is deducted from the fund's unfranked income and treated as an expense of the fund, with the result that no corporation tax is payable.

The situation for each tax group is:

- UK individual non-tax payers can use the income tax voucher issued by the CIS to reclaim the 20% income tax;
- UK individuals basic rate tax payers have no further tax liability and lower rate tax payers can recover the excess;
- higher rate tax payers have a further tax liability of 20% of the grossed-up value of the distribution.

For corporate holders (including collective investment schemes, pension funds and charities) interest distributions are taxed as interest received in the normal way. However, with effect from 1 April 2001, if such holders are the beneficial owners of the units/shares they may receive interest distribution gross without deduction of tax.

ISA managers may receive these distributions gross without deduction of income tax or will reclaim the tax deducted from HMRC. Individuals who hold their units/shares via an ISA will receive the gross value of interest distributions and the income will, therefore, be tax-free.

3.4 The Position of Non-resident Unit/Shareholders

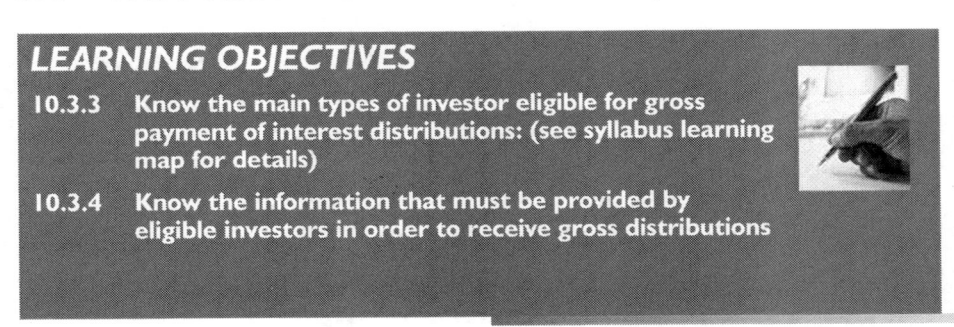

> **LEARNING OBJECTIVES**
>
> 10.3.3 Know the main types of investor eligible for gross payment of interest distributions: (see syllabus learning map for details)
>
> 10.3.4 Know the information that must be provided by eligible investors in order to receive gross distributions

The Finance Act 1994 allows for the payment of interest distributions, without the deduction of income tax, to shareholders who are not ordinarily resident in the UK.

Ordinary residence means that the residence is not casual and uncertain, but that the individual who resides in the UK does so in the ordinary course of his/her life. Someone who is not ordinarily resident may visit the UK but cannot stay for more than six months or habitually stay for substantial periods, eg, three months each year.

To pay interest gross to a non-resident, the CIS must receive a completed declaration form in which the unit/shareholder declares that he is not ordinarily resident or, if a company, not resident in the UK.

The declaration must meet the following detailed conditions:
- it must be in a form approved by HM Revenue & Customs;
- it must be made in writing to the CIS, although the forms will probably be dealt with by the registrar;
- it must contain the name and principal residential address of the unit/shareholder and an undertaking that he will notify the CIS registrar if he becomes ordinarily resident in the UK;
- if made by personal representatives, it must contain the name and principal residential address of the deceased holder immediately before death; and
- if made by a company, it must contain the name of the company, the address of its registered principal office, and an undertaking to inform the CIS registrar if it becomes resident in the UK.

The CIS registrar can continue to pay gross relying on the declaration unless they receive a notification of change of residence or are otherwise notified that the unit/shareholder may be ordinarily resident, or resident, in the UK.

HM Revenue & Customs has prepared guidance notes covering these declarations.

In October 2002, HM Revenue & Customs announced a relaxation of the requirement for overseas investors who wish to receive gross interest from CISs to make a declaration that they are not ordinarily resident (NOR) in the UK.

This is intended to make UK CISs more attractive to foreign investors and allow them to compete on a more equal footing with overseas competitors.

The change removes the need for overseas investors to make declarations so long as they invest:

- in a special share class which is not marketable to UK residents; and
- through a reputable local intermediary, such as a bank or other authorised financial institution.

3.5 Capital Taxes

> **LEARNING OBJECTIVES**
> 10.3.5 Understand the potential liability to UK Capital Gains Tax on the disposal of units/shares

CISs provide a tax efficient investment with each fund being exempt from CGT on transactions within the fund, subject to the fund not being seen as 'trading'.

On the disposal of units/shares, however, a unit/shareholder may, depending on personal circumstances, be liable to pay CGT on the increase in value. For 2008/09 tax year an individual's first £9,600 of gains on disposals of assets are exempt from CGT.

Gains in excess of this figure were previously added to the individual's other income and taxed at the rates applicable. However from the 2008/09 tax year a specific rate of CGT has been set at 18%.

The capital gain on income shares is calculated by deducting the original purchase cost, less the amount of equalisation shown in the first tax credit voucher following the purchase, from the sale proceeds.

The capital gain on accumulation shares is calculated by deducting the total amount of reinvested net income added to the original cost (including equalisation, since this was not repaid) from the sale proceeds.

For assets acquired prior to 6 April 1998, there is additional tax relief as the acquisition cost is indexed to allow for inflation. The basis of indexation is the change in the Retail Price Index (RPI) from the time of purchase (or in the case of reinvested income, from the date of reinvestment) to the time of sale, or from 31 March 1982 in the case of investment before that date. Equalisation is eligible for indexation allowance from the date of allocation.

Indexation stops at 5 April 1998 and is replaced by taper relief, whereby the taxable gain is reduced according to the length of time that the assets have been held. Such relief cannot be used to create or increase a loss.

Gains arising before 31 March 1982 are not subject to CGT. To calculate the indexation relief which may be deducted from any gain, the following formula is used:

$$\text{Purchase Cost} \times \frac{(\text{Index month sold} - \text{Index month bought})}{\text{Index month bought}} = \text{Indexation relief}$$

Where the investment was purchased prior to 31 March 1982 then the purchase cost, may at the option of the investor, be valued as at 31 March 1982 and the **index month bought** will be that of March 1982.

> **LEARNING OBJECTIVES**
>
> 10.3.6 Understand the use of 'Bed & ISA or 'Bed & Spouse' maximise use of Capital Gains Tax relief/allowance

Bed & Breakfast was the name given to a process whereby an investor could utilise their annual capital gains tax allowance to offset gains made by their investments. The process involved the investor selling the holding one day and buying it back the next.

Changes in the 1998 Finance Act means that if the same investment is re-acquired by the same person within 30 days of a sale, the purchase, sale and any gain are linked together. This means that the **Bed & Breakfast** option of selling one day and buying back the next no longer a practical way of realising profit or loss for CGT purposes.

However, it is still open to an investor to sell a holding, subscribe the proceeds to an ISA and then for the ISA manager to buy back the holding within the ISA. The investor will have established a loss or gain on the sale which can be used as part of that investor's CGT allowance for that year and will continue to hold the stock albeit through the ISA manager; this process is known as **Bed & ISA**.

If a holding is transferred between husband and wife, any capital gains tax liability is transferred to the spouse with the holding. There is no gain or loss incurred at the point of transfer. Any gain arising on a subsequent sale by the receiving spouse would be calculated by reference to the original cost and any indexation plus any applicable taper relief. The receiving spouse who subsequently sold the holding would be liable for any CGT. Thus, it is possible to maximise the use of CGT allowances of both spouses.

3.6 Inheritance Tax (IHT)

> **LEARNING OBJECTIVES**
>
> 10.3.7 Know the implications of share values for Inheritance Tax purposes for domiciled and non-domiciled holders

Inheritance tax does not affect a CIS itself but, as with any other investment, units/shares in such a scheme will be included as part of an individual's estate for IHT purposes. Any gifts of shares made within seven years of the shareholder's death must also be included in any calculation of IHT liability, although relief may be available.

AFMs/CIS registrars will receive requests from solicitors or relatives dealing with an estate for a valuation for probate purposes and for establishing the inheritance tax liability (if any). For such purposes, the value of any property is the price that the property might reasonably be sold for on the open market. Accordingly, the value placed on shares for such purposes is the manager's quoted price on the date of the holder's death. If the death occurred on a day when no price was published, eg, Saturday, then the last published price, eg, that on the Friday, may be used (Taxation of Chargeable Gains Act 1992, S272(5)).

If the dealing days are infrequent, a special price may be calculated if there is a significant movement in the market value between the days on which prices are normally published. If not, then the last published price is used.

It may be advantageous to use the value of shares at the date of sale, rather than the date of death, for the calculation of the IHT liability. This depends on the assessment carried out within 12 months of the date of death of the sale proceeds of all an estate's qualifying investments. This is likely to apply if, following the date of death, there has been a significant fall in the stock market and the value of the qualifying investments.

In October 2002, HM Revenue & Customs announced that holdings of overseas investors in UK-based CISs would be exempt from inheritance tax. This announcement was part of a package of measures designed to increase the attractiveness of UK-based funds to overseas investors and allow UK fund managers to compete on a more equal footing with their overseas rivals.

4. REPORTING OF INVESTOR INFORMATION TO HMRC

LEARNING OBJECTIVES

10.4.1 Understand the background and purpose of reporting obligations arising under the **Taxes Management Act** and the **EU Savings Directive**

10.4.2 Know the requirements in relation to the following: payments to be reported; reporting dates; paying agents; reportable persons; withholding tax

4.1 Information Reporting Regime

The Chancellor extended information reporting obligations on UK banks and other financial companies with effect from 6 April 2001.

The new reporting regime requires UK CIS operators to report (to HM Revenue & Customs) details of interest distributions paid to UK, and many non-UK, investors. At the same time, they will still be obliged to deduct tax on interest distributions, except where holders are otherwise eligible to receive gross payments.

4.1.1 Why have reporting obligations been extended?

In June 2000, EU member states agreed to a proposal for a directive based on information exchange between tax authorities on interest payments. This was accepted as an alternative to a pan-European withholding tax on interest.

Besides introducing legislation extending information reporting, the UK Chancellor also introduced legislation to allow HM Revenue & Customs to exchange the information reported with overseas tax authorities on a reciprocal basis (Finance Act 2000, Section 146). The stated aim of the extended reporting requirements is to '…help HM Revenue & Customs to co-operate more effectively with tax authorities in other countries to combat international tax evasion and avoidance'. The European Savings Tax Directive requires EU countries to introduce similar legislation to give effect to the information exchange.

4.1.2 What Payments are Reportable?

Only interest distributions need be reported. CISs making dividend distributions and all unauthorised unit trusts (which make annual payments) are unaffected.

Not all interest distributions are reportable. The ones that are reportable are those paid to an individual in the UK or an individual in a fully reportable country (EU countries, UK overseas territories, crown dependencies and certain double tax agreement partners, namely Australia, Canada, Japan, South Korea, New Zealand, Norway and the US). Interest distributions paid to:

- corporate bodies;
- individuals in non-fully reportable countries; and
- ISA investors, do not need to be reported.

4.1.3 When are Notices to make a Return Issued?

CISs need only report information if they receive a notice to do so from HMRC. However, notices are issued as a matter of course. Usually notices will be issued in the January before the end of every tax year. Though, strictly, notices should be served on the trustee of each unit trust and the ACD of each OEIC, to simplify matters HMRC has said it will issue the notices to AFMs, requesting information for all the CISs under their management. The trustee or OEIC will remain responsible for the accuracy of the information.

If a CIS that is issued a notice to make a return fails to do so, a penalty of up to £300 and a further penalty of up to £60 for each day the return is late will be imposed. Incorrect returns completed negligently or fraudulently carry more severe penalties.

4.1.4 What Information must be Reported?

The information required to be reported differs, depending upon whether the interest distribution is paid gross by virtue of a NOR declaration – Form R105(AUT) or R105(OEIC) or meet sother eligibility criteria.

If an investor has filed a NOR declaration the fund must report the:

- name and principal residential address of the individual beneficially entitled to the interest distribution; and
- amount of interest distribution paid.

The address required to be returned will be the registered address which will also be the address on the NOR declaration, but may be another address, for example, a correspondence address known to the AFM.

If an investor has not filed a NOR declaration, the AFM must report the:

- name and address of the individual to whom the interest distribution has been paid;
- amount of interest distribution paid; and
- amount of tax deducted from the payment.

The address required to be returned will be the registered address but, if a different address is held, which is known to be the address of the person to whom the interest is paid, that address should be returned instead. An example is a holding registered in the names of the trustees but on which interest is paid to a beneficiary.

4.1.5 Restricting Returns to Individuals in the UK and Fully Reportable Countries

Only interest distributions paid to individuals in the UK and fully reportable countries need be reported, but AUTs and CISs may choose to return payments made to all individuals. An AFM with IT systems that do not allow easy identification of payments made to individuals in non-fully reportable countries may wish to do this. The AFM will need to consider:

- the ability of their IT systems to identify the relevant individuals;
- data protection considerations.

4.1.6 The EU Directive on the Taxation of Savings and Investment

During 2003 a much broader and far reaching directive was adopted by the EC. The enabling legislation was included by the UK in the Finance Act 2003. The final UK regulations, issued by HM Revenue & Customs, are now implemented. The principal effect of the directive is to create an exchange of information between members of the EU and certain other countries relating to savings income, to ensure that the savings income of individuals is properly taxed.

Some countries, such as Luxembourg, have decided to apply a withholding tax regime rather than exchange information. The tax will increase in stages over several years to give such countries an incentive to apply the exchange of information regime.

The objective of HM Revenue & Customs, therefore, is to collect details of relevant overseas residents who have received savings income payments from UK-based paying agents. The information will be exchanged with tax authorities in other countries who operate under the directive. This builds upon the interest reporting regime introduced by HM Revenue & Customs since April 2001 but is much broader in application, with more funds, products and investors being brought within the scope of the rules.

As a first stage, with effect from 1 January 2004, the directive required paying agents (fund managers for example) to establish the identity and residence for tax purposes of reportable persons. This entailed system changes to accommodate new data and complex additional processing steps when taking new clients on and when administering many changes in the register from this date.

The second stage, for payments made with effect from 1 January 2005, was to produce reports which include the relevant details together with information about any savings income payment to HM Revenue & Customs. The savings income referred to is primarily distribution payments and redemption proceeds from certain unit trusts or OEICs.

Generally, the rule is for a fund with over 15% invested in relevant securities, the paying agent must report savings income paid to reportable persons and, when it has 40% invested in relevant securities, it has to report sale or redemption proceeds. Complex rules exist for calculating the relevant securities percentages.

The rules are covered in more detail below.

Paying Agents

A paying agent is someone who pays savings income to reportable persons. The requirement is that a paying agent identifies reportable persons, identifies savings income payments to them and reports the key information to HMRC. The agent is not required to report payments made to other paying agents such as nominee companies etc.

If there are a number of intermediaries between the originator of the payment and the beneficiary, the paying agent is the last in the chain. For example, ISA payments are included in the reporting requirement. So an investor who has moved abroad, but continues to retain an ISA which they took out while resident in the UK, will be included in the reports to HM Revenue & Customs. In these cases, the units/shares will be held by the ISA manager (either solely or jointly) on behalf of the investor and may be registered in the name of the ISA manager's nominee company; it is the ISA manager who will make a separate report as the paying agent.

Reportable Persons

Reportable persons are called Relevant Payees (RPs) or Residual Entities (REs). RPs are individuals resident outside the UK and in the prescribed territories (see Table 1 in the section on Withholding Tax). Reporting will be based on the details held for these payees as at 1 January 2004 until they create a new contractual relationship with the fund (or paying agent) whereupon all the required data must be obtained.

Paying agents do not have to identify all RPs themselves for non-face-to-face business but they are the responsible party. It is permissible to use certified copies of documents via Independent Financial Advisers (IFAs) etc, subject to some rules covering the certification process similar to the anti-money laundering requirements. Some of the certification requirements may involve investors in additional costs.

Where an apparent RP claims he is not the beneficial owner, he can opt to advise the paying agent (AFM) of the true beneficiary and the paying agent should then report that detail.

If the RP makes a further purchase, or redeems a holding of units/shares, full identification documents and tax residence details for overseas investors will be required. For holdings which were purchased prior to 1 January 2004, any record of identification held on the system will suffice. Where address changes occur to an RP, or to a UK resident moving to a prescribed territory, or to another non-UK location, records have to be updated. The present, simpler standards will apply providing that no change of a contractual nature has occurred after 1 January 2004. Only where a contractual change has occurred after 1 January 2004 will all documentation need to be investigated.

The other reportable person is the Residual Entity (RE). Examples of these are trusts and unincorporated bodies, ie, not legal persons, such as investment clubs which could be deemed to be residual entities by HM Revenue & Customs. Companies, UK partnerships and most taxed business entities are excluded. There is scope for some entities to be registered as UCITS for the purpose of the scheme and detailed rules are available from HMRC. Professional or corporate trustees, if identifiable, do not need to be reported.

As a general rule, HM Revenue & Customs would expect the paying agent to update or complete records where there is reasonable opportunity but accepts there may be reasonable basis for not holding all information at the outset of a contractual relationship.

A complete review and updating of a client register may be needed in the event of a company takeover, merger or restructuring as the new contractual relationship would trigger this. The new register would need to comply with the post 1 January 2004 rules.

A complete review of client records to establish the identities of the paying agents, RPs and REs will need to be undertaken for the first return.

Savings Income

AFMs, as paying agents, will need to apply the limits applicable to trigger savings income reporting. These are 15% of the fund in relevant securities for distributions and for sales (redemptions) the fund has 40% or more of these securities. There are options to declare either the amount of the savings income contained in the payment or the whole amount which is clearly the more practical. Relevant securities are debt claims which include negotiable debt securities such as corporate bonds and gilts. Where the 15% and 40% limits cannot be ascertained it appears the paying agent might be able to report all payments to RPs and REs.

There are two ways to determine the 15% and 40% limits. These are to measure them (without further guidance it seems to be a continuous measurement as sales could occur any day) or to prescribe them in literature such as a trust deed or prospectus, which may not be practicable. The measurement option raises many questions such as at what point the 15% or 40% is established for a distribution or sale proceeds payment and guidance is now available from HMRC. One possible option is to take an annual test and apply it for a 12 month period.

AFMs need to understand the rules for the securities caught by the provisions in order to calculate the limits on their funds. There are some transitional provisions for negotiable debt securities which may be excluded from the limits and may include many of the existing bonds in portfolios. It is feasible that a fund with over 60% in bonds could be paying interest to investors but would not be caught by the 15% or 40% rules due to the exclusion of negotiable debt securities from the calculation. It would, however, be caught by the existing interest reporting return.

Reporting

There is a hierarchy of returns and it will not be necessary to repeat an entry on an interest reporting return if it is already on the Savings Directive scheme return. The return may be made on paper or by magnetic media by 30 June annually.

The basic required data for all new clients (including new parties to joint accounts) will be:

- name;
- address;
- country of residence (established by passport or ID card);
- tax identification number; or
- date and place (town and country) of birth from passport.

For existing contractual relationships as at 1 January 2004 it is only necessary to show the name, address and country of residence as shown on the paying agent's records, along with details of payment etc. Only when the contractual relationship is changed is it necessary to undertake the new identification procedure.

For payments to REs, only the name, address and amount of the payment is required.

Withholding Tax (WHT)

Jersey, Guernsey and the Isle of Man have followed the example of Luxembourg, Belgium and Austria in applying a withholding tax. This is deducted from dividends paid to non-residents. This tax became effective from 1 January 2005 at a rate of 15%, rising to 20% in 2007 and then to 35% from 2010 or until the exchange of information is agreed by all other countries in negotiation with the EC.

One of the provisions of the Savings Directive is that an investor may elect to receive their income without deduction of WHT by producing a tax certificate from their local tax authority. In this case exchange of information, as completed in other EC countries, will take place.

CIS administrators will need to include in their withholding tax systems the following:

> Table 1: The prescribed territories are those prescribed in regulations to which the scheme rules will apply. These will include, for purposes of the scheme:
> - EU member states (other than the UK) (including the accession countries, ie, those scheduled to join);
> - all dependent and associated territories applying the same measures as member states (Jersey, Guernsey, Isle of Man, Anguilla, Montserrat, British Virgin Islands, Turks and Caicos Islands, Cayman Islands, Netherlands, Antilles and Aruba).

For the funds caught by these rules, the accurate application of the 15% and 40% rules is critically important as it triggers the deduction of tax and production of vouchers etc.

> - deduction of tax at the point of distribution;
> - deduction of tax from sale proceeds (the rate of this could involve some complex calculations);
> - production of tax deduction vouchers for investors;
> - accounting for the tax to the local tax authorities;
> - exchange of information returns as specified by the local tax authorities (likely to be largely based on the UK model).

END OF CHAPTER QUESTIONS

Think of an answer for each question and refer to the appropriate section for confirmation.

Question		Answer Reference
1.	On what basis is an authorised CIS taxed?	Section 1.1
2.	How is an authorised CIS's taxable profit determined?	Section 1.3
3.	What administration arrangements are needed for the AFM's periodic charge to be charged to capital?	Section 1.5
4.	What sort of tax can be relieved under Double Taxation Agreements?	Section 2
5.	What CGT liabilities can an authorised CIS incur?	Section 2.1
6.	Why are many CISs not registered for VAT?	Section 2.2
7.	What is the difference between stamp duty and stamp duty reserve tax?	Section 2.3
8.	Briefly describe the situations in which stamp duty arises.	Section 2.3
9.	What is the tax position of UK unit/shareholders in respect of: a) dividend distributions? b) interest distributions?	Sections 3.1, 3.2
10.	What type of distribution can be paid gross to non-resident investors and how is this achieved?	Section 3.4
11.	How is a shareholder's CGT liability calculated on a disposal of income shares?	Section 3.5
12.	Why have the reporting obligations on banks, CISs and other financial companies regarding interest payable been extended?	Section 4.1.1
13.	When are notices issued requesting interest payments be reported?	Section 4.1.3
14.	What penalties may be enforced against an AFM for failing to make a return of interest paid to the tax authorities?	Section 4.1.3
15.	What may an investor do to avoid a withholding tax being made on the amount paid to them from a CIS?	Section 4.1.6

Chapter 10
TAXATION OF
COLLECTIVE
INVESTMENT SCHEMES

GLOSSARY

Accumulation Units/Shares
Units/shares where net income is automatically reinvested and is reflected in the price of the units/shares. The unit/shareholder benefits from not having to pay an initial charge on the reinvested income.

Alternative Investment Market (AIM)
The successor to the unlisted securities market. A market open to companies which do not fulfil the requirements of the Stock Exchange for a full quotation. The companies listed on AIM are often small and developing with little track record.

Annual Management Charge
A charge usually in the order of 0.75% to 1.75% of the value of the fund levied for the management of the collective investment scheme.

Authorised Corporate Director (ACD)
A body corporate and an authorised person given powers and duties under Open-Ended Investment Companies Regulations 2001 to operate an OEIC.

Authorised Fund Manager (AFM)
A firm authorised and regulated by the FSA, eg, for the provision of fund management services and the operation of collective investment schemes.

Authorised Unit Trust (AUT)
A unit trust scheme authorised by the Financial Services Authority. Authorised unit trusts can be offered for sale to the general public.

Back-to-back Borrowing
A method of hedging foreign exchange risk if, for example, a CIS's base currency is sterling and the investments are based on a foreign currency.

Bear
A person who sells shares he or she does not hold in the hope of buying them back at a lower price. The term describes someone who thinks a price will fall. A bear market is one where prices are under the primary influence of sellers.

Bearer Shares
Units or shares which transfer by hand without the need for registration of the change of ownership.

Bed & ISA
The selling of an investment to create a loss or gain for capital gains tax purposes and then using the cash proceeds to subscribe to an ISA and repurchase the investment within the ISA wrapper.

Bed & Spouse
A bed and breakfast type transaction where one spouse sells an investment establishing a gain or loss for capital gains tax purposes and the other purchases the same investment back in their name. Transfers of investments between spouses is also common in order to maximise the use of capital gains tax allowances of both spouses.

Bid/Offer Spread
The difference between the bid and offer prices, expressed as a percentage of the offer price of units in a unit trust.

Bid Price
The price paid to unit holders redeeming their units in a unit trust. In the case of large deals a lower price may be payable.

Blue Chip
Originally an American expression to denote the shares of companies which are well established, usually large and highly regarded.

Book/Box
The stock of units/shares owned by an manager of a CIS acting as principal. Incoming investors buy their units/shares from the manager. If the manager acts only as agent in the issue of units/shares, then units/shares are transferred directly into the unit/shareholder's name (ie, not from the manager). The box allows the manager to avoid unnecessary creation and cancellation of units/shares by taking in units/shares from holders who wish to redeem and resell them to new investors.

Bull
Someone who expects a share/unit price will rise. A bull market is one which is primarily influenced by buyers.

Business Day
Any day other than a Saturday, Sunday, Christmas Day, Good Friday or a bank holiday under the Banking and Financial Dealings Act 1971.

Cancellation Rights
Under the FSA's Conduct of Business Rules, Section 6 there are certain circumstances under which an investor has the right to cancel a purchase of units or shares, but cancellation rights only apply if the investment was made through an independent financial adviser, or after receiving advice from a company representative of the fund manager. They are not available for execution-only transactions or if terms of business with the IFA exclude cancellation rights.

Capital Gains Tax (CGT)
Capital gains tax is payable by the individual taxpayer at the rate equivalent to the taxpayer's highest rate of tax on gains (£9,200 for 2007/2008 and £9,600 for 2008/2009) arising from the sale of securities.

Collective Investment Schemes (CIS)
A generic term encompassing authorised unit trusts, common investment funds, CISs and investment trust companies.

Collective Investment Scheme Sourcebook (COLL)
Part of the FSA handbook covering those rules relating to the operation of collective investment schemes such as unit trusts and open-ended investment companies.

Commission
A fee usually paid out of charges in addition to the price of units or shares. It is payable to the third party – a stockbroker or independent financial adviser. Normally 3%. Also paid by ACDs to stockbrokers on share purchases, eg, 0.25% for UK deals (see also *Renewal Commission*).

Conduct of Business Rules Sourcebook
Part of the FSA handbook covering those rules relating to the conduct of business by companies authorised by the FSA to conduct investment and other business under the Financial Services and Markets Act.

Contract Note
A document sent to the investor on a purchase or sale being made, detailing the price at which the units or shares were bought or redeemed.

Conversion Factor
Income units/shares and accumulation units/shares are linked by a conversion factor so from day to day the two types of unit/share will always move in line. Each time the income units/shares are quoted XD the conversion factor is adjusted, so there will be a proportionate difference between the two types of unit/share. The conversion factor tells you that each accumulation unit/share is the equivalent of that number of income units/shares. The factor is calculated to five significant figures.

Conversion Notice
Notice given by a unit/shareholder in a CIS to the AFM to convert from a holding of one type of share to another. Charges may be made for such conversions.

CREST
Computerised system for the transfer of uncertificated shares on the Stock Exchange.

Cum Distribution
Units or OEIC shares are assumed to be cum distribution (ie, the buyer is entitled to the next income distribution and the seller is not) unless they are expressly stated to be ex-distribution.

Dematerialisation
A term used to describe the process of ceasing to issue unit or share certificates to investors.

De Minimus
Below the level to be taken into account, eg, where the amount available for distribution to unit/shareholders in a CIS is below the minimum laid down by scheme regulations.

Depositary
A body corporate such as a bank or insurance company designated as an authorised person to whom property of a UK CIS is entrusted. Broadly similar to a trustee of a unit trust.

Derivative
Financial instrument whose value is dependent upon the value of an underlying asset. These options and futures are derivatives as they are a spin-off from shares, bonds etc.

Dilution Adjustment
An adjustment made by the AFM where a single pricing method of valuation of a CIS is in operation. It is used to compensate the value of the fund which otherwise would fall in respect of large sales. The AFM determines the expected net effect of the dealing activity during the day and establishes an approximate cost of underlying transactions. The single price is then adjusted and the quote price is calculated to reflect the dilution adjustment.

Dilution Levy
An AFM may be permitted to require payment of a dilution levy because of reduction in the value of CIS property as a result of costs incurred in dealing in investments and any spread between buying and selling prices of such investments.

Distributor Status
Where an offshore fund that has been certified by HM Revenue & Customs (HMRC) as a distributing fund for UK tax purposes pursuant to ICTA 1988 and, therefore, all capital gains made by those residents for tax purposes in the UK are not subject to income tax as at the date of realisation.

Distribution/Dividend Warrant
A warrant is similar to a cheque and is used as a method for paying income to unit/shareholders.

Dual-Pricing
Method historically used for pricing unit trusts (but not OEICs). Bid and offer prices are established whereby the manager will purchase units from a holder at a bid price and sell at the offer price. There are therefore two prices reached after valuation. Dual-pricing is not generally found in overseas investment markets.

Earnings
This is a company's net profit after tax, less minority interest and preference dividends. In other words, it is the profit available for equity holders.

Electronic Message Exchange (EMX)
Service for fund managers and IFAs to allow the ability to trade electronically and to exchange information about investments.

Electronic Trading
Effecting transactions, buying and selling, via an electronic system such as the electronic messaging exchange (EMX).

Eligible Market
A securities market in which a unit trust or a CIS can invest, either within the EU on which transferable securities are traded or any other market agreed between the manager and the trustee/depositary as eligible because it meets certain criteria, eg, adequate liquidity.

European Currency Unit (ECU)
A former unit of currency made up of a basket of EU currencies and used for the settlement of transactions by EU central banks. Such settlements are now made in euros, the single currency used by many of the EU member states.

Ex-Distribution (XD)
Ex-distribution means that the seller is entitled to the next distribution and the buyer is not.

Ex-Distribution Price
A price which entitles a seller of units/shares to the next income payment but which precludes the buyer from it. A unit trust or a CIS with an ex-distribution price is denoted in the financial press by XD. If XD is not quoted on the contract note it is assumed it is cum-div and they will receive the distribution. Such notation will not appear on accumulation unit/share contracts.

Exit Charge
With effect from 1 November 1994, under revised FSA regulations, unit trust managers and consequently AFMs of CISs have been given the option to levy a charge on redemption of units/shares in place of or in combination with their initial charge. This charge is referred to as an exit charge.

Fair Value Pricing (FVP)
Fair value pricing involves the use of a fund manager's estimate of the value of a security at a valuation point to produce a fairer net asset value. This is proposed by the FSA as a method for producing a fairer valuation where a market on which a security is traded is closed.

Financial Ombudsman Service (FOS)
Deals with complaints arising from investments. Previously there were multiple ombudsmen depending on how investments were purchased. Now all complaints are dealt with by the Service.

Financial Promotions

Financial adverts and other promotional material covered by the FSA's financial promotions rules, such as:

- Adverts in newspapers and magazines (including leaflet inserts).
- Product brochures, leaflets and other sales literature.
- Direct mail shots.
- Posters.
- TV and radio adverts.
- Promotional emails and text messages.
- Adverts on websites, including product providers' own sites.

Financial Services Authority (FSA)

The FSA, formerly the Securities and Investments Board (SIB), is an agency designated by HM Treasury and funded by the financial services industry to oversee the system of self-regulation. The website address is www.fsa.gov.uk

Forward Pricing

A system of pricing where investors deal blind, ie, the price of the units/shares at which they sell or buy is determined on the next valuation of the fund.

Franked Income

Dividends from UK companies are paid after the company has paid corporation tax. This income is referred to as 'franked' and is not subject to further corporation tax in the hands of the unit trust/CIS.

Fund Supermarkets

Intermediary type companies which offer to investors and IFAs a wide range of funds, often from a large number of fund management groups. The benefit to the investor is that they can have all their holdings in one place and receive just one statement. (See also *Platforms*).

Futures and Options Association (FOA)

The FOA is an industry association for firms and institutions carrying on business in futures, options and other derivatives.

Gearing

The relationship between borrowing and capital. High gearing means that prior charges are large in relation to the rights of shares. Low gearing means the reverse.

Hedging

The process of protecting CIS's assets from the effects of exposure to currency fluctuations or other investment risks. This may be done using back-to-back loans (ie, borrowing a foreign currency against a sterling deposit) or, with certain restrictions, forward currency transactions or the use of derivatives such as futures and options.

Historic Pricing
A system of pricing where dealing prices are based on the most recent valuation of the fund.

ISA
A tax-favoured scheme introduced by the Labour government from 6 April 1999. ISAs have taken the place of personal equity plans (PEPs). There are now two types of ISA – cash and stocks, and shares. The maximum amount that may be invested in the tax year is £7,200.

Income Units/Shares Income Allocation Dates
Investors holding such units/shares are entitled to receive regular income payments. The payments are usually made twice a year, but can be quarterly or monthly.

Indexation Relief
The adjustment made to reflect inflation when calculating a capital gain for tax purposes.

Initial Charge
A charge levied on investors when first investing in a unit trust/OEIC. The charge, which is typically levied at 5%, is calculated as a percentage of the price and is additional to the price paid for the units/shares.

Initial Offer Price
The price at which units/shares are available to the public in a new CIS for a limited period which may not exceed 21 days.

Initial Yield
An estimated figure which indicates how much income a new unit trust/CIS buyer might expect to receive in the first year of his investment. This is not the only basis of preparing an estimate. Estimated gross yield is calculated before allowing for tax credit amounts.

Investment Company with Variable Capital (ICVC)
An ICVC is more commonly known as an open-ended investment company (OEIC).

Investment Management Association (IMA)
Following the merger of the Fund Managers Association with AUTIF, the new trade body representing the industry has been renamed the Investment Management Association (IMA). The website address is www.investmentuk.org.uk

Income Share
Income shareholders in an investment trust company have the right to:

1. all the income received from the underlying portfolio and distributed as dividends and

2. a fixed repayment of capital when the company is wound up.

In Specie Dealings
An ACD can arrange for the issue of shares in return for certain investments, and this, for example, would be a method of converting an investment trust into a CIS. Similarly, the AFM can agree with a

shareholder for shares to be redeemed by way of a transfer of a suitable proportion of the CIS's portfolio of equal value.

Instrument of Incorporation
Legal document which sets out the constitution and internal regulations of an OEIC. Broadly similar to a Companies Act company's Memorandum and Articles of Association.

Interim Accounting Period
One or more periods ending on dates prior to the end of a CIS's annual accounting period in respect of which interim distributions of income are paid.

Investment Trust
An investment trust is simply a listed public company whose business it is to hold and manage a portfolio of investments. The shares are dealt on the Stock Exchange at prices which depend upon supply and demand and which are not necessarily related to the value of the company's assets. 85% of its income must be distributed.

Key Facts/Key Features Document (KFD)
A document drawn up for all potential investors containing essential information about CIS to enable them to determine whether they should invest and what their rights are.

Liquidity
The part of CIS portfolio which is held in cash or near-cash. This may include some gilt-edged securities and certificates of deposit.

Market Capitalisation
The total value of a listed company's issued securities at their current stock market prices. This figure should include all the different types of security issued by the company, but is often used in relationship to the equity market capitalisation.

Markets in Financial Instruments Directive (MiFID)
Establishes a set of EU rules on the information that must be supplied to consumers when financial services are sold at a distance, eg, via the internet, and sets minimum periods of withdrawal from distance contracts. MiFID was implemented in November 2007 and took the place of the Investment Services Directive.

Mixed Funds
Funds which may invest in a wide range of transferable securities and certain other investments. This provides greater flexibility to fund managers by allowing different security types to be mixed in the same CIS.

Money Market Fund
An unit trust/CIS which invests in deposits and other money market instruments, eg, Treasury Bills.

Near Cash
Assets which may be converted into cash very quickly, eg, Treasury Bills and Certificates of Deposit.

Net Asset Value (NAV)
This is the value of the underlying shares held in the portfolio based on quoted mid-market prices, together with other assets, less liabilities, divided by the number of shares in issue. NAV is quoted in pence per unit/share.

Nominal (or Par) Value
The face value of a share as against its market value. For example, a company may have an issued capital of £10m, divided into 40 million shares of 25p. Par values may be of any amount. They have no real significance, being purely a matter of law and book keeping.

Nominee
This usually refers to a legal entity which holds shares on behalf of others. It can be a method of concealing the beneficial owner.

No Par Value Shares
Shares are issued by companies with a nominal, par or face value of say 10p, 50p etc. This is to comply with legal regulations. This causes confusion in some minds because when those shares are issued they are usually offered for sale at a price higher than par value than the 10p, 50p. Many overseas companies and CISs do not have to comply with such regulations.

Notified Point
Regular point chosen by the AFM of a CIS, by which a decision is made to issue or cancel units/shares. An authorised fund manager should agree a period of time with the depositary during which it will give instructions to issue or cancel units. Where the authorised fund manager operates a box with the principal aim of making a profit, this period will be short (for example, two hours); otherwise a longer period (for example, up to the next valuation point but in all cases within 24 hours) may be acceptable, provided the principles in (2) are followed. Under the COLL sourcebook the AFM has flexibility to agree the period for notification with the trustee/depositary.

Non-Certified Shares
Shares for which no certificate is issued to the unit/shareholder.

Off-The-Page Advertisement
Advertisements which appear in the press and which contain application forms for purchasing shares. If used, the investor does not have rights to cancel the investment.

Open-Ended Investment Companies (OEICs)
Open-Ended Investment Companies (pronounced 'oiks'), which is a body corporate established for collective investment purposes.

Operational Risk Management

The management of risk which is defined as the risk of loss resulting from inadequate or failed internal processes, people and systems or from external events. Such risks arise from failures in corporate governance, IT, outsourcing and business continuity etc.

Paying Agent

As indicated under the European Savings and Investment Directive, it is the person or firm which makes payment of any distribution of income or the proceeds of redemption to the owner or beneficial owner of the relevant units or shares. It is the paying agent who reports to the tax authorities information to be exchanged with other EU tax authorities or deducts withholding tax.

Personal Equity Plan (PEP)

An investment plan managed by a plan manager, approved by HMRC, and managed in accordance with PEP regulations. Any gain from a PEP does not attract capital gains tax and interest income, after reclaiming the tax from HMRC, is paid gross. No new subscriptions have been permitted in PEPs since 6 April 1999, though existing PEPs opened before that date can continue. (See *ISAs*).

Periodic Charge

See *Annual Management Charge*.

Platforms

A term being used to describe firms, like fund supermarkets, who offer a range of suppliers' products such as ISAs, life and pensions products and equities and a single administration service for the investor/IFA. They may also offer various, often online, tools for dealing, valuation and product selection.

Portfolio Turnover Rate (PTR)

The rate at which the assets of the CIS (shares, bonds etc) are bought/sold during any one period.

Pound Cost Averaging

A feature of the regular investment of a fixed sum. Because the fixed sum buys more units/shares when the price is lower and fewer when it is higher, the effect is to make the average price paid for the units/shares bought lower than the average price ruling over the period of saving.

Product and Management Directives

Directives adopted and issued by the European Commission relating to Undertakings for Collective Investment in Transferable Securities (UCITS).

Product Particulars

Factual information about the investment, which must accompany notices of the right to cancel. The purpose is to ensure that the investor knows what he or she is acquiring. Details include the investment objectives, dealing procedures, charges, the yield, dealing spread and the name of the trustee/depositary.

Prospectus
Every CIS is required to have a prospectus. It contains details which investors and professional advisers would reasonably require before making a judgement about the merits of investing in a company.

Qualified Investor Scheme (QIS)
FSA CIS sourcebook (COLL) introduced FSA authorised collective investment schemes for non-retail investors. Such schemes are for sophisticated investors, ie, those with significant knowledge of investment, either private individuals or businesses. They are less heavily regulated than ordinary retail schemes.

Quorum
The minimum number of persons entitled to vote who must be present or represented at a meeting in order for it to transact business. The quorum requirements will be set out in the fund prospectus.

Recognised Investment Exchange (RIE)
An investment exchange in relation to which a recognition order is in force. The Treasury may make regulations setting out requirements which must continue to be complied with. An example of an RIE is the LSE.

Redemption Charge
See *Exit Charge*.

Registrar
The company which maintains the register of shareholders and issues share certificates.

Regular Income Plans
The use of several income-oriented CISs to provide an investor with either a monthly or quarterly income.

Relevant Payees
A term used to describe those individuals resident for tax purposes in EU member states or prescribed territories, such as the Channel Islands, to whom payments are made and in respect of whom information is exchanged between EU tax authorities. Relevant payees include individuals who hold investments in one EU country and are resident for tax purposes in another.

Renewal Commission
A fee (typically 0.5%) paid to IFAs, usually on an annual basis, out of the ACD's charge. It is paid on funds which remain in the CIS. The purpose is to encourage long-term investment and remunerate the IFA for servicing the client. Also known as 'trail commission'.

Renunciation Form
The form which may appear on the back of a unit/share certificate or may be separate and which the holder(s) sign(s) when selling units/shares back to the Manager/ACDs. The form is the formal transfer of legal title to the Manager/ACDs of the units/shares being redeemed.

Reportable Persons
Persons whose details and transactions (distributions of income and capital repayments) are reported to HM Revenue & Customs under the Savings Directive.

Residual Entities
A term used under the EU Savings and Investment Directive to describe those non-legal entities, such as a trust, who may themselves be paying agents (see *Paying Agent*).

Rights Issue
An issue of new shares to existing shareholders in a fixed proportion to their holdings, usually at a price which is below the current stock market price of existing shares. Does not apply to CISs.

Savings Plan
Schemes run by CISs enabling investors to purchase units/shares conveniently on a regular, usually monthly, basis. Similar schemes are offered by some investment trusts.

Scrip Issue
A scrip issue is an issue of shares to existing shareholders in a set proportion to their existing shareholding, eg, a 1 for 10 scrip issue gives a shareholder one free share for each ten held. In reality, merely an adjustment to the number of shares, not to their total value.

Securities and Investments Board (SIB)
The former name of the Financial Services Authority.

Share Exchange Schemes
A scheme run by a CIS enabling investors to exchange existing equity holdings for shares in a CIS.

Share Yield
The share yield is a percentage of the quoted price of shares in a CIS, representing the prospective annual income of the CIS for its current annual accounting period, after deduction of all charges. The yield is expressed gross of tax.

Simplified Prospectus (SP)
Designed to provide investors with key information about a UCITS fund. AFMs may use their discretion to produce and issue a simplified prospectus to prospective investors instead of key features documents.

Single Pricing
Pricing system widely used outside the UK, where CISs quote only one price instead of a bid and an offer price. A sales charge is usually added when units are purchased. OEICs always use single pricing of units/shares.

Soft Commissions
Commissions for financial services paid in kind rather than in cash, eg, provision of research free of charge.

Statement of Recommended Practice (SORP)

A SORP provides standards for the preparation of accounts. A new SORP covering both unit trusts and OEICs has been issued by the Investment Management Association (IMA).

Sub-division of Units/Shares

If the price of units/shares increases substantially over a period, the Manager/ACD may split the units/shares in the ratio of, for example, 4 for 1. The net result is a five-fold increase in the number of units/shares and a reduction in the price per unit/share by a factor of 5.

Subordinated Loan

A loan which is junior in claim on assets to other debt, ie, repayable only after other debts with a higher claim have been satisfied.

Tax Credit

Dividend distributions, whether paid or reinvested, are treated as the top slice of income and carry a tax credit of 10%. A tax credit voucher is usually issued half-yearly. Investors liable to tax at the basic rate or lower rate band will have no further liability to tax. Higher rate taxpayers will have a further liability to tax. The tax credit is only reclaimable if the income arises within an ISA, however, this tax benefit ceased on 5 April 2004.

Trail Commission

Commission usually paid annually for introducing IFAs to encourage long-term investment. Also referred to as 'renewal commission'.

Trust Deed

An instrument in writing by which a unit trust scheme is normally constituted.

Trustee

An institution, such as a bank or insurance company, which acts as custodian of a unit trust fund's assets on behalf of unit holders and watches their interests generally. Broadly similar to a depositary in a CIS.

Ultra Vires

Beyond the powers of.

Umbrella Funds

A single authorised CIS with any number of constituent parts, providing the opportunity for unitholders/shareholders to switch all or part of their investment from one part to another. Each part may have an entirely separate portfolio.

Unfranked Investment Income
Income from overseas units/shares, government securities and bank deposits which unlike UK share dividends, has not already borne UK corporation tax and is called 'unfranked' and is subject to corporation tax in the hands of the CIS. CISs investing only in gilt-edged securities, local authority stocks and other fixed interest securities are exempt from paying corporation tax and are liable instead to the basic rate of income tax on the income from these investments.

UCITS
A European directive governing Undertakings for Collective Investment in Transferable Securities. It is designed to harmonise the operation of collective investment schemes which includes authorised unit trusts throughout the EU, with a view to facilitating the sale of funds in other member states.

Warrant
An equity warrant offers the holder the right to buy the underlying equity at a predetermined price on specified dates, or at any time, up to the end of a predetermined time period. A warrant differs from an option in that options usually have a life of less than one year. Warrants are usually issued by companies or by securities houses and have a life span of more than one year. The exercise of a company-issued warrant will result in an increase of the capital of that company. (See also *Distribution/Dividend Warrant*).

Withholding Tax (WHT)
Tax deducted from dividends paid by foreign companies to non-residents. 15% is a common figure.

ABBREVIATIONS

ABI	Association of British Insurers
ACD	Authorised Corporate Director
ACT	Advance Corporation Tax
AFM	Authorised Fund Manager
AGM	Annual General Meeting
AUT	Authorised Unit Trust
AUTIF	Association of Unit Trust and Investment Funds
BACS	Bankers' Automated Clearing Service
BACSTEL	Bankers' Automated Clearing Service Telecommunications Link
CAD	Capital Adequacy Directive
CC	Competition Commission
CCSS	CREST Courier and Sorting Services
CGT	Capital Gains Tax
CIS	Collective Investment Scheme
COLL	Collective Investment Scheme Sourcebook
DATA	Depositary and Trustee Association
DBV	Delivery by Value
DMD	Distance Marketing Directive
DPA, 1998	Data Protection Act, 1998
DTA	Double Taxation Agreements
DTI	Department of Trade and Industry
DTR	Double Taxation Relief
EC	European Community
ECU	European Currency Unit
EEA	European Economic Area
EGM	Extraordinary General Meeting
EMX	Electronic Message Exchange
EPM	Efficient Portfolio Management
EU	European Union
FII	Franked Investment Income
FOA	Futures and Options Association
FOFs	Futures and Options Funds

FOS	Financial Ombudsman Service
FSA	Financial Services Authority
FSA.IPRU (INV)	FSA's Interim Prudential Sourcebook (Investment)
FSACOBR	Financial Services Authority Conduct of Business Rules
FSCS	Financial Services Compensation Scheme Limited
FSMA, 2000	Financial Services & Markets Act, 2000
FVP	Fair Value Pricing
GFOFs	Geared Futures and Options Funds
GOPS	Government and other Public Securities
HMRC	HM Revenue & Customs
IAQ	Investment Administration Qualification
ICTA, 1988	Income and Corporation Taxes Act, 1988
ICVC	Investment Company with Variable Capital
IFA	Independent Financial Advisers
IMA	Investment Management Association
ISA	Individual Savings Account
ISD	Investment Services Directive
IT	Information Technology
ITC	Investment Trust Company
JMLSG	Joint Money Laundering Steering Group
KFD	Key Features Document
LSE	London Stock Exchange
MiFID	Markets in Financial Instruments Directive
MLRO	Money Laundering Reporting Officer
NOR	Not Ordinarily Resident
NURS	Non-UCITS Retail Schemes
OEIC	Open-Ended Investment Company
OFT	Office of Fair Trading
PAIF	Property Authorised Investment Fund
PEP	Personal Equity Plan
PIA	Personal Investment Authority
PTR	Portfolio Turnover Rate
QIS	Qualified Investor Scheme
RE	Residual Entity
RIY	Reduction in Yield

RP	Relevant Persons
RPI	Retail Price Index
SDRT	Stamp Duty Reserve Tax
SIB	Securities and Investments Board
SOCA	Serious Organised Crime Agency
SORP	Statement of Recommended Practice
SP	Simplified Prospectus
SRO	Self-Regulated Organisations
SYSC	Senior Management Arrangements, Systems and Controls
TCGA, 1992	Taxation of Capital Gains Act, 1992
TER	Total Expense Ratio
TPA	Third Party Administration
UCITS	Undertakings for Collective Investments in Transferable Securities
XD	Ex-Dividend

# APPENDIX A

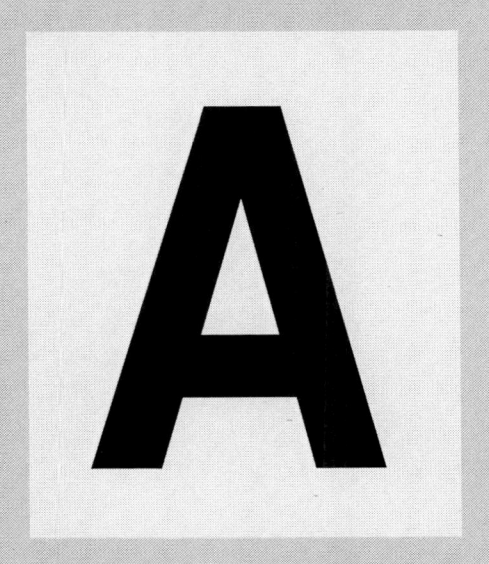

1.	IMA-FUND CATEGORIES/SECTOR CLASSIFICATION	261
2.	NOTICE OF AN EXTRAORDINARY GENERAL MEETING	262
3.	SCHRODERS KEY FEATURES AND APPLICATION FORMS FOR UNIT TRUSTS	263
4.	SCHRODER UK LARGE CAP FUND – FINAL REPORTS AND ACCOUNTS	276
5.	CONTRACT NOTES	298
6.	FORM OF RENUNCIATION AND STOCK TRANSFER FORM	308
7.	INTEREST DISTRIBUTION VOUCHER AND WARRANT (INCOME UNITS)	314
8.	DIVIDEND DISTRIBUTION VOUCHER AND WARRANT (INCOME UNITS)	315
9.	INTEREST DISTRIBUTION VOUCHER (ACCUMULATION UNITS)	316
10.	DIVIDEND DISTRIBUTION VOUCHER (ACCUMULATION SHARES)	317
11.	DISTRIBUTION MANDATE FORM	318
12.	DATA REQUIRED FOR MONTHLY SDRT COMPUTATION	319

Collective Investment Schemes Administration

APPENDIX I

A. Funds Principally Targeting Income

Immediate Income	
UK Gilts	
UK Index Linked Gilts	
High Yield	
UK Corporate Bond	
UK Strategic Bond	
UK Global Bond	
UK Equity & Bond Income	
Growing Income	
UK Equity Income	

B. Funds Principally Targeting Capital

Capital Growth/Total Return	Capital Protection
UK All Companies	Money Market
UK Smaller Companies	Guaranteed/Protected Funds
Japan	
Japanese Smaller Companies	
Asia Pacific including Japan	
Asia Pacific excluding Japan	
North America	
North America Smaller Companies	
Europe including UK	
Europe excluding UK	
European Smaller Companies	
Cautious Managed	
Balanced Managed	
Active Managed	
Global Growth	
Global Emerging Markets	
UK Zeros	

C. Specialist Sectors

Specialist *	
Technology & Telecommunication	
Personal Pensions	
Absolute Return	

*Funds with a single country (other than UK, Japan or US) or a single sector theme.

Collective Investment Schemes Administration

APPENDIX 2

Notice of an Extraordinary General Meeting

XYZ Investment Fund (ICVC)

1 Abbey Buildings, London, EC3X 5NV

NOTICE IS HEREBY GIVEN that an extraordinary general meeting of the above company will be held at 1 Abbey Buildings, London, EC2X 5NV on 30th September 20XX at 2pm.

1. To approve a scheme of amalgamation with ABC Investment Fund, as set out in the circular to holders dated XX September 20XX

    2--- and the reports of the ACD and the auditors.

2. To approve a change in investment objective of the XYZ Investment Fund as set out in the circular to holders.

By order of the ACD   9th September 20XX

B A Smith

for XYZ Investment Funds

Note:

Shareholders of the company entitled to attend and vote are entitled to appoint one or more persons to act as proxies to attend and vote instead of them. A proxy so appointed need not be a shareholder of the company. The form of proxy for use at the meeting must be deposited, together with any power of attorney or authority under which it is signed at the principal office of the company, 1, Abbey Buildings, London, EC2X 5NV not later than 48 hours before the time appointed for the meeting or adjourned meeting. An appropriate form of proxy is enclosed with this report. Shareholders who complete proxy forms will not be precluded from attending the meeting and voting in person if they so wish.

Note:

The above notice assumes there are no other directors in office other than the Authorised Corporate Director.

APPENDIX 3

Example Key Features Document

(NB: AFMs may use a Document which incorporates a simplified Prospectus and Key Features)

Schroders - Key Features for unit trusts

(excluding Multi-Manager Portfolios) May 2005

Schroders' broad and flexible product range gives you the flexibility to invest in a number of different ways, according to your individual circumstances.

This document contains the key features for a **unit trust investment** (outside a tax-efficient ISA wrapper) into Schroders' funds.

To discuss the most suitable fund and the best route for your investments you should speak to an authorised financial adviser. Before you invest you must read the following key features before completing the application form:

Contents

1.0 The Funds

2.0 Information for all investors

3.0 Unit trust investments (outside an ISA)

4.0 Further information for all investors

5.0 Unit trust application form

Note: Statements will be sent twice a year as at 5 April and 5 October

Unit Trust Key Features

Your Investment

A unit trust is a type of fund which allows you to gain exposure to a selection of different underlying shares or other securities. Each fund has a specific aim which determines the types of shares or securities in which it invests.

1.0

The Fund

AIMS OF EACH UNIT TRUST

Schroder Corporate Bond Fund

Aims to achieve a high-level of income from a diversified portfolio of fixed interest securities. It will invest primarily in corporate bonds and convertible bonds issued by UK companies.

Schroder European Fund

Aims to achieve capital growth by investing in European stockmarkets, excluding the UK.

Schroder European Alpha Plus Fund

Aims to achieve capital growth by investing in European companies. The fund may also invest in companies headquartered or quoted outside Europe which have material or critical operations within, or derive significant business from, Europe. Fixed interest securities may also be included in the portfolio.

Schroder European Small Companies Fund

Aims to achieve capital growth by investing in smaller companies listed on European stockmarkets (excluding the UK).

Schroder Far East Fund

Aims to achieve capital growth by investing in the stockmarkets of the Far East and Asia (including Japan).

Schroder Gilt & Fixed Interest Fund

Aims to achieve a high-level of income with the potential for capital growth, from investment in a diversified portfolio of sterling denominated fixed interest securities.

Schroder Global Emerging Markets Fund

Aims to achieve capital growth over the longer term by investing in the world's emerging markets.

Schroder Income Fund

Aims to achieve a growing level of income. It will invest primarily in UK shares which will seek to pay out an above-average income.

Schroder Japan Alpha Plus Fund

Aims to achieve total return primarily through investment in Japanese companies. In order to achieve the objective the manager will invest in a focused portfolio of securities.

Schroder Managed Wealth Portfolio

Aims to provide a total return primarily through investment in collective investment schemes, as well as directly held transferable securities, derivatives, cash, deposits, warrants and money market instruments. The fund may also gain exposure to alternatives, including hedge funds, private equity and property, through investment in transferable securities which themselves invest in these asset classes.

Schroder Medical Discovery Fund

Aims to achieve capital growth by investing in healthcare, medical services and related product companies on a worldwide basis.

Schroder Monthly High Income Fund

Aims to achieve a high level of income from a diversified portfolio of debt securities, including unrated issues and those of non-investment grade.

Schroder Pacific Fund

Aims to achieve capital growth by investing in equities on the stockmarkets of the Asia Pacific ex Japan region.

Schroder Recovery Fund

Aims to achieve capital growth through investing in companies that have suffered a set back in terms of profit or share price, but whether the management and prospects are believed to be good.

Schroder Strategic Bond Fund

Aims to achieve a total return from a diversified portfolio of global debt securities. The full spectrum of available securities including non-investment grade, will be utilised. The portfolio will consist of sterling denominated securities or other securities, hedged back into sterling.

Schroder Tokyo Fund

Aims to achieve capital growth through investing in companies listed on the Japanese stock markets.

Schroder UK Alpha Plus Fund

Aims to provide capital growth through investment in UK and other companies. In order to achieve the objective the manager will invest in a focused portfolio of securities.

Schroder UK Equity Fund

Aims to achieve a high total return, focusing on both capital and income growth. It will invest in companies listed on the UK stockmarket.

Schroder UK Large Cap Fund

Aims to achieve capital growth by investing in companies listed on the FTSE 100 index.

Schroder UK Midi 250 Fund

Aims to achieve capital growth primarily through investing in a smaller than normal number of shares listed in the FTSE 250 ex-investment trusts index.

Schroder UK Select Growth Fund

Aims to achieve capital growth by investing in a smaller than normal number of shares listed on the UK stockmarket.

Schroder UK Smaller Companies Fund

Aims to achieve capital growth by investing in smaller companies which are listed in the UK.

Schroder US Small & Mid Cap Fund

Aims to achieve capital growth and income primarily through investment in equity securities of smaller and medium-sized US companies.

Schroder US Smaller Companies Fund

Aims to achieve capital growth by investing in smaller companies listed on the US and Canadian stockmarkets.

Important Information

Please note that this key features document is not applicable to Schroders Multi-Manager Portfolios. Please read the separate key features before applying.

RISK FACTORS

If you invest in unit trusts you should be aware that there are risks involved.

- Most importantly, you may not get back what you originally invested when you sell. Both your initial capital sum and the income the investment may pay can go down as well as up due to price fluctuations in the financial markets outside Schroders' control.
- You should be aware that the past performance of your investment is not an indicator of its future performance.
- Exchange rate changes may cause the value of overseas investments to rise and fall.
- If you have received investment advice from an authorised financial adviser, you will qualify for cancellation rights. These enable you to cancel your investment within 14 days, however you should be aware that although you will not have to pay the initial charge, you may not get back the amount you invested if the unit price has fallen since you invested.
- If you have not received advice from an authorised financial adviser, you will not qualify for cancellation rights.
- If you choose a fund which invests in assets that are not denominated in sterling, then you should be aware that if sterling appreciates against the currency in which the investments are being made this can have a negative effect on your sterling quoted price.
- If the income received by fund is insufficient to pay management charges, this amount will be deducted from capital, thereby eroding the funds' capital value.
- There is no guarantee that the tax and regulatory characteristics of your investment will not change in the future and, if this were to happen, you could incur taxes or costs that are not paid through Schroders or imposed by it.

RISKS AFFECTING SPECIFIC FUNDS

- Less developed markets are generally less well regulated than the UK, they may be less liquid and may have less reliable custody arrangements. These markets involve a higher than normal degree of risk and thus should be regarded as long-term in nature. Unit trusts that invest in this kind of market are **Schroder Pacific Fund, Schroder Far East Fund** and the **Schroder Global Emerging Markets Fund**.

- A more concentrated portfolio - an average fund will include between 80 and 150 different companies in its portfolio. However, **Schroder European Alpha Plus Fund, Schroder Japan Alpha Plus Fund, Schroder Medical Discovery Fund, Schroder Recovery Fund, Schroder UK Alpha Plus Fund, Schroder UK Select Growth Fund, Schroder UK Large Cap Fund and Schroder UK Mid 250 Fund** all invest in a smaller than usual number of stocks (approximately 50-80) and can invest heavily in specific types of companies or sectors. This stock concentration carries more risk than funds spread across a larger number of companies.

- Smaller companies may be less liquid than larger companies and price swings may therefore be greater than in larger company funds. The following funds all invest in smaller companies: **Schroder UK Smaller Companies Fund, Schroder US Smaller Companies Fund, Schroder US Small & Mid Cap Fund, Schroder European Smaller Companies Fund**.

- Deducting annual charges from capital can result in the income paid by the fund being higher than would otherwise have been the case and the growth in the capital sum being eroded. Unit trusts that deduct part or all of their annual charges from capital are: **Schroder Income Fund, Schroder Monthly High Income Fund, Schroder Strategic Bond Fund, Schroder Corporate Bond Fund and Schroder Gilt & Fixed Interest Fund**.

- The **Schroder Monthly High Income Fund, Schroder Strategic Bond, and the Schroder Corporate Bond Fund** will invest in high-yielding bonds - 'non-investment grade' bonds. The risk of default is higher with 'investment grade' bonds. Higher yielding bonds may also have an increased potential to erode your capital sum than lower yielding bonds.

- **Schroder Gilt & Fixed Interest Fund** - more than 35% of the property of the fund consists, or is likely to consist, of Government securities.

- This is a risk that if the assumed size of new funds is not achieved, the proportion of charges and expenses allocated to the investment may be higher and the value of the investment consequently reduced.

- Concentrated sectors - investments which focus on specific sectors carry more risk than funds spread across a number of different industry sectors. **Schroder Medical Discovery Fund** invests in concentrated sectors.

- When investing n the **Schroder Global Emerging Markets Fund** investors should be aware that these markets have greater price volatility, substantially less liquidity and significantly smaller market capitalisation of their security markets.

- **Schroder Managed Wealth Portfolio, Schroder Recovery and Schroder Strategic Bond Fund** may use increased investment powers available to them under UCITS 3 legislation. These powers, which include the potential to have higher cash holdings and use derivatives as investments rather than for efficient management purposes, may increase volatility of the funds. Further details are available in the fund's prospectus.

2.0

Information for All Investors

The Schroder Unit Trusts Limited Prospectus (retail) (as amended from time to time) sets out the terms and conditions of your investment. The terms and conditions of this document together with the Schroders' application form set out the terms on which Schroders provide services to you in relation to your investment. These items are, and all future communications will be, produced in English and shall be governed in accordance with English law and Schroders and you agree that the English courts will have exclusive jurisdiction in respect of any dispute between you and Schroders. There is no minimum duration to your agreement with Schroders.

The following features apply to investments in unit trusts, please refer to the relevant other sections for specific features of each type of investment.

What is the unit trust initial charge?

The initial unit trust charge is 5.25% for all funds except Schroder Monthly High Income Fund, Schroder Corporate Bond Fund and Schroder Strategic Bond Fund. For these three funds, the initial charge is 3.25%.

What is the annual management charge?

The annual management charge of all funds is 1.50% with the exception of the following funds: Schroder Monthly High Income Fund (1.25%) Schroder Corporate Bond Fund (1%) Schroder Strategic Bond Fund (1%) and Schroder Gilt & Fixed Interest Fund (0.5%). The tables on the following pages show how the charges we take out of your investment can affect what you might get back. They are designed to help you compare our charges with other funds in the industry.

How will I receive my income?

There are two types of units available - income units and accumulation units. If you choose accumulation units the income generated from your investment is not paid directly to you, but is paid into the fund and increases the value of the units. Any tax credit payments received are re-invested to buy additional units on your account. If you choose to invest in income units any income (including tax credit payments received) will be paid into your bank account by Direct Credit. Income arising in respect of income units will be paid out monthly, quarterly or half-yearly depending on the distribution frequency of the relevant unit trust.

If I sell my holdings how quickly will I get my proceeds?

You can instruct Schroders or your financial adviser to sell units in writing, by telephone or by signed fax. We will sell your holdings on the day of receipt of your instructions, provided they are received before the fund's next valuation point. We will then send a cheque for the proceeds to you by the close of business four workings days later, provided we have received a signed confirmation. If (after you have sold your units) you have less than the minimum investment of £1,000 for regular savers we may sell all your remaining units on your behalf. Sales of units will take place at the next selling price determined at the valuation point following the receipt by Schroders of instructions from you. A redemption charge up to a maximum of 1.5% of the value of the units being redeemed may be charged at the manager's discretion. Where you wish to redeem units to the value of £15,000 or more, the manager may elect to deal at the cancellation price.

Money Laundering

The Money Laundering Regulations 2003 (as amended from time-to-time) require us to make checks on various transactions. Independent documentary verification may be required for both the identity and permanent address of the applicant opening an Account. This may also apply to existing account holders. This may also apply to existing account holders. Processing of your instruction or payment due to you may be delayed, pending receipt of satisfactory evidence. Signing of the application form represents permission from you to make any necessary electronic searches of the electoral roll and credit reference agencies. These agencies may keep a record of our enquiry.

Please pay for any lump sum investment by a cheque drawn on your personal (or joint) bank or building society account, as this reduces the need for us to obtain documentary evidence. Where you are investing money using a building society branch cheque or banker's draft, please arrange for them to certify, on the cheque, the name and account number of the client from whose account payment is being drawn, together with the branch stamp.

Stamp Duty Reserve Tax (SDRT)

SDRT is a tax on certain dealings in units of unit trusts. The cost will be recovered directly from the fund itself, however Schroders reserves the right to charge unitholders at the time of dealing in cases of exceptionally large deals (ie, repurchases of at least £100,00). Dealings in units in Schroder Corporate Bond Fund, Schroder Monthly High Income Fund, Schroder Gilt & Fixed Interest Fund and Schroder Strategic Bond Fund are exempt from SDRT.

How did we do our calculations in this document? (Please note this information refers to all Charges and Expense sections.)

We chose our minimum investment amount of £1,000 for all our investments. We then deducted the initial costs represented by the 'spread'. This is the difference between the buying price of units and the price you would get if you sold immediately. If you would like to find out what the most recently quoted spread is, please contact Schroders or your financial adviser. We then assumed that a unit trust outside an ISA investment grows at 6.0% a year. This is a standard growth rate, which will allow you to compare charges with other unit trusts. We also made allowance for the annual charge and administration charges that are deducted from the funds. These include the annual fund management charge plus other expenses such as fees to suppliers including Auditors, Trustees etc. We have shown these charges after tax relief where appropriate. Costs of dealing in the underlying securities are not included.

The effects of charges and expenses are set out in tables within the unit trust, Charges and Expenses section.

3.0

Unit Trust investments (outside an ISA)

Your Schroders Unit Trust (outside a ISA)

To invest in a Schroders Unit Trust you will need a lump sum of at least £1,000. If you wish to top-up your investment you can do so with any amount over £500. As an alternative, you may invest from £50 a month (except for Schroder Managed Wealth Portfolio). You can start and stop investing whenever you like by informing us in writing.

If a holding falls below the minimum holding then the manager reserves the right to redeem the units on behalf of the holder. The manager reserves the right to reduce or waive the minimum investment levels. The manager reserves the right to reject, on reasonable grounds, any application for units in whole or in part, in which event the manager will return by post, any money sent, or the balance, for the purchase of units which are the subject of the application, at the risk of the applicant.

Risk Factors

Please refer to the risk factors listed in section 1.0.

How do I invest?

Complete and return the application form at the end of this booklet or send clear written instructions. Alternatively, telephone 0800 718788 (Dealing) or 0800 718777 (Investor Services). Lump sum and regular savings investments will be invested on the basis of the relevant unit price calculated at the next valuation point following receipt of monies.

If Schroders has purchased income units on your behalf, but is unable to establish your correct banking details in order to pay by BACS credit transfer, Schroders will issue a cheque. Your distributions will then be held in a designated account until contact is made.

You should make your cheque payable to Schroder Unit Trust Limited if you are investing a lump sum. If you are investing on a monthly basis, your Direct Debit will be collected on or around the 10th of each month.

Can I cancel/withdraw my application?

Your unit trust will be opened immediately. You are entitled to a 'cancellation' period of 14 days if you have received advice from an authorised financial adviser. During this time, if you change your mind, simply complete and return the cancellation form (which will be sent to you with your contract note).

Where you are investing through the regular savings option it is also recommended that you instruct your bank to cancel the direct debit. There is no right to cancel after this cancellation period. If you have invested a lump sum, and you exercise your cancellation rights, we will return the amount you have invested or the lower value if the unit price has fallen in the meantime. You may not, therefore, get back the amount you originally invested.

What documentation will I receive?

Shortly after you invest you will receive a confirmation letter and, if applicable, a name slip which should be returned as instructed. It will show the price at which you have bought your units. We do not issue unit certificates so we suggest that you retain the contract note. You will receive a short form Manager's Report and Accounts twice a year giving current details of investments and a commentary from the fund manager. The long form Manager's Report and Accounts is available on request. You will also receive a statement twice a year as at 5 April and 5 October.

What are my tax liabilities?

These depend on your personal circumstances. Lower and basic rate taxpayers will have no income tax liability but they may be liable to capital gains tax when selling units. Higher rate taxpayers must be liable to further tax on income, and for capital gains tax when selling units. Capital gains released within the fund are exempt from capital gains tax.

3.1

Unit Trust charges and expenses
How will charges and expenses affect my investment?

What is the unit trust initial charge?

The initial unit trust charge is 5.25% for all funds except Schroder Monthly High Income Fund, Schroder Corporate Bond Fund and Schroder Strategic Bond Fund. For these three funds, the initial charge is 3.25%.

Investing in a Schroder Unit Trust outside an ISA

Please be aware when you read the following tables that they are designed to demonstrate the impact of charges and expenses on your investment based on the assumptions in section 3.1. These figures will vary depending on the actual return from the funds.

"What you might get back" is not guaranteed, it shows the effect of charges and expenses on an investment of £1,000, assuming growth of 6% a year.

Note: The figures do not allow for any discount that you may receive when you invest.

Schroder Income Fund Initial Costs 5.89%, Annual charge and administration charges 1.61%, Gross income yield 4.14%.

Income Funds

All five income unit trust funds have broadly similar charges. The table below shows Schroder Income Fund as an example. Annual charges and expenses in income funds are deducted from capital. Other expenses are deducted from income (see Risk Factors in section 1.0).

At End of Year	Investment to Date	Income Units			Accumulation Units	
		Effect of Deductions to Date	Income to Date	What you might get back 6.0%	Effect of Deductions to Date	What you might get back 6.0%
	£	£	£	£	£	£
1	1,000	79	31	951	79	983
3		122	95	972	124	1,074
5		171	160	994	179	1,172
10		327	329	1,050	364	1,460

The last line in the table shows that over 10 years the effect of the total charges and expenses could amount to £327 for income units and £364 for accumulation units. Putting it another way, this would have the same effect as bringing investment growth from 6.0% a year down to 3.9% a year for income units and accumulation units.

Other Income Funds

To give you an idea of how the charges and expenses on the other income funds could affect returns, this table outlines the reduction in rates of return from 6.0% a year after taking account of charges.

Effective reduction in investment growth from 6.0% to the following % per annum	Income Units	Accumulation Units
Schroder Corporate Bond Fund	4.6	4.6
Schroder Gilt & Fixed Interest Fund	5.1	5.1
Schroder Monthly High Income Fund	4.4	4.4
Schroder Strategic Bond Fund	4.6	4.6

Capital Growth Funds

All 18 growth unit trust funds have broadly similar charges. The table shows Schroder UK Equity Fund as an example. Annual charges and expenses in capital growth funds are deducted from income. Where there is insufficient to cover expenses, the balance may be taken from capital (see Risk Factors in section 1.0).

Schroder UK Equity Fund

Initial Costs 5.84%, Annual charge and administration charges 1.61%.

At End of Year	Investment to Date £	Effect of Deductions to Date £	Income Reinvested — What you might get back 6.0% £
1	1,000	78	984
3		124	1,074
5		178	1,173
10		364	1,461

The last line in the table shows that over 10 years the effect of total charges and expenses could amount to £364 if you reinvested income. Putting it another way, this would have the same effect as bringing investment growth from 6.0% a year down to 3.9%.

Other Capital Growth Funds

To give you an idea of how the charges and expenses on the other capital growth funds could affect returns, this table outlines the reduction in rates of return from 6.0% a year after taking account of charges.

Effective reduction in investment growth from 6.0% to the following % per annum	%
Schroder European Fund	3.8
Schroder European Alpha Plus Fund	3.6
Schroder European Smaller Companies Fund	3.5
Schroder Far East Fund	3.8
Schroder Global Emerging Markets Fund	3.8
Schroder Japan Alpha Plus Fund	3.9
Schroder Managed Wealth Portfolio	3.9
Schroder Medical Discovery Fund	3.7
Schroder Pacific Fund	3.7
Schroder Recovery Fund	3.9
Schroder Tokyo Fund	4.0
Schroder UK Alpha Plus Fund	3.9
Schroder UK Select Growth Fund	3.7
Schroder UK Large Cap Fund	3.9
Schroder UK Mid 250 Fund	3.9
Schroder UK Smaller Companies Fund	3.7
Schroder UK Small & Mid Cap Fund	3.9
Schroder US Smaller Companies Fund	3.9

All source: Schroders, March 2005

The charges and expenses are correct at the Funds' last reporting period.

4.0

Further information for all investors

How much will any advice cost?

We will only provide you with information about Schroders products and will not offer any advice based on individual circumstances.

If you are in any doubt whether a product is suitable for you, you should consult a financial adviser. In some cases they will receive commission from Schroders. This is taken from our charges and the amount will depend on the size of your investments and the period over which you make or retain them. They will give you details of the amount of commission they will receive as a result of your investment. Where commission is not paid, you may have to pay a fee to your adviser.

Who is the unit trust manager?

Schroder Unit Trusts Limited, 31 Gresham Street, London EC2V 7QA. Schroder Unit Trusts Limited is authorised and regulated by the Financial Services Authority and is entered on the FSA register under register number 197288. The principal business of the manager is the management and administration of collective investment schemes.

Who are the trustees?

JP Morgan Trustee and Depository Company Limited, Chaseside, Bournemouth BH7 7DA.

Who is the administrator?

International Financial Data Services administers your investment on behalf of Schroder Investments Limited.

What is the administration address?

Schroders, PO Box 6100, Basildon SS15 5NJ.

Where can I find the latest prices and yields for my funds?

The buying and selling prices and income yield can be found on the unit trusts prices pages of the Financial Times newspaper, or on the internet at: **www.schroders.co.uk/prices**

What price will I get when I place my deal?

Dealing will be carried out on a forward basis. This means that the price at which you buy units will not be available when you place your deal. Your confirmation letter will show the price at which you have bought your units. The price of units is calculated at a set valuation point on each business day.

Details of valuation points are available from Schroders or your financial adviser. If you place a deal after the valuation point, the price you receive will be the price valued on the following business day. All cash received will, pending investment, be credited to a non-interest bearing client money account. Where you wish to redeem units to the value of £15,000 or more, the manager may elect to deal at the cancellation price.

What happens if Schroders is unable to contact me?

If a client fails to make contact with Schroders for a period of six years, Schroders reserves to right to retain the proceeds of any individual cash balances that remain unclaimed. We will make all reasonable attempts to contact the client including writing to them at their last known address and ensuring that there have been no further transactions on their account during this time. Please note that if at any time the client resumes contact with Schroders, Schroders will repay all amounts owing.

Who can I complain to if I am not satisfied with the service I receive?

You can write to the Head of Investor Services, Schroders, PO Box 6100, Basildon SS15 5NJ. If Schroders fails to resolve your complaint satisfactorily you also have the right to refer the complaint to the Financial Ombudsman Service, South Quay Plaza, 193 Marsh Wall, London E14 9SR. You can also request a copy of the Plan Manager's written internal complaints procedures by writing to the above address or contacting Schroders Investor Services on 0800 718777.

In the event of Schroders being unable to meet its liabilities, you may be entitled to compensation under the Financial Services Compensation Scheme. Currently, the maximum level of compensation you can receive from the Scheme for a claim against an investment firm is £48,000 (100% of £30,000 and 90% of the next £20,000) per person. For further information on the scheme you can contact the Financial Services Authority, or the Financial Services Compensation Scheme or visit www.fscs.org.uk

APPENDIX 4

Schroders UK Alpha Plus Fund

Final Reports and Accounts May 2007

Investment Objective and Policy
Schroder UK Alpha Plus Fund

The Fund's investment objective is to aim to achieve capital growth through investing in UK and other companies. In order to achieve the objective the manager will invest in a focussed portfolio of securities.

The emphasis of the Fund will be investment in UK companies. The Fund may also invest in companies headquartered or quoted outside the UK where those companies have material or critical operations within, or derive significant business from, the UK. Fixed interest securities may be included in the portfolio.

Investment will be in directly held transferable securities. The Fund may also invest in collective investment schemes, warrants and money market instruments.

Financial highlights

Selling price	1.6.07	1.6.06	% change
A Income units	107.90pxd	87.92pxd	22.73
A Accumulation units	115.10p	92.65p	24.23
	31.7.07	31.7.06	
Final distribution per A Income unit	1.3185p	0.7095p	

Fund information

Launch date	24 June 2002	
Launch price	50.00p per A Income unit 50.00p per A Accumulation unit	
Accounting dates	Interim	Final
	30 November	31 May
Income allocation date		Final
		31 July

Total expense ratio

	For the year to 31.5.07	For the year to 31.5.06
A Income units	1.65% #	1.65%
A Accumulation units	1.65% #	1.65%

The Total expense ratio includes VAT recoverable on registrar's fees (registrar's fees now form part of administration charges).

Richard Buxton
Fund Manager

Richard Buxton graduated from Oxford University where he read English. His investment career spans twenty-one years and has seen him work at Brown Shipley Asset Management and Baring Asset Management. Richard join Schroders in 2001 and, as well as managing Schroder UK Alpha Plus Fund, is also Head of UK Equities.

Investment Review

From 1 June 2006 to 1 June 2007 the price a A Income units on a selling price to selling price basis rose 22.73% in comparison with an increase of 18.39% in the FTSE All Share Index (Source: Thomson Financial Datastream).

UK share prices have now risen strongly for over four years, driven by a favourable combination of strong company profits, takeover activity and a healthy global economy. Investor confidence has remained high in this environment and, as a result, the FTSE All Share Index has surged to a level not seen before. Against this background of strong returns, the Schroder UK Alpha Plus Fund has continued to perform well. Over the period in question, the Fund posted returns that were markedly ahead of the broader UK stockmarket. This performance has also enhanced the Fund's impressive long-term track record, which places it among the top performing funds in its sector since its launch in July 2002.

The Fund's success stems from our focus on high quality companies whose long-term prospects seem to have been overlooked or misunderstood by investors. Stockmarkets tend to act somewhat irrationally, with share prices often driven by short-term sentiment rather than a realistic assessment of a company's strengths or long-term potential. However, by taking a longer-term view, it is possible to identify companies with healthy balance sheets, successful business models and excellent prospects that are not yet being fully appreciated by the market. Strong returns can then be generated when investors finally come to recognise these long-term strengths.

> Please remember that past performance is not a guide to future performance and it might not be repeated. The value of investments and the income from them may go down as well as up and investors may not get back the amount originally invested. Because of this, you are not certain to make a profit on your investments and you may lose money.

Over the past year, we have seen a wide range of companies within the portfolio being well rewarded by the market. Among these were holdings like retailer Alliance Boots, whose attractive long-term growth prospects led to a takeover earlier this year. Shares in the company rose over 60% during the period as a result. Engineering components specialist Invensys has also been a strong performer since we purchased a stake in February. The shares have since risen over 30% following clear evidence of the company's continued recovery - having previously taken on too much debt, Invensys has now announced its first annual profit for six years.

We are still finding a wide range of attractive opportunities in the UK. On this basis, we feel the range or profitable, well-run companies held in the portfolio will continue to provide strong support to fund performance in the medium to longer term.

21 June 2007

Net Asset Value and Comparative Tables

Schroder UK Alpha Plus Fund
Unit price range

Year to 31 Dec	A Income Units		A Accumulation units	
	Highest buying	Lowest buying	Highest buying	Lowest buying
	p	p	p	p
2002	53.98	41.42	53.98	41.42
2003	63.39	39.52	64.42	39.52
2004	68.90	55.91	70.39	57.37
2005	84.69	61.54	88.54	63.93
2006	103.30	80.71	108.80	84.38
2007 to 31 May	115.90	94.38	122.10	99.46

Net Income

Year to 31 Dec	A Income units Pence per unit	A Accumulation units Pence per unit
2002	Nil	Nil
2003	1.1175	1.1228
2004	1.0177	1.0439
2005	0.4107	0.4266
2006	0.7095	0.7417
2007 to 31 May	1.3185	1.3894

New asset value

As at 31 may	Net asset value £000's	Net asset value per unit p	Number of units in issue*
2005	441,941	64.46	685,610,947
2006			
A Income units	429,817	88.26	486,987,598
A Accumulation units	246,707	92.26	265,257,780
2007			
A Income units	668,689	107.86	619,959,740
A Accumulation units	565,058	115.04	491,187,235

* including notional units for income reinvested where applicable.

Please remember that past performance is not a guide to future performance and it might not be repeated. The value of investments and the income from them may go down as well as up and investors may not get back the amount originally invested. Because of this, you are not certain to make a profit on your investments and you may lose money. The Fund may invest in assets which are not denominated in sterling. Exchange rate changes may cause the value of these overseas investments to rise or fall. The Fund invests in a small number of stocks and can invest heavily in specific types of companies, sectors or regions. This stock concentration carries more risk than funds spread across a large number of companies. For these reasons, the purchase of units should not normally be regarded as a short term investment.

The Financial Services Authority's Collective Investment Schemes sourcebook (COLL) requires the Manager to prepare accounts for each annual and half yearly accounting period, in accordance with United Kingdom Generally Accepted Accounting Practice, which give a true and fair view of the financial position of the Fund and of its net income/expenditure and the net gains/losses on the property of the Fund for the year. In preparing the accounts the Manager is required to:

- select suitable accounting policies and then apply them consistently;
- comply with the disclosure requirements of the Statement of Recommended Practice for Authorised Funds issued by the IMA in December 2005;
- follow generally accepted accounting principles and applicable accounting standards;
- prepare the accounts on the basis that the Fund will continue in operation unless it is in appropriate to do so;
- keep proper accounting records which enable it to demonstrate that the accounts as prepared comply with the above requirements.

The Manager is responsible for the management of the Fund in accordance with its Trust Deed, the Prospectus and the COLL and for taking reasonable steps for the prevention and detection of fraud, error and non-compliance with law or regulations.

The Manager's report and accounts for the year ended 31 May 2007 were signed on 13 July 2007 on behalf of the Manager by

H.J. Macey
R.E. Stoakley
Directors

Report of the Trustee

Schroder UK Alpha Plus Fund
Statement of the Trustee's responsibilities in relation to the accounts of the Fund

The trustee is responsible for the safekeeping of all of the property of the Fund (other than tangible moveable property) which is entrusted to it and for the collection of income that arises from that property.

It is the duty of the trustee to take reasonable care to ensure that the Fund is managed by the authorised fund manager in accordance with the Financial Services Authority's Collective Investment Schemes sourcebook (COLL) and the Fund's Trust Deed and the Prospectus, as appropriate, in relation to the pricing of, and dealings in, units in the Fund; the application of income of the Fund; and the investment and borrowing powers of the Fund.

Trustee's Report for the accounting period from 1 June 2006 to 31 May 2007
Schroder UK Alpha Plus Fund (The Fund)

Having carried out such procedures as we consider necessary to discharge our responsibilities as trustee of the Fund, it is our opinion, based on the information available to us and the explanations provided, that in all material respects the authorised fund manager:

(i) has carried out the issue, sale, redemption and cancellation, and calculation of the price of the Fund's units and the application of the Fund's income in accordance with the COLL as appropriate, and, where applicable, the Fund's Trust Deed and Prospectus; and

(ii) has observed the investment and borrowing powers and restrictions applicable to the Fund.

Bournemouth
18 June 2007

J.P. Morgan Trustee and Depositary
Company Limited
Trustee

Report of the Independent Auditors

Schroder UK Alpha Plus Fund

Independent auditors' report to the Unitholders of Schroder UK Alpha Plus Fund (The Fund)

We have audited the accounts of Schroder UK Alpha Plus Fund for the year ended 31 May 2007 which comprise the statement of total return, the statement of change in unitholders' net assets, the portfolio statement, the balance sheet, the summary of material portfolio changes, the related notes and the distribution table. These accounts have been prepared under the accounting policies set out therein.

Respective responsibilities of the Manager and Auditors

The Manager's responsibilities for preparing the annual report and accounts in accordance with applicable law and United Kingdom Accounting Standards (United Kingdom Generally Accepted Accounting Practices) are set out in the Statement of the Manager's Responsibilities.

Our responsibility is to audit the accounts in accordance with relevant legal and regulatory requirements, International Standards on Auditing (UK and Ireland) and the requirements of the Collective Investment Schemes sourcebook. This report, including the opinion, has been prepared for and only the unitholders of the Fund as a body in accordance with paragraph 4.5.12 of the Collective Investments Schemes sourcebook and for no other purpose. We do not, in giving this opinion, accept or assume responsibility for any other purpose or to any other person to whom this report is shown or into whose hands it may come save where expressly agreed by our prior consent in writing.

We report to you our opinion as to whether the accounts give a true and fair view and are properly prepared in accordance with the Statement of Recommended Practice for Authorised Funds issued by the IMA in December 2005, the Collective Investment Schemes sourcebook and the trust deed. We also report to you if, in our opinion, proper accounting records for the Fund have not been kept or if the accounts are not in agreement with those records, and whether the information given in the Manager's Report is consistent with the accounts. In addition, we state whether we have obtained all the information and explanations necessary for the purposes of our audit.

We read the other information contained in the annual report and consider whether it is consistent with the audited accounts. This other information comprises only the Investment Review and the other items set out of pages 1 to 4 and 26. We consider the implications for our report if we become aware of any apparent misstatements or material inconsistencies with the accounts. Our responsibilities do not extend to any other information.

Basis of audit opinion

We conducted our audit in accordance with International Standards on Audit & Accounting policies (UK and Ireland) issued by the Auditing Practices Board. An audit includes examination, on a test basis, of evidence relevant to the amounts and disclosures in the accounts. It also includes an assessment of the significant estimates and judgements made by the Manager in the preparation of the accounts, and of whether the accounting policies are appropriate to the Fund's circumstances, consistently applied and adequately disclosed.

We planned and performed our audit so as to obtain all the information and explanations which we considered necessary in order to provide us with sufficient evidence to give reasonable assurance that the accounts are free from material misstatement, whether caused by fraud or other irregularity or error. In forming our opinion we also evaluated the overall adequacy of the presentation of information in the accounts.

Opinion

In our opinion the accounts :

- give a true and fair view in accordance with United Kingdom Generally Accepted Accounting Practice of the financial position of the Fund at 31 May 2007 and of the net income and the net gains on the property of the Fund for the year end; and

- have been properly prepared in accordance with the Statement of Recommended Practice for Authorised Funds issued by the IMA in December 2005, the Collective Investment Schemes sourcebook and the trust deed.

We have obtained the information and explanations we consider necessary for the purposes of the audit.

In our opinion the information given in the Investment Review and the other items set out on pages 1 to 4 and 26 is consistent with the accounts.

London
13 July 2007

PricewaterhouseCoopers LLP
Chartered Accountants
& Registered Auditors

The accounts are published at www.schroders.co.uk, which is a website maintained by the Manager. The maintenance and integrity of the Schroders website is the responsibility of the Manager; the work carried out by the auditors does not involve consideration of these matters, and accordingly, the auditors accept no responsibility for any changes that may have occurred to the accounts since they were initially presented on the website. Visitors to the website need to be aware that legislation in the United Kingdom governing the preparation and dissemination of the accounts may differ from legislation om their jurisdiction.

Statement of Total Return

Schroder UK Alpha Plus Fund
For the year ended 31 May 2007

	Notes	2007 £000's	2007 £000's	2006 £000's	2006 £000's
Net gains on investments during the year	2		194,440		154,054
Income	3	27,849		14,026	
Expenses	4	(14,950)		(8,991)	
Net income before taxation		12,899		5,035	
Taxation	5	(65)		(45)	
Net income after taxation			12,834		4,993
Total return before distribution			207,274		159,047
Finance costs: Distributions	6		(12,835)		(4,995)
Change in net assets attributable to unitholders			194,439		154,052

Statement of Change in Unitholders' Net Assets

For the year ended 31 May 2007

	2007 £000's	2007 £000's	2006 £000's	2006 £000's
Net assets at the start of the year		676,524		441,941
Movement due to sales and repurchases of units				
Amounts received on creation of units	403,509		156,203	
Less: Amounts paid on cancellation of units	(47,084)		(77,312)	
		356,425		78,891
Stamp duty reserve tax		(466)		(327)
Change in net assets attributable to unitholders (see above)		194,439		154,052
Retained distribution on Accumulation units		6,825		1,967
Net assets at the end of the year		**1,233,747**		**676,524**

Portfolio Statement as at 31.5.07

Schroder UK Alpha Plus Fund

	Holding at 31.5.07	Market value £000's	% of total net assets
Oil & Gas 14.80%			
(2006 – 15.75%)			
BG Group	7,928,814	61,171	4.96
BP	10,230,000	57,748	4.68
Dana Petroleum	2,857,700	32,463	2.63
Wood Group (John)	10,032,890	31,152	2.53
		182,534	14.80
Basic Materials 8.71%			
(2006 – 7.60%)			
BHP Billiton	3,690,958	45,399	3.68
Xstrata	2,138,647	62,042	5.03
		107,411	8.71
Industrials 13.10%			
(2006 – 15.60%)			
Charter	4,213,615	43,463	3.52
Experian Group	7,288,845	45,829	3.72
Invensys	12,387,908	48,282	3.91
Rolls-Royce Group	4,840,847	24,095	7.95
		161,669	13.10
Consumer Good 4.86%			
(2006 – 0.00%)			
Burberry Group	3,853,518	26,319	2.13
Unilever	2,161,088	33,670	2.73
		59,989	4.86
Health Care 4.42%			
(2006 – 3.34%)			
GlaxoSmithKline	2,327,731	30,493	2.47
Shire	2,021,717	23,978	1.95
		54,471	4.42

	Holding at 31.5.07	Market value £000's	% of total net assets
Consumer Services 21.43%			
(2006 – 23.66%)			
Alliance Boots	3,579,828	40,398	3.27
British Airways	4,042,588	18,980	1.54
Home Retail Group	4,416,331	20,823	1.69
Next Group	1,481,708	32,731	2.65
Reuters Group	8,822,344	55,360	4.49
Tesco	6,278,519	28,803	2.34
Whitbread	1,649,289	31,229	2.53
WPP Group	4,828,544	36,069	2.92
		264,393	21.43
Telecommunications 3.04%			
(2006 – 0.00%)			
Vodafone Group	23,772,847	37,561	3.04
		37,561	3.04
Utilities 2.49%			
(2006 – 4.96%)			
Drax Group	3,836,457	30,720	2.49
		30,720	2.49
Financials 23.20%			
(2006 – 26.34%)			
3i Group	2,515,797	30,542	2.48
Barclays	4,876,893	35,211	2.85
British Land	1,516,374	21,927	1.78
HSBC Holdings	5,165,460	48,220	3.91
Man Group	5,001,192	29,382	2.38
Old Mutual	14,522,980	25,154	2.04
Provident Financial	4,528,177	35,818	2.90
Resolution	5,329,935	33,685	2.73
Standard Chartered	1,539,967	26,333	2.13
		286,272	23.20
Technology 1.59%			
(2006 – 0.00%)			
Misys	7,773,213	19,550	1.59
		19,550	1.59
Portfolio of investments		1,204,600	97.64
Net other assets		29,147	2.36
Net assets		1,233,747	100.00%

Unless otherwise stated the above securities are ordinary shares or common stock and admitted to official stock exchange listings.

Balance Sheet

Schroder UK Alpha Plus Fund

As at 31 May 2007

	Notes	2007 £000's	2007 £000's	2006 £000's	2006 £000's
Assets					
Portfolio of investments			1,204,600		657,891
Debtors	7	10,732		8,817	
Cash and bank balances		28,470		19,009	
Total other assets			39,202		27,826
Total assets			**1,243,802**		**685,717**
Liabilities					
Creditors	8	(1,881)		(5,738)	
Distribution payable on A Income units		(8,174)		(3,455)	
Total other liabilities			(10,055)		(9,193)
Total liabilities			**(10,055)**		**(9,193)**
Net assets attributable to unitholders			**1,233,747**		**676,524**

Summary of Material Portfolio Changes *

Schroder UK Alpha Plus Fund

For the year ended 31 May 2007

Total purchases for the period (see note 13) £607,605,240

Purchases	Cost £000's
Invensys	35,992
WPP Group	32,093
Dana Protection	30,639
Experian Group	30,261
BT Group	30,210
Provident Financial	30,016
Vodafone Group	29,955
Next Group	29,114
Unilever	27,259
Shire	25,482
Rolls-Royce Group	24,215
British Land	22,571
British Airways	19,967
BHP Billiton	19,535
ITV	19,492
Misys	19,327
BG Group	16,332
HSBC Holdings	14,456
BP	13,662
Resolution	11,786

Summary of Material Portfolio Changes *

Schroder UK Alpha Plus Fund

For the year ended 31 May 2007

Total sales for the period (see note 13)   £255,334,244

Sales	Cost £000's
BT Group	38,513
BAA	33,835
ITV	22,835
Wolseley	22,139
British Land	19,317
BAE Systems	18,189
Intercontinental Hotels Group	18,182
British Sky Broadcasting Group	15,698
Man Group	12,233
MFI Furniture Group	11,220
Standard Chartered	9,594
Shire	9,571
PartyGaming	7,267
HBOS	7,240
Burberry Group	4,722
Drax Group	4,513
Unilever	265

* Material portfolio changes are exceeding 2% of the net assets of the Fund at the start of the period with a minimum of the twenty largest purchases and sales shown.

Notes to the Accounts

Schroder UK Alpha Plus Fund

1. Accounting policies

Basis of accounting

The accounts have been prepared under the historical cost basis, as modified by the revaluation of investments, and in accordance with the Statement of Recommended Practice for Authorised Funds (new SORP) issued by the IMA in December 2005 which was adopted during the year. The presentation of the accounts has been changed to comply with the new SORP and comparative amounts have been stated in line with the new presentation requirements. Except for the change in valuation policy as described below, none of these changes have any impact on the return for the period or the total net assets of the Fund.

Income

Dividends receivable from equity investments are recognised net of attributable tax credits and are credited to income when they are first quoted ex-dividend. Interest receivable from bank deposits is accounted for on an accruals basis. Underwriting commissions are included in income except where the Fund is required to take up shares. In these cases commission is deducted from the capital cost of those shares on a proportional basis.

Special dividends

Special dividends are treated as income or capital depending on the facts of each particular case.

Expenses

Expenses of the Fund are allocated against income except for Stamp Duty Reserve Tax and costs associated with the purchase and sale of investments and the Manager's periodic charge which are allocated to the capital of the Fund.

Taxation

Corporation tax is charged on the income liable to corporation tax less deductible expenses.

Deferred taxation is provided for on all timing differences that have originated but not reversed by the balance sheet date, other than those differences regarded as permanent. Any liability to deferred taxation is provided for at the average rate of taxation expected to apply. Deferred tax assets and liabilities are not discounted to reflect the time value of money.

Distributions

The income available for distribution is the total income earned by the Fund, less deductible expenses and taxation allocated to income. This income is distributed annually on 31 July.

Valuation

Listed investments of the Fund have been valued at market value at 18:00 on the balance sheet date. Market value is defined by the new SORP as fair value which generally is the bid value of each security.

The accounting policy has been changed from the previous period to comply with the requirements of the new SORP. As the restatement of the prior year comparatives is not required by the new SORP, the value of investments for the prior year is shown at mid-market value in line with the previous accounting policy.

If comparative information had been restated, the nature of the main adjustments required would be to reduce the value of the investments by the spread between mid-market and bid-market values with an equal reduction in net gains on investments.

Foreign currencies

Transactions in foreign currencies are translated into sterling at the exchange rate prevailing on the date of the transaction. Assets and liabilities valued in foreign currencies have been translated into sterling at the exchange rates prevailing at the balance sheet date.

2. Net gains on investments

The net gains on investments during the period comprise:

	2007 £000's	2006 £000's
Non-derivative securities	194,440	154,054
Net gains on investments	**194,440**	**154,054**

3. Income

	2007 £000's	2006 £000's
UK dividends	25,232	12,585
Overseas dividends	558	253
Bank interest	2,057	1,133
Underwriting commission	0	58
Exchange rate gains on withholding tax received	2	(3)
Total income	**27,849**	**14,026**

4. Expenses

	2007 £000's	2006 £000's
Payable to the Manager, associates of the Manager and agents of either of them:		
Manager's periodic charge	13,650	7,993
Administration charge	1,202	926
	14,852	8,919
Payable to the Trustee, associates of the Trustee and agents of either of them:		
Trustee's fees	83	59
Safe custody fees	4	3
Transaction charges	2	2
	89	64
Other expenses		
Audit fee	9	8
	9	8
Total expenses	**14,950**	**8,991**

5. Taxation

(a) Analysis of the tax charge for the year

	2007 £000's	2006 £000's
Overseas withholding tax	64	39
Adjustments in respect of prior periods	1	3
Total current tax (Note 6(b))	**65**	**42**

No provision for corporation tax has been made as expenses exceed the income liable to corporation tax.

(b) Factors affecting the current tax charge for the year

The tax assessed for the year is different from that calculated when the standard rate of corporation tax for authorised unit trusts of 20% (2006-20%) is applied to the net income before taxation. The differences are explained below.

	2007 £000's	2006 £000's
Net income before taxation	**12,899**	**5,035**
Net income for the year before taxation multiplied by the standard rate of corporation tax	2,580	1,007
Effects of:		
Income not subject to corporation tax	(5,046)	(2,520)
Overseas withholding tax	64	39
Income taxable in different periods	0	4
Movement in excess management expenses	2,466	1,509
Adjustments in respect of prior periods	1	3
Current tax charge for the year	65	42

(c) Factors that may affect future tax charges

At the year end, there is a potential deferred tax asset of £6,187,102 (2006 - £3,724,856) in respect of unutilised management expenses and £121,951 (2006 - £57,030) in relation to eligible unrelieved foreign tax available for double taxation relief. It is unlikely the Fund will generate sufficient taxable profits in the future to utilise these amounts and therefore no deferred tax asset has been recognised in the year or prior year.

6. Finance costs

Distribution and interest payable

The distribution takes account of income received on the creation of units and income deducted on the cancellation of units, and comprises:

	2007 £000's	2006 £000's
Final Dividend distribution	14,999	5,423
Add: Income deducted on cancellation of units	268	143
Deduct: Income received on creation of units	(2,432)	(571)
Total finance costs	**12,835**	**4,995**
Net income per Statement of Total Return	12,834	4,993
Transaction charges taken to capital	2	2
Movement in undistributed income	(1)	0
Net distribution for the period	**12,835**	**4,995**

Details of the distribution per unit are set out in the table on page 25

7. Debtors

	2007 £000's	2006 £000's
Amounts receivable for creation of units	5,923	5,159
Accrued UK dividends	4,339	3,521
Accrued bank interest	173	71
Overseas withholding tax	100	66
VAT refund	197	0
Total debtors	**10,732**	**8,817**

8. Creditors

	2007 £000's	2007 £000's	2006 £000's	2006 £000's
Amounts payable for cancellation of units		0		179
Purchases awaiting settlement		0		4,535
Accrued expenses				
Managers and Agents				
Manager's periodic charge	1,546		872	
Administration charge	285		104	
		1,831		976
Trustee and Agents				
Trustee's fees	8		6	
Safe custody fees	1		1	
		9		7
Other accrued expenses		9		8
Stamp duty reserve tax payable		32		33
Total creditors		**1,881**		**5,738**

9. Contingent liabilities

There were no contingent liabilities at the balance sheet date (2006 - Nil).

10. Related party transactions

The Manager and the Trustee actively co-operate to exercise control over the Fund and are therefore related parties by virtue of their controlling influence.

Amounts paid during the year or due to the Manager or the Trustee at the year end are disclosed under Expenses, Finance costs and Creditors in the Notes to the Accounts. Bank interest paid or payable to the Fund by the Trustee is disclosed in Income and Debtors in the Notes to the Accounts.

Transactions relating to the creation and cancellation of units and the purchases and sales of investments which pass through, but are not for the benefit of, either related party are disclosed in the Statement of Change in Unitholders' Net Assets and the Summary of Material Portfolio Changes respectively. Amounts due to or from the Fund at the year end in relation to these transactions are disclosed under Debtors and Creditors in the Notes to the Accounts. Cash and bank balances with the Trustee are disclosed in the Balance Sheet.

11. Unit classes

The Fund currently has two unit classes: A Income units and A Accumulation units. The annual management charge is based on the average value of the Fund, calculated on a daily basis, and covers the remuneration of the Manager, the Investment Adviser and their overhead expenses and for each unit class is as follows:

A Income units	1.50%
A Accumulation units	1.50%

The net asset value of each unit class, the net asset value per unit and the number of units in issue in each class are given in the Net Asset Value and Comparative Tables on page 4. The distribution per unit class is given in the Distribution Table on page 25. Both classes have the same rights on winding up.

12. Derivative and other financial instruments

In accordance with the investment objective, the Fund may hold certain financial instruments. These comprise:
- securities held in accordance with the investment objective and policies;
- cash and short-term debtors and creditors arising directly from operations.

Under normal circumstances, the Manager would expect substantially all of the assets of the Fund to be invested in securities appropriate to the Fund's investment objective. Cash and near cash may only be held to assist in the redemption of units, the efficient management of the Fund or for purposes regarded as ancillary to the Fund.

The Fund has little exposure to credit risk. The main risks arising from the Fund's financial instruments are market price, foreign currency, liquidity and interest rate risks. The Manager's policies for managing these risks are summarised below and have been applied throughout the year and the prior year.

Market price risk

The Fund's investment portfolio is exposed to market price fluctuations which are monitored by the Manager in pursuance of the investment objective and policy. Adherence to investment guidelines and to investment and borrowing powers set out in the Trust Deed, the Prospectus and in the COLL mitigates the risk of excessive exposure to any particular type of security or issuer.

Foreign currency risk

The Fund can invest in overseas securities and the balance sheet can be significantly affected by movements in foreign exchange rates. The Fund has not hedged the sterling value of investments that are priced in other currencies.

Income received in other currencies is converted to sterling on or near the date of receipt. The Fund does not hedge or otherwise seek to avoid currency movement risk on accrued income.

Currency risk profile

The currency risk profile of the Fund's net assets and liabilities at the balance sheet date was as follows:

Currency	Monetary exposure £000's	Non-monetary exposure £000's	Total £000's
Sterling			
2007	28,603	1,204,600	1,233,203
2006	17,940	657,891	675,831
US dollar			
2007	544	0	544
2006	693	0	603

Liquidity risk

The Fund's assets comprise mainly of readily realisable securities. The main liability of the Fund is the redemption of any units that investors wish to sell.

Interest rate risk

Interest receivable on bank deposits or payable on bank overdraft positions will be affected by fluctuations in interest rates.

Interest rate risk profile of financial assets and financial liabilities

The interest rate risk profile of financial assets and liabilities at the balance sheet date was as follows:

Currency	Floating rate financial assets £000's	Financial assets not carrying interest £000's	Total £000's
Sterling			
2007	28,470	1,214,592	1,243,062
2006	19,009	666,015	685,024
US dollar			
2007	0	543	543
2006	0	693	693

Currency	Floating rate financial liabilities £000's	Financial liabilities not carrying interest £000's	Total £000's
Sterling			
2007	0	9,858	9,858
2006	0	9,193	9,193

There are no material amounts of non interest bearing financial assets, other than equities, which do not have a maturity date.

Floating rate financial assets and financial liabilities

Sterling denominated bank balances and bank overdrafts bear interest rates based on SONIA.

Fair value of financial assets and financial liabilities

There is no material difference between the value of the financial assets and liabilities, as shown in the balance sheet, and their fair value.

13. Portfolio transaction costs

	2007 £000's	2007 £000's	2006 £000's	2006 £000's
Analysis of total purchase costs				
Purchases in period before transaction costs		604,045		457,096
Commissions	857		632	
Taxes	2,703		2,163	
Total purchase costs		3,560		2,795
Gross purchase total		**607,605**		**459,891**
Analysis of total sales costs				
Gross sales before transaction costs		255,662		381,962
Commissions	(328)		(498)	
Total sales costs		(328)		(498)
Total sales net of transaction costs		**255,334**		**381,464**

Distribution Table

Schroder UK Alpha Plus Fund

Final distribution for the year ended 31 May 2007

Group 1	Units purchased prior to 1 June 2006
Group 2	Units purchased on or after 1 June 2006

	Net income 2007 p per unit	Equalisation 2007 p per unit	Distribution payable 31.7.07 p per unit	Distribution paid 31.7.06 p per unit
A Income Units				
Group 1	1.3185	-	1.3185	0.7095
Group 2	0.7171	0.6014	1.3185	0.7095
A Accumulation Units				
Group 1	1.3894	-	1.3894	0.7417
Group 2	0.7809	0.6085	1.3894	0.7417

Equalisation applies to units purchased during the distribution period (Group 2 units). It is the average amount of income included in the purchase price of Group 2 units and is refunded to the holders of these units as a return of capital.

Being capital it is not liable to income tax but must be deducted from the cost of units for capital gains tax purposes.

Corporate Unitholders

Corporate unitholders receive the dividend distribution payment as detailed below:

- 90.60% of the total distribution together with the tax credit is received as franked investment income.

- 9.40% of the distribution is deemed to be an annual payment received after deduction of income tax at the lower rate and is liable to corporation tax. It is not franked investment income.

General Information

Schroder UK Alpha Plus Fund

Manager
Schroder Unit Trusts Limited
31 Gresham Street
London EC2V 7QA
Authorised and regulated by the Financial Services Authority

Registrar*
International Financial Data Services Ltd
IFDS House
St Nicholas Lane
Basildon
Essex SS15 5FS

Investment Adviser
Schroder Investment Management Limited
31 Gresham Street
London EC2V 7QA
Authorised and regulated by the Financial Services Authority

Administration details
Schroders
FREEPOST
RLTZ-CHSY-HBUT
PO Box 1102
Chelmsford
Essex CM99 2XX
Investor Services 0800 718 777
Dealing 0800 718 788
Fax 0870 043 4080

Trustee
J.P. Morgan Trustee and Depositary Company Limited
Chaseside
Bournemouth BH7 7DA
Authorised and regulated by the Financial Services Authority

Independent Auditors
PricewaterhouseCoopers LLP
Southwark Towers
32 London Bridge Street
London SE1 9SY

- The Manager has delegated the function of Registrar to International Financial Data Services Limited.

Authorisation

The Fund is an authorised unit trust and is constituted pursuant to the COLL and is structured as a trust. The Fund is a UCITS scheme for the purpose of the categorisation of the COLL.

Initial Management Charge

The issue price of the units reflects an initial management charge of 5.25% of the creation price (this is the same as 4.99% of the buying price). This is retained by the Manager.

The Prospectus and the Simplified Prospectus are available on request or can be downloaded from our website www.schroders.co.uk

APPENDIX 5

Contract Notes

North Finchley Financial Advisors Ltd
High Street
Finchley
London
NW1 3DW

5 October 2007

Your client's reference number:
0123456789
Your financial adviser reference number:
141739
Transaction reference:
0000001234

Your Client's M&G Investment.

Dear Sirs

Thank you for advising your client to invest with M&G. Full details appear on the following pages.

Details have also been sent to your client.

Settlement for this transaction is due on 12 June 2007.

Total Amount due to be paid £0.00

If you have any questions, please contact our **Financial Advisers Helpline** free on **0800 328 3191**, quoting your reference number. Our lines are open from 8am to 6pm, Monday to Friday. For your security and to improve the quality of our service we may record and randomly monitor telephone calls.

Important notes:

This is an important document. Please retain it for your records.

Yours faithfully

Deborah Carter

Deborah Carter - Customer Relations Director
M&G Securities Ltd

Collective Investment Schemes Administration

Registered holder: Alan Jones

Your client's reference number:
0123456789
Your financial adviser reference number:
141739
Transaction reference:
0000001234

Details of your investment.

Important notes:

The price basis is "forward" which means we buy and sell shares/units using the prices calculated at the valuation point **after** we receive your instruction. The time of the transaction is available on request.

For further details regarding **all** charges and information relating to share/unit classes please refer to your Key Features document.

Recovery Fund
Sterling Class X Accumulation Shares

Transaction date	Transaction description	Shares	Share price (p)	Amount (£)
06/06/2007	Sale	4,649.866	215.060	10,000.00
Total invested into this fund				**10,000.00**

A redemption charge is payable in respect of these shares in accordance with your Key Features document.

This is a sub-fund of M&G Investment funds (3), a UK authorised open-ended investment company.

Total Amount due to be paid £0.00

Collective Investment Schemes Administration

Registered holder: Alan Jones

Your client's reference number:
0123456789

Your financial adviser reference number:
141739

Transaction reference:
0000001234

Commission details.

North Finchley Financial Advisors Ltd

Lump sum subscriptions

Fund name	Lump sum subscription (£)	Renewal rate	Initial rate	Lump sum initial paid (£)
Recovery Fund Sterling Class X Accumulation Shares	10,000.00	0.50%	3.00%	300.00

Important notes:

This statement about commissions forms part of the Key Features.

All commission will be paid by M&G.

In addition to the initial commission shown above, M&G will pay North Finchley Financial Advisors Ltd renewal commission at the rate of 0.50% of the value of your holding in the fund noted above. If your holding were worth £1,000, M&G would pay them £5.00. If your holding were worth £2,000, M&G would pay them £10.00. This commission is accrued annually to 30 September and payable in mid November.

Collective Investment Schemes Administration

North Finchley Financial Advisors Ltd
High Street
Finchley
London
NW1 3DW

Your client's reference number:
0123456789
Your financial adviser reference number:
161064
Transaction reference:
0000001234

5 October 2007

Your M&G withdrawal contract note.

Dear Sirs

We have received your client's recent withdrawal request. Please note that payment cannot be made until a Form of Renunciation has been completed in full by all registered holder(s) and returned to us. A summary of their withdrawal is shown below and full transaction details appear on the following page(s).

Details have also been sent to your client.

Funds	Amount
Corporate Bond Fund	
Sterling Class A Accumulation Shares	£23,037.56
Total withdrawal proceeds	**£23,037.56**

We would like to take this opportunity to thank you for investing with us - we hope that the investment(s) you have sold met your needs and we look forward to providing you with further investment products in the future.

If you have any questions, please contact our **Financial Advisers Helpline** free on **0800 328 3191**, quoting your reference number. Our lines are open from 8am to 6pm, Monday to Friday. For your security and to improve the quality of our service we may record and randomly monitor telephone calls.

Yours faithfully

Deborah Carter

Deborah Carter - Customer Relations Director
M&G Securities Ltd

Important notes:

This is an important document, please retain it for your records.

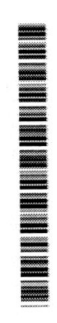

Collective Investment Schemes Administration

Registered holder: Alan Jones

Your client's reference number:
0123456789
Your financial adviser reference number:
161064
Transaction reference:
0000001234

Details of your withdrawal.

Corporate Bond Fund
Sterling Class A Accumulation Shares

Transaction date	Transaction description	Shares sold	Share price (p)	Amount (£)
5/06/2007	Withdrawal	64,011.000	35.990	23,037.56
Total withdrawal proceeds from this fund				**23,037.56**

This is a sub-fund of M&G Investment Funds (3), a UK authorised open-ended investment company.

Important notes:

For further details regarding all charges and information relating to your investment please refer to your Key Features document.

Settlement will be released within four working days of satisfactory receipt of requested documents.

This contract is your record of the date, price and the amount of your redemption. You should keep it for Capital Gains Tax purposes in the future.

Collective Investment Schemes Administration

North Finchley Financial Advisors Ltd
High Street
Finchley
London
NW1 3DW

Your client's reference number:
0123456789
Your financial adviser reference number:
143921
Transaction reference:
0000001234

5 October 2007

Your Client's M&G Investment.

Dear Sirs

Thank you for advising your client to invest with M&G. Full details appear on the following pages.

Details have also been sent to your client.

Settlement for this transaction is due on 11 June 2007.

Total Amount due to be paid £0.00

If you have any questions, please contact our **Financial Advisers Helpline** free on **0800 328 3191**, quoting your reference number. Our lines are open from 8am to 6pm, Monday to Friday. For your security and to improve the quality of our service we may record and randomly monitor telephone calls.

Yours faithfully

Deborah Carter

Deborah Carter - Customer Relations Director
M&G Securities Ltd

Important notes:

This is an important document. Please retain it for your records.

Collective Investment Schemes Administration

Registered holder: Alan Jones

Your client's reference number:
0123456789
Your financial adviser reference number:
143921
Transaction reference:
0000001234

Details of your investment.

Important notes:

The price basis is "forward" which means we buy and sell shares/units using the prices calculated at the valuation point **after** we receive your instruction. The time of the transaction is available on request.

For further details regarding all charges and information relating to share/unit classes please refer to your Key Features document.

Dividend Fund
Sterling Class A Income Shares

Transaction date	Transaction description	Shares	Share price (p)	Amount (£)
05/06/2007	Sale			310.00
	Initial charge			-12.40
	Amount invested	408.399	72.870	297.60
Total invested into this fund				**297.60**

This is a sub-fund of M&G Investment funds (3), a UK authorised open-ended investment company.

Total Amount due to be paid £0.00

Collective Investment Schemes Administration

Registered holder: Alan Jones

Your client's reference number:
0123456789
Your financial adviser reference number:
143921
Transaction reference:
0000001234

Commission details.

North Finchley Financial Advisors Ltd

Lump sum subscriptions

Fund name	Lump sum subscription (£)	Renewal rate	Initial rate	Lump sum initial paid (£)
Dividend Fund Sterling Class A Income Shares	310.00	0.50%	3.00%	9.30

In addition to the initial commission shown above, M&G will pay North Finchley Financial Advisors Ltd renewal commission at the rate of 0.50% of the value of your holding in the fund noted above. If your holding were worth £1,000, M&G would pay them £5.00. If your holding were worth £2,000, M&G would pay them £10.00. This commission is accrued annually to 30 September and payable in mid November.

Important notes:

This statement about commissions forms part of the Key Features.

All commission will be paid by M&G.

Collective Investment Schemes Administration

North Finchley Financial Advisors Ltd
Hight Street
Finchley
London
NW1 3DW

Your client's reference number:
0123456789

Your financial adviser reference number:
150287

Transaction reference:
0000012343

5 October 2007

Your M&G withdrawal contract note.

Important notes:

This is an important document, please retain it for your records.

Dear Sirs

We have received your client's recent withdrawal request. Please note that payment cannot be made until a Form of Renunciation has been completed in full by all registered holder(s) and returned to us. A summary of their withdrawal is shown below and full transaction details appear on the following page(s).

Details have also been sent to your client.

Funds	Amount
Extra Income Fund	
Sterling Class A Income Shares	£4,992.81
Total withdrawal proceeds	**£4,992.81**

We would like to take this opportunity to thank you for investing with us - we hope that the investment(s) you have sold met your needs and we look forward to providing you with further investment products in the future.

If you have any questions, please contact our **Financial Advisers Helpline** free on **0800 328 3191**, quoting your reference number. Our lines are open from 8am to 6pm, Monday to Friday. For your security and to improve the quality of our service we may record and randomly monitor telephone calls.

Yours faithfully

Deborah Carter

Deborah Carter - Customer Relations Director
M&G Securities Ltd

Collective Investment Schemes Administration

Registered holder: Alan Jones   s

Your client's reference number:
0123456789
Your financial adviser reference number:
150287
Transaction reference:
0000012343

Details of your withdrawal.

Extra Income Fund
Sterling Class A Income Shares

Transaction date	Transaction description	Shares sold	Share price (p)	Amount (£)
5/06/2007	Withdrawal	657.000	759.940 xd	4,992.81
Total withdrawal proceeds from this fund				**4,992.81**

This is a sub-fund of M&G Investment Funds (2), a UK authorised open-ended investment company.

Important notes:

Further payments will be made in due course in respect of Distributions or Tax Repayments.

If the Fund you have redeemed is quoted as "xd" please refer to your Key Features document for further details.

For further details regarding all charges and information relating to your investment please refer to your Key Features document.

Settlement will be released within four working days of satisfactory receipt of requested documents.

This contract is your record of the date, price and the amount of your redemption. You should keep it for Capital Gains Tax purposes in the future.

Collective Investment Schemes Administration

APPENDIX 6

Form of Renunciation

M&G Form of Renunciation.

Please note that the proceeds from the repurchase do not become payable until this form (if applicable), properly signed and completed, has been received at our Chelmsford office. Terms and Conditions apply.

Please complete this Form of Renunciation in BLOCK CAPITALS in blue or black ink and return it to:
M&G Securities Limited, PO Box 9039, Chelmsford CM99 2XG.

- Insert FULL names and addresses of all holders
- Section 3 must be fully completed
- Payment will be made to all holders and sent to the first holders registered address UNLESS Section 4 overleaf is completed

1 Personal details.

Your M&G reference number: 0123456789

Holding designation, e.g 'A a/c' (if applicable):

First holder
- Full name
- Address
- Postcode
- Telephone number (inc. area code)

Second holder
- Full name
- Address
- Postcode

Third holder
- Full name
- Address
- Postcode

Fourth holder
- Full name
- Address
- Postcode

2 Shares to be repurchased.

Transaction Reference: 0000001234

3 Declaration. - All holders must sign this section and state their capacity where applicable*

I/We being the registered shareholder(s) hereby acknowledge that I/we are no longer interested in the shares as stated on the Contract Note to which this Form of Renunciation relates.

First holder
- Capacity
- Date

Second holder
- Capacity
- Date

Third holder
- Capacity
- Date

Fourth holder
- Capacity
- Date

* When Corporate bodies are renouncing shares/units, this form should be completed by the Company and signed by two Directors or a Director and a Secretary, stating capacities, or authorised signatories. Alternatively, a Company may execute this form under seal.

Please continue overleaf to section 4 - Payment Details

Collective Investment Schemes Administration

4 Payment details. - All holders must sign this section and state their capacity* where applicable

Only complete this section if you wish the cheque for this repurchase to be made payable specifically to one or more of the registered holders and sent to either their registered address or to their bank account, or to the client bank account of the intermediary who placed the repurchase. M&G do not accept responsibility for the quotation of bank/building society account numbers, please ensure that you check the details of this section before you submit this form.

Please tick the relevant box; cheque to registered address; cheque to bank
Please pay

Name(s)		OR	Send payment to the following Bank or Building Society	☐
Please send payment to the following registered address	☐		Name and full postal address	
			Bank or Building Society	
Postcode			Postcode	

First holder
Capacity
Date

Name(s) of account holder(s)

Second holder
Capacity
Date

Branch sort code   Bank account number

Third holder
Capacity
Date

Bank/Building Society reference number

Fourth holder
Capacity
Date

* When Corporate bodies are completing this section, two Directors or a Director and a Secretary (stating capacities) should sign this form, or authorised signatories.

Alternatively, a company may execute this form under seal.

Please note that signatures of all holders are required to authorise payment as above.

Contacting us.

Call us on:
0800 390 390
8am to 6pm
Monday to Friday
9am to 1pm Saturday

Write to us at:
M&G Customer Relations
PO Box 9039
Chelmsford
CM99 2XG

Minicom:
0800 917 2296

See our home page on:
www.mandg.co.uk
email us on:
info@mandg.co.uk

Collective Investment Schemes Administration

APPENDIX 6A

Stock Transfer Form

Guidance for the completion of the stock transfer form for UK unit trusts and open-ended investment companies

Introduction

Historically, the common stock transfer form used to effect a transfer of company shares or stock has also been used for UK unit trusts and open-ended investment companies (funds). From 15 December 2007, however, new legislation imposed a requirement on fund managers to verify the identity of all registered holders of their funds as well as any other beneficial owners and controllers. For this reason, it was necessary to introduce a bespoke form for UK investment funds.

These guidance notes relate solely to the Stock Transfer Form for UK Unit Trusts and Open-Ended Investment Companies.

Completion of the form: front

The top section deals with the units/shares as they are registered currently:

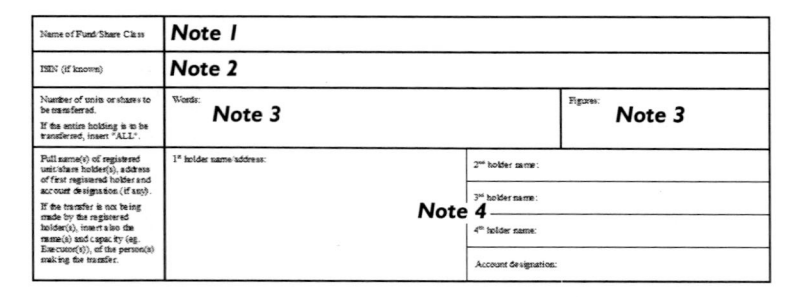

Name of Fund/Share Class	Note 1		
ISIN (if known)	Note 2		
Number of units or shares to be transferred. If the entire holding is to be transferred, insert "ALL".	Words: Note 3		Figures: Note 3
Full name(s) of registered unit/share holder(s), address of first registered holder and account designation (if any). If the transfer is not being made by the registered holder(s), insert also the name(s) and capacity (eg. Executor(s)), of the person(s) making the transfer.	1st holder name/address: Note 4	2nd holder name:	
		3rd holder name:	
		4th holder name:	
		Account designation:	

Note 1: Enter the name of the fund in which the units/shares are held including the name of the class (if applicable), for example:

ABC European Fund, Income Shares; or

XYZ UK Equity Fund, Class 'A' Shares

Note 2: Enter the ISIN code if it is known. ISIN stands for International Securities Identification Number and is a unique reference code which is given to each share class of a fund.

Note 3: Enter the number of unit/shares to be transferred in both words and figures. If the entire holding is to be transferred, 'All' may be entered in both boxes, instead of an actual number.

Note 4: These boxes should be used to enter the full name(s) and address (including postcode) in which the units/shares are registered currently. If the holding is designated (for example, 'ABC Account'), the designation should be entered in the box provided.

The middle section is where the current holders (the transferor(s)) execute the transfer and authorise the units/shares to be re-registered:

Note 6a — I/We hereby transfer the above units/shares out of the name(s) aforesaid to the person(s) named below and request that such entries be made in the register as are necessary to give effect to this transfer.

☐ I/We hereby certify, <u>if the box to the left is ticked</u>, that this transfer is not for consideration in money or money's worth and is exempt from SDRT by virtue of paragraph 6(2) of Schedule 19 to the Finance Act 1999.

Note 6b — ☐ I/We hereby certify, <u>if the box to the left is ticked</u>, that this transfer is exempt from SDRT by virtue of paragraphs 6(3) - 6(5) of Schedule 19 to the Finance Act 1999 (charities, intra-group transfers etc.) and attach evidence as to facts of the transfer, which give rise to such exemption. (Important: see "Stamp Duty Reserve Tax" below).

Stamp of the institution lodging this form (if any): **Note 7**

Signature(s) of transferor(s)

1. ....
2. ....
3. .... **Note 5**
4. ....

All transferors must sign. Bodies corporate should execute under their common seal, or otherwise as determined by their Memorandum and Articles of Association.

Date:

Note 5: All current registered holders must sign here. If someone is signing on behalf of a holder, with power of attorney for example, the document appointing them (or a properly certified copy) must be attached if it has not already been lodged with the Registrar.

Note 6a: The first box should be ticked if the transfer is exempt from SDRT because no consideration in money or money's worth is given in connection with the surrender of the units/shares. This will be the case, for example, when the units/shares are being transferred as a gift or distributed to the beneficiaries of a trust or deceased estate. It is also likely to be the case when the legal title to units/shares is being transferred to or from a nominee with no change of the underlying beneficial ownership.

Note 6b: The second box should be ticked **only** if the transfer **is** for consideration in money or money's worth **and** the transfer is exempt from SDRT by virtue of paragraphs 6(3) – 6(5) of Schedule 19, Finance Act 1999. Where this box is ticked, supplementary evidence will need to be provided to substantiate the entitlement to the exemption. For example, a transfer of units/shares for consideration in money or money's worth to a charity may be exempt under paragraph 6(3) of Schedule 19, Finance Act 1999, but additional evidence must be provided that the transferee is both a charity and one that is tax exempt, in order to support this position.

Note that only one box should be ticked; usually this will be the first box. Leaving both boxes blank, will indicate that the unit/shares are being transferred to someone that has purchased them from the current holder or they are otherwise being exchanged for something of value in monetary terms and that the transfer therefore gives rise to a liability to SDRT (other than in the limited circumstances mentioned under Note 6b). In these cases, the Manager* will calculate any liability to SDRT according to the market price of the units/shares and certain other factors on the date the Registrar1 receives the transfer, and may require the amount concerned to be sent to them to pay into the fund before they will register the transfer.

Note 7: This box is for the stamp of any firm that is lodging the form with the Registrar on behalf of either the current or new holder(s) and with whom the Registrar or Manager should correspond in the event of a query.

* The Registrar and the Manager may or may not be the same person.

Collective Investment Schemes Administration

The bottom section provides spaces for the details of the transferee(s) in whose names the units/shares are to be registered going forward:

| Full name(s), date(s) of birth and full postal address(es) (including postcode) of the person(s) to whom the security is transferred*, and any account designation. In each case please state title or salutation (eg. Mr., Mrs., Miss. etc.). Note that only the 1st holder's address will appear on the register of title. *Please see "Customer Due Diligence For Anti-Money Laundering Purposes" overleaf. | 1st holder name/address:

 Date of Birth:

 3rd holder name/address:

 Date of Birth:

 Account designation: **Note 9** | 2nd holder name/address:

Note 8
 Date of Birth:

 4th holder name/address:

 Date of Birth: |

Note 8: These boxes must contain the full name(s), address(es) (including postcode) and date(s) of birth of the person(s) to whom the units/shares are being transferred. They must be completed in BLOCK CAPITALS.

Note that only the address of the first named holder will usually be entered on the register. The remaining details are required by the Manager in connection with its customer due diligence obligations (see below).

Note 9: Any designation (for example, 'ABC Account') that the new holder(s) wish to be included on the register for identification purposes may be added here.

Back

The reverse of the form deals entirely with the Manager's legal obligations to undertake 'customer due diligence' measures in relation to the transferee(s) (to whom the shares are being transferred).

The explanation at the top concerns mainly the Manager's obligation to verify the identities of both the transferees and any other beneficial owners or controllers, for which they may require documentary evidence or may undertake searches of electronically-held records. In connection with this, the table below must be completed as necessary and the declaration signed. The table is used to list the names of any beneficial owners or controllers that may exist other than the transferee(s).

What constitutes a beneficial owner for these purposes depends upon whether the units/shares are being transferred to a company or to one or more individuals who may be acting as trustees.

For companies, the beneficial owners that must be listed are any shareholders or other individuals that ultimately own or control more than 25% of the voting rights or are entitled to more than 25% of the company's capital profits. Note that they may not necessarily be the actual shareholders in the company. Directors of a company do not need to be listed unless they fall within this definition. For trusts and other similar arrangements, the beneficial owners are individuals that are nominated to benefit from more than 25% of the trust property, as well as any trustees that may exist in addition to the transferee(s) or others that may exercise control over them.

Name	Capacity (eg. trustee, partner, shareholder, beneficiary etc.)
	Note 10

If there is insufficient space above to list all the relevant individuals, please tick here ☐ and continue onto a separate sheet of paper, which should be stapled to this form.

I/We hereby certify that the above is a complete list of the beneficial owners and controllers as described above and that they are known to me/one or more of us or, in the case of a class of beneficiary, that the description is appropriate and accurate.

To be signed by one or more of the transferees named overleaf, in whose names the units/shares will be registered.

Signature(s):

1. ....

2. ....

Note 11

3. ....

4. ....

Note 10: The names of any beneficial owners or controllers should be entered in the left-hand column with a brief description of their capacity entered on the right. This box should be completed on BLOCK CAPITALS.

If the transferee(s) are the only beneficial owner(s) of the units/shares, simply enter 'TRANSFEREE' or 'TRANSFEREES' as appropriate on the first line of the left column.

If there are other beneficial owners, but none has an interest that exceeds 25% (see above), 'NONE' should be entered in the left column and the relevant description (usually, this will be 'SHAREHOLDER' or 'BENEFICIARY') to the right.

Where a trust or arrangement is established for unspecified individual beneficiaries – the trustees may, for example, have discretionary powers to identify who should receive payments out of the trust property on an ad hoc basis, or an arrangement such as a charity may have been established for the general benefit of a section of the community – these are referred to as 'classes' of beneficiary. In these cases, a description of the class of beneficiary should be entered in the table (this may extend across both columns). Note that all additional trustees or controllers must be listed individually.

The table can be used to provide the names of up to ten beneficial owners or controllers. If there are more than ten, a tick should be placed in the small box immediately below the table and details of the others provided on a separate sheet.

Note 11: One or more (if there are any) of the transferees should sign here to certify both that the table above has been completed properly and that any beneficial owners or controllers that may be listed are known to at least one of those who sign.

APPENDIX 7

Interest Distribution Voucher and Warrant (Income Units)

THE M&G GILT AND FIXED INTEREST INCOME FUND
Managers: M&G Securities Limited, M&G House, Victoria Road, Chelmsford, CM1 1FB

INCOME TAX VOUCHER
ISIN CODE: GB0005495709

Group	Units	Gross Interest Distribution	UK Income Tax Deducted at the Basic Rate	Net Interest Distribution	Equalisation	Total Amount Payable

Dist No.	Distribution	Rate per unit	Holding as at	Distribution period From — To	Date payable

A warrant is attached for the distribution payable in respect of this holding of INCOME units.

From
COUTTS & CO.,
Custodial Services,
New London Bridge House,
25 London Bridge Street,
London SE1 9SG

Any correspondence concerning this holding should be addressed to the Managers, as above, quoting the following A/c No.

WE HEREBY CERTIFY that an amount of income tax equal to that shown as the UK income tax deducted at the basic rate will be accounted for to the Inland Revenue
COUTTS & CO.,
Trustee.

SPECIMEN

If you have any enquiries or require any information about your holding please telephone the Customer Services Department on 01245 390390.

This voucher should be retained as evidence of UK income tax deducted at the basic rate in respect of which you may be entitled to claim payment or relief. A charge may be made for a replacement.

NOTES RELATING TO THE M&G GILT AND FIXED INTEREST INCOME FUND

1. INCOME TAX

Your income tax return should show separately the amounts shown in the gross interest, income tax deducted and net interest boxes. The UK income tax deducted at the basic rate is available to be set off against any income tax chargeable on your total income. If the UK tax deducted at the basic rate exceeds your income tax liability, you are entitled to have the excess repaid to you by the Inland Revenue. Higher rate tax payers will have further tax to pay.

2. NON-RESIDENT UNITHOLDERS

Investors who are not normally resident in the UK and who have completed the relevant NOR declaration will receive some or all of the interest distribution gross. They may also receive some of the interest distribution after deduction of UK tax at the basic rate. This tax may be refundable to a non-resident if a claim is made to the Financial Intermediaries and Claims Office at Lynwood House, Thames Ditton, Kingston - upon - Thames, Surrey KT7 0DP.

3. CORPORATE UNITHOLDERS

Corporate unitholders will receive the interest distribution as interest, it is not reclassified as an annual payment.

4. EQUALISATION

For taxation purposes this item is treated as a return of capital. It is not subject to tax and accordingly does not carry a tax credit. The equalisation amount is a deduction from the base cost for capital gains tax purposes. Units on which equalisation is payable are designated group 2.

THE M&G GILT AND FIXED INTEREST INCOME FUND

9
To: COUTTS & CO.
15 Lombard Street, London EC3V 9AU

18-00-01
38034141

M&G PAY

SPECIMEN

MILLIONS	HUNDRED THOUSANDS	TEN THOUSANDS	THOUSANDS	HUNDREDS	TENS	UNITS	PENCE

THE SUM OF £

This warrant must be presented for payment through a banker within six months

Distribution Account
The M&G Gilt and Fixed Interest Income Fund
For Coutts & Co.

Trustee

Collective Investment Schemes Administration

APPENDIX 8

Dividend Distribution Voucher and Warrant (Income Units)

M&G The M&G Australasian Fund
Managers: M&G Securities Limited, M&G House, Victoria Road, Chelmsford, CM1 1FB

TAX CREDIT VOUCHER
ISIN CODE: GB0005494173

Dividend Distribution Rate per Unit (p)	Holding as at	Distribution Period From	to	Date Payable

A warrant is attached for the distribution payable in respect of this holding of INCOME units.

Dist No.	Distribution	Group	Units	Tax Credit	Dividend Distribution Payable	Equalisation

Total of Dividend Distribution and Equalisation Amounts payable

Lloyds Bank PLC, Trustee

Any correspondence concerning this holding should be addressed to the Managers, as above, quoting the following A/c No.

If you have any enquiries or require any information about your holding please telephone the Customer Services Department on 0800 390390. We may record and randomly monitor telephone calls.

This voucher should be retained as evidence to support your tax return. A charge may be made for a replacement.

1. Income Tax
Your income tax return should show, in the separate sections provided, the amounts of the dividend distribution and tax credit disclosed overleaf.

2. Dividend Distributions
The tax credit is available to be set off against any income tax chargeable on your total income. If you are a UK resident no part of the tax credit is payable to you. If you are liable to pay income tax at rates in excess of the basic rate, the amount upon which the Inland Revenue will assess you is the total of the amounts shown as dividend distribution and tax credit.

3. Corporate Unitholders
A unitholder within the charge to UK corporation tax receives the dividend distribution excluding any equalisation as unfranked income to the extent that the gross income less tax from which the dividend distribution is made is not franked investment income.

Where the gross income from which the dividend distribution is made is not wholly franked investment income, part of the distribution is received as an annual payment from which income tax at the lower rate has been deducted.

For distribution periods beginning on or after 6th April 1999, the maximum amount of income tax, if any, that may be reclaimed from the Inland Revenue is the corporate unitholder's portion of the Trustees' net liability to corporation tax in respect of the gross income.

0.00% of the total dividend distribution together with tax credit is received as franked investment income.

100% of the dividend distribution is received as an annual payment received after deduction of income tax at the lower rate and is liable to corporation tax. It is not franked investment income.

£0.00 is the Trustees' net liability to corporation tax in respect of the gross income (distribution periods beginning on or after 6th April 1999 only).

0.00p is the Trustees' net liability to corporation tax per unit.

4. Equalisation
For taxation purposes this item is treated as a return of capital. It is not subject to tax and accordingly does not carry a tax credit. The equalisation amount is a deduction from the base cost for capital gains tax purposes. Units on which equalisation is payable are designated group 2.

5. Group 2 Units
Group 2 units are the units purchased by you during the accounting period and which you held at close of business on the period end date shown overleaf. They may constitute all or part of your holding. On a first distribution any units bought in the initial launch period are categorised as group 1 units.

M&G The M&G Australasian Fund

To: LLOYDS BANK PLC
Unit Trust Trusteeship Department

30-19-05
000119   00050274

PAY *SPECIMEN.*

MILLIONS	HUNDRED THOUSANDS	TEN THOUSANDS	THOUSANDS	HUNDREDS	TENS	UNITS	PENCE

THE SUM OF £

Distribution Account
The M&G Australasian Fund
For M&G Securities Limited

Secretary

This warrant must be presented for payment through a banker within six months.

ACCOUNT PAYEE

Collective Investment Schemes Administration

APPENDIX 9

Interest Distribution Voucher (Accumulation Units)

THE M&G GILT AND FIXED INTEREST INCOME FUND
Managers: M&G Securities Limited, M&G House, Victoria Road, Chelmsford. CM1 1FB

INCOME TAX VOUCHER
ISIN CODE: GB0005495923

Group	Units	Gross Interest	UK Income Tax Deducted at the Basic Rate	Net Interest	Equalisation	Total Amount Transferred

The total amount transferred from Income Account to Capital Account in respect of this holding of ACCUMULATION Units is made up as shown on this voucher.

Dist No.	Distribution	Rate per unit	Holding as at	Distribution period From — To	Date of Transfer

SPECIMEN

From
COUTTS & CO.,
Custodial Services,
New London Bridge House,
25 London Bridge Street,
London SE1 9SG

Any correspondence concerning this holding should be addressed to the Managers, as above, quoting the following A/c No.

WE HEREBY CERTIFY that the amount of income tax equal to that shown as the UK income tax deducted at the basic rate will be accounted for to the Inland Revenue.
COUTTS & CO.,
Trustee.

H

The income in respect of Accumulation Units is not distributed, but is retained in the Fund and is reflected in the price of the Units

If you have any enquiries or require any information about your holding please telephone the Customer Services Department on 01245 390390.

This voucher should be retained as evidence of UK income tax deducted at the basic rate in respect of which you may be entitled to claim payment or relief. A charge may be made for a replacement.

NOTES RELATING TO THE M&G GILT AND FIXED INTEREST INCOME FUND

1. INCOME TAX

Your income tax return should show separately the amounts shown in the gross interest, income tax deducted and net interest boxes. The UK income tax deducted at the basic rate is available to be set off against any income tax chargeable on your total income. If the UK tax deducted at the basic rate exceeds your income tax liability, you are entitled to have the excess repaid to you by the Inland Revenue. Higher rate tax payers will have further tax to pay.

2. NON-RESIDENT UNITHOLDERS

Investors who are not normally resident in the UK and who have completed the relevant NOR declaration will receive some or all of the interest distribution gross. They may also receive some of the interest distribution after deduction of UK tax at the basic rate. This tax may be refundable to a non-resident if a claim is made to the Financial Intermediaries and Claims Office at Lynwood House, Thames Ditton, Kingston - upon - Thames, Surrey KT7 0PD.

3. CORPORATE UNITHOLDERS

Corporate unitholders will receive the interest distribution as interest, it is not reclassified as an annual payment.

4. EQUALISATION

For taxation purposes this item is treated as a return of capital. It is not subject to tax and accordingly does not have any UK income tax deducted at the basic rate. Units on which equalisation are payable are designated group 2.

5. CAPITAL GAINS TAX

The base cost should be increased by the amount of the net interest.

Collective Investment Schemes Administration

APPENDIX 10

Dividend Distribution Voucher (Accumulation Shares)

M&G **The M&G Australasian Fund**
Managers: M&G Securities Limited, M&G House, Victoria Road, Chelmsford, CM1 1FB

TAX CREDIT VOUCHER
ISIN CODE: GB0005494066

Dividend Distribution Rate per Unit (p)	Holding as at	Distribution Period From	To	Date of Transfer

The total amount transferred from Income Account to Capital Account in respect of ACCUMULATION Units is made up as shown on this voucher.

Dist No.	Distribution	Group	Units	Tax Credit	Dividend Distribution	Equalisation

Total of Dividend Distribution and Equalisation Amounts Transferred

Lloyds Bank PLC, Trustee

Any correspondence concerning this holding should be addressed to the Managers, as above, quoting the following A/c No.

The income in respect of Accumulation Units is not distributed, but is retained in the Fund and is reflected in the price of the Units.

If you have any enquiries or require any information about your holding please telephone the Customer Services Department on 0800 390390. We may record and randomly monitor telephone calls.

This voucher should be retained as evidence to support your tax return. A charge may be made for a replacement.

1. Income Tax
Your income tax return should show, in the separate sections provided, the amounts of the dividend distribution and tax credit disclosed overleaf.

2. Dividend Distributions
The tax credit is available to be set off against any income tax chargeable on your total income. If you are a UK resident no part of the tax credit is payable to you. If you are liable to pay income tax at rates in excess of the basic rate, the amount upon which the Inland Revenue will assess you is the total of the amounts shown as dividend distribution and tax credit.

3. Corporate Unitholders
A unitholder within the charge to UK corporation tax receives the dividend distribution excluding any equalisation as unfranked income to the extent that the gross income less tax from which the dividend distribution is made is not franked investment income.

Where the gross income from which the dividend distribution is made is not wholly franked investment income, part of the distribution is received as an annual payment from which income tax at the lower rate has been deducted.

For distribution periods beginning on or after 6th April 1999, the maximum amount of income tax, if any, that may be reclaimed from the Inland Revenue is the corporate unitholder's portion of the Trustees' net liability to corporation tax in respect of the gross income.

0.00% of the total dividend distribution together with tax credit is received as franked investment income.

100% of the dividend distribution is received as an annual payment received after deduction of income tax at the lower rate and is liable to corporation tax. It is not franked investment income.

£0.00 is the Trustees' net liability to corporation tax in respect of the gross income (distribution periods beginning on or after 6th April 1999 only).

0.00p is the Trustees' net liability to corporation tax per unit.

4. Equalisation
For taxation purposes this item is treated as a return of capital. It is not subject to tax and accordingly does not carry a tax credit. The equalisation amount is a deduction from the base cost for capital gains tax purposes. Units on which equalisation is payable are designated group 2.

5. Group 2 Units
Group 2 units are the units purchased by you during the accounting period and which you held at close of business on the period end date shown overleaf. They may constitute all or part of your holding. On a first distribution any units bought in the initial launch period are categorised as group 1 units.

6. Capital Gains Tax
Your base cost should be increased by the total amounts shown in the dividend distribution and equalisation boxes.

SECURITIES & INVESTMENT INSTITUTE

Collective Investment Schemes Administration

APPENDIX 11

Distribution Mandate Form

To: The Registrar,

Insert FULL TITLE of Company or Sub-fund	

Insert ACCOUNT No. if known (see note A)		Insert any designation recorded in respect of the holding(s)	

See NOTE B — Please forward, until further notice, all Distribution Warrants that may from time to time become due on any Shares now standing, or which may hereafter stand in my (our) name(s) of the survivor(s) of us in the Company's books to.

Insert in block capitals FULL NAME AND ADDRESS of the bank, company, firm or person to whom distributions are to be sent. (See note C)

. . . .
. . . .
. . . .
. . . .

or, where payment is to be made to a Bank, to such other Branch of that Bank may from time to time request. Your compliance with this request shall discharge the Authorised Corporate Director's liability in respect of such distributions.

ALL SHAREHOLDERS PLEASE SIGN HERE (Office holders should state the capacity in which they sign e.g. Director)

(1) Signature . . . .
Name in full . . . .
Address . . . .
(BLOCK CAPITAL)
. . . .
. . . . .Post Code . . . .

(3) Signature . . . .
Name in full . . . .
Address . . . .
(BLOCK CAPITAL)
. . . .
. . . . .Post Code . . . .

Any changes of address may be notified by quoting former and present address

(2) Signature . . . .
Name in full . . . .
Address . . . .
(BLOCK CAPITAL)
. . . .
. . . . .Post Code . . . .

(4) Signature . . . .
Name in full . . . .
Address . . . .
(BLOCK CAPITAL)
. . . .
. . . . .Post Code . . . .

Please complete the unshaded areas

Date . . . . 19 . . . .

NOTES:
- **A** The XYZ ICVC account number is obtainable from statements relating to distribution payments or from the share certificate(s).
- **B** If instructions are recieved less than one month before a distribution is payable it may not be possible to apply them to that distribution.
- **C** Directions as to the account with a bank or building society to be credited with distributions MUST be given to the branch or office concerned and should NOT be included in the form by the shareholder(s).
- **D** Where the instructions are in favour of a bank (or building society) this form should be sent to the branch concerned for the completion of the boxes below.
- **E** XYZ ICVC do not accept any responsibility for the quotation of building society account numbers and the quotation of any such number is entirely at the risk of the unitholder. This does not apply where special arrangements have been made between XYZ ICVC and the building society concerned.

TO BE COMPLETED BY BRANCH BANK

Bank's Reference Numbers and Details:-

(1) Sorting Code Number. | 05 | - | - |

(2) Name of bank and Title of Branch

(3) Account Number (if any) | 06 |

STAMP OF BANK BRANCH

APPENDIX 12

Data Required for Monthly SDRT Computation

	WEEK (w)									
	1		2		3		4		5	
	Number of Shares	Value (£)	Number of Shares	Value (£)	Number of Shares	Value (£)	Number of Shares	Value (£)	Number of Shares	Value (£)
Issues (incl. 3rd party transfers liable for SDRT)										
Week w	330,000		110,000		400,000		200,000		600,000	
Week w+1	110,000		400,000		200,000		600,000		80,000	
(I)	440,000		510,000		600,000		800,000		680,000	
Surrenders (incl. 3rd party transfers liable for SDRT)										
Week w	500,000	160,000	30,000	9,600	100,000	32,000	650,000	208,000	150,000	48,000
Week w+1	30,000		100,000		650,000		150,000		950,000	
(S)	530,000		130,000		750,000		800,000		1,100,000	
Calculation (only if S>I)										
I/S x value of week w surrenders =		132,830		n/a		25,600		n/a		29,673
Plus										
Week w non pro-rata in-specie redemptions	5,000	1,600	3,750	1,200	0	0	0	0	1,500	480
Sub-Total 'A'		134,430		10,800		25,600		208,000		30,153
Calculation (where applicable)										
(N) Value of Non-Exempt assets		1,500,000		1,500,500		1,500,250		1,500,600		1,400,000
(E) Value of Exempt assets		500,000		501,000		500,500		500,600		450,000
Sub-Total 'B' (i.e.(N/N+E) x Sub-Total 'A')		100,823		8,097		19,196		155,969		22,818
SDRT Due		504.12		40.49		95.98		779.85		114.09
(Sub-total 'B' x 0.5% to nearest penny)								Total SDRT for Month =		1534.53
DECLARATION										
Week w Pro-rata In-Specie Redemptions	10,000		0		3,300		0		1,200	
Week w Exempt 3rd Party Transfers	600		1,000		2,000		600		4,500	

Collective Investment Schemes Administration

MULTIPLE CHOICE QUESTIONS

Tick one answer for each question. When you have completed all questions, refer to the end of this section for the correct answers.

1. Which of the following does not apply to a unit trust?

    A They are 'open ended'

    B They directly reflect the value of the underlying assets

    C Unit trust holders are the beneficial owners of the property of the scheme

    D Unit trust units are usually bought and sold via the Stock Exchange

2. Which ONE of the following does not have to be included in a unit trust deed?

    A Name of the scheme

    B Base currency

    C Duration of the scheme

    D Authorised status

3. When an initial offer of shares is made, how long after the ACD has received the price from the purchaser has he got to pay the depositary for those shares?

    A By the close of the third business day after the monies are received

    B By the close of the fourth business day after the monies are received

    C At the end of the third business day after the twenty-one day initial offer period expires

    D At the end of the fourth business day after the twenty-one day initial offer period expires

4. The annual accounting period of XYZ ICVC ends on 30 June each year. When is the latest date by which the ACD must publish the annual report?

    A 31 August

    B 30 September

    C 31 October

    D 30 November

5. A manager sells units at 200p. The unit price falls. How soon after dealing day must the manager issue cancellation notices to investors who have received investment advice in order that the shortfall provisions may apply? Within:

    A 5 days

    B 8 days

    C 10 days

    D 15 days

Collective Investment Schemes Administration

6. Under the Money Laundering regulations, financial institutions are required to keep records of customers and transactions for a minimum period after the relationship with the customer has ended. This period is at least:

   A 3 years

   B 5 years

   C 7 years

   D 12 years

7. A cash investment has been made by the ACD on Wednesday 10 February. When is the latest date he may pay the depositary?

   A 12 February

   B 13 February

   C 14 February

   D 15 February

8. If the annual general meeting of shareholders in an OEIC is called by the ACD and a quorum is not present, which of the following should happen?

   A Within 30 minutes the chairman should adjourn the meeting for not less than seven days thereafter

   B The chairman should get acceptance from those present to conduct the business

   C The chairman should write to the FSA informing them of what has happened

   D The ACD should re-circulate all members and call another meeting for one month after

9. In respect of a unit trust, which one of the following has ultimate responsibility for the register of unit holders?

   A The manager

   B The trustee

   C A registrar appointed by the manager

   D Either the manager or the trustee, as nominated in the trust deed

10. When an investor receives a final response from an OEIC in regard to a complaint regarding his investment, how long has the investor to refer the matter to the Financial Ombudsman Service?

    A 4 weeks

    B 8 weeks

    C 6 months

    D 12 months

11. Trustees to unit trusts must have a gross capital of at least:

    A £4m

    B £20m

    C £25m

    D £100m

12. An OEIC's liability to corporation tax is calculated on the balance of taxable income after the deduction of chargeable management expenses. Which of the following is not a chargeable expense?

    A Depositary's fees

    B Financial Services Authority fees

    C Auditor's fees

    D Stockbroker's fees

13. Which TWO of the following categories of asset in UCITS Retail Schemes have permitted investment borrowing powers?

    I Government and Public Securities

    II Gold

    III Derivatives

    IV Immovables (ie, real property)

    A I and III

    B II and III

    C II and IV

    D I and II

14. When distribution warrants are paid out to unit holders, how long are they normally valid from the date shown on the warrant?

    A 3 months

    B 6 months

    C 9 months

    D 12 months

15. On the winding up of a unit trust, which TWO of the following actions should the trustee take?

    I Pay unclaimed distribution payments into court 12 months after distribution date
    II If a relevant pension scheme, proceeds of realisation may be paid in accordance with distribution arrangements in the trust deed
    III Make a further distribution to existing holders to that already paid, if surplus funds available
    IV Keep any surplus for a further five years after distribution date

    A I and IV
    B II and III
    C I and II
    D III and IV

16. Which ONE of the following statements regarding the launch of an OEIC is FALSE?

    A An OEIC initial offer cannot exceed 21 days but must always be kept open for the whole of this period
    B An ACD cannot issue shares other than at the fixed initial price
    C If an ACD makes a preliminary charge it may make discounts from that charge
    D Shares are treated as issued during an offer period once the ACD has, prior to the close of the offer, agreed to sell shares or received an order

17. Which two of the following are the responsibility of the trustee/depository?

    I Creation and cancellation of units
    II Being custodian of the assets of the fund
    III Selecting the advertisements for the fund
    IV Selecting investments for the fund

    A I and II
    B II and III
    C III and IV
    D IV and I

18. With a securities company OEIC which is dedicated to investment in transferable securities, what is the limit on the percentage of transferable securities which are not approved securities, ie, those not officially listed?

    A 5%
    B 10%
    C 20%
    D 50%

19. Excluding back-to-back borrowing, what is the limit on borrowing on the value of an OEIC in one business day?

   A 2%

   B 5%

   C 10%

   D 20%

20. Which TWO of the following statements relating to the Register of Shareholders are TRUE?

   I Every OEIC must maintain a register of shareholders which must include all shareholders

   II The register may be closed for up to 30 days each calendar year

   III The register must be kept at the head office of the OEIC

   IV The register must contain the person designated in the instrument of incorporation (usually the ACD)

   A I and II

   B II and IV

   C III and IV

   D I and IV

21. An OEIC's annual accounting reference date is 31 December. When is the latest annual income date it may have?

   A 31 March

   B 30 April

   C 31 May

   D 30 June

22. All collective investment scheme operators are required to have complaints procedures. Which TWO of the following statements regarding complaints are FALSE?

   I Records of complaints must be kept for 5 years

   II Any complainant must be informed of receipt of complaint within 5 days

   III A return of complaints must be made annually to the Financial Services Authority

   IV Within 4 weeks of receiving a complaint, the complainant must be sent a final response or holding response

   A I and II

   B II and III

   C I and III

   D II and IV

23. When an OEIC pays an interest distribution, income tax has to be paid to HMRC. When must this be paid?

   A At the end of the month after the distribution is paid

   B At the end if the quarter in which the distribution is paid

   C The day following payment of the distribution

   D Two months after the end of the month the distribution is paid

24. On the advice of an Independent Financial Adviser, an investor buys 1,000 units at 200p. The investor receives his contract note and a cancellation rights notice the following day. He returns his cancellation notice 10 days after receipt with a letter requesting the return of his money. At the time of receipt by the manager the buying price is 199p and the selling price is 197p. Which ONE of the following statements is correct?

   A The manager must refund the £2,000 paid

   B The manager must pay the current buying cost of £1,990

   C The manager must refund £1,970

   D The manager is not obliged to accept the cancellation notice

25 The maximum penalty on conviction for assisting a money launderer is?

   A Unlimited fine

   B 5 years imprisonment and/or fine

   C 10 years imprisonment and/or fine

   D 14 years imprisonment and/or fine

ANSWERS TO SAMPLE MULTIPLE CHOICE QUESTIONS

1. D
2. C
3. B
4. C
5. B
6. B
7. D
8. A
9. D
10. C
11. A
12. D
13. A
14. B
15. C
16. A
17. A
18. B
19. C
20. B
21. B
22. C
23. B
24. B
25. D

WORKBOOK INDEX

Approval	51	Complaints Handling	47
Approved Money Market Instruments	104	Compliance	51
Approved Securities	102	Conduct of Business Sourcebook (COBS)	22
Auditor's Report	203	Consolidation	165
Auditors	94	Corporation Tax	213
Authorised Corporate Director (ACD)	87	Creation of Units/Shares	138
Authorised Fund Manager (AFM)	10, 85	Creation Prices	125
Authorised Fund Manager's Report	194	Data Protection Act (DPA)	29
Authorised Unit Trusts (AUTs)	67, 86	Data Protection Directive	29
Balance Sheet	200	Dealing Cut-off Point	26
Bankers Automated Clearing Services (BACS)	183	Dealing Process	135
		Dealing Spread	125
Bearer Unit/Shareholders	162	Delivery By Value (DBV)	112
Bed & Breakfast	231	Depositary	91
Bed & ISA	231	Deposits	104, 109
Borrowing	109	Derivatives	25, 28, 105, 110
Cancellation	52, 138	Dilution Adjustment	128
Cancellation Notice	54	Dilution Levy	128
Cancellation Prices	125	Direct Credit	184
Capital Gains Tax (CGT)	219	Discounts	141
Capital Requirements Directive (CRD)	41	Distance Marketing Directive (DMD)	43
Capital Taxes	230	Distribution	27, 178, 185
Cash/Near Cash	107	Distribution Table	201
Certificates	158	Distribution Warrants	184
Charges	27	Dividend Distributions	227
Classes of Shares	129	Dual-Pricing	120
Classes of Units	129	Effective Yield	179
Collective Investment Scheme Sourcebook (COLL)	11, 23, 93	Electronic Message Exchange (EMX)	144
		Eligible Assets Directive (EAD)	39
Commission Disclosure	146, 149	Eligible Markets	102
Commissions	141	Endowment Policies	15
Comparative Table	195	Equalisation	186
Compensation	50		

Errors	131, 140	Investment Management Association (IMA)	8
Exchange of Units/Shares	164	Investment Trust Company (ITC)	14
Expenses	27	Investment Trusts	14
Fair Value Pricing (FVP)	26, 133	ISAs	166
Financial Promotion	51	Key Facts	149
Financial Services Act 1986	21	Key Features	147
Financial Services and Markets Act 2000 (FSMA 2000)	21	Key Features Document (KFD)	27
		Legislation	21
Financial Services Compensation Scheme (FSCS)	50	Manager's Box	136
Form of Renunciation	137	Manual Records	29
Forward Pricing	130	Market Abuse Directive (MAD)	43
FSA Comparative Tables	206	Market Due Diligence review	102
FSA Handbook	22	Markets in Financial Instruments Directive (MiFID)	40
Gold	109	Material Portfolio Changes	201
Government and Public Securities (GAPS)	103	Meetings	57
Hard Disclosure	149	Mixed Funds	25
Hedging	105	Money Laundering	31
Historic Pricing	130	Money Laundering Regulations 2007	31
Holder Reconciliation Requests	159	Money Laundering Sourcebook	31
In Specie Cancellation	169	Non-life Products	146
In Specie Deals	139	Non-UCITS Retail Schemes (NURS)	11, 25, 108
In Specie Issues	169	Notional Broking Charges	122
Income	27	Offshore Funds	15
Income Distributions	182	Open-Ended Investment Companies (OEICs)	4, 68, 87
Income Payment	175		
Income Tax	213	Overseas Investments	17
Incorrect Prices	134	Overseas Transfers	30
Inheritance Tax (IHT)	232	Paying Agents	235
Initial Charge	124	Pound Cost Averaging	13
Initial Offer Period	25, 75	Price Publication	27
Instruments of Constitution	69	Pricing	75
Instruments of Incorporation	70	Pricing Checks	133
Insurance Bonds	15	Pricing Controls	131
Interest Distributions	228	Pricing Methods	119

Term	Page
Principles-based Regulation	21
Proceeds of Crime Act 2002	31, 35
Product Disclosure	146
Product Directive	100
Property Income Distributions (PIDs)	178
Prospectus	70
Qualified Investor Scheme (QIS)	11, 27, 111
Qualifying Money Market (QMM)	132
Qualifying Money Market Funds (QMMFs)	111
Quoted Bid Price	125
Real Property	109
Redemption Arrangements	26
Registration	155
Regulation	21
Reportable Persons	236
Reporting	237
Reporting Regime	233
Retirement Income	16
Risk Management Process	106
Savings and Investment Products Regulations 2004	56
Savings Income	237
Savings Plans	166
Scheme Structure	72
Senior Management Systems and Controls (SYSC) Sourcebook	90
Serious Organised Crime Agency (SOCA)	34
Settlement	167
Share Classes	72
Shareholder Rights	44
Shares	104
Short Report	25, 197
Shortfall	55
Simplified Prospectus	149
Single-Pricing	120, 127
Specialist Sectors	17
Stakeholder Products	56
Stamp Duty	221
Stamp Duty Reserve Tax (SDRT)	221
Statement of Recommended Practice (SORP)	25, 198
Stock Transfer Act 1963	159
Stocklending	113
Sub-Division	165
Sub-Registers	166
Tax Rates	214
Taxable Income	215
Taxes on Income	226
Termination	79
The Long Report	194
Total Asset Value	125
Transferable Securities	101, 108
Transfers	159
Treating Customers Fairly (TCF)	46
Trust Deeds	70
Trustee	91
Two-hour Notification Limit	26
UCITS Directive	4, 37
UCITS Management Directive	38
UCITS Retail Schemes	11
UCITS Schemes	101
Underlying Tax	218
Unit Trusts	3
Valuation	131
Value Added Tax (VAT)	220
Voting	60
Warrants	104
Winding up	79
Withholding Tax (WHT)	218, 238

SYLLABUS LEARNING MAP

COLLECTIVE INVESTMENT SCHEMES ADMINISTRATION

SYLLABUS 4.1 / WORKBOOK EDITION 5 COMPARISON

Syllabus Unit/Element		Workbook Chapter/Section
ELEMENT 1	**INTRODUCTION TO COLLECTIVE INVESTMENT SCHEMES**	**CHAPTER 1**
1.1	**The Introduction of Collective Investment Schemes**	
	On completion, the candidate should:	
1.1.1	*know* why Collective Investment Schemes were introduced and how they are used	Section 1
1.1.2	*know* the influence of the following on the development of schemes:	
	• Launch of fixed trusts	Section 1
	• Introduction of flexible trusts	Section 1
	• EU and the introduction of UCITS	Sections 1.2, 2, 2.3
1.1.3	*know* the principal types of funds available by asset class and the IMA performance categories	Section 2.2
1.1.4	*know* what statistical reporting is made by AFMs to industry and government bodies	Section 2.2
1.1.5	*know* the comparative features, advantages and disadvantages in contrast to other forms of investment (direct and indirect)	Sections 3.2, 4
1.1.6	*know* the key differences between onshore and offshore funds	Section 4.4
1.1.7	*understand* how schemes can be used to meet different investment objectives	Section 5
1.1.8	*know* the purpose of authorising Collective Investment Schemes and the classification of those schemes by the FSA	Section 3.1
ELEMENT 2	**REGULATORY CONTROLS**	**CHAPTER 2**
2.1	**UK Regulation and Legislation**	
	On completion, the candidate should:	
2.1.1	*know* the requirements of the Conduct of Business Rules relating to authorisation of Collective Investment Scheme Operators (	Section 1.1
2.1.2	*know* the framework of UK regulation and the purpose of the following:	Sections 1.2, 1.3
	• The FSA Collective Investment Schemes Sourcebook (COLL)	
	• The OEIC Regulations 2001	
2.1.3	*know* the reasons for the Data Protection Act 1998 and the responsibilities of investment groups	Section 2
2.2	**The Prevention of Financial Crime**	
	On completion, the candidate should:	
2.2.1	*know* the requirements of The Proceeds of Crime Act 2002, The Money Laundering Regulations 2003 and The Joint Money Laundering Steering Group guidance as they apply to:	Section 3
	• control systems	
	• record keeping	
	• staff training	
	• reporting procedures	
	• roles and responsibilities of a Money Laundering Reporting Officer	
2.2.2	*be able to apply* the Money Laundering requirements for new and existing clients	Section 3.5
2.2.3	*know* what is satisfactory evidence and when it is required	Section 3.5
2.2.4	*understand* the importance of verification	Section 3.5
2.2.5	*be able to apply* the actions required if inadequate evidence is provided	Section 3.3, 3.4
2.2.6	*understand* the importance of being able to recognise a suspicious transaction	Section 3.4

Syllabus Unit/Element		Workbook Chapter/Section
	and the procedures for reporting it	
2.2.7	*understand* the role of the FSA and other crime prevention agencies in relation to Money Laundering and financial crime prevention	Section 3.7
2.2.8	*know* the requirements firms and individuals need to meet in relation to Money Laundering and financial crime prevention and the implications of not meeting the requirements	Section 3.3, 3.7
2.3	**European Union Directives**	
	On completion, the candidate should:	
2.3.1	*know* the purpose of the following EU directives:	
	• Undertakings of Collective Investment in Transferable Securities Directive (UCITS)	Section 4.1
	• Eligible Assets Directive (EAD)	Section 4
	• Markets in Financial Instruments Directive (MiFID)	Section 4.3
	• Capital Requirements Directive (CRD)	Section 4.4
	• Distance Marketing Directive (DMD)	Section 4.5
	• Market Abuse Directive (MAD)	Section 4
	• European Savings Directive (EUSD)	Section 4
2.4	**Rights and Protection of Unit/Shareholders**	
	On completion, the candidate should:	
2.4.1	*know* the outcomes arising from the FSA's principles-based approach to treating customers fairly (TCF)	Section 5.4
2.4.2	*know* the regulatory procedures for handling customer complaints	Section 5.5
2.4.3	*know* the role of the Financial Ombudsman Service	Section 5.6
2.4.4	*understand* the circumstances under which the Financial Services Compensation Scheme pays compensation and know the compensation payable	Section 5.7
2.4.5	*know* the circumstances under which cancellation rights are available to investors including under the EU Distance Marketing directive	Section 7
2.4.6	*be able to calculate* cancellation proceeds including shortfall when applicable	Section 7.4
2.4.7	*understand* the protection provided by stakeholder products	Section 8
2.4.8	*understand* the rights of unit/shareholders in relation to changes to the fund and the protection afforded by meetings	Sections 9, 10
ELEMENT 3	**CONSTITUTION**	**CHAPTER 3**
3.1	**Establishment of a Scheme**	
	On completion, the candidate should:	
3.1.1	*know* the alternative constitutional structures of authorised Collective Investment Schemes	Section 1
3.1.2	*understand* the process and requirements of authorisation	Section 1.4
3.1.3	*know* the purpose of the following documents:	Section 1.4, 2, 2.4
	• Instrument of Incorporation (OEIC)	
	• Trust Deed (Unit Trust)	
	• Prospectus and Simplified Prospectus	
	• Key features/key facts	
	• Marketing plan	
	• FSA Application Form and Solicitor's Certificate	
3.2	**Scheme Structure**	
	On completion, the candidate should:	
3.2.1	*know* the differences between single fund and umbrella schemes	Section 3
3.2.2	*know* the permissible share and unit classes issued by schemes	Section 3.1
3.2.3	*know* the following characteristics of scheme constitution:	Section 4

Syllabus Unit/Element		Workbook Chapter/Section
	• issue and cancellation (on a continuing basis)	
	• limited issue	
	• limited redemption	
	• guaranteed	
3.2.4	*understand* the treatment of the following in respect to the initial offer period:	Section 5
	• share and unit issue	
	• large market movement	
	• pricing	
	• settlement	
3.3	**Termination /Re-organisation of Collective Investment Schemes**	
	On completion, the candidate should:	
3.3.1	*know* the process and relevant regulatory requirements in relation to:	
	• termination	Section 7
	• conversion	Section 6
	• amalgamation	Section 6
	• reconstruction	Section 6
ELEMENT 4	**ROLES AND RESPONSIBILITIES**	**CHAPTER 4**
4.1	**The Role of the Authorised Fund Manager (AFM)**	
	On completion, the candidate should:	
4.1.1	*know* the role of the AFM in relation to the following:	Section 1
	• making investment decisions	
	• box management	
	• investor transactions (AFM as agent or principal)	
	• maintaining register of holders	
	• maintaining other client and scheme records	
	• valuation and pricing	
	• distribution of income	
	• voting	
	• issuing reports	
	• compliance with investment and borrowing regulations	
	• marketing the fund	
4.1.2	*Know* the scope for delegation by the AFM of:	Section 3.4
	• investment management	
	• fund accounting	
	• registration and client administration	
4.1.3	*know* the FSA's requirements for the outsourcing of delegated activities	Section 3.4.1
4.2	**Depositaries, Trustees and Custodians**	
	On completion, the candidate should:	
4.2.1	*know* the role and responsibilities of depositary or trustee in relation to the following:	Section 4
	• protecting investors	
	• oversight of the AFM in relation to scheme management	
	• custody of the funds assets	
	• registers and sub registers	
	• delegation	
	• issuing and cancelling units	
	• valuation	
	• accuracy of prices	

Syllabus Unit/Element			Workbook Chapter/Section
		• breach reporting	
4.3		**The Auditors**	
		On completion, the candidate should:	
4.3.1		*know* the requirements for appointment of the auditors	Section 5
4.3.2		*know* the auditors' rights, obligations and responsibilities for the following:	Section 5
		• conducting an audit	
		• reporting to the FSA	
		• reporting to shareholders/unit holders	
ELEMENT 5		**INVESTMENT AND BORROWING POWERS**	**CHAPTER 5**
5.1		**General Principles**	
		On completion, the candidate should:	
5.1.1		*understand* the requirement for a prudent spread of risk and the principles of investment and borrowing powers	Section 1
5.1.2		*know* the basis for investment or borrowing limits, the factors used in and obligations attached to valuing scheme property	Sections 1, 5
5.2		**Rules Relating to Investment**	
		On completion, the candidate should:	
5.2.1		*know* the definitions of:	Section 2.1
		• eligible markets	
		• transferable securities	
		• approved securities	
		• derivatives	
		• approved derivatives	
		• off-exchange derivatives	
5.2.2		*know* the specific limits applying to:	
		• UCITS funds	Section 2
		• Non-UCITS retail funds	Section 3
		• Qualified Investor Schemes (QIS)/Qualifying Money Market schemes (QMM)	Section 2
5.3		**Borrowing and Stock Lending Powers**	
		On completion, the candidate should:	
5.3.1		*know* the definitions, uses and restrictions of stock lending	Section 6
5.3.2		*know* the restrictions and powers relating to cash, borrowing, stock lending and the exceptions applying	Section 7
ELEMENT 6		**INVESTOR TRANSACTIONS**	**CHAPTER 6**
6.1		**Information available to Investors**	
		On completion, the candidate should:	
6.1.1		*know* the AFM's responsibilities to make available and/or supply the following:	Section 11
		• Prospectus	
		• Simplified prospectus (NOTE: Clive to update)	
		• Key features/key facts	
		• Report and accounts (including short reports)	
		• Trust Deed/Instrument of Incorporation	
6.2		**Valuation/Pricing/Charges**	
		On completion, the candidate should:	
6.2.1		*know* how and when valuations are made including frequency	Introduction
6.2.2		*be able to calculate* the price of units and shares using the different methods permitted by the FSA	Introduction, Sections 2, 3

Syllabus Unit/Element			Workbook Chapter/Section
6.2.3		understand how prices are calculated for funds with multiple share classes	Section 2
6.2.4		know the charges that may be made by the AFM	Sections 2, 3
6.2.5		understand the AFM's discretion in setting dealing prices under single and dual pricing	Sections 2.5, 3
6.2.6		know the requirements for price publication	Introduction
6.2.7		know the requirements for notification to the depositary/trustee	Section 6
6.2.8		know the definitions, uses and requirements of forward and historic pricing	Sections 3, 4
6.2.9		know what constitutes a pricing error, the consequences and the action to be taken by the AFM and trustee/depositary	Sections 5, 9
6.3		**Buying, Selling and Exchange of Shares/Units**	
		On completion, the candidate should:	
6.3.1		understand how different classes are used for different types of investor	Section 3.3
6.3.2		know the difference between an exchange and a conversion	**Chapter 7, Section 6, 7**
6.3.3		be able to apply the IMA's suggested formula to ensure proper and fair exchange of shares/units	**Chapter 7, Section 7**
6.3.4		be able to calculate the number of units following conversion	**Chapter 7, Section 6**
6.3.5		understand the AFMs' discretion in relation to:	Section 3, 8.2
		• large redemptions	
		• in specie transactions	
		• dilution levy/dilution adjustment	
		• Stamp Duty Reserve Tax	
6.3.6		be able to calculate purchase consideration and redemption proceeds using the different methods permitted by the FSA	Sections 2, 3, 4
6.4		**Investing through Intermediaries**	
		On completion, the candidate should:	
6.4.1		know the methods by which investor transactions are executed	Section 10
6.4.2		know the documentation required in relation to the execution of investor transactions	Section 11
6.4.3		understand how commissions and discounts affect investor transactions	Section 10
6.4.4		know the definition, role and function of intermediaries	Section 10
6.4.5		understand the treatment of distributions of income and other rights	Ch 8, Introduction
6.4.6		understand the difference between investing direct with the AFM or via a an intermediary	Section 10
ELEMENT 7		**REGISTRATION AND SETTLEMENT**	**CHAPTER 7**
7.1		**Registration**	
		On completion, the candidate should:	
7.1.1		know the requirements for the establishment, maintenance and contents of a Register	Sections 1, 4
7.1.2		understand who can be registered as a holder of units/shares	Section 2
7.1.3		know the status of the Register as proof of ownership	Section 2
7.1.4		know the process for rectification of registration errors	Section 2
7.1.5		understand the registration treatment of third party interests	Section 2
7.1.6		understand the entitlement to inspection	Section 2
7.1.7		know the requirements for the collection of beneficial holder details	Section 3.1.1
7.2		**Transfers of Title**	
		On completion, the candidate should:	
7.2.1		understand the processes and information requirements relating to transfers by the holder, in favour of the AFM, and by the operation of law	Section 3

Syllabus Unit/Element		Workbook Chapter/Section
7.2.2	*Know* the differences between transfers	Section 3
	• by the holder	
	• to the AFM	
	• to third parties	
	• by operation of law	
7.2.3	*understand* the objectives of introducing electronic transfer of title for Collective Investment Schemes	Section 3.4
7.3	**Sub-Division and Consolidation**	
	On completion, candidates should:	
7.3.1	*know* the Capital Gains Tax implications of conversions on a value-for-value basis	Sections 6, 7
7.3.2	*know* the AFM's procedures for sub-dividing or consolidating units/shares	Section 8
7.4	**Sub-Registers for Savings Plans and ISAs**	
	On completion, candidates should:	
7.4.1	*know* the requirements governing the sub-registers for savings plans and ISAs	Section 9
7.4.2	*know* the rights of holders on sub-registers	Section 9
7.4.3	*know* who has responsibility for sub-registers	Section 9
7.5	**Settlement**	
	On completion, the candidate should:	
7.5.1	*know* the regulatory requirements for settlement	Section 10
7.5.2	*understand* the different methods of settling investor transactions:	Section 10
ELEMENT 8	**DISTRIBUTION OF INCOME**	**CHAPTER 8**
8.1	**Income and Distributions**	
	On completion, the candidate should:	
8.1.1	*know* the sources of income	Section 1
8.1.2	*understand* the different treatment of income for income and accumulation shares/units	Section 1.1
8.1.3	*be able to apply* the timetable for distribution of income	Section 1.1
8.1.4	*be able to calculate* the available income	Section 1.3
8.1.5	*know* the requirements for calculation of the effective yield	Section 1.5
8.1.6	*know* the difference between dividend, interest and property income distributions and the relevant criteria	Section 1.4
8.1.7	*know* the customary payment processes and their associated requirements for the following:	Section 2
	• tax vouchers	Section 2
	• BACS	Section 2.1
	• distribution warrants	Section 2.2
8.1.8	*know* the treatment of unclaimed distributions	Section 2.2
8.2	**Income Equalisation and Tax Vouchers**	
	On completion, the candidate should:	
8.2.1	*know* the contents of tax vouchers in relation to distributions, including requirements for corporate investors	Section 2.3
8.2.2	*know* the definition of equalisation and its treatment in respect to investor's tax liability	Section 3
8.2.3	*understand* the equalisation rate calculation	Section 3
8.2.4	*know* how equalisation is shown on tax vouchers	Section 2.3
8.2.5	*understand* the alternative methods of delivering tax voucher information	Sections 2.3, 2.4
	• single tax vouchers	
	• composite tax vouchers	

Syllabus Unit/Element		Workbook Chapter/Section
	• electronic tax vouchers	
ELEMENT 9	**INVESTOR COMMUNICATIONS**	**CHAPTER 9**
9.1	**Annual and Half Yearly Reports and Accounts**	
	On completion, the candidate should:	
9.1.1	*know* the FSA requirements in relation to the reports and accounts	Sections 1, 3, 4
9.1.2	*understand* the purpose and benefits of short reports	Section 1
9.1.3	*know* the difference in content between short reports and long form report and accounts	Section 1
9.1.4	*know* the requirements of the Statement of Recommended Practice (SORP) in relation to the content of the long form annual and half yearly reports and accounts:	Section 2
	• the statement of total return	
	• the statement of movement in unit/shareholders' funds	
	• the balance sheet	
	• the portfolio statement	
	• summary of material portfolio changes	
	• notes to the accounts	
	• distribution tables	
9.1.5	*know* the main differences between interim and final reports and accounts	Section 1.2
9.1.6	*understand* what investors should look for in the reports and accounts	Sections 5, 6
9.1.7	*know* the different methods by which reports may be delivered to investors	Section 5
ELEMENT 10	**TAXATION**	**CHAPTER 10**
10.1	**Corporation Tax and Income Tax on the Fund**	
	On completion, the candidate should:	
10.1.1	*understand know* the basis on which authorised Collective Investment Schemes are taxed	
	• Corporation Tax	Section 1.1
	• Capital Gains Tax exemption	Section 2.1
	• income tax on interest received	Section 1.3
	• payment dates and returns made	Section 1.1
	• deductible and non-deductible expenses	Section 1.4
10.1.2	*know* the tax treatment of different types of income distribution	Sections 1.2, 1.3
10.2	**Other Taxes**	
	On completion, the candidate should:	
10.2.1	*know* the types of overseas taxes on income received in the UK from an overseas company and the treatment of such taxes as they affect the income available for distribution	Section 2
10.2.2	*know* the treatment of VAT on umbrella-type schemes	Section 2.2
10.2.3	*know* the situations in which UK Stamp Duties are likely to arise	Section 2.3
10.2.4	*understand* the treatment of Collective Investment Schemes for Stamp Duty Reserve Tax (SDRT) and exemptions:	Section 2.3
	• basic treatment	
	• in specie contributions and redemptions	
	• fund reconstructions and mergers	
10.2.5	*know* the HM Revenue & Customs' information requirements, timetable for returns and payments, and penalties, in relation to SDRT	Section 2.3
10.2.6	*know* AFM's options in making an SDRT provision	Section 2.3
10.3	**Taxation Implications for Investors**	
	On completion, the candidate should:	

Syllabus Unit/Element		Workbook Chapter/Section
10.3.1	*know* the income tax, Corporation Tax and Capital Gains Tax implications for the following investors:	Sections 3.1, 3.3
	• corporate (including other Collective Investment Schemes)	
	• individuals (tax payers, non-tax payers and ISA investors)	
10.3.2	*know* the taxation treatment of dividend and interest distributions	Sections 3.2, 3.3
10.3.3	*know* the main types of investor eligible for gross payment of interest distributions:	Sections 3.3, 3.4
	• corporate (including other Collective Investment Schemes)	
	• ISA plan managers	
	• charities	
	• pensions funds	
	• non-residents	
10.3.4	*know* the information that must be provided by eligible investors in order to receive gross distributions	Section 3.4
10.3.5	*understand* the potential liability to UK Capital Gains Tax on the disposal of shares/units	Section 3.5
		Section 3.5
10.3.6	*understand* the use of "Bed & ISA" or "Bed & Spouse" to maximise use of Capital Gains Tax relief/allowance	Section 3.5
10.3.7	*know* the implications of share values for Inheritance Tax purposes for domiciled and non-domiciled holders	Section 3.6
10.4	**HM Revenue & Customs Information Reporting**	
	On completion, the candidate should:	
10.4.1	*understand* the background and purpose of reporting obligations arising under the Taxes Management Act and the EU Savings Directive:	Section 4
10.4.2	*know* the requirements in relation to the following:	Section 4
	• payments to be reported	
	• reporting dates	
	• paying agents	
	• reportable persons	
	• withholding tax	

Examination Specification

Each examination paper is constructed from a specification that determines the weightings that will be given to each element. The specification is given below.

It is important to note that the numbers quoted may vary slightly from examination to examination as there is an element of flexibility to ensure that each examination has a consistent level of difficulty. However, the number of questions tested in each element should not change by more than plus or minus 2.

Examination specification 50 multiple choice questions		
Element number	Element	Questions
1	Introduction to Collective Investment Schemes	3
2	Regulatory Controls	8
3	Constitution	3
4	Roles and Responsibilities	3
5	Investment and Borrowing Powers	4
6	Investor Transactions	9
7	Registration and Settlement	7
8	Distribution of Income	5
9	Investor Communications	3
10	Taxation	5
	Total	50

CANDIDATE UPDATE

Candidates are reminded to check the 'Candidate Update' area of the Institute's website (www.sii.org.uk) on a regular basis for updates that could affect their examination as a result of industry change.

pre exam stress ?

Studying for a Securities & Investment Institute qualification is hard work and we're sure you're putting in plenty of hours, but don't lose sight of your goal! This is just the first step in your career, there is much more to achieve!

The securities and investments industry attracts ambitious and driven individuals. You're probably one yourself and that's great, but on the other hand you're almost certainly surrounded by lots of other people with similar ambitions. So how can you stay one step ahead during these uncertain times?

post exam success !

Using your new SII qualification* to become an Associate (ASI) member of the Securities & Investment Institute could well be the next important career move you make this year, and help you maintain your competence.

Join our global network of over 40,000 financial services professionals and start enjoying both the professional and personal benefits that SII membership offers. Once you become a member you can use the well recognised ASI designation after your name; the further acknowledgment you deserve for achieving your award.

(* ie, IAQ, IFQ, SII Certificate Programme)

Turn over to find out more about SII membership

> " ... competence is not just about examinations. It is about skills, knowledge, expertise, ethical behaviour and the application and maintenance of all these "
>
> April 2008
> FSA, Retail Distribution Review Interim Report

Becoming an Associate member of SII offers you...

- ✓ Use of the SII CPD Scheme
- ✓ Unlimited free CPD seminars
- ✓ Highly recognised designatory letters
- ✓ Free access to online training tools including Professional Refresher and Infolink
- ✓ Free webcasts and podcasts
- ✓ Unlimited free attendance at SII Professional Interest Forums
- ✓ SII publications including S&I Review and Regulatory Update
- ✓ 20% discount on all SII conferences and training courses
- ✓ Ask an Expert - online question and answer service
- ✓ Invitation to SII Annual Lecture
- ✓ SII Select Benefits — our exclusive personal benefits portfolio

Plus many other networking opportunities which could be invaluable for your career.

Joining Fee: £25
(waived for online applications)

Annual Subscription: £105 (pro rata)

To upgrade your student membership to Associate,

get in touch...

SECURITIES & INVESTMENT INSTITUTE

+44 (0)20 7645 0650
memberservices@sii.org.uk
www.sii.org.uk/membership

# SECURITIES & INVESTMENT INSTITUTE

The Securities & Investment Institute is the professional body for qualified and experienced practitioners of good repute engaged in a wide range of securities and other financial services businesses. The Institute's purpose is to promote high standards of personal integrity, business ethics and professional competence and to create opportunities for practitioners to meet for professional and social purposes. Please call 020 7645 0600 or visit www.sii.org.uk for more information.

ASSOCIATE STATUS

Associate status is a professional designation offered by the Securities & Investment Institute in recognition of the achievement of a benchmark qualification. Through Associate status, the Institute offers practitioners the opportunity to meet regulatory requirements to maintain competence. Upon achieving the Investment Administration Qualification (IAQ) individuals become eligible for Associate status. The use of the designatory letters 'ASI' demonstrates a high level of competency within the financial services industry and a commitment to high standards and professional integrity. For further information please telephone the Membership Department on 020 7645 0650.

CONTINUING COMPETENCE

On successful completion of the IAQ, and to meet regulatory requirements, individuals will be required to keep their industry knowledge up-to-date by undertaking Continuing Competence. The Institute offers an extensive range of courses, conferences and workshops which provide excellent opportunities to keep in touch with industry developments. Telephone our Client Services team on 020 7645 0680 for more information. Membership of the Institute provides access to a programme of free Continuing Professional Development (CPD) Events and information on a range of topics on the website. See the Membership section of our website (www.sii.org.uk) or telephone the Membership Department on 020 7645 0650.

LEARNING RESOURCES EVALUATION FORM

FROM: _____

FIRM: _____

TEL NO: _____

PUBLICATION: _____

DATE OF PURCHASE: _____

Please use numbers 1 – 4 to indicate your views.
1 = Excellent / Strongly Affirmative, 2 = Good / Affirmative, 3 = Adequate / Slightly Negative, 4 = Poor / Strongly Negative

Q1. Are you satisfied with our speed of response to your order?
Q2. Did your publication arrive in good condition?
Q3. Do you find the layout and presentation helpful to your studies?
Q4. Does the book cover everything you feel it should?
Q5. Is it relevant to your training needs?
Q6. Please expand upon your views here, or tell us anything that may help us with our continuous improvement programme:

_____
_____
_____
_____

When completed, please fax to **020 7645 0601** or post to:
Learning & Resources, Securities & Investment Institute, 8 Eastcheap London EC3M 1AE

We phone a proportion of our customers to follow up their evaluation. If you do NOT want to be contacted, please tick this box: ☐

SII External Specialists
Joining The Team

SECURITIES & INVESTMENT INSTITUTE

— network with your peers
— qualify for the SII's CPD Scheme
— keep up-to-date with your industry knowledge
— attend our Annual External Specialists event

If you would like to become one of our External Specialists and help the Institute then we would very much like to hear from you.

SII Workbooks

Authors
Experienced freelance authors with experience in the financial sector, and who have had published work in their area of specialism, are sought. Requirements include:

- updating a specific Institute workbook as per a new syllabus and industry changes
- ensuring that the syllabus (with regard to new/altered syllabus sections/learning objectives) is covered
- addressing workbook review comments where necessary

Workbook Reviewers
Individuals with a high-level of knowledge of the subject area are sought. Requirements include:

- highlighting any inconsistencies against the syllabus
- ensuring that the coverage is sufficient
- providing a review of the workbook
- assessing the author's interpretation of the workbook

Also sought.....workbook proofreaders and technical support.

SII Examinations

Exam Question Writers/Editors
Subject specialists are sought to write questions for specific SII exam subjects. Requirements include:

- being able to produce SII exam standard questions to agreed deadlines
- ensuring that questions are written/edited against the learning objectives
- knowledge of the subject a distinct advantage though not essential

Exam Advisors
Advisors ensure the accuracy and relevance of the examination. Requirements include:

- attending panel meetings
- supporting the Examination Manager with occasional examination-related issues
- offering advice and guidance on industry changes that may affect the exam

Also sought.....syllabus and exam panel members.

> *Being an Item Writer enables me to contribute to the work of the Institute. It is an opportunity to give something back after having received so much from others. As a side benefit, writing good items requires accurate knowledge, so it is an incentive to keep up-to-date with developments in the industry.*
>
> Paul Banji, Project Manager, Regulatory Management

SII's Suite of Workbooks and Exams

The Institute is looking for external specialists in the following subject areas.....

Investment Administration Qualification (IAQ)
Exams & Workbooks

The SII Investment Administration Qualification (IAQ) is a practitioner-led programme for administration and operations staff. It equips individuals with an overview of the financial services industry and its regulation, and of their particular industry sector.

- Introduction to Securities & Investment
- FSA Financial Regulation
- Asset Servicing
- Collective Investment Schemes Administration
- CREST Settlement
- Exchange-Traded Derivatives Administration
- Global Securities Operations
- ISA & CTF Administration
- IT in Investment Operations
- Operational Risk
- OTC Derivatives Admin
- Principles of Financial Regs
- Private Client Administration

Certificates
Exams & Workbooks

The SII Certificate programme is designed specifically to meet the requirements of individuals working in the securities and derivatives markets who need to obtain Financial Services Authority (FSA) Approved Person status.

- FSA Financial Regulation
- Securities
- Derivatives
- Securities & Financial Derivatives
- Investment Management
- Principles of Financial Regulation
- Financial Derivatives
- Investment & Risk

Diploma
Exams only

The SII Diploma is the UK's leading postgraduate finance qualification. The exams reflect situations and issues that practitioners will encounter and require students to apply their knowledge to answer case studies, write reports and explain techniques and terms.

- Bond and Fixed Interests
- Financial Derivatives
- Fund Management
- Global Operations Management
- Interpretation of Financial Statements
- Investment Analysis
- Management Studies
- Private Client Investment Administration and Management
- Regulation and Compliance

SII Masters
Exams only

The SII Masters (SIIM) in Wealth Management, the first qualification in the SII Masters Programme, offers wealth managers, IFA's and private client managers a postgraduate level qualification encompassing the knowledge needed to give a high quality service to clients.

- Financial Markets
- Portfolio Construction Theory
- Applied Wealth Management

Certificate in Corporate Finance
Exams only

The Certificate In Corporate Finance is aimed at individuals working in corporate finance and related areas, such as venture capital, who need to demonstrate a sound understanding of both regulatory and technical aspects of the subject.

- Corporate Finance Regulation
- Corporate Finance Technical Foundations

International Certificate in Financial Advice (ICFA)
Exams & Workbooks

ICFA is a quality benchmark for firms to ensure that their financial advisers understand the fundamentals of financial advice. It is a global qualification that reflects the knowledge and skills base required to advise private clients in the retail sector of the industry.

- International Certificate in Financial Advice (ICFA)

Islamic Finance Qualification (IFQ)
Exams & Workbooks

Developed in conjunction with Ecole Supérieure des Affaires in Beirut, the IFQ is a ground-breaking qualification that covers Islamic finance from both a technical and Sharia'a perspective, providing the first international benchmark in the area of Islamic finance.

- Islamic Finance Qualification (IFQ)

Advanced Certificates
Exams & Workbooks

The Advanced Certificate programme offers staff a range of post-benchmark qualifications. The aim of the Advanced Certificates is to make available to staff and their firms a career pathway that is on a par with the senior qualifications available to sales staff.

- Advanced Global Securities Operations
- Advanced Investment Schemes Administration
- Advanced Operational Risk

SII Mission statement:

> **To set the standards of professional excellence and integrity for individual practitioners and to provide the means of attaining them.**

If you're interested in joining the team contact us now:

john.o'keeffe@sii.org.uk or call **020 7645 0624**

A dedicated website area for SII external specialists.....**www.sii.org.uk/specialists**

SII CPD Scheme:	SII External Specialists:	SII Membership:
www.sii.org.uk/cpdscheme	www.sii.org.uk/specialists	www.sii.org.uk/membership

ORDER FORM | WORKBOOKS & eLEARNING PRODUCTS | SECURITIES & INVESTMENT INSTITUTE

Workbooks
The Securities & Investment Institute produces workbooks which are specifically aimed at those who work in the securities and investment industry, not only in the UK but also overseas.
Price: £75 (except for Advanced Operational Risk: £25).

eIAQ - elearning product
eIAQ, which is recommended for IAQ™ examination preparation, is an online study tool to be used in conjunction with Securities & Investment Institute workbooks.
Price: £35 per single user licence
(Discounts are available on large orders: call 020 7645 0680 for details)

Revision Express - elearning product
Revision Express consists of revision questions and is recommended for IAQ™ and Certificate examination preparation.
Price: £35 per single user licence
(Discounts are available on large orders: call 020 7645 0680 for details)

Link Pack = an SII Workbook + an SII elearning product
You can purchase an SII workbook (IAQ or Certificate) plus an SII elearning product (either eIAQ or Revision Express Online) for a combined price of just **£100** (a saving of £10).

PERSONAL DETAILS

Full name: _____ Date of Birth: _____
Firm/Organisation name: _____ Email: _____
Address: Home ☐ / Work ☐
_____ Postcode: _____ Daytime telephone: _____

☐ I enclose a cheque for £............... **Please make cheques payable to Securities & Investment Institute & cross 'Account Payee Only'.**

☐ Please charge to our Account *(customer number)*: _____

☐ I authorise you to debit my payment card with the amount of £............... **Please fill out your card details fully: no goods will be dispatched without a signature.**

Card number: ☐☐☐☐ ☐☐☐☐ ☐☐☐☐ ☐☐☐☐   ☐ Amex ☐ Delta/Switch ☐ Eurocard ☐ MasterCard ☐ Visa

Expiry date: ☐☐☐☐   Issue date: ☐☐☐☐   Switch only issue number: ☐☐☐☐

Signature: _____

Card holder's address: *(if different from above)*
☐☐☐☐☐☐☐☐☐☐☐☐☐☐☐☐☐☐☐☐☐☐☐☐☐☐☐
☐☐☐☐☐☐☐☐☐☐☐☐☐ Postcode: ☐☐☐☐☐☐

Date: _____

Please note: purchases made with a credit card will incur a 2% surcharge to cover administration & handling fees. This does not apply to debit card transactions.

IAQ — The **IAQ™** is a practitioner-led programme for administration and operations staff. It equips individuals with an overview of the financial services industry and its regulation as well as providing a detailed picture of their particular industry sector.

	Workbook (£75)	Revision Express (£35)	eIAQ (£35)	Link Pack (£100)
Asset Servicing	☐	☐	☐	☐
Collective Investment Schemes Admin	☐	☐	☐	☐
CREST Settlement	☐	☐	☐	☐
Exchange-Traded Derivatives Admin	☐	☐	☐	☐
FSA Financial Regulation	☐	☐	☐	☐
Global Securities Operations	☐	☐	☐	☐
Introduction to Securities & Investment	☐	☐	☐	☐
International Introduction to Securities & Investment	☐	☐	☐	☐
ISA & CTF Administration	☐	☐	☐	☐
IT in Investment Operations	☐	☐	☐	☐
Operational Risk	☐	☐	☐	☐
OTC Derivatives Administration	☐	☐	☐	☐
Principles of Financial Regulation	☐	☐	☐	☐
Private Client Administration	☐	☐	☐	☐

The SII **Certificate programme** is designed specifically to meet the requirements of individuals working in the securities and derivatives markets who need to obtain Financial Services Authority (FSA) Approved Person status.

	Workbook (£75)	Revision Express (£35)	Link Pack (£100)
FSA Financial Regulation	☐	☐	☐
Securities	☐	☐	☐
Derivatives	☐	☐	☐
Securities & Financial Derivatives	☐	☐	☐
Investment Management	☐	☐	☐
International Certificate in Investment Management	☐	☐	☐
Principles of Financial Regulation	☐	☐	☐
Financial Derivatives Module	☐	☐	☐
Investment & Risk	☐	☐	☐
Commodity Derivatives	☐	☐	☐

International Workbooks — Workbook (£75)
International Certificate in Financial Advice	☐
Islamic Finance Qualification	☐
Dubai Rules & Regulations	☐

Advanced Certificates Workbooks — Workbook (£75)
Advanced Global Securities Operations	☐
Advanced Operational Risk (£25)	☐
Advanced Investment Schemes Admin	☐

Introduction to Investment	☐
International Introduction to Investment	☐

Introduction to Investment is the ideal induction qualification for new staff across the industry. It is appropriate for students preparing to enter the industry (for example as part of a Higher or Further Education programme) or for those newly recruited to the industry as part of their in-house induction programme.

TO ORDER: tick the box(es) above and enter the sub-total, delivery (if applicable) and full total in the TOTAL box.

SUB-TOTAL: £ _____   Delivery: £ _____   TOTAL: £ _____

DELIVERY CHARGES
1 workbook = £10.00 outside London (free within London)
2-5 workbooks = 10% of cost of total order
Over 5 workbooks = FREE

Then photocopy this form and **fax to 020 7645 0601** OR post to:
Client Services, Securities & Investment Institute, 8 Eastcheap, London EC3M 1AE
Telephone: 020 7645 0680 Facsimile: 020 7645 0601 Email: clientservices@sii.org.uk
For more information about these products visit **www.sii.org.uk**

International: Overseas and Channel Islands orders, contact Client Services on **+44(0)20 7645 0680**, or email **clientservices@sii.org.uk**

The SII would like to keep you informed of products and services that may be of interest to you. If you do not wish to receive this information, please tick this box. ☐

A Registered Charity number 1036566. Registered office as above. VAT registration number 644 8569 95. A company limited by guarantee and registered in England and Wales number 2687534.

elearning
....helping you prepare for your exam

You've bought the workbook.....
...now test your knowledge before your examination

SII elearning products are high quality, interactive and engaging learning tools and revision aids which can be used in conjunction with SII workbooks, or to help you remain up to date with regulatory developments in order to meet compliance requirements.

Revision Express Online

Developed for those taking the IAQ™ and the Certificates programmes, and used in conjunction with the workbook, Revision Express Online is an internet-based revision aid that consists of tests that are designed to look and feel like the exam that candidates will face.

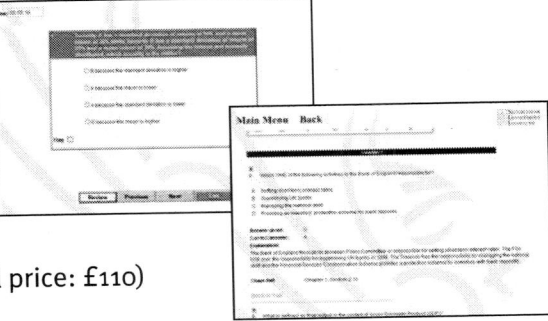

Key Features of Revision Express Online

- A large database of over 200 questions per title
- Edition accurate: only current versions are available
- Remembers all past test results, even after logging off

Price per module: £35
Price when purchased with the SII workbook: £100 (normal price: £110)

eIAQ

eIAQ is an interactive and engaging online study tool to be used with the SII's IAQ™. It contains graphics, exercises and incorporates the questions from Revision Express Online. For the Introduction to Investment Award, the product is called eINTRO.

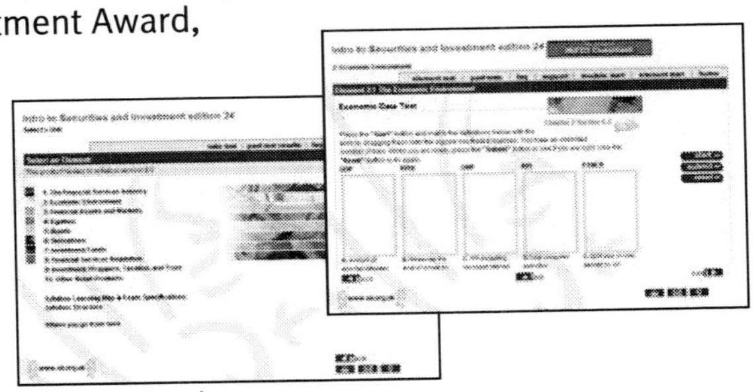

Key Features of eIAQ

- Exam-focused: covers the key points of the syllabus
- Questions throughout as well as at the end of each unit
- Interactive exercises

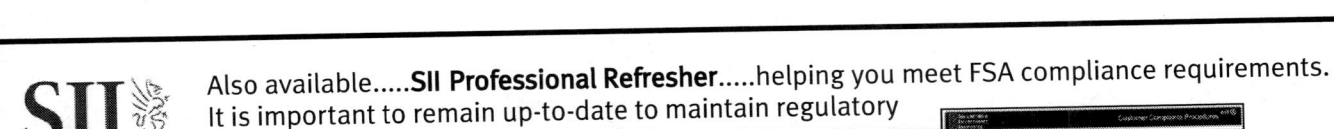

Price per module: £35
Price when purchased with the SII workbook: £100 (normal price: £110)

SII PROFESSIONAL REFRESHER

Also available.....**SII Professional Refresher**.....helping you meet FSA compliance requirements. It is important to remain up-to-date to maintain regulatory compliance and demonstrate continuing learning. In order for firms to meet compliance requirements, SII is pleased to offer SII Professional Refresher as an easy and cost-effective training solution.

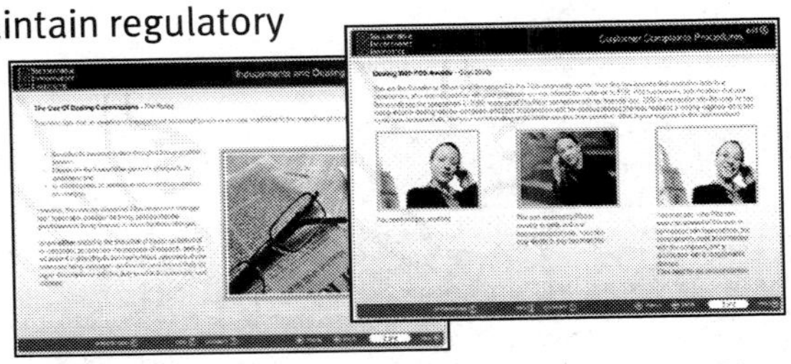

Current modules include:

- Anti-Money Laundering
- Training & Competence
- Price Stabilisation
- Approved Persons Regime
- Market Abuse
- Financial Promotions
- Customer Complaints Procedure
- UK Regulatory Structure
- Best Execution
- Financial Ombudsman Service
- Client Classifications
- Permissions Regime
- Inducements & Dealing Commissions
- Investment Business on the Internet

Price: £80 (free to all SII members, except student members)

Coming Soon...... **Revision Express Interactive**

Revision Express Interactive is an new engaging online study tool to be used in conjunction with SII IAQ™ and the Certificates programme workbooks. It contains graphics, exercises and revision questions.

Key Features of Revision Express Interactive

- Questions throughout to reaffirm understanding of the subject
- Special end of module practice exam to reflect as closely as possible the standard you will experience in your examination*
- Interactive exercises throughout
- Extensive glossary of terms
- Useful associated website links

* (please note, however, they are not the SII examination questions themselves)

Price per module: £35
Price when purchased with the SII workbook: £100
(normal price: £110)

Revision Express Interactive will initially be available for the SII Certificate subjects
- Securities
- Derivatives
- Financial Derivatives
- Securities & Financial Derivatives
- Investment & Risk
- Investment Management
- FSA Financial Regulation
- Principles of Financial Regulation

Coming Soon!

As each IAQ™ syllabus and workbook are updated, we will be producing Revision Express Interactive modules for all subjects.

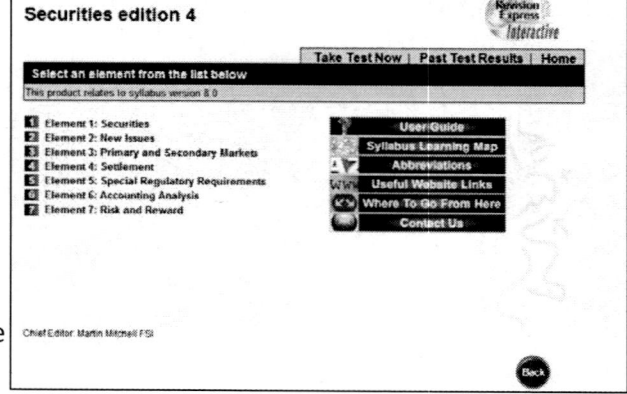

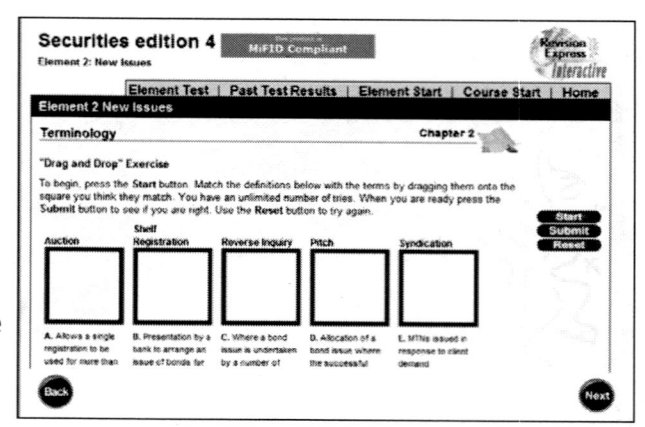

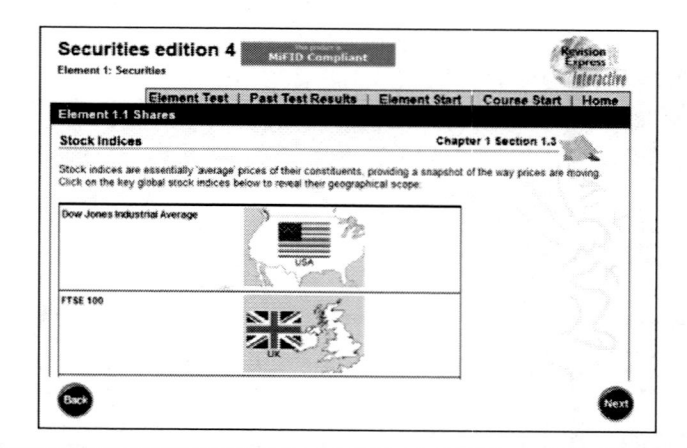

For more information on our elearning products call:
+44(0)20 7645 0756

Or visit our web site at:
www.sii.org.uk/elearning

To order call SII elearning products call Client Services on:
+44(0)20 7645 0680

NOTES

NOTES